NAHUA HORIZONS

NAHUA HORIZONS

Writing, Persuasion, and Futurities in Colonial Mexico

EZEKIEL G. STEAR

THE UNIVERSITY OF
ARIZONA PRESS
TUCSON

The University of Arizona Press
www.uapress.arizona.edu

We respectfully acknowledge the University of Arizona is on the land and territories of Indigenous peoples. Today, Arizona is home to twenty-two federally recognized tribes, with Tucson being home to the O'odham and the Yaqui. Committed to diversity and inclusion, the University strives to build sustainable relationships with sovereign Native Nations and Indigenous communities through education offerings, partnerships, and community service.

© 2025 by The Arizona Board of Regents
All rights reserved. Published 2025

ISBN-13: 978-0-8165-5455-3 (hardcover)
ISBN-13: 978-0-8165-5291-7 (paperback)
ISBN-13: 978-0-8165-5292-4 (ebook)

Cover design by Leigh McDonald
Tianguis glyph adapted from *Matrícula de Huexotzinco*, World Digital Library
Designed and typeset by Sara Thaxton in 10.5/14 Warnock Pro with Golden WF and Adrianna Condensed

Publication of this book is made possible in part by a subvention from Auburn University's College of Liberal Arts and Department of World Languages, Literatures, and Cultures.

Library of Congress Cataloging-in-Publication Data
Names: Stear, Ezekiel G., 1977– author.
Title: Nahua horizons : writing, persuasion, and futurities in colonial Mexico / Ezekiel G. Stear.
Description: [Tucson] : University of Arizona Press, 2025. | Includes bibliographical references and index.
Identifiers: LCCN 2024016412 (print) | LCCN 2024016413 (ebook) | ISBN 9780816554553 (hardcover) | ISBN 9780816552917 (paperback) | ISBN 9780816552924 (ebook)
Subjects: LCSH: Nahuatl literature—16th century—Criticism, Textual. | Nahuas—History—16th century. | Nahuas—Social conditions—16th century. | Mexico—History—16th century.
Classification: LCC PM4068 .S74 2025 (print) | LCC PM4068 (ebook) | DDC 897/.45209—dc23/eng/20240921
LC record available at https://lccn.loc.gov/2024016412
LC ebook record available at https://lccn.loc.gov/2024016413

Printed in the United States of America
♾ This paper meets the requirements of ANSI/NISO Z39.48-1992 (Permanence of Paper).

To Olivia and our children, our future

CONTENTS

List of Illustrations ix
Acknowledgments xi

Introduction 3

1. Problems of Perpetuity in the *Lienzo de Quauhquechollan* and the *Tira de Tepechpan* 33

2. Futurities of Well-Being in Books 10 and 11 of the *Florentine Codex* 79

3. Warning, Reconnaissance, and Return in the *Anales de Juan Bautista* 115

4. Didactic Horizons in the *Crónica mexicayotl* 149

Epilogue 175

Notes 197
References 227
Index 259

ILLUSTRATIONS

Figures

1. Plate 4, *Tira de Tepechpan* — 4
2. *Lienzo de Quauhquechollan* — 34
3. Year 9 Reed (1527), *Tira de Tepechpan* — 36
4. The alliance scene in Quauhquechollan, *Lienzo de Quauhquechollan* — 44
5. Aztlan in the *Códice Boturini* (*Tira de la peregrinación*) — 46
6. The alliance proceeds to the south, *Lienzo de Quauhquechollan* — 47
7. Retalhuleu, *Lienzo de Quauhquechollan* — 54
8. Jorge de Alvarado attacks the place glyph in Almolonga, *Lienzo de Quauhquechollan* — 57
9. Standard glyph of a *tianguis* (marketplace) near Chimaltenango, *Lienzo de Quauhquechollan* — 58
10. *Tlamemehque*, male and female, between Ollintepeque and Los Encuentros, *Lienzo de Quauhquechollan* — 59
11. Founding Tepechpan, *Tira de Tepechpan* — 64
12. Tlatoani Cristóbal Maldonado, 1540, *Tira de Tepechpan* — 67
13. Santa María Magdalena, church-and-convent complex in Tepechpan — 68
14. Skulls show deaths by epidemics, *Tira de Tepechpan* — 72

15. San Martín de Caballero, church and convent,
    Huaquechula, Puebla   73
16. Book 10, chapter 27, f. 55v–56r, *Florentine Codex*   83
17. Three plants representing *centli ina*, *Florentine Codex*   102
18. *Tlacoxivitl*, *Florentine Codex*   105
19. Peyote and its ingestion, *Florentine Codex*   106
20. The mushroom *teonanacatl* and bipedal bird,
    Florentine Codex   107
21. A *ticitl* gives a topical application of *toloa*,
    Florentine Codex   109
22. Rainbows depicted in the *Florentine Codex*   142
23. Opening section known as the *Crónica mexicayotl* in
    the *Codex Chimalpahin*   151
24. A Hispanicized portrait of Fernando Alvarado
    Tezozomoc in the *Tlalamatl Huauhquilpan*   157
25. East side of the Secretaría de Relaciones Exteriores, with
    a reconstruction of the façade of the Tecpan of Tlatelolco   189

Maps

1. Mesoamerica during the sixteenth century   2
2. The region of the Valley of Mexico and Tlaxcala during
   the sixteenth century   2

Table

1. Nahua healers (*titicih*) who contributed to research on
   healing plants, Books 10 and 11 of the *Florentine Codex*   94

ACKNOWLEDGMENTS

This project began at an intensive Nahuatl summer course, with the Instituto de Docencia e Investigaciones Etnológicas de Zacatecas (IDIEZ) at Vanderbilt University in Nashville, Tennessee, in 2011. I learned from amazing, dedicated instructors from Chicontepec, Veracruz: Delfina de la Cruz, Victoriano de la Cruz, Sabina Cruz de la Cruz, and Ofelia Cruz Morales. Surely thanks go to my first teachers of the language, Sabina and Ofelia: *tlazcamati miac*. That summer John Sullivan also taught a class on manuscript reading. Once, while commenting on the annual festival of corn and fertility in Chicontepec in honor of the deity Chicomexochitl, he explained that Nahua rituals are teleological: they aim to achieve specific objectives.

I was beginning my doctoral coursework then in Spanish colonial literature at the University of Kansas. I turned Sullivan's insight over in my mind. If their rituals serve teleological purposes today, then perhaps they always had. If so, rituals would also carry narratives—*stories*—that look not just to the past but also to times ahead. In this intersection between Nahua studies and the arts of persuasion I began a line of investigation into Nahua texts from the sixteenth and seventeenth centuries. My profound thanks go to John Sullivan for his kindhearted and abiding encouragement to study Nahuatl and Nahua culture, as well as his friendship, advice, and assistance with translations and resources that have enriched this study.

During my graduate studies and since, Santa Arias has been a fantastic mentor. She has given to me generously of her time and her wise professional advice. I am deeply grateful to her. ¡Muchísimas gracias, Santa! Verónica Garibotto, Patricia Manning, and Robert Schwaller all asked challenging questions and pushed me to keep developing my approach. Rocío Cortés also gave valuable observations and critiques, especially regarding the writings of Fernando Alvarado Tezozomoc and Domingo Chimalpahin. My fellow graduate students shared camaraderie and discussions on research and life. I recall with great appreciation productive conversations with Jacob Rapp, Tiffany Creagan-Miller, Edma Delgado, Pablo Celis, Matías Beverinotti, Tamara Mitchell, Katya Soll, Luis Cortés, David Dalton, Javier Barroso, Ian Gowan, and Elizabeth Villalobos.

A special thank-you goes to John F. Schwaller and the Association of Nahuatl Scholars. He has consistently invited me to their yearly gathering and is always available with helpful suggestions on where to learn more and go deeper into the sources. I'm very appreciative to James Maffie for our conversations on ways in which philosophy can help us understand Nahua ethics and how they have imagined times to come. I thank Camilla Townsend, Louise Burkhart, Alan and Pamela Sandstrom, Gordon Whittaker, and Andrew Laird for their comments on my ideas. I am appreciative to Julia Madajczek for her feedback on the book's theoretical frame as well as to Molly Bassett and Jerome Offner for their readings and comments on drafts of the introduction and chapter 1. This welcoming community of scholars—hard-working, generous, and wise—is a model of interdisciplinary collaboration.

A generous grant from the College of Liberal Arts of Auburn University provided the funding that made on-location and archival research possible in Guatemala and Central Mexico. I remember the warm welcome and assistance of the University Francisco Marroquín in Guatemala City. Thank you to Luis Figueroa and to the Secretario General (Provost) Ricardo Castillo for taking time to talk about the *Lienzo de Quauhquechollan*. Thanks go to Katherinne del Valle and Brenda Galindo for coordinating my visit. I am especially appreciative to Brenda and her husband, Gabriel, for taking me to locations in Guatemala that the *lienzo* depicts (Iximché, Chichicastenango, Chimaltenango, Los Encuentros, La Antigua). At the Archivo General de la Nación (AGN) in Mexico City I am grateful to Hidekel Maldonado Hernández and Eunice Ruiz Zamudio for helping me access archival documents while navigating COVID-19 protocols. I am thankful to Diana Garcia Pozas, Ingrid Vásquez, Carlos Alberto Neyra, and Miguel Ángel Gasca Gómez, across town in Chapultepec at the Biblioteca Nacional de Antropología e Historia (BNAH), who helped me with documents cordially. During the same trip, I had the great fortune of visiting Eduardo de la Cruz at IDIEZ in Zacatecas. I owe a debt of gratitude to him for tutoring me remotely and patiently walking through the stories and wisdom of his ancestors. *Tlazcamati miac ipan paquiliztli.* I am looking forward to seeing how his vision for teaching, research, and traditional culture in Chicontepec will continue to grow.

During the writing and publishing process, the University of Arizona Press has been very supportive. Since our first communication, I have appreciated the synergy and interest in making this study available. I am grateful to Kristen Buckles for her support, patience, and availability. I also express my sincere thanks to the anonymous reviewers of the book. Their suggestions, corrections, and insights have brought a new level of clarity to my arguments. I thank everyone at the press—all have been down the road of submission, editing, and final proofs many times—for sharing their knowledge. My appreciation goes as well to Luz Campbell for crisp and engaging cartography. I also thank the graduate assistants who helped me at various stages: Piero Garibaldi, Arturo Moreno, and Carlos Cano. Ultimately, I take responsibility for the study's strengths and weaknesses as well as for the translations in the following pages, which, unless indicated, are mine.

I am grateful to friends who have supported me over the years and at pivotal moments. Josiah Pruiksma, John Bawden, Darrick Taylor, Joseph and Monique González, as well as Christopher García and Juan Tavárez have always given their friendship along with fascinating, satisfying conversation. Special thanks go to Loknath Persaud and Juan Manuel Sánchez at Pasadena City College. I am grateful to my friends in Mexico City who have taught me so much and encouraged me to spread the word about the wonders of Mexico: Edgar Leija, Paco and Erika Rincón, Laura Barranco Mancera, and many more. *¡Gracias de todo corazón!*

In the end, there would be no book without the undying support of my family. I thank my mother, Mary Kay, and my late father, Ken, for their sacrifices and examples of hard work, integrity, and trust. Most of all, thanks go to my wife, Olivia. She encouraged me to go to graduate school in the first place and has been a source of inspiration all along the way. Our boys, Lukas and Thomas, only toddlers when we spent that summer at Vanderbilt, have now grown into adolescents and have been to Mexico with me, visiting many sites this book discusses. Our girls, Aurora and Bernadette, have filled my years since graduate school with many joys. Looking forward, this book and the rest of our lives together learning, traveling, and discovering are the best thank-you I can think of.

NAHUA HORIZONS

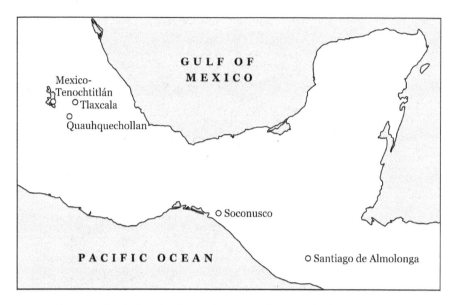

MAP 1 Mesoamerica during the sixteenth century. Cartography by Luz Campbell, 2024.

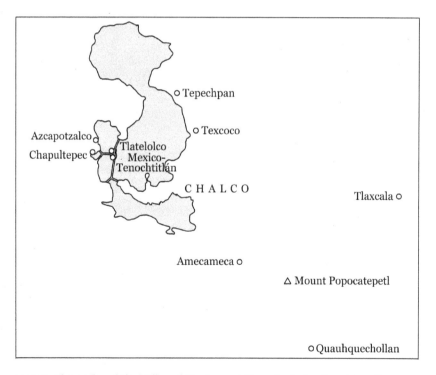

MAP 2 The region of the Valley of Mexico and Tlaxcala during the sixteenth century. Cartography by Luz Campbell, 2024.

• • • •

Introduction

In the year *ome acatl* (2 Reed [1351]), four couples left the city of Tenochtitlan, the capital of the Mexica (the Aztecs). They went to attend a sacrifice in Tepechpan, a community called an *altepetl*, allied with the neighboring Texcoco, one of the most influential towns in the Valley of Mexico at the time.[1] They crossed earthen causeways that joined the island city with the surrounding land and walked along the northwest shore of Lake Texcoco. One of the men carried a bundle on his back, the contents of which remained sealed to observers of the pictorial document that preserves this scene, the *Tira de Tepechpan*, plate 4 (see figure 1). At the pyramid of Tepechpan, the couples participated in the sacrifice of a snake, a butterfly, and a bird (Diel 2008, 36).[2] This event is one moment in the 286 years of the timeline the *tira* (long strip of paper) presents (ca. 1310–ca. 1596). The pictorial gives parallel histories: Tepechpan's is on a register above the linear display of years, while the history of the Mexica and of other towns unfolds below that line, a format that prioritizes events in Tepechpan. At various points along the tira, Tepechpan anticipated future conditions and set goals. Elsewhere in the Valley of Mexico a heart sacrifice took place, in Colhuacan, in the same year of 2 Reed, as the tira records on its lower register (Diel 2008, 36–37).[3] Over the nearly three centuries the text records, Tepechpan navigated rapid shifts in political power, military confrontations, natural and demographic crises, and ac-

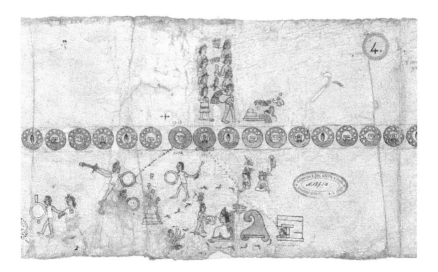

FIGURE 1 Plate 4, *Tira de Tepechpan*, Biblioteque National de France, Fonds Mexicain 88-6.

cessions of rulers, all while maintaining a strong sense of the past and a continuous identity.

The Mexica couples that migrated likely intended to settle in Tepechpan, sealing their journey by sacrificing the same animals as at the founding ceremony of Tepechpan seventeen years earlier (Diel 2008, 24). The men's face paint and loincloths show they are warriors, yet of lower status than the men of Tepechpan (Diel 2008, 38). The women's bound hair indicates they were married (Olko 2014, 37). The migrant couples used a ritual to link themselves, their work, and potentially their offspring to Tepechpan.

The journey of the Mexica couples and their sacrifice per the norms of a smaller group outside Tenochtitlan confronts us with cultural combinations in a time before the Spanish had entered the region. In fact, the scene takes place even before the Mexica controlled the area. Of course, the fact that these representations come from a Tepechpaneca perspective casts the goals of the Mexica in a particular light. The painters of the pictorial have designed a context in which the eight Mexica migrants reorient their loyalty to Tepechpan, investing their lives in that altepetl. Understanding that the micro-patriotism of the altepetl reached deep into the past in Central Mexico (Lockhart 1985, 477; Connell 2011, 148; Carballo 2020, 8), this scene shows that perspectives regarding times to come also varied between *altepeme* (pl. of altepetl). Seventy years later, in 1521, the consensus on power relationships had changed. In Mexica pictorials from shortly after the Spanish invasion, they represented themselves as the most influential altepetl of the region.[4] Thus, the difference of viewpoint suggests that even during times of Mexica hegemony other altepeme did not always take their perspective, or their imperial goals, as given. This difference of perspective during the Postclassic Period reveals the future as a long-standing polemic between Nahuatl-speaking groups. After the conquest, controversies surrounding the future gained a new intensity as the Spanish empire, with its globalizing designs along religious, political, and economic lines, occupied the region.

In the chapters that follow, I argue that Nahuas in the colonial period used culturally specific tools of persuasion in texts to convince their Indigenous readers to act for the benefit of their communities, despite the hardships of colonialism. These discourses concerning future conditions and plans for times ahead I refer to as *Nahua futurities*, based on the work of contemporary Indigenous scholars. Convincing through writing is a fundamentally linguistic endeavor. Thus, the chapters focus on how words, narrative tropes, imagery, and features of the Nahuatl language itself—in pictorials and alphabetic texts—reveal writers' strategies to help lead their communities. The texts I have selected for this study represent time as a crucial concern for Nahuas. I analyze the *Florentine Codex* (1578), the *Anales de Juan Bautista* (1582), and a narrative selection known as the "Crónica mexicayotl" (1609), showing how Native writing subjects used alphabetic Nahuatl to communicate their future expectations and goals. Books 10 and 11 of the *Florentine Codex* come from the complex collaboration between Bernardino de Sahagún and Nahua contributors—elders, polyglot scribes, painters, and Indigenous physicians—and convey futurities of healing and well-being. The *Anales de Juan Bautista* started off as a tribute register, yet its Nahua amanuenses turned it into a record of events from mid-sixteenth-century Mexico-Tenochtitlan. These annals disclose economic and political anxieties regarding tribute while also providing practical models for engaging the Spanish as their rule wore on. The *Crónica mexicayotl*, a compilation of the memories of Mexica elders, again results from a collaboration, this time between two Nahuas: the Amequemeca historian Domingo Chimalpahin and the Mexica noble Fernando Alvarado Tezozomoc. The chronicle aims to ensure the education of young nobles would continue in a world of disappearing traditional knowledge. Pictographic texts in this study also reveal Nahua futurities. The *Lienzo de Quauhquechollan* (1530s), a narrative map depicting an alliance between Nahua warriors and Spanish forces to invade Guatemala, documents the early execution of long-term plans for expanding Nahua linguistic, economic, and political influence in Central America. The *Tira de Tepechpan* (ca. 1596), with its sacrificial episodes, also features accessions of altepetl rulers (*tlatoque*). Leaders in Tepechpan used the tira for nearly three centuries to outline the future actions and cultural development of their communities before and after the arrival of the Spanish. In both cases, Nahuas actively engaged in predicting future conditions, influencing outcomes, and shaping local cultures.

This study corrects the pervasive presentation of the Nahuas as passive receptors of cultural change instead of active interpreters of events and builders of their own futures. My analyses shed light on Nahuas' deliberations on how they should approach the problematic of the future. Nahua futurities as ways of knowing and writing allowed them to look beyond the losses the Spanish inflicted.[5] The effort expended in future-oriented writing projects reveals the writers' concern for the preservation of knowledge for their times and for readers beyond their lives. Likewise, Nahua futurities reveal that the Spanish did not control all they wrote: Nahuas' future-leaning discourses expose fissures in the invaders' epistemological regime. Certainly Nahua knowledge(s) were under unprecedented threats from the Spanish. As Rolando Vázquez (2011, 30) observes, "knowledge has been part and parcel of the modern/colonial systems of oppression and destitution. The epistemic territorial practices are such that all that lies outside their realm is made invisible, is excluded from the real, and is actively distained, even unnamed." The Spanish aimed to exclude Nahuas and their knowledge(s) from reality. However, as we shall see, Spanish epistemes had their blind spots. The same practices of exclusion from Spanish knowledge ironically opened discursive possibilities for the Nahuas. In the texts under consideration, Nahuas consistently posited distinct futures from the Spanish imperialist projects, charting out paths and action guides for times ahead.

The study's methodology centers on what I term *Nahua tools of persuasion*.[6] Instead of describing their writing as "rhetoric," a term with

Greco-Roman and Renaissance connotations, I opt for *persuasion* and *convincing* to describe how these texts convey Nahua futurities. In the texts I examine in *Nahua Horizons: Writing, Persuasion, and Futurities in Colonial Mexico*, the following tools of persuasion operate in an interlocking, nonhierarchical manner:

(a) *Gathering Strength*: By interpreting their surroundings as manifestations of a profoundly animated cosmos, Nahuas have used writing and images to build strength. Attestations of *chicahua* (to strengthen) and its grammatical iterations show how groups fortified themselves for coming times.[7]

(b) *Reciprocity*: Plans to support reciprocal relationships between Nahuas in their communities and between Nahuas and their deities constituted knowledge concerning the future. Nahua texts encourage expanding networks of mutual giving in order to bring about positive outcomes for their communities. Additionally, reciprocity allows communities to seek and forge balanced paths through life.

(c) *Repetition*: In pictorial texts, iterations of an image, colors, or glyphs emphasize plans for future action. In alphabetic texts, the repetition of words, phrases, situations, and relationships between humans and deities underscores forward-leaning content. Causes or origins can join repeated elements in an image or text (metonymy). Also, repetition can move from small to large, such as when a part represents a whole (synecdoche).

(d) *Questioning-as-Persuasion*: Even in cases when listeners know the answer, a speaker may use questions to emphasize an imbalance or situation in need of correction. For instance, in the *Anales de Juan Bautista* (see chapter 3), this technique draws attention to widespread complaints regarding Spanish tribute demands.

(e) *Specific Features of Nahuatl*: Grammatical features of Nahuatl became tools of persuasion writers used to convince their audiences. These features, each of which I will discuss in its time, include omnipredicativity, hyper-trophism, and syntactic parallels.[8]

The above summary of my approach to close readings of the texts in this study by no means exhausts Nahua writers' strategies for approaching the future. Each text examined uses multiple Nahua tools of persuasion to convince audiences to build futures, often with aims that contest or depart from the designs of Spanish colonizers.

Before proceeding, I recognize that a number of factors complicate this study. My etic perspective, even as postcolonial and postmodern, carries its own colonial echoes. As Terry Goldie (1995, 263) has observed, Western scholars and audiences often commodify Indigenous textual production as a means to recuperate a lost spirituality characteristic of the postmodern, globalized world. One intellectual option for recovering lost interconnectedness with a wider reality is to gravitate toward Indigenous aesthetics. Art historians Carolyn Dean and Dana Leibsohn (2003) have critiqued academics' fascination with so-called hybridity, an interest that often, and curiously, impels researchers toward what they already assume. They have observed that Western academic debate around cultural hybridity furthers the assumption of the centrality of all things European. Academic dialogue on hybridity also takes for granted a derivative, inferior status of Indigenous art and other cultural products that combine regional and Western characteristics (Dean and Leibsohn 2003, 6). On the one hand, we academics fetishize Indigenous cultural production and yet value it in terms of its parallels with European forms. On the other hand, the fascination with hybridity has led us to rely for too many years on descriptive approaches that downplay Indigenous agency. For these reasons I share Dean and Leibsohn's (2003, 8–9) concern regarding the study of cultural hybridity. Equally limiting in the conventional notion of cultural "hybridity" is its assumption that acquiring or using a technology or material object of European origin carries the disavowal of Indigenous identity. Rather, as Kelly McDonough (2024, 14–15) has observed, Indigenous epistemologies are "always-in-process" and incorporate ideas and technologies into larger "Indigenous repertoires." Adoption does not mean dilution of identity. In terms of this study, this concern likewise covers "syncretism," a category that also assumes that foundational, nonintentional mixing rather than individual and collective agency has been responsible for religious diversity. The overapplication of these merely descriptive categories works to explain away complex phenomena that occur in networks of individual and collective agency and contingency. Thus, hybridity and syncretism further the pervasive exclusion of Nahuas' choices by which they have shaped their futures.

Deformed interpretations of Indigenous cultures touch on deeper complications: how can we be sure that what Nahuas have chosen as their cultural forms and practices represent futurities? James Lockhart (1992, 243) has famously observed that when Spanish and Nahua cultures "ran parallel, the Nahuas would soon adopt the relevant Spanish form without abandoning the essence of their own form." This tendency led to inaccurate interpretations on the part of the Spanish and Nahuas of each other's actions and intentions, mutual interpretive entanglements that Lockhart (1992, 445) termed the "double mistaken identity." Monolithic colonial projects, whether they involved Westernization, Christianization, or the ubiquitous and ongoing promotion of a common mestizo identity, have overlooked local concerns and goals.[9]

Considering these complications, far from placing all Nahuatl speakers under one cultural banner, in these pages I recognize the local nature of the expectations and goals each of the texts I examine represents. I assume no unitary Nahua identity but recognize multiple horizons they have pursued in writing. Quite often, attention to ways in which Nahua writing does not run "parallel" to Westernizing projects reveals locally specific futurities. Thus, by centering my analysis on future-oriented discourses that produce dissonance, I aim to avoid pitfalls in my interpretations. Rather than seeking a single, static, or authentic Nahua perspective, my intention is to illustrate the continuous evolution of Nahua futurities. Now, I shift to the analytical precedents for studying Indigenous futurities, including Nahua futurities, in this book.

INDIGENOUS FUTURITIES

Anishinaabe author Grace Dillon first employed the term *Indigenous futurities* in her volume *Walking the Clouds* (2012), a science fiction collection by Indigenous writers. Dillon (2012, 1–2) framed the term as analogous to Afrofuturisms, a sci-fi genre that opened space for the work of writers of color in a heteronormative, white-male-dominated creative field. Subsequent Indigenous scholarship has built on this precedent and elaborated larger epistemological fronts. Futurities generate knowledge(s) and practices. As Noelani Goodyear-Kaʻōpua (Kānaka Maoli) (2019, 86) explains, "*futurity* is not just another way to say 'the future." Futurities are ways that groups imagine and produce knowledge about futures." Laura Harjo (Mvskoke) (2019, 216) has theorized that Indigenous futurities come from collective reflection based in humans' and more-than-humans' "responsibility to one another." This ethical orientation means Indigenous futurities manifest themselves through action: Harjo (2019, 30) comments, "Mvskoke people are performing futurity in everyday spaces, and this is powerful." Indigenous futurities have their origins in specific places and in day-to-day life (Goodyear-Kaʻōpua 2019, 98). Place plays a key role in planning for the future as a starting point and as an imagined transformed destination; place helps envision maps from the present to a desired future (Harjo 2019, 25). *Way-finding* thus emerges as a central element of Indigenous futurities, a commitment that requires the strengthening of shared knowledge. Harjo (2019, 100) explains, "way-finding involves recuperating and strengthening these knowledge pathways that remind us of the array of knowledge we carry in our bodies." Embodied knowledge in turn provides a continuum of contact with deceased relatives: the present generation connects with ancestors and envisions times beyond the horizons of this historical moment (Recollet 2016, 94; Goodyear-Kaʻōpua 2019, 86–87; Harjo 2019, 199). By implication, the connection with ancestors means that even now Indigenous peoples are living out their own "ancestors' and relatives' unactivated [sic] possibilities" (Harjo 2019, 5, 34). Yet not all Indigenous scholars agree that all ancestral dreams are precursors to the present. Emalani Case (Kānaka Maoli) (2021, 62) points out that projecting the dreams of the present onto the past may prove problematic. Instead, Case (2021, 52) proposes an adaptive, agentive vision of Indigenous futurity as "our current actions and our attempts to create the conditions in which our future generations can continue to see their desires into fruition." Being present does not mean presentism, and opening conditions for Indigenous futurities prepares for multiple perspectives that will exist in times ahead. Indigenous futurities thus incorporate multiple perspectives of deceased kin and Native communities today.

At this point I ask: is it problematic to retroactively apply twenty-first-century Native American scholars' concepts as an approach to Nahua texts from five hundred years ago? The origin and development of the concept already show generalizability across regions. With reference to the historical displacement of the Mvskoke from the current southeastern United States to Oklahoma, Harjo (2019, 219) describes a network of Indigenous futurities between ancestors and individuals alive today. While during the forced relocation some lost their lives on the Trail of Tears, others imagined and lived out future plans in Oklahoma. Likewise, subsequent Mvskoke generations have advocated for protecting their ancestral lands in Alabama and Georgia.

The way-finding aspect of Indigenous futurity also resonates with deeply rooted Nahua lifeways. Before and after the Spanish invasion, Nahuas have emphasized balanced living on the path of life. Right living, in the Nahua worldview, *cualli nehnemi* (walking well), relies on the metaphor of proceeding step-by-step in a balanced manner.[10] For Nahuas writing in the early colonial era that inherited their predecessors' traditions, good living depended on acting in harmony with their surroundings (L. Burkhart 1986, 107–12; 1989, 134). This Nahua approach to life resonates with other Indigenous peoples in the Americas who conceive of correct action in terms of a conscientious and centered path (Hester and Cheney 2001, 319–25; S. Pratt 2002, xi–xv, 78–106; Hester 2012, 602). As Brian Yazzie Burkhart (Cherokee) (2003, 17) observes, Amerindians are more concerned with a way of life than with an aim for life. I recall that the migrant couples in the *Tira de Tepechpan* also sought a path from Tenochtitlan to Tepechpan to start a new phase of life there. Consequently, the approach of Nahua futurities places a label on phenomena that were already underway, as communities in ancestral times and during the Spanish invasion found balanced paths ahead. The examples I provide in the remainder of this introduction and in the book's chapters illustrate particular Nahua futurities prior to and after the Spanish invasion.

The study draws on further analytical precedents from Nahua studies and related fields—ethnohistory, anthropology, philosophy, and religious studies—which I reorient to learn how Nahuas have used texts to articulate their expectations and goals. My focus on the convincing power of the texts and their epistemological content places my contribution within literary and postcolonial studies, in an interdisciplinary network. I observe that divergent anticipations and goals contribute to cultural (mis)interpretation. My approach sheds light on Nahua culture by examining the future-oriented content of their texts, which diverged from Spanish objectives.

We are increasingly aware of how Nahuas relied on their traditions to find strategic paths forward during the colonial era. Stephanie Wood, in *Transcending Conquest* (2003), shows how Natives who produced pictorial and alphabetic texts re-envisioned their past as one of continuity with their ancestors and reframed the Spanish invasion as a comparatively minor event. Likewise, McDonough has demonstrated in *The Learned Ones* (2016) that Nahuas adopted alphabetic text and adapted it to a wide array of needs—economic, religious, linguistic, and artistic—and have maintained an unbroken chain of textual production in Nahuatl and Spanish from the sixteenth century to the present. As McDonough also shows, colonial-era Nahua texts serve as sources of language revitalization and cultural information for contemporary Nahuas.[11] In her study *Indigenous Science and Technology* (2024), McDonough provides examples of how Nahua observations of the world include predicting the weather (54) and influencing outcomes in hunting and trapping (65–69). Native intermediaries during the colonial period also played a crucial role in negotiating the future on behalf of their communities. Yanna Yannakakis, in *The Art of Being in Between* (2008), draws attention to Native interpreters, notaries, and other intermediaries in the Sierra Norte of Oaxaca, 1660–1810. Yannakakis demonstrates the dynamism of peripheral areas for shaping identity and future trajectories within Native communities.[12] These studies represent a growing orientation toward bringing Indigenous agency, concerns, and sovereignty to the fore.

Regarding the overlapping area of the development of futurities in other communities in the colonial era, Hispanized, urban communities in Mexico also envisioned days ahead during the colonial period. Matthew O'Hara's *History of the Future in Colonial Mexico* (2018) provides case studies of "future-making." O'Hara focuses on religious and economic life in Central Mexico from the colonial period to independence. In distinction to the Hispanizing processes O'Hara discusses, the current book shows how Nahua leaders re-evaluated ancestral knowledge as a basis for long-term engagements with the Spanish. While O'Hara's focus on the rise of creole culture distances itself from the attention to Nahua sources in this study, Peter Villella's *Indigenous Elites and Creole Identity in Colonial Mexico, 1500–1800* (2016) explains how Indigenous elite families during the sixteenth century transitioned to a Christian and Hispanic identity as a means to preserve the legal rights they possessed prior to the Spanish.[13] These literary and ethno-historical studies of Native documents and mediators reposition Nahua voices as protagonists of their futures.

Other studies in the philosophies and religions of the Nahuas have shed further light on how they inform the sacred and how the sacred informs them. James Maffie's *Aztec Philosophy: Understanding a World in Motion* (2014) gives a systematic approach on how Nahuas have viewed reality, emphasizing continuities from ancient times to the present. With a similar attention to continuity, Guilhem Olivier's *Mockeries and Metamorphoses of an Aztec God: Tezcatlipoca, Lord of the Smoking Mirrors* (2003) emphasizes the ritual phenomenology of Nahuas over time and geographic regions. Olivier examines the origins of Nahua deities during the Postclassic Period, which he traces ultimately to Tezcatlipoca, who expresses his potential through many beings.[14] Molly Bassett, in *The Fate of Earthly Things: Aztec Gods and God-Bodies* (2015), also examines the pivotal role of Nahua ritual experience in their cultural survival. Bassett delves into how Nahuas from ancient memory have built and maintained complex linguistic and ritual phenomena centering on localized embodiments of deities. She explains that Nahuas who build physical representations of their deities in turn receive assistance from the very deities their work has animated.[15] As we shall see, making deities entails proposing a series of future actions. Whereas these studies concern continuities between the Postclassic Period and the colonial era, my analyses shed light on the understudied area of expectations and goals as discursive resources for Nahuas in the wake of the Spanish invasion.

Until now, documentary investigation has produced a limited study of Nahua discourses of futurity. Concerning Nahua views of days to come during the Postclassic Period, Elizabeth Boone (1992, 2007) has examined the tonalpohualli calendar, describing how divinatory calendars helped the *tonalpouhque* (diviners) provide prognostications for rulers (*tlatoque*). Surge Gruzinski (2013, 50) describes calculated practices for cultural survival in Mexico-Tenochtitlan after its surrender to the Spanish, which he calls a "personal palimpsest" with a focus on survival. Camilla Townsend (2019) has also described postinvasion Mexica perspectives on their future.[16] In this burgeoning line of investigation, *Nahua Horizons: Writing, Persuasion, and Futurities in Colonial Mexico* brings the problematic of the future to the forefront.[17] My study also includes non-Mexica Nahua perspectives, groups that lived first under Mexica dominance and later under the Spanish.[18]

In the remainder of this introduction, I consider concepts undergirding the texts I examine. Nahua futurities existed prior to Spanish colonization during the Postclassic Period. I review how Nahuas generated and diffused knowledge regarding the future with attention to the figures of the *tlamatini* and the *tlacuilo*. The Nahua understanding of change leads me next to review scholarly approaches to the ubiquitous yet enigmatic concept of *teotl*. I consider teotl as both metaphysical concept and as phenomenological experience. I then turn to the role of strengthening (chicahua) and of that which gives strength (*chicahualiztli*). Finally, I review prevailing representations of time in Mesoamerica and in early modern Europe before proceeding to an overview of the chapters.

READING THE COSMOS

Colonizers brought radical changes to Mesoamerica. Epidemics decimated Indigenous populations. Spanish lawmen and clergy dismantled Native institutions. Nahua elders explained their losses to the Franciscan friar Bernardino de Sahagún, as recorded in the *Florentine Codex* in concrete terms: "qujtqujque in tlilli, in tlapalli, in amoxtli, in tlacuilolli qujqujque in tlamatiliztli: mochi qujqujque in cujcaamatl, in tlapitzolli" (They took away the wisdom. They took away all the books, the songs, the wind instruments [*FC*, Bk. 10, f. 141v; 11:191]).[19] The diphrastic kenning "In tlilli in tlapalli," "it is the red, it is the black," refers to pictographic representation as a tool for recording information and interpreting experience. The loss of the red and black ink of the codices carried with it the more devastating loss of the ability to transmit knowledge to posterity, an aspect of Nahua futurities.

A particular aspect of knowledge suppression in the colonial project was to end Nahuas' ability to keep traditional time. As Vázquez (2011, 36) explains, "all that is excluded from the epistemic territory of modernity is that which does not fit into its notion of time." The imposition of a universal, linear conceptualization of time consequently shook the foundations of Nahua "time-place," which is "heterogeneous, not homogenous. It is plural, not singular. . . . Instead of speaking of time *per se*, therefore, we should speak of times . . . just as we speak of the qualitatively different times of a person's life" (Maffie 2014, 419–20, 422–23). For the Nahuas, the contours of time varied like topography between locales. Thus, Mexico-Tenochtitlan, Tepechpan, and other altepeme each marked time with their own calendars (Hassig 2001, 27–28). Yet all these communities had similarities in their timekeeping: while advancing forward, Mesoamerican cyclical time was cumulative in that the future was embedded in the past so that repetition was guaranteed (D. Tedlock 1985, 64; L. Burkhart 1989, 72; Boone 2007, 13–14). The Spanish disruption of Nahua time-place fragmented local histories and the transmission of knowledge to future generations.

Pictorial arts aided the recitation of complex histories before and after the conquest. For time immemorial, communities used the pictorial genre of the *xiuhpohualli* (yearly account) to keep records of important events in an altepetl (Lockhart 1992, 378). The narrative perspectives in the xiuhpohualli were collective. Yet, rather than rely on a central compiler, perspectives rotated between narrators in a single text (C. Townsend 2009, 626–27). Multiple vantage points confirmed the importance of the events they described. The correlation between place and the xiuhpohualli genre reminded local residents of their participation in cosmic and social processes unfolding in their immediate surroundings (R. Cortés 2011, 1). Reverberations of the xiuhpohualli appear in postconquest texts that Natives painted and wrote.[20] The xiuhpohualli documents that recorded various perspectives in an altepetl assumed that what had occurred before could repeat in future events.

While the xiuhpohualli represented an altepetl, rulers also sought individual advice on how to achieve balance. The details of how one could live a balanced life depended on the amount of solar energy an individual had received at birth, as revealed through the 260-day tonalpohualli solar calendar (McKeever Furst [1995] 1997, 35–37; Berdan 2014, 199).[21] Based on one's date of birth, each person received a portion of the sun's *tona* (heat, warmth), which carried with it a destiny and set of personality traits (Soustelle [1970] 2002, 112–13). These parameters shaped an individual's *tonalli*, a conduit of energy located in the head.[22] A closely related resource for understanding time, interpreting the tonalpohualli calendar, and recommending proper actions was the *tonalamatl* genre, or pictorial books of divination. The tonalamatl formed practical guides to living, concerned with everyday orderliness (Boone 2007, 18–20). These guides for action allowed the *tonalpouhque*, the specialists who read the tonalamatl, to give advice for living in the present and preparing for things to come (Boone 2007, 51–52). Nahua writers in the colonial period thus inherited remnants of this role of keeping and interpreting calendars.[23] During the colonial period, in a manner similar to their predecessors' tonalamatl action guides, Nahua futurities provided strategies for extending balanced living into the years ahead.

In addition to the tonalpouhque, rulers sought answers to their pressing questions from the *tlamatinime*, the keepers of wisdom. The *tlamatini* (sing.) was the principal didactic figure before the Spanish invasion, whose knowledge, as "a first-hand, embodied process" included information from the five senses as well as intuitive knowledge gained through meditation on the interconnectedness of reality (Maffie 2008b, 46; McDonough 2024, 46–47, 230n118). As men and women (Boone 2005, 11), the tlamatinime embodied "the wisdom contained in the painted books" (Boone 2000, 25). The *Florentine Codex* explains that a good tlamatini "ticitl piale machice temachtli" (serves as a physician. He makes one whole); in addition, a tlamatini is "tenonotzani, teixtlamachtiani, teixcuitiani" (an advisor, a counselor, a good example [*FC*, Bk. 10, f. 19v; 11:29]). The tlamatinime saw times to come and committed their knowledge to paper. They specialized in observing and interpreting astronomical movements as individual destinies. They spoke with deities: in fact, these specialists were associated with Quetzalcoatl, tutelary numen of the Toltecs, whose patronage included codex making and artisanal goods (Florescano 1999, 168; Duverger 2000, 473). The tlamatinime received training in the calmecac schools, where they also would teach and train Nahua nobles. The tlamatinime meditated on reality, which included interpreting the past and present and anticipating the future (León-Portilla [1963] 1975, 22–23). Through song-poems, called *in xochitl in cuicatl* (flower-songs), they reflected on the nature of being and on the meaning of human action.[24] Their songs often used semantic couplets called *difrasismos* in order to convey metaphorical meanings. One such difrasismo, *in xochitl in cuicatl*—"it is the flower; it is the song"—evokes the becoming of the universe in all its ordinary, and at times marvelous, operations. Learning and teaching about that unfolding were core activities of the tlamatinime. The knowledge of the tlamatinime thus gave them vital visionary roles.

The role of the tlamatini paralleled the occupation of the tlacuilo, the traditional painter of graphic information. This artisan's name comes from the Nahuatl verb *icuiloa*, to write or paint (Karttunen 1992, 97). A tlacuilo could also be male or female.[25] Prior to the conquest, *tlacuiloque* (pl. of tlacuilo) were specialists in pictorial representations of song-poems in codices that the tlamatinime kept in the calmecac schools (León-Portilla 1956, 227–28). The tlamatinime were the custodians of the codices, due to their priestly and divinatory status. In turn, the tlacuiloque painted accordion-folding codices (*amoxtli*) and murals under the sages' direction (Boone 2000, 24). Thus, the tlamatinime and the tlacuiloque shared the role of generating and diffusing knowledge regarding times ahead—including conditions to expect and how one should act. Although the Spanish invasion displaced these figures, Nahuas continued to use the term *tlacuilo* to denote a painter or writer in the colonial period (Molina [1571] 2008, 2:120r; Lockhart 1992, 326).

In sum, tradition already meant advising those to come. The Nahuas' concept of the earth itself reflects a path-finding approach to the future. The advice of tlamatinime and tlacuiloque constituted futurities in the calmecac that helped the young navigate the risks and opportunities of life. *Tlalticpac*, Nahuatl for the world, means "on the point or summit of the earth" (Launey 1992, 126). Bernardino de Sahagún recorded the advice of Nahua elders, "conjtotivi, ca tlachichiqujlco in tivi, in tinemj tlalticpac, njpa tlanj, njpa tlanj: in campa tonchicopentonjz, in campa tonchicoeoaz vmpa tonvetziz, vmpa timotepexiujz" (They went saying that indeed on a jagged edge we go, we live on earth. Here is down, over there is down. Wherever you go out of place to the side, wherever you take off to the side, there you will fall, there you will throw yourself over the precipice) (Sahagún [1578] 1969, 6:125). This advice signals a consensus that the best way through life consists of a middle path of self-control, avoiding extreme attitudes and behaviors.[26] Nahua writers, faced with new colonial challenges, continued to provide guides for future readers.

COSMIC MOVEMENTS, UNFOLDING FUTURES

As mentioned, Nahuas perceived the universe as an unfolding process encompassing matter, plants, animals, humans, and other forms of life.

They wrote texts that reflected their pantheistic belief that all reality is teotl. If teotl is all, then teotl underlies Nahua discourses related to the future. While accounting for regional variations in deity representations poses a challenge to this metaphysical view, attention to pantheism provides insights into how Nahuas sought to persuade their communities to prepare for uncertain times after the Spanish invasion.

James Maffie's work explains ways in which tlamatinime sages, tonalpouhque calendar readers, and other specialists interpreted the operations of teotl. Maffie (2014, 172) argues that preconquest and colonial-era sources show that teotl moves constantly in three basic ways: *ollin*, *malinalli*, and *nepantla*. Readable within the cosmos, ollin is the back-and-forth cyclical energy completion associated with the sun's movement across the sky (Aguilar-Moreno 2007, 208). Nahuas viewed ollin and the Fifth Sun as one and the same.[27] This daily motion orders the cosmos and links to human rituals via heart sacrifice (McKeever Furst [1995] 1997, 13–14; Read 1998, 26, 115). Thus, any succession of cosmic events implies patterned, repeating movements. Even though the postconquest continuation of Nahua culture did not mean the end of the cosmic age, new circumstances encouraged colonial-era Nahua writers to look beyond a traditional understanding of the Fifth Sun.[28] Their experience of this crisis of the conceptualization of time led them to assume parallel linear temporalities in which humans' present actions shape future outcomes. The texts they produced show Nahua writers' multiple experiences of Spanish colonialism, which, in turn, made their futurities plural, even in the face of universalizing, Western time.

As ollin provides the conditions for life, malinalli—twisting and turning cosmic forces—results in growth, fertility, and regeneration (López Austin 1997, 117–19). The New Fire Ceremony, which renewed ritual time, centered on a spinning fire drill (Read and González 2002, 120; Maffie 2014, 318). The Nahuas observed malinalli in the twisting of roots, cornstalks, and all other plants (B. Tedlock and D. Tedlock 1985). Malinalli also refers to a type of grass used to make rope (*mecatl*). By extension, in pictorial documents rope-like ties join members of a genealogy, whose connecting lines have the name *tlacamecayotl*, highlighting the processes that bind humans together, like rope (Kellogg 1995, 175). Malinalli thus carried with it expectations for the commencement of cosmological cycles, future growth, and survival.

Nepantla, Maffie's third category of cosmic movement, has fascinated scholars, who have tended to explain it more as an abstraction rather than an ethical orientation anchored in Nahua sources. Louise Burkhart recalls that *nepantlismo* as an approach to Nahua culture held sway among academics during the 1990s.[29] She explains that the term originated from an elder's comment to Diego Durán regarding the Nahuas' slow and partial adoption of Christianity:

> Todavía estamos nepantla . . . que quiere decir "estar en medio." . . . Me dijo que, como no estaban aún arraigados en la fe, que no me espantase; de manera que aún estamos neutros, que ni bien acudían a la una ley, ni a la otra, o por mejor decir, que creían en Dios y que juntamente acudían a sus costumbres antiguas y ritos del demonio. (Durán 1967, 1:237)

> [We are still nepantla . . . which means "to be in the middle." . . . He told me that I should not be alarmed that they were not yet rooted in the faith. "It just that we are still neutral": they followed neither one law nor the other well, which is to say, that along with believing in God, they kept participating in their ancient customs and rituals of the devil.]

Durán's project of conversion met not with indifference but with the desire to follow what seemed best to Nahuas drawing from both traditions. However, by elaborating a heuristic based on nepantla alone, scholars have generalized the specific comment of the elder across time and regions. Even so, and despite interpretive limits, I submit that nepantla remains valuable for understanding futurities. Burkhart (1989, 87–129, 170–83) has also shown the importance of nepantla as an ethical category of way-finding, of middling behavior that shaped Nahua responses to Christianity. Thus, nepantla primarily manifests itself through ethics.

A more productive approach to nepantla, consequently, is to emphasize its role in optimal living. Nepantla entails active mutual exchanges, based on *nepanotl*, which denotes action performed in a reciprocal manner (Campbell 1985, 212; Karttunen 1992, 169; Busto 1998, 7–21). Alan Sandstrom (1991) and Catharine Good Eshelman (2005) have elaborated on the importance of reciprocal gift giving in Nahua groups. Giving and receiving gifts are regular occurrences in many communities today. Nahuas have also placed great emphasis on reciprocity with deities through their proper observance of rituals, both in the Postclassic Period (L. Burkhart 1989, 142; Nichols and Rodríguez-Alegría 2017, 598; 184) and in contemporary Nahua groups (Sandstrom 1991, 170, 205; Good Eshelman 2005). Living a balanced life and path-finding requires reciprocity. Communities found their way forward listening to advice from the tlamatinime and the tlacuiloque, as discussed here. They also forged ways ahead by constructing powerful, extraordinary beings to guide them.

TEOTL, *TETEO*, AND PHENOMENOLOGY

Invoking deities' assistance to solve problems or heal infirmities opens a sphere of collaborative ritual activity. Molly Bassett's work on deity embodiment comes to bear here. Nahuas have interacted with their deities as singular (teotl) or in their multiplicity (*teteo*).[30] Bassett (2015, 57) recalls that teotl as an impersonal cosmic force originated with the Danish scholar of religion Arild Hvidtfeldt, who compared teotl to the Polynesian belief in *mana*, an animistic power that one gains by properly carrying out rituals.[31] Several studies of Mesoamerican pantheism resonate with Hvidtfeldt's view, including Alfredo López Austin's approach to teotl as an archetypal energy (1997, 10) and James Maffie's (2014) categories of cosmic movement. However, Anastasia Kalyuta (n.d.) has noted limitations in Hvidtfeldt's theory, drawing attention to his limited data set.[32] Working from Europe in the 1950s, he based most of his ideas on Arthur Anderson and Charles E. Dibble's translation of the *Florentine Codex*. Paul Kirchhoff (1960), anthropologist and contemporary of Hvidtfeldt, also noted that the Danish scholar relied on stadial theories regarding the development of religion and societal organization. The implicit assumption that all societies pass through a similar developmental trajectory does not sufficiently explain local variations in belief and practice. Hvidtfeldt's influence thus belies the overreach of his metaphysical and meta-social framework. Consequently, for now, a consensus on a definition or unified interpretation of teotl has not prevailed.

Whatever teotl may mean, it represents a gathering of metaphysical and concrete concerns. Bassett (2015, 127) has summarized her view: "Teotl is neither the monotheistic God, the polytheistic gods, nor simply god. Instead, (1) a *teotl* has *axcaitl* (possessions, property); (2) a *teotl* has a *tonalli* (heat; day sign; fate, fortune, privilege, prerogative); (3) a *teotl* has a *neixcahuilli* (an exclusive thing, occupation, business, pursuit); (4) a *teotl* is *mahuitzic* (something marvelous, awesome, worthy of esteem); and (5) *tlazohca* (valuable, beloved)."[33] Yet how does an impersonal force come to have property, a fate, an occupation, and how does it receive love?

In practice teotl did not exist as an abstraction or invisible force. Only beings that Nahuas could see, touch, and with whom they could conduct two-way communication made rituals viable. Consequently, despite his generalization of the mana principle to teotl, Hvidtfeldt's groundbreaking work continues to influence scholarship with regard to the *teixiptla*, which refers to myriad ways in which Nahuas construct physical representations of their deities (Bassett 2015, 61). In terms of Nahua futurities, repositioning the conversation around the ritual materiality of teotl (or teteo, pl.) offers the advantage of shedding light on aims Nahuas had when making specific ritual objects. Beyond an immediate ritual need, the construction of a deity carries a larger goal, such as the petition for rain (Heyden 1991; Ruiz Medrano 2016).

As Nahua communities embody and build numens, they reveal their aims and seek to activate potential they believe they share with their deities. In this study, I assume that both teotl-as-metaphysics and teotl-as-phenomenology shed light on ways in which the Nahuas have prepared for days ahead, before and after the Spanish invasion. Moreover, my intervention includes pointing out how deity representations allow for the expression of Nahuas' tools of persuasion; that is, how Nahuas portray the sacred (teotl) has a direct bearing on how they convince their readers to act. Representations of teotl and teteo take on human and animal qualities as Nahuas collaborate to give the cosmos its faces.

The Nahuas knowingly build their deities. This conscious construction of sacred beings stretches the credulity of Westerners—from missionaries to enlightened scientists, to postmodern intellectuals—who are amazed that Nahuas accept as essential that which they know they have made. However, as Bruno Latour (2010, 31) has noted, Westerners, through an ongoing series of cultural revolutions, also "replace the ancient idols that lie broken at their feet only with another statue, it too made of stone on a pedestal."[34] Western notions of authenticity and artificiality have little to do with Nahuas' interactions with their deities.

Rather, Nahuas take on a reciprocal relationship of care with the more-than-human. As Miguel León-Portilla (1993, 43–44) explains, the term

> *tlamacehua* denotes the primary and essential relation human beings have with their gods. These, through their own penance and sacrifice, deserved—brought into existence—human beings. The gods did this because they were in need of someone who would worship them, someone who would provide the gods with sustenance so that they could continue [to] foster life on earth. They could not, however, do this without human cooperation. There was to be a reciprocal obligation between the gods and humanity. People also had to perform *tlamacehualiztli* (. . . the act of deserving through sacrifice), including the bloody sacrifice of offering human beings.

Nahuas saw themselves as cosmic caretakers: they "needed the gods, but the gods needed them" (Köhler 2001, 131). Nahuas' beliefs regarding their extraordinary beings have derived from their empirical observations of nature over millennia (McKeever Furst [1995] 1997); from dreams (Durán 1967, 1:132); and through the use of psychotropic plants (Laack 2019; Nesvig 2021). These experiences, through the mediation of tlamatinime sages, found expression in sculpture, painting, or costumed deity representations. Each of these was a teixiptla, a highly animated image that drew an extraordinary being (teotl) from the cosmos and anchored it to the physical present. I will treat the concept of teixiptla in more detail shortly.

If we return to the journey of the Mexica couples to Tepechpan, a greater significance of their actions begins to emerge. They were born as members of the altepetl of Tenochtitlan. However, they viewed the world as animated, with each altepetl under the protection of its own deities. They took for granted that the deities of Tepechpan exercised influence over that altepetl. Their participation and the objects they carried—even if observers cannot see them inside the bag they brought—added to the energy expended for the deities. In return, the sacrifice would instantiate benefits they hoped to gain, presumably as residents of Tepechpan (Diel 2008, 36). Their ritual efforts added to the confluence of energy there. The problem remains of identifying the animals' associations to Tepechpaneca deities. The butterfly, snake, and bird, while open to various interpretations, anchor the scene in ritual time and by virtue of their combined presence. These glyphic elements represent a common phenomenon, the agglomeration of zoomorphic images in the representations of a deity. How is it that multiple animals stand for a specific being? Katarzyna Mikulska has described how depictions of deities reflect their ritual functions at particular times. Rather than possessing a set of canonical characteristics, Mikulska (2022, 456) proposes that a deity's identity

> was defined in the very moment of creating his/her image with particular graphic signs, in this way crystallizing certain of his/her multiple properties, important at a very precise moment (or in the ritual, when it occurred in real life). Some of these signs correspond clearly to what we consider names of a god, but there is hardly ever just one of them, as the distinct qualities of a god could be expressed as different names. Perhaps we should see the Mesoamerican gods not as distinguishable identities, but rather as a temporarily crystallized mosaic of different properties sometimes expressed also as names.

Mikulska's comments shift focus away from descriptions of deities as reified essences and toward dynamic, multidimensional goals of a Nahua group. Her concept of "mosaic gods" encapsulates the variety of representations of a given deity within the ritual aims of its community. Thus, a sacrifice of multiple animals in Tepechpan may evoke the deity associations I mentioned earlier (snake ~ Quetzalcoatl; butterfly ~ Itzpapalotl; bird/eagle ~ Huitzilopochtli).[35] The scene enlarges the social network to include the Mexica newcomers, the animals offered to the sun, and the environment. For Nahuas at the time and today, the physical surroundings of a community form a vital part of their social network (McDonough 2024, 76).[36] However, and more importantly, the three animals together gather strength and establish reciprocity, opening up a future for a growing altepetl. For the scene's painter, the deities required sacrifice and the Mexica couples' allegiance. The eight Mexicas who journeyed to Tepechpan crossed over into its historical narrative and the associated horizon.

As a part of preparing for rituals, Nahua specialists make images, sculptures, paintings, and costumes for deity impersonators, all of which become visual ceremonial focal points. A teixiptla possesses sight. Alfredo

López Austin (1988, 1:196–97) and Frances Karttunen (1992, 114) parse the related term *ixiptlayotl* as beginning with *ixtli* (the eye). Bassett (2015, 141) points out that ixtli also implies "face" or "surface." Taking into account *xip*—peeling, flaying, and shaving (Karttunen 1992, 325)—Bassett (2015, 132) arrives at an amplified definition of teixiptla: "someone's surface-flayed thing."[37] The covering of a teixiptla and the fact that the object had eyes meant that ritual participants experienced exchanging visual contact with their deity (Gell 1998, 118; Bassett 2015, 156). Exchanging gazes reached a new intensity when the teixiptla was a person. Regarding human sacrifice at the Templo Mayor, David Carrasco (1999, 83) explains, "the major ritual participants were called *in ixiptla in teteo* (deity impersonators, or individuals, or objects whose essence had been cosmo-magically transformed into gods)." Here I note that the diphrastic kenning "in ixiptla in teteo" means literally "it is its surface-flayed thing; it is someone's teotl." This expression recognizes simultaneously that humans have made the being, that it belongs to a particular Nahua group (e.g., "someone's"), and that it has a forward-looking, temporary existence in this mode. *Teixiptlahuan* (pl., per Bassett)—constructed, named, and allowed to endure for a set time—served specific ritual ends (Clendinnen 1991, 251). During rituals, the Nahuas interacted with their guardians and had the potential of touch with a being they considered living.

Closely related to the teixiptla, sacred bundles called *tlaquimilolli* contained physical parts of a deity and served as the most important ritual object in an altepetl. A tlaquimilolli held parts of the body of the deity who founded the altepetl (Bassett 2015, 191), a constitution with consequences. Looking ahead, the community's future prospects depend on how well they did their work as custodians of the bundle.[38] Gerónimo de Mendieta recorded a description his fellow Franciscan Andrés de Olmos provided of the tlaquimilolli of Tezcatlipoca in Tlamanalco:

> envolvían estas mantas en ciertos palos, y haciendo una muesca o agujero al palo, le ponían por corazón unas pedrezuelas verdes y cuero de culebra y tigre, y a este envoltorio decían tlaquimilolli, y cada uno le ponía el nombre de aquel demonio que le había dado la manta, y este era el principal ídolo que tenían en mucha reverencia, y no tenían en tanta como a este a los bastiones o figuras de piedra o de palo que ellos hacían. (Mendieta [1595] 1870, 80)

[They wrapped these cloths around certain sticks and after making a slot or hole in the stick, they put small green stones into it as a heart, and covered the stick with snake and tiger skin. This bundle they called a tlaquimilolli, and they gave the same name to each one as the demon who had given it its wrapping. This was the main idol that they held in great reverence, beyond that which they gave to the shrines or the figures they made of stone or wood.]

The care and reverence for the tlaquimilolli that Olmos observed shows Tlamanalco saw its own future tied together with Tezcatlipoca's. In chapter 4, I conduct a close reading of the account of the tlaquimilolli of Huitzilopochtli in the *Crónica mexicayotl*. In cases of deity bundles, materiality reveals futurity. Both the teixiptla and the tlaquimilolli embody deities, which make visible their past dealings with an altepetl and open future possibilities for communities who construct and care for them, in a process of focusing cosmic energy.

GATHERING STRENGTH

Deity construction requires physical energy. Nahuas expend strength in order to gain strength. Throughout this study, I refer to linguistic attestations of strength in descriptions of future plans. As we shall see, Nahuas have gathered strength for military endeavors, building projects, the healing arts, and educational initiatives. In the *Florentine Codex* alone, Joe Campbell has identified some 216 attestations of the verb *chicahua* (to strengthen).[39] As one example, warriors preparing for combat would ask a seer (tonalpouhqui) to read their tonalli. The most favorable prognostications would call a warrior's tonalli by the name *tonalchicahuac* (from tonalli, "solar head energy," and chicahuac, "it is strong"). This intense amount of solar energy indicated that a young man would draw on additional force, which would allow him to triumph (Olivier 2003, 18). Identifying objectives and gathering strength to reach them are crucial concerns in Nahua futurities. Proposing a future to audiences throughout the Nahua region meant communicating how to gather the strength to reach it.

Further examples of Nahua futurity from prior to Spanish arrival illustrate gathering strength as a key approach to times ahead. The education of warriors in the *telpochcalli* entailed periods of fasting and sexual abstinence as a means to prevent young men from lowering their life-force (Olivier 2003, 27). Fernando de Alva Ixtlilxochitl (Ixtlilxochitl 1976, 171) recorded how the first Chichimec lords, after leaving their homeland of Chicomoztoc-Colhuacatepetl, fasted in order to merit their title of tlatoque. Fasting and abstinence saved energy for the battlefield, where the warriors could expend their force for the altepetl and earn prestige. Sacrifice played a political role for the Mexica both on the battlefield and in Tenochtitlan. As Ross Hassig (1988, 10, 121, 128) recounts, the *xochiyaoyotl* (flower wars) had the objective of taking prisoners as sacrifices. It is difficult to overstate the importance and lasting impact of sacrifice in the capital.

Simultaneous to the rise of the flower wars came the reforms of the *cihuacoatl* (royal advisor) Tlacaelel, who served three tlatoque (Itzcoatl, Moteuczoma Ilhuicamina, and Axayacatl). Tlacaelel explicitly articulated the aim of feeding the sun (Tonatiuh) with the energy of sacrificed hearts (*yollotli*).[40] This need to keep the sun moving motivated the wars and tribute collection of their empire. Whether by ritual fast or sacrifices, the Mexica worked from the present in order to influence political and economic outcomes.

In the Postclassic Period, Mexica rulers developed state-centered discourses driven by concerns for the future. With increasing power and aspirations, Mexica tlatoani Itzcoatl ordered the burning of codices that depicted weakness, aiming to shape a glorious historical narrative for future generations (C. Townsend 2019, 33–34). This rewriting of history, although censorial and propagandistic, also strengthened noble houses. In these cases, reaching the future entailed ensuring success and survival, both of which Nahua leaders did not leave to chance. Thus, Nahua futurities in the colonial period built on ancestral precedents. The Spanish invasion merely intensified discussions about future times. The final portion of the introduction explains impacts of postconquest ideological shifts on concepts related to time itself.

TIME AND CHANGE

In the face of the commonplace of Western time as linear and Nahua time as cyclical, it is worth considering ways in which conceptualizations of time as linear already existed in Mesoamerica. In fact, even for the West, the sixteenth and seventeenth centuries hold the origins of linear time as we recognize it. In the Nahua region, the coordination between the tonalpohualli and the xiuhpohualli on the surface refers to cyclical time. Yet from the examples of ancestral Nahua futurities, it remains clear that linear progressions existed between problems Indigenous leaders perceived and solutions. Tlacaelel's establishment of the Mexica military-sacrificial complex provided a future narrative for Tenochtitlan. Likewise, in Tepechpan, the community already had a linear framework to anticipate conditions, set goals, and emplot their actions. Thus, the view that events occur in succession and that present actions influence future outcomes existed in the Postclassic Period, via linearity in political scenarios.

At the same time, and an ocean away, I also take care to not assume that medieval Iberians conceived of time as strictly linear. In fact, in terms of religion and agriculture, cycles influenced the daily experiences of most people. As Camarin Porter (2010, 1351) explains, "a plurality of 'times' existed. Sources reveal not only contemporary consciousness of a linear, Christian cosmology, but also a diversity of temporal cycles, such as the liturgical calendar and the agricultural seasons." Further, as Hayden White (1987, 9) has explained, medieval European annals recorded local events, such as floods, harvests, and plagues, with only a vague reference to the theological framing of the Gregorian calendar. Local concerns often figured more prominently in conceptualizations of time. Viviana Díaz Balsera (2018, 8) points out that commoners used the services of "folk practitioners" in order to "find lost objects or goods, to discover the origin or cause for illnesses when actors could not determine them, and for fortune-telling."[41] These divinatory practices depart from a unified, orthodox view of history as a single timeline and place emphasis on local concerns and contingencies.[42]

Nevertheless, in medieval Christendom the view of a present age with a coming end prevailed. Hassig (2001, 1) has described the conventional Western view of linear time: "originating in a religious concept of a beginning and an end, and later harnessed to the Enlightenment notion of progress, change for the West is ongoing, continuous, and cumulative but not repetitive." Further, although the future comes as an "outgrowth of the past, it is not deterministically embedded in it" (Hassig 2001, 1).[43] The linear organization of time implies that humans have the potential to reach goals, only not yet. Spain's history carried with it imperial objectives, the teleologies of religious conversion, and economic expansion.

Spain's ideological goals of Christianization and economic control in Central Mexico depended on a sequential logic of linear time. Aníbal Quijano (2008, 190) has pointed out how colonizers worked to replace Native customs by encouraging the imitation of European culture. Beginning in the sixteenth century, a confluence of ideologies, based on race, capitalism, and Europe as the model of progress, coalesced in what Quijano has termed "the coloniality of power."[44] With the *reconquista* of the Iberian Peninsula, Spain's leaders Fernando de Aragón and Isabella de Castilla began to view their newly formed kingdom as the protagonist in the providential mission of Christianizing the globe. According to Enrique Dussel (1981, 38), the Moorish occupation of Spain led to a blending of medieval feudalism with Islamic theocracy that produced patriotism in early modern Spain "akin to 'temporal messianism' in which the destiny of the nation and the destiny of the Church were believed to be united. Hispanic Christianity . . . was unique in that the nation had been elected by God to be the instrument for the salvation of the world." Papal bulls granted privileges to the Spanish Crown, facilitating Spanish colonialism.[45] For Castilian nobles, fortune-seeking hidalgos, and the clergy, the time had come for Spain to assert itself on the world stage.

The twelve Franciscan friars who reached Mexico in 1524 intensified Spanish providentialism with the belief that their evangelization would catalyze the Second Coming. Franciscan enclaves promoted the views of Joachim de Fiore, whose apocalyptic expectations of a coming of the age of the Holy Spirit fueled Portuguese and Spanish colonialism (Florescano 1992, 319).[46] Nahuas' proximity to clergy and colonial administrators meant exposure to ideologies that posited the teleology of a worldwide Spanish Christian utopia.

The imperial project to make Spain the first to spread Christianity to the globe occurred simultaneously with their economic expansion. In an ironic twist, the surge of Christian Spain's commerce catalyzed incipient processes of secularization. Immanuel Wallerstein (1979, 278–79) has described "the secular trends of capitalism" as central to the rise of the modern world system. The rapid expansion of Spain's worldwide economy established "regular trade between Europe and the rest of the inhabited world" (Wallerstein 1974, 102). After the gold from Mesoamerica and the Andes ran out, silver bullion from Potosí and other mines gave a bonanza to Spain, a flow of currency with no foreseeable end.[47] To my mind, this rapid accumulation of silver shifted Spain's attention away from traditional agricultural cycles and toward an open-ended epoch of shipping and trade. These commercial activities reveal a conceptualization of time resembling the modern, secular, and linear view of what Walter Benjamin (1973, 263) described as "homogeneous, empty time."[48] In effect, the universalizing designs of Spain conspired to interrupt and displace Nahua futurities.

In light of these considerations, when the Nahuas met the Spanish, they encountered an agglomeration of views on time. Western, linear time had its origins in Christianity. Yet religious conversion alone cannot account for the shift toward linear conceptualizations of time. Commercial and legal influences turned Spain's attention to aggrandizing the nation and the individual. For Spanish colonizers, the view of time as open or growing potential had only begun to form as a process of secularization. The Spanish had begun to dissociate their temporal actions from the Final Judgment. Consequently, if the Spanish imposed a linear view of time, they also imposed economic exclusion and with it uncertainty regarding any universal future.

To review my main argument, for the Nahuas in the sixteenth and seventeenth centuries, the future became a problematic yet productive resource. Circumstances were not altogether new, yet life had changed to the point that traditional wisdom no longer provided satisfactory explanations of Nahua writers' lived experiences. As such, they took on the task of proposing future trajectories. Their path seeking continued to aim for balance, echoing the tradition of the tonalamatl and the xiuhpohualli calendars, but their texts portrayed a range of human activity no longer based exclusively on one's tonalli. Nahua writers echoed the tlacuiloque tradition of ordering events on paper (Farriss 1987, 574; Lockhart 1992, 398; C. Townsend 2009, 645–46). However, under the influence of the Gregorian calendar they began arranging events that reflected open-ended chronological schemes.

OVERVIEW OF THE CHAPTERS

In the following chapters, I examine Nahua futurities in colonial-era pictorial and alphabetic texts. Chapter 1, "Problems of Perpetuity in the

Lienzo de Quauhquechollan and the *Tira de Tepechpan*," examines Nahua futurities in both pictorials. Tlacuiloque from Quauhquechollan painted a narrative map—the *Lienzo de Quauhquechollan* (ca. 1530s)—of their military alliance with the Spanish for the purpose of invading Guatemala, first with Pedro de Alvarado and later with his brother Jorge. Florine Asselberg's (2008) pivotal study shows how the lienzo provided Native warriors with legal precedents for privileges in the colonial order. My examination reveals Indigenous representations of events in linear progressions. The narrative begins with a ceremony intended to gather strength (chicahua) in the teixiptlahuan of various deities for use in subsequent battles against Kiché and Kaqchiquel Mayas. Unfolding events disclose Quauhquechollan's economic and political goals. As detailed in chapter 1, Tepechpan depicted their community life as a linear progression. The *Tira de Tepechpan* (ca. 1596) documented their efforts to maintain political and economic agency under the Mexica and later under the Spanish. Tlacuiloque in Tepechpan composed their tira to record past achievements and to demonstrate the altepetl's strength for proceeding into unknown years ahead.

Chapter 2, "Futurities of Well-Being in Books 10 and 11 of the *Florentine Codex*," focuses on human well-being. I begin with considerations of the Colegio Imperial de la Santa Cruz in Tlatelolco as a center of advanced studies for Native nobles, where they also preserved traditional knowledge from surrounding Nahua groups. The Colegio provided the space and resources for Nahua healers to contribute to texts on curative powers of regional plants, as in the collaboration between the Native physician Martín de la Cruz and the Nahua scholar of Latin Juan Badiano in 1552. In the 1570s, sixteen more Nahua healers would contribute material to Bernardino de Sahagún's extensive *Historia universal* (1578) that communicates Nahua futurities of healing through samplings of traditional approaches to well-being. This material comprises sections of books 10 and 11 of the codex that Sahagún did not translate into Spanish. Compared to the whole text, this editorial inconsistency draws my attention to understudied futurities in the information the sixteen Nahua healers provided on the human body, and their practices. Despite the interference of Sahagún, his Christianized scribes, and colonial administrators to suppress future-oriented information in the text, Native authorial contributions remain. I argue that the contributions of the sixteen healers, despite their fragmented expression, reveal cracks in the epistemological project of colonization. The Western organization and categories do not erase the fact that the codex presents the human body as a pathway of cosmic energy that, moving forward, required human effort to maintain and regenerate.

Chapter 3, "Warning, Reconnaissance, and Return in the *Anales de Juan Bautista*," moves from Tlatelolco to San Juan Moyotlan, the southwest quarter (*calpolli*) of Mexico-Tenochtitlan. There, these annals detail how Native scribes, through representations of a crisis in Mexica leadership, wrote future-oriented discourses in response to Spanish law, economics, and religion. A group of Nahua scribes, charged with keeping a census of tribute payments, followed the xiuhpohualli tradition, expanding the text's content to various events in mid-sixteenth-century Mexico-Tenochtitlan. I contend that while the Spanish set about weakening ancestral institutions that supported Nahua laws, economics, and religion, the scribes empowered themselves to reestablish a conceptual map of order in the city, with the regeneration of the altepetl in mind. In reporting the happenings of their day, these writers conveyed aims for economic and social cohesion. The *Anales de Juan Bautista*, a textual project without direct clerical supervision, walked a fine line. The scribes juxtaposed views critical of colonial directives while they kept their own voices at a safe distance from censure. Thus, they relayed the very words of a religious rebellion aimed at restoring ancestral beliefs and the cries of rioters who protested the Spanish monetization of tribute. Near the end of the *Juan Bautista* text, the return of the spirit of Moteuczoma I (Ilhuicamina) addresses imbalances, which they saw in the Native hierarchy and in the city's ritual life.[49]

Chapter 4, "Didactic Horizons in the *Crónica mexicayotl*," centers on education linked to the noble families of Mexico-Tenochtitlan. I show how a memory-preserving collaboration known as the *Crónica mexicayotl* (1609) proposed a futurity of education in order to compensate for the destruction of the ancestral house of learning, the calmecac, which had previously prepared Mexica and Tlatelolca elites to govern. Drawing on research by Susan Schroeder and Camilla Townsend, I argue that Domingo Chimalpahin and Fernando Alvarado Tezozomoc's collaboration signifies shared concerns about the future. My analysis also reveals linkages between the educational aims of the text and a project to rebuild the *tecpan*, the Native seat of government in Tlatelolco. Strengthening education and rebuilding governmental infrastructure reflect simultaneous work to preserve the nobles' waning influence.

The epilogue revisits the book's main argument—that Nahua pragmatism fired under ongoing coloniality motivated Native writers to generate knowledge about times to come. Nahua futurities appeared in the *Lienzo de Quauhquechollan*, the *Tira de Tepechpan*, the *Florentine Codex*, the *Anales de Juan Bautista*, and the *Crónica mexicayotl*. In *Nahua Horizons: Writing, Persuasion, and Futurities in Colonial Mexico*, my readings of colonial-era Nahuatl texts further our understanding of how they planned long-term engagements with the Spanish and in counterdistinction to settler colonizers' objectives. This fresh way of studying Nahua colonial texts has implications for teaching and research. The approach opens up further study of Nahua futurities in colonial and contemporary texts. In advancing this approach I invite further investigation and debate. Nahua futurities reveal understudied and complex counterdiscourses. In the cases I analyze, the internal deliberations of Nahua communities on how to approach the problem of the future contributed to their survival. By focusing on the aims of Native writing subjects, my approach explains how Nahuas have used writing and pictorial representations to shape their culture, working within pressures of colonial institutions and going beyond limits the Spanish imposed. Nahua writers have forged paths ahead, relying on their tried knowledge that even beyond the vanishing point, the world will continue moving, and humans will continue gathering strength and building within it.

CHAPTER 1

Problems of Perpetuity in the *Lienzo de Quauhquechollan* and the *Tira de Tepechpan*

A thin trail of dust appeared to the north above a long line of marching men. As the bearded leader and his horse came into view, residents of Quauhquechollan saw a red banner flapping from the staff he carried. The company crossed the Huitzilihuitl River and approached Quauhquechollan, a city one day's walk south of the volcano Popocatepetl.[1] Men from Castilan—as the Nahuas called Spain—had visited them twice already. The first time, they came from the east, with three thousand Tlaxcalan warriors. On that occasion, Quauhquechollan joined the Tlaxcallans to defeat the Mexica, who had taken tribute from them for more than a generation.[2] After that victory, the Quauhquecholteca made an alliance with the leader, Hernán Cortés, in the year in the foreigners' calendar, 1520. Three years later, after Cortés and the Tlaxcalans conquered Tenochtitlan, another horseman, Pedro de Alvarado, passed near Quauhquechollan. With his Tlaxcalan allies and warriors from Quauhquechollan, he conquered towns to the south in Oaxaca and Chiapas. By the time the third Spaniard appeared in 1527, with wooden cross aloft and crimson banner unfurled, the city saw his group as allies and defeaters of their common enemy the Mexica. This distinction earned the outsiders the right to ask Quauhquechollan to send warriors again, this time to help conquer the distant land of Guatemala.[3] Jorge de Alvarado promised them lands, titles, and rapiers as part of their compensation;

and why should Quauhquechollan not believe? They already saw that many of the Tlaxcalan allies wore rapiers, rode horses, and farmed their ancestral lands without paying tribute.[4] Thus, they renewed their alliance with the Spanish and began a campaign that culminated later that year in the founding of a Spanish capital in Guatemala—Santiago de Almolonga. These events grew so important to the trajectory of Quauhquechollan that the community's record-keeping painters (tlacuiloque) committed the events of the Guatemala campaign to a multipaneled canvas, known today as the *Lienzo de Quauhquechollan* (see figure 2).[5]

Some twenty-three years later, circa 1550, and many days' walk to the north over Popocatepetl and across Lake Texcoco, a tlacuilo labored on a long strip of *amatl* paper. He added to a timeline that stretched more than two hundred years into the past, with scores of illustrations concerning his town of Tepechpan. He also noted the year 9 Reed (1527) as important because of the influence of a new ruler in Tenochtitlan,

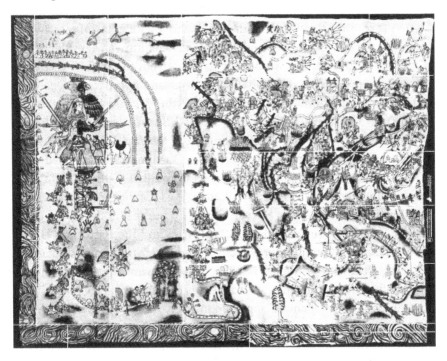

FIGURE 2 *Lienzo de Quauhquechollan.* Digital restoration courtesy of Universidad Francisco Marroquín / Banco G&T Continental. © 2007 Universidad Francisco Marroquín, Guatemala.

Hernán Cortés. He painted the hidalgo from Extremadura with a wide-brimmed hat, blue jacket, and red boots. Cortés would appear with many other rulers, both Nahua and Spanish, on this pictorial timeline that documented events of the altepetl of Tepechpan (ca. 1302–ca. 1596). The tlacuilo included Cortés in the lower portion of the timeline, dedicated to events in Mexico-Tenochtitlan (see figure 3).[6] Lori Boornazian Diel (2008), in her study of the *Tira de Tepechpan*, explains that four tlacuiloque painted images above the timeline of repeating signs and numbers follow their local calendar conventions.[7] Time spiraled forward, following cycles while advancing into what had not yet occurred. The painter's composition also recalls Cortés's journey to Spain in 1528 to argue for the legal validation of his conquest of Mexico to emperor Charles V. Cortés traveled with a group of Nahua rulers (tlatoque) (Noguez 1978, 1:120–21; Diel 2008, 99–100). For the Nahua audience of the tira, who were more concerned with local than with imperial politics, the journey to Spain suggested potential for gain through collaboration with the Spanish and "the continuing importance of Indigenous rulership" (Diel 2008, 100). Now that Tepechpan was no longer a subject of the Mexica, the future, in alliance with the Spanish, presented new possibilities.

This chapter focuses on Nahua futurities in the *Lienzo de Quauhquechollan* and the *Tira de Tepechpan* in the wake of the Spanish invasion. My analysis concerns rituals, economics, and political autonomy. Place and time became sources of uncertainty; yet place and time continued, rooted in intergenerational knowledge(s) and practices. After a period of initial optimism regarding potential benefits, each community experienced disappointment when the Castilians broke their promises. Laura Harjo (2019, 82) has observed that in many Indigenous communities—including the Mvskoke and the Diné (Navajo)—maps serve as a "tool of futurity." By mapping space in a meaningful way, Indigenous peoples draw connections between themselves and what is most valuable to them. Even on colonized land, Native groups can build forward-looking "emergence geographies" to locate themselves within an intelligible and legible landscape and cosmos (Harjo 2019, 40). To the extent that these Nahua communities made strategic use of space, they also made use of linear time. As Ryan Crewe (2018, 503) has noted, Nahua communities in Central Mexico at that time "reframed the past in order to gain leverage over an uncertain future."[8] The passage of time and what the future may

FIGURE 3 Year 9 Reed (1527), *Tira de Tepechpan*. Biblioteque National de France, Fonds Mexicain 13-14.

hold form central concerns in both the *Lienzo de Quauhquechollan* and the *Tira de Tepechpan*. At the point of the documents' composition, the past remained as an abiding presence and resource.

In light of this re-evaluation of group experience, I recall Antony Easthope's (1991, 182) description of linear time as a "continuous succession of nows identical in kind." Facing a potentially unending stream of the present, Quauhquechollan and Tepechpan needed to press on, narrativizing the liminal postinvasion years of optimism, disappointment, and preparation for events their ancestors had not experienced. Quauhquechollan and Tepechpan faced uncertainty. Would existing trade routes continue as valid under the foreigners? Would Native tlatoque (rulers) still have a say in local government? How would the population loss from foreign diseases affect Tepechpan's ability to provide for itself and to pay the tribute the Spanish now required? How could both towns negotiate with the Spanish, who now held the ability to raise or lower tribute?

In this chapter, I argue that Quauhquechollan and Tepechpan painted images and used alphabetic writing to strengthen collective identity and confront problems of perpetuity. The makers of the *Lienzo de Quauhquechollan* sought to record their triumph in Guatemala, proving their warriors' skills in battle and their earned right to farm and trade for a prosperous future.[9] How does an altepetl earn and deserve the right to farm and live on the land? From ancient times, they did so via cooperation with their nobles and deities. My analysis shows how tlacuiloque of Quauhquechollan presented tools of persuasion to convince their altepetl that their alliance with the Spanish and with multiple deities would allow them to occupy Guatemala and establish trade and agriculture there. Deity representations in the lienzo come to the fore since in Mesoamerica "military victory was manifest evidence of the superior power of the victor's gods" (Díaz Balsera 2008, 322n48).[10] I argue that the tlacuiloque used the opening scene of the lienzo to make a visual representation of a composite teixiptla—"mosaic deities," per Katarzyna Mikulska (2022)—combining the power of at least six deities, five from their altepetl and one the Spanish carried. This complex deity construction, I argue, reveals a retrospective interpretation, which occurred during the fourteen years between the foundation of Santiago de Almolonga in 1527 and its destruction in a landslide in 1541. The lienzo captures the optimism of a brief period when the goals of the Alvarado brothers and Quauhquechollan overlapped, under the expectation that favorable conditions would continue.[11] The animated view of the world in the lienzo resonates with the view of "the land as a living ancestor" (Case 2021, 11). Maintaining reciprocity with the land, the Quauhquecholteca continued socio-cosmic relationships Spanish colonizers did not control. Since the community held the map, it held the future of its identity.[12] As the narrative unfolds, the tlacuiloque used self-comparison and metonymy to represent the Quauhquecholteca as legitimate co-rulers of Guatemala. As we shall see, they showed the efficacy of the ritual energy they accrued in the opening scene via timely releases of strength and deployments of strategy on the battlefield.

Concerning the *Tira de Tepechpan*, I argue that as the tlacuiloque and the annotators made additions to the document, they aimed for future balance of their noble houses. The tira's emphasis changed over time, with the lasting aim of securing benefits for Tepechpan's Native rulers (Diel 2008, 73). In the Postclassic Period, the tlacuiloque used representations of the proper performance of rituals in their altepetl to show they knew the way forward. After the arrival of the Spanish, however, the tlacuiloque—and later annotators—shifted their emphasis to representations of their leaders' appropriations of Western cultural forms, most notably Christianity, alphabetic writing, and the clothing of Spanish elites. The bulk of the alphabetic annotations in the tira focused on "autonomy and identity" through the noble lineage of Tepechpan from ancient times (Diel 2008, 90). As a window onto Tepechpan's futurities, representations of rituals, royal unions, lineages, and postconquest building projects all reveal internal deliberations, which drew on all available evidence to approach times ahead.[13] As we shall see, royal lineages also allowed towns to gain cabecera status. A cabecera designation ensured a degree of political autonomy, since each cabecera managed its own political affairs, its use of natural resources, and its labor.[14]

A number of considerations deserve attention before I continue. The Nahua tools of persuasion in these two texts prioritize their communities. Concerning this linkage with future expectations, Diel (2008, 1) observes that "for the Indigenous peoples of Central Mexico, history was a political argument, a tool of persuasion that could be manipulated to argue for power and status in the pre-conquest and colonial worlds, hence the micropatriotic focus of many of these histories." I note that this same micropatriotic tendency of Nahua texts results in selectivity in their content in the texts I examine here. Quauhquechollan and Tepechpan recorded events that cast themselves in a positive light and moved them toward their objectives of economic and political stability (Asselbergs 2008, 185–86; Díaz Balsera 2008, 325n59). I also acknowledge that within their local concerns, pictorial representation became polysemic, open to various interpretations. This flexibility allowed Native nobles and their tlacuiloque to adapt the message to their political ends and to particular audiences (Umberger 1981, 11). During the Spanish invasion, Nahuas saw new opportunities to rise—a minor altepetl could grow in regional importance during the era of chaos and reorganization the foreigners brought (Lockhart 1985, 477). Polyvalence also allowed for these texts' enduring relevance. In fact, the *Lienzo de Quauhquechollan*, as with other Indigenous maps, "is still coming into being, and in flux, because all of its elements, uses, and destinations change" (Harjo 2019, 194). Thus, even today these documents remain open, anticipating the participation of their communities in the future. As I will show, over time, the makers of the *Lienzo de Quauhquechollan* and the *Tira de Tepechpan* added to and reinterpreted the content of their texts as they responded to emerging challenges.

Beyond uses of the documents within their communities, their makers communicated their aims to surrounding Indigenous groups and to the Spanish. Since the *Lienzo de Quauhquechollan* represents a particular example in the *probanza* genre (Asselbergs 2008, 244–45) and the *Tira de Tepechpan* emphasized merit based on affiliation with the Spanish (Diel 2008, 129–30), my analysis reveals Nahua futurities as arguments for autonomy. Despite Spanish efforts to impose centralized power, Quauhquechollan and Tepechpan envisioned paths forward and anticipated the Spanish would not have the final say in their futures.

METHODOLOGY

Recalling the Nahua tools of persuasion, my analysis in this chapter focuses on way-finding as futurity. I consider way-finding closely related to the Nahua concern to form and maintain relationships of reciprocity between humans and between humans and deities. This task of way-finding often exceeds the dimensions of Western cartography. As Harjo (2019, 617) observes, "Western spatial imaginaries are not complex enough to imagine and carry out Indigenous futurities, and therefore Indigenous communities conceiving of Indigenous geographies is critical." Likewise, although outside observers may not understand the locations an Indigenous map represents, nor the breadth of its epistemological implications, it remains clear that the map serves as one of the "way-finding tools that operate to create a map to the next world" (Harjo 2019, 38). In the *Lienzo de Quauhquechollan*, its makers were concerned with gathering strength through ritual measures before starting on the road to Guatemala. Repeating images of combatants and weaponry signals a conversation between the makers of the lienzo and those who were on the ground regarding how they found their way ahead during the campaign and what forays into Guatemala meant for their desired future. Narrative arcs disclose these deliberations. Among a number of knowledge-protecting measures in Mesoamerican-made maps from the colonial period—such as the *Relaciones geográficas*—was the use of the map as a repository of narrative (McDonough 2019, 476). With these considerations, I approach the texts under examination in this chapter. In addition to Nahua tools of persuasion, in this chapter I draw on multiple findings from Nahua studies and other disciplines.

Previous studies have used literary theory to analyze the *Lienzo de Quauhquechollan* and the *Tira de Tepechpan*. Florine Asselbergs (2008, 5), in her study of the lienzo, expressed her approach as concerned with the "structure and rhetoric (*i.e.*, convincing power) of the text."[15] Drawing on approaches from narratology, she incorporates the concepts of narrative focalization and fabula. Focalization refers to the viewpoint of a narration (Bal 2004, 263–96; Asselbergs 2008, 32). Asselbergs (2008, 24) defines fabula as "a series of logically and chronologically related events caused or experienced by actors, or the basic story material."[16] Asselbergs's landmark study of the lienzo reconstructs a narrative that explains the community's motivation to compose the map and how Quauhquechollan used the document. Along the lines of persuasion, I will develop more fully the epistemological horizons—the Nahua futurities—in the lienzo, which its makers laid out in ritual terms.

As for the *Tira de Tepechpan*, Diel (2008, 8) has used poststructuralist approaches from Jacques Derrida and Roland Barthes that consider "language and discourse" as "inherently multivalent"; accordingly, a text does not "have a single unitary meaning, but rather multiple and unstable meanings."[17] Following that line of reasoning, it would be possible to view many futures from any point along the tira's timeline. However, limiting my scope here, I have chosen to focus on the overall shift from depictions of proper ritual performance to the gradual, strategic appropriation of Western cultural forms as part of a vision of balance for times ahead. The abiding aim was to maintain economic and political stability for Tepechpan's rulers.

My close readings focus on repetition, comparison, and metonymy. By repetition, I mean the recurrence of signs and meanings that disclose values and aims informing these pictorials at the time of their composition. Repetition emphasizes the importance of a person, scene, or group (Asselbergs 2008, 29, 209), within what Elizabeth Boone (1994, 20) has called a "semasiographic" system in which "the pictures are the texts. There is no distinction between word and image."[18] As discussed in the introduction, the agglomeration of aspects of a deity resulting in an efficacious ritual image called a teixiptla also relies on iterations of images. Iconography in such cases carries with it orality. As Michael Launey (2004, 7) has observed, regarding the expressive economy of Nahuatl, "one-word answers constitute full-fledged sentences." Thus, every image represents an utterance, communicating narrative elements.[19] By the approach of comparison, I refer to those that the makers of these documents conducted: that is, self-comparisons to other Indigenous groups, or their comparisons between their deities and those of other groups.[20]

Finally, by metonymy, I refer to relationships of causality and origins between images. For example, smaller scenes throughout the lienzo connect to the initial alliance scene. The meaning of *macehual*, what one deserves, what one attains or enjoys (Lockhart 2001, 223), recalls that the commoners deserved to farm the land (Reygadas-Robles 2020, 182). In an altepetl, nobles and commoners were thus bound in a network of metonymies and stories that comprised their social worlds of relationships between humans and between humans and more-than-humans. The noble enclaves who sponsored the *Lienzo de Quauhquechollan* and the *Tira de Tepechpan* brought with them "cuitlapilli, atlapilli" (the tail, the wings) of society, a difrasismo that refers to the macehualli commoners as the totality of society and rulers' responsibility for their well-being (C. Townsend 2019, 74).

Synecdoche, a type of metonymy, also appears, in which a part of a group signifies the whole. For instance, representations of small groups of warriors in the lienzo refer to the thousands that went to Guatemala. Another important use of synecdoche comes in the relationships between the tlatoque (nobles) and the macehualli (commoners). In Nahua societies, the tlatoani (chief speaker) stood for the altepetl. Since the tlatoani represents the altepetl, synecdoche lies at the heart of Nahua political life. Further, synecdoche reflects that "most or all of the information on a single page of a codex relates to most or all of the other information on that page" (Offner 2014, 46) and that "the 'message' of such documents is the entire page" (Offner 2014, 47). Rarely mutually exclusive, repetitions, self-initiated comparisons, and metonymies in the texts open a window onto their makers' experiences, anticipations, and objectives. This chapter's analysis begins with an examination of the lienzo, moves into analysis of the tira, and concludes with considerations on the two communities' areas of mutual concern regarding times ahead.

A NARRATIVE MAP

The *Lienzo de Quauhquechollan* measures 2.35 × 3.25 meters (10.7 × 7.7 ft) and is painted on sixteen strips of cotton cloth sewn together. It represents an alliance the nobles of Quauhquechollan made with Spanish forces from 1521 to 1527. They allied with Hernán Cortés, later with Pedro de Alvarado, and eventually undertook the incursion into Guatemala with Pedro's younger brother Jorge. From the left section of the lienzo, the road enters Guatemala via the isthmus of Tehuantepec. Battles ensued against the Ki'ché and Kaqchiquel Mayas as the alliance made its way east to where they founded Santiago de Almolonga. A sizable section of the narrative map has been torn from the right-hand side at an unknown date, obscuring the alliance's campaigns to the east of the new capital.[21] The content and tools of persuasion in the lienzo point to its use by an Indigenous audience that would have viewed it as a part of oral performances (Asselbergs 2008, 26, 255). Its makers later added strips of paper as labels for locations and individuals key to their narrative and objectives. Likely they used the slips of paper as evidence for Spaniards of Quauhquechollan's role in the Guatemala campaign (Asselbergs 2008, 230). The lienzo thus has legal dimensions, along with other documents the community produced.[22] The lienzo was likely composed during the 1530s in the Valley of Almolonga, between the surrender of Kaqchiquel forces in 1530 and the 1541 landslide that wiped out the fledgling capital and displaced its Indigenous, Spanish, and African inhabitants (Asselbergs 2008, 227, 229, 255). The *Lienzo de Quauhquechollan* takes its place among the lienzos other communities produced for their internal needs (Mundy 1996, 111; J. Gillespie 2004, 119–20).[23] My contribution is to explain how the lienzo's makers constructed a deity mosaic in the opening scene to amass the energy necessary to conquer Guatemala, expand Quauhquecholteca economic influence, and establish their own noble lineages in the conquered territory.

THE ALLIANCE

When the Spanish and the accompanying contingents of Mexica and Tlaxcalteca warriors entered Quauhquechollan, they gathered local deities in combination with the war banner of the Spanish (see figure 4). By recalling that the alliance served to strengthen all forces, in this section I provide evidence that the scope of this initial gathering connected altepetl and cosmos. The core ritual space of an altepetl recapitulated all of reality: ceremony and cosmos fused together in community life (Florescano 1999, 229–30). One implication of the concentration of cosmic energy in the ceremonial center is that all things of the altepetl, its possessions (*altepetlahuiztli*), had the potential for ritualized movement. Since Quauhquechollan allied with Jorge de Alvarado voluntarily (Asselbergs 2008, 142, 238; Díaz Balsera 2008, 326n63), I observe representational similarities between them based on a supposition of equality. The Natives and Spanish in the scene are of approximately the same size and face one another. The alliance as a joining of human forces, through ritual, as we shall see, also became an alliance of deities, a mosaic of numena with the aim of taking Guatemala. In distinction to Asselbergs (2008, 221), I contend that for the Quauhquecholteca, the gathering of power and temporal transition did not mean the end of a cosmic age, merely the end

FIGURE 4 The alliance scene in Quauhquechollan, *Lienzo de Quauhquechollan*. Digital restoration courtesy of Universidad Francisco Marroquín / Banco G&T Continental. © 2007 Universidad Francisco Marroquín, Guatemala.

of Mexica control, as evinced in their locally specific approach to deity construction. Assuming the continuing validity of ritual actions always performed in the world of the Fifth Sun, the Quauhquecholteca built a teixiptla to embody the strength of multiple deities to prepare for battle and for uncertainties ahead.

The two parties made the alliance within the city walls and under the auspices of a double-headed bird. The resemblance of the animal to the bi-cephalic eagle of the Habsburg crest comes as no surprise. The widespread Indigenous use of European-style heraldry shows not unreflective imitation but rather a strategic deployment of cultural forms. Mesoamericans used European heraldic elements to gain status in the Spanish legal system and to protect themselves from abuses by colonial administrators and clergy (Wood 1991, 179; 2003, 57; Gutiérrez 2015, 51).[24] The Habsburg eagle motif appears in other Native pictorials (Gutiérrez 2015, 58).[25] Since the objectives of a Nahua group led them to make mosaic deities, appropriating heraldic elements did not preclude the incorporation of older visual elements. Ancestral deities were never far off. María Castañeda de la Paz (2009, 152) explains the assistance that Native painters sought by embedding images of ancestral beliefs in colonial heraldry: "the inclusion of the headdress of Otontecuhtli in the blazon of Coyoacan or the shield and colors of Xipe Totec in that of Tlacopan were 'hidden' yet important iconographic elements that would guarantee the protection of these patron gods." The animals, humans, ritual objects, and colors in the alliance scene together reveal careful selections the tlacuiloque made to enhance the audience's understanding of the alliance.

The concentric organization of the opening scene emphasizes the strength Quauhquechollan built through its alliance with the Spanish. The scene features a core of animated beings engaged in a ritualized exchange, enveloped by layers of cloth, feathers, stone, and water. Each of these materials had ritual significance. Sturdy walls to the north and east, the Pacific Ocean to the west, and the Huitzilihuac River to the northeast encircle the ritual space, enabling Nahua warriors and the Spanish to gather energy for the upcoming battles. The extensive walls around the city, by showing strength, draw on the chicahua linguistic complex. As I explained in the book's introduction, the verb *chicahua* (to strengthen) describes processes by which Nahuas have exerted work in order to accomplish their goals. Demonstrated efforts to build strength reveal a futurity of military strength, representative of objectives of the leaders of Quauhquechollan. Further evidence comes from Spanish sources, which recount the importance of Quauhquechollan as a regional center, the size of its military-aged population, and the strength of its walls. Hernán Cortés (1993, 92, 110) estimated that five to six thousand people lived in Quauhquechollan and that some twelve thousand tribute-paying households surrounded the city. The hidalgo described the four high walls and narrow entries that protected Quauhquechollan (H. Cortés 1993, 92), which Juan de Torquemada ([1615] 1986, 1:518) corroborated. Depicting strong walls implies the need to protect the acts inside them. Here the alliance uses that protection to gather further strength.[26] Thus, to my mind the tlacuiloque depicted the defensive walls that stood at the time to protect and strengthen their ritual preparations for the Guatemala campaign.

As for the bodies of water around the scene, I recall Molly Bassett's observation that the contributors to Book 11 of the *Florentine Codex*, while hesitant to identify the ocean as a deity, did describe it as marvelous (*mahuitzic*): "inic mitoa teoatl, camo teotl, zan quitoznequi mahuistic huei tlamahuizolli" (it is called *teoatl* [sea], not that it is a god; it only means wonderful, a great marvel [*FC*, Bk. 11, f. 223r; 12:247]). The Nahuas attributed an intense cosmic energy to the ocean (Bassett 2015, 124). By including living animals (fish and turtles) in the movements of the ocean, the tlacuiloque underscored the marvelous cosmic animations attending the alliance. By the same token, the opening scene of the *Tira de la peregrinación* (*Codex Boturini*) also shows the nomadic Chichimeca group that became the Mexica emerge from their island home, where water surrounded and protected them (see figure 5). Inside the limits of the Huitzilihuac River, the dual walls, and the churning ocean, the tlacuiloque depicted a gathering of intense ritual energy. The protective power of walls and bodies of water shrouded—as the dressing or wrapping of a deity embodiment (teixiptla)—the powerful animated beings inside the city.

Below the bi-cephalic eagle, in the middle of the scene sits a glyph of Quauhquechollan as a hill atop a temple, divided into four calpolli, each with a representative image on a chevron resembling Spanish heraldry. The residents of a calpolli, an ancestral, internal division of an altepetl,

FIGURE 5 Aztlan in the *Tira de la peregrinación* (*Códice Boturini*). Instituto Nacional de Antropología e Historia (INAH).

often had kinship ties (Hicks 1982, 230–31). These units also shared draft labor projects and military service on a rotating basis (Lockhart 1992, 14–20). The number of calpolli in Quauhquechollan at the time of the initial alliance remains unknown. However, from after the Guatemala campaign the *Mapa de Quauhquechollan* (ca. 1540s) shows that ten calpolli comprised the altepetl (Asselbergs 2012, 227). A contingent of warriors left with Pedro de Alvarado in 1522 and another in 1527 with Jorge de Alvarado, while a substantial number remained in Quauhquechollan. As for the chevron, the digital restoration has made its images only partially discernible. Francisco de Paso y Troncoso (1892–93) described plumage in the top-left quadrant, an eagle's head in the top-right, and arrangements of feathers in the bottom portions. These images parallel subsequent depictions of leading warriors in the lienzo who represent noble houses of the calpolli (Asselbergs 2008, 139, 144). In fact, as the warriors departed toward the south, four of them wore back racks, which identify them as leaders—one carries a radial arrangement of feathers, two have feathers tied to the tops of poles, and a fourth wears a jaguar skin with an eagle's head. All four hold swords and have beards, embodying Nahua and Spanish strength together (see figure 6). The choice of accouterments suggests deity imitation, a core aspect of a teixiptla.[27] It is

FIGURE 6 The alliance proceeds to the south, *Lienzo de Quauhquechollan*. Digital restoration courtesy of Universidad Francisco Marroquín / Banco G&T Continental. © 2007 Universidad Francisco Marroquín, Guatemala.

reasonable that the tlacuiloque of the community would include representatives of their deities in the shield in the center of the first scene and in their leaders' back racks. Attention to the beings represented in the scene shows further evidence of deity embodiment.

Several extraordinary beings and leaders share space and participate in the alliance ceremony that builds a collective teixiptla. The double-headed eagle above the joining forces represents both the Habsburg crest of Charles V and the patron deity of Quauhquechollan (Asselbergs 2008, 139). Katarzyna Mikulska's concept of mosaic deities, reviewed in the introduction, provides a useful approach to meanings associated with this compound numen. Mikulska (2022) argues that the visual representations of deities have less to do with innate characteristics and more to do with the aims of the altepetl that depicts them. The name of the town breaks down to "Quauh-" (*cuauhtli* = eagle), "-*quechol-*" (dark swan), and the locative "-*tlan*." Expanding the etymology reveals its meaning as a place abounding in the energy that comes from the combination of "cuauhtli" and "quecholli," a combined form of an eagle and a dark-colored species of swan (Asselbergs 2008, 241).[28] Pairing the eagle with the dark quecholli swan forms the linguistic attestation of "cuauhquechol," which translates as "Eagle Swan," not as a *cygnus* but as "connoting musicianship or transport to the other world" (Bierhorst 2010, 35). While I recognize the risk of treating secondary sources—Mikulska and Bierhorst—as primary sources, as we shall see, the ensuing action of the lienzo confirms persuasive approaches the tlacuiloque have employed here, through ways in which Quauhquechollan named its main deity. The altepetl, in conjunction with the double-headed numen, would produce and draw energy for their future success in the military campaign.

Other references to the eagle evoke Huitzilopochtli, the Mexica tutelary deity. The hummingbird (*huitzilihuitl*), an avatar of Huitzilopochtli (López Wario 2008, 154), also adorns the river north of town that bears its name (Huitzilihuac, "hummingbird like river").[29] There the tlacuiloque painted hummingbirds in a repeating pattern. Feathers also indicate extraordinary transformative power, independent of any particular deity (Russo 2002, 232–34). Heron feathers designated rulers and warriors in nearby Tlaxcala (Nicholson 1967, 73–75; McDonough 2016, 72). The references to Huitzilopochtli and war-making join further symbols of strength: the *macuahuitl*—a standard Aztec war club with embedded flint serrations—appears in the marvelous eagle's west-facing claw, while its east-facing claw grips a Spanish steel sword. The positioning of weapons is of particular interest to me. To my mind, the west-facing claw gripping the macuahuitl references the alliance's victories against the Mexica, while its east-facing claw gripping the steel sword references the force the alliance will display in Guatemala. The subsequent action in the lienzo bears out the importance of the double-headed eagle and other powerful beings in the alliance scene.

The doubling of animals continues in the twisting of a pair of canine-like beings under the two-headed eagle. These fierce animals face to the right to where the mass of the battles will unfold. The Alvarado brothers had a reputation for throwing their enemies to their infamous mastiffs (Asselbergs 2008, 89, 108, 180, 236, 242). The interlocking canines may also evoke a Mesoamerican understanding of local authority as images of the double-headed jaguar or puma had previously (Holland 1963, 103–4; Huerta Ríos 1981, 226; Olivier and Guerrero Rodríguez 1998, 127). Their twisted shape is powerful and recalls the importance of malinalli motion in the cosmos. Accordingly, "twisting transforms something disorderly and deranged into something orderly and well arranged; something weak into something strong; something useless into something useful" (Maffie 2014, 263). Thus, the twisted animal represents a ritually charged weapon within a mosaic of deities built for war. By joining powerful animals to the ritualized scene of the alliance, the tlacuiloque indicate a gathering of the energy of human and more-than-human entities.

Inside the city walls under the protection of the animated beings discussed so far, human agents accumulated strength toward their shared goal of the conquest of Guatemala. A Quauhquecholteca lord (possibly the tlatoani) embraces Cortés, a gesture that for the Nahuas signaled successful negotiations and served as a prelude to a feast, which made a legal transaction official (Lockhart 1985, 475–76). Gift giving for the Nahuas calls for a reciprocal response from the receiving party: one gives in order to receive later (Good Eshelman 1994, 144; Maffie 2019, 10).[30] Far from placing themselves under the Spanish, during this ritual parlay the Quauhquecholteca directed their strength to giving as a way to elicit future compensation. The Native nobles wear Spanish cloaks (*mantos*), sandals, and traditional headgear. Fully clothed, they show their high status (Sullivan and Knab 2003, 101; Olko 2014, 85–92). In this scene, the tlacuiloque portrayed their lords as equals to the Spanish: Malintzin stands close behind Cortés, combining the two as one figure of authority.[31] Other figures in the scene summarize separate historical events: when Cortés and Malintzin arrived to Quauhquechollan in 1520, both Alvarado brothers accompanied them (Asselbergs 2008, 140–41).[32] The number of figures present in the scene adds power to both parties in the alliance.

I now analyze why the tlacuiloque included the Spanish battle standard, specifically the cross of Santiago and the red flag in Jorge de Alvarado's hands during the alliance scene. A superficial reading would suggest the emblems as evidence of acceptance of the Spanish religion. However, evidence is lacking that the Spanish during the expedition made coordinated efforts to proselytize. Moreover, the depiction of the emblems recalls the images of a deity bundle (*tlaquimilolli*) in Nahua migration pictorials from the sixteenth and seventeenth centuries, including the *Mapa de Sigüenza*, the *Tira de la peregrinación* (*Códice Boturini*), and the *Codex Aubin* (1576).[33] Given these numerous incidences of deity-carrying narratives, I propose that Jorge de Alvarado's battle standard reveals a Nahua interpretation and depiction of a Spanish deity. Prior to exposure to the tenants of Christianity, the sight of the staff for the Nahuas likely evoked the importance of carrying a deity into battle. Nahua ritual precedents offer evidence for my claim. Unfurling banners denoted releases of malinalli energy (Maffie 2014, 325). In fact, the Mexica annual festival of Panquetzaliztli used unfurled banners in ceremonies of renewal (Schwaller 2019, 8–9, 42–29). Further evidence regarding Spanish inaction during the expedition also comes to bear. Spaniards do not always carry the cross and banner in this lienzo: Quauhquecholteca leaders carry it into battle in later scenes (Asselbergs 2008, 131). Finally, if any clergymen accompanied the Alvarado brothers' expeditions, there is no evidence in Spanish chronicles or otherwise that they proselytized Indigenous peoples (Gall 1967, 42–43). Thus, cross preceded creed. The actions of the Nahua combatants, who had limited knowledge of Christianity, suggest they treated the cross of Santiago as part of the mosaic of deities in the opening scene. Consequently, how the Nahuas used the cross in subsequent battles reveals that the tlacuiloque considered it a source of strength.[34] As with the Nahuas' back racks, battles released the accumulated energy of the Spanish battle cross.

Chromatic content also manifests strength. Colors the tlacuiloque employed in the alliance show how they set out to animate the persons and deities they depicted. The left eagle, though faded blue today, once had a covering of gold leaf that wore off over time (Paso y Troncoso 1892–93, 1:71–72). The term for gold in Nahuatl, *teocuitlatl* (sacred excrement), comes from "teotl," an extraordinary sacred entity, and "cuitlatl," that is, an "extrusion" (Lockhart 2001, 234) that the earth pushes out. Nahuas described the metal as "mahuitztic" (worthy of esteem, awesome, marvelous).[35] Considering the earth a sacred body, they elevated the shimmer and heat of excrement to a glowing metal that subterranean movements produced (Bassett 2015, 111–12). The crown above the two-headed eagle recalls that gold was "in tlazotli, in necuiltonolli, in netlamachtilli, intonal, imaxca, inneixcahuil in tlatoque, in totecuihuan" (the wealth, the good fortune of rulers, our lords; it is their prerogative, their property, their exclusive thing [*FC*, Bk. 11, f. 213v; 12:233]). In the traditional cosmovision, the earth also gave birth to precious stones, particularly *teoxihuitl* (turquoise) and *chalchihuitl* (jade) (Johansson 2012, 135–44). Nahuas described teoxihuitl as marvelous (*FC*, Bk. 11, f. 205v), which explains the great trade network that transported turquoise to Central Mexico from Zacatecas and from as far north as Chaco Canyon in current New Mexico (Bassett 2015, 125). Turquoise and jade colors fill the alliance scene. The clothing of the Quauhquecholteca noble, of Malintzin, and of Jorge de Alvarado forms part of their centrality in the scene. Ana Díaz (2020a) recalls that clothing serves a key pictorial convention for identifying deities and ancestors and for representing specific characteristics of their power. Likewise, the blue steel of the drawn sword, the blue altepetl glyph in the center, and the formidable ocean and Huitzilihuac River assemble strength through vivid color. Taken together, the chromatic range in the opening alliance evokes an animated, pantheistic metaphysics at a ritual event joining Quauhquechollan with Spanish forces.

CONQUERING SOUTH

Ensuing actions unwrap the collected teixiptlahuan of the opening scene and regather them at inflection points in the map's narrative: at the transition into Guatemala, during the founding of Santiago de Almolonga, and at strategic incursions into marketplaces (*tianguis*). Regarding the metonymic wrapping of multiple elements into smaller units, Asselbergs (2008, 150) has observed that "obviously the battles for these places were waged by armies, not just by the few individuals depicted in the lienzo."[36] The recurring appearance of back racks in battles thus denotes victories of calpolli groups and not of individual warriors. Recalling that victories provide evidence of the superiority of the deities they have constructed and animated, the synecdoche (one-as-many connotation) of the warriors would have been central to the oral performances in which the tlacuiloque recounted the alliance, conquest, and migration into Guatemala. Throughout the journey, the power of deities proved decisive. Keeping the use of metonymy and parallelisms as a main technique of the lienzo in mind reveals how the tlacuiloque released the energy of their mosaic of deities in retellings of their narrative.

Marching south out of Quauhquechollan, the alliance conquered beyond the limits of previous Mexica expansion. They came first to a region Pedro de Alvarado had taken four years earlier with Indigenous allies in 1523 (Asselbergs 2008, 40). Military precedents of the Mexica must have given the Quauhquecholteca warriors points of comparison. The Mexica tlatoani—Moteuczoma I (Ilhuicamina), who ruled from 1440 to 1468, and Ahuitzotl, who reigned from 1486 to 1502—more than doubled the size of the empire, and each left a mark on Quauhquechollan. Of the nine place glyphs south of Quauhquechollan Asselbergs (2008, 145) has identified, Huehuetlan coincides with the list of Ahuitzotl's conquests in the *Codex Mendoza* (f. 13r). The *Codex Mendoza* also corroborates Ahuitzotl's conquest of Tehuantepec and of Chiapan further south (f. 13r).[37] Other sources confirm his conquest of Soconusco, pictured in the *Lienzo de Quauhquechollan* at the edge of Guatemala.[38] Since Pedro de Alvarado had taken these lands previously, when Jorge de Alvarado arrived in 1527, they easily retook them (Asselbergs 2008, 169). By taking these lands with little resistance and extending their conquest further, the tlacuiloque represented Quauhquechollan as the strategic superior to the Mexica. In 1523, older adults in Quauhquechollan would have remembered Ahuitzotl as the warlord who absorbed Zapotec and Mixtec lands. These comparisons would in turn evoke meanings associated with Ahuitzotl. The tlatoani was named after a water-dwelling predator famous for luring humans to their deaths (McDonough 2024, 37, 66–68). Perhaps some would have even remembered the days of Moteuczoma Ilhuicamina. When the Alvarado brothers arrived, the Quauhquecholteca saw an opportunity. Comparing the previous five decades of their history to the possibilities ahead of them, Quauhquechollan moved beyond what the previously dominant Mexica had achieved.

Establishing a Quauhquecholteca outpost in Guatemala gave further strategic benefits. As Camilla Townsend (2019, 10–11) has observed, "the Spaniards would offer one advantage—they were even more powerful than the Mexica, which meant not only that they could defeat them but also that they could insist that all intervillage warfare cease in the regions they controlled. Many opted for that possibility and thus gave victory to the newcomers." The outsiders offered privileges and economic gain in addition to the oft-cited allure of war technologies (L. Burkhart 2010, 98; Matthew 2012, 46). Through an act of comparison to their recent past, they reflected that their tribute to the Spanish would not consist of human captives, which the Mexica had required after defeating a town (Hassig 1988, 22). Consequently, standing at the edge of Guatemala, the Quauhquecholteca paused between a past as subjects of the Mexica and what appeared as their future allied with the Castilians.

INTO GUATEMALA

Entering K'iché lands, the alliance halted to discuss perils and opportunities (see figure 7). Arriving in Soconusco, which marked the boundary of the Mexicas' former territory, the Spanish had no alternative but to depend on Nahua experience. In 1524, Pedro de Alvarado invaded this region with a force of Mexica, Tlaxcalteca, Cholulteca, and Zapoteca warriors (Matthew and Fowler 2020, 131). Pedro's earlier foray had caused complications, which Jorge and the Quauhquecholteca had to confront. The older Alvarado, when he entered Guatemala, formed an alliance with the Kaqchiquel kingdom of Iximché (Lovell 2019, 426). Pedro de Alvarado had come, as he put it, "para atemorizar la tierra" (to strike fear into the land) (Lovell 2019, 430–31n18). However, once the Kaqchiquel saw Pedro's tactics of torture and intimidation, they ended the alliance and became his enemies.[39] These considerations must have informed the discussion at Soconusco, which the Kaqchiquel called Retalhuleu.[40] Jorge

FIGURE 7 Retalhuleu, *Lienzo de Quauhquechollan*. Digital restoration courtesy of Universidad Francisco Marroquín / Banco G&T Continental. © 2007 Universidad Francisco Marroquín, Guatemala.

de Alvarado sat in his folding curule chair, projecting authority, but he also recognized the risk of proceeding without the guidance of the Nahua guides. This pause reveals Spanish apprehension and an opportunity for the Quauhquecholteca to offer their reconnaissance and intelligence. The lienzo presents Quauhquechollan as loyal compared to their mutual enemy, the Kaqchiquel, who had abandoned their alliance with the Spanish.

Before proceeding, it is worth noting how Retalhuleu provided a reassembling of sacred elements of strength from the opening scene. The strategic pause is framed between two rivers, a detail the tlacuiloque considered important enough to repeat and that recalls the river and ocean surrounding the opening alliance. In the sequence at Retalhuleu, Native allies face Jorge de Alvarado. As synecdoche, the three figures recall the totality of the alliance, repeating the initial joining of forces. The presence of personages from the opening scene, by extension, includes all the objects and their chromatic values the tlacuiloque used to depict their teixiptla—thousands of macuahuitl war clubs, hundreds of swords, the precious stones Quauhquechollan gifted to Jorge de Alvarado, the calpolli deities made present in the warriors' back racks, and the cross-and-banner of Santiago. The ceiba tree at Retalhuleu has a massive arrow shot through it, which indicates conquest (Asselbergs 2008, 151). I observe that the projectile's orientation points east, aligning with elements of the opening scene: the fantastical mastiffs and the Spanish sword in the east-facing claw of the double-headed eagle-swan. These parallels show steady progress toward the establishment of Santiago de Almolonga.

The ceiba tree and arrow also represent linguistic parallels with the teixiptla scene in Quauhquechollan. Within the Retalhuleu scene, crimson feathers appear in the shield of the scout returning to inform the company. Similar red feathers serve as guides on the arrow shot through the tree. Warriors and rulers wore the reddish feathers of the *quecholli* (spoon-billed roseate swan) into battle (Hajovsky 2015, 81–82). In fact, Alonso de Molina's ([1571] 2008, 2:96v) definition of "quecholli" as "pluma otra rica" (another fine feather) enhances the status that these feathers conferred to their bearer. Recalling the east-facing bird of the double-headed crest/deity of the altepetl, it becomes clear that the Quauhquecholteca combatants have carried—perhaps all the way from Central Mexico—valuable quecholli feathers as preparation for battle. Showing quecholli feathers in the arrow and on the shield reiterates the name of the altepetl, which the tlacuiloque have depicted as a place of abundant eagle and swan feathers. In sum, I observe that the gathering of feathers released its power into regions Nahuas had not conquered, paralleling the strength of the collective teixiptla image of the opening scene. Further, I recall the importance of periodic oral performances of the narrative of the lienzo (Asselbergs 2008, 33). This portion at Retalhuleu would have required shifts in the narration to remind listeners of shared goals of conquest and of Quauhquechollan's vital role in reconnaissance. Such a performance may have employed forms of the word *quecholli* and others related to the expenditure of gathered energy for warfare, including *mitl* (arrow) and *chimalli* (shield). As a parallel to the double-headed eagle, the ceiba also functioned as a conduit for cosmic energy between different realms, perhaps between chaos and order.[41] These elements together gather energy present in the collective teixiptla of the opening before entering Guatemala to settle there on a permanent basis.

ALMOLONGA

The foundation of Santiago de Almolonga holds high importance in the lienzo's organization and economic objectives. That foundation also recalls the accumulated energy of the teixiptla from the first scene. Through demonstrations of strength (chicahua), the warriors opened space and time for their future residence. On July 25, 1524, Pedro de Alvarado had taken the Kaqchiquel capital of Iximché, whose name he changed to Santiago de Guatemala.[42] Yet this was the extent of that foray. The renewed efforts of Jorge de Alvarado and the alliance in 1527 show that Pedro's earlier campaign was insufficient to advance into areas beyond Iximché.[43] Kaqchiquel resistance continued with roadblocks to slow them and traps they dug full of sharpened stakes to impale the Nahuas (Asselbergs 2008, 132–34). Near Chimaltenango, the lienzo represents a figure swinging from a gallows with his face covered: via metonymy, this figure may represent a number of Kaqchiquel lords Jorge de Alvarado executed, including Kaji' Imox, Kiywit Ka'oq, or Chu'y Tz'ikinu', the probable ruler of Iximché.[44] The demise of Kaqchiquel rule meant the possibility of Quauhquecholteca political influence in the region. In the ensuing confusion, alliance members gathered building materials from the abandoned city of Tzalcualpa, south of Chimaltenango, to build a permanent settlement (Sáenz de Santa María 1991, 34–35).[45] The alliance's goal of eliminating Kaqchiquel opposition led them to move the capital to Almolonga. With this objective in mind, the Nahuas focused on extending their economic and political influence into the future.

After the Spanish invaded Kaqchiquel land, killed their leaders, and found building materials, the foundation of the second capital of the Spanish in Guatemala, Santiago de Almolonga, occurred on November 22, 1527. Almolonga is the most likely site for the composition of the lienzo, due to its importance as a military achievement of the alliance. Further, from Almolonga the tlacuiloque could have climbed the Volcán de Agua to see and draw the surrounding area (Fuentes y Guzmán 1932, 55–56; Asselbergs 2008, 190, 222). The tlacuiloque confirmed Almolonga's importance: after achieving military victories in Chichicastenango, Chimaltenango, and Iximché, they regathered the teixiptla's strength in Almolonga, as various marketplaces also suggest. The taking of Chimaltenango served as such a pivotal event that the tlacuiloque again used synecdoche to represent the mounted Jorge de Alvarado, to represent the whole alliance, as he attacks the place glyph itself (*chimal-*, shield, and *-tenango*, walled place) with his lance (see figure 8). News of the alliance's

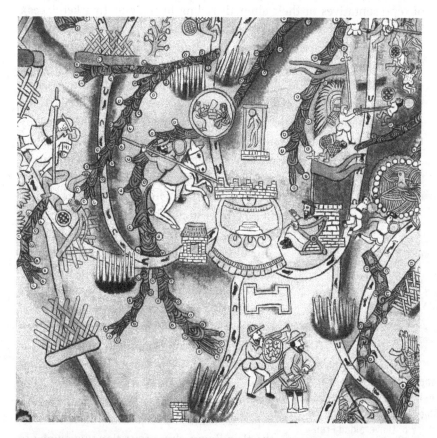

FIGURE 8 Jorge de Alvarado attacks the place glyph in Almolonga, *Lienzo de Quauhquechollan*. Digital restoration courtesy of Universidad Francisco Marroquín / Banco G&T Continental. © 2007 Universidad Francisco Marroquín, Guatemala.

victory in Chimaltenango spread to other Nahua communities.[46] To the Quauhquecholteca, recording victory in Chimaltenango over Kaqchiquel lands demonstrated the might of their collective teixiptla compared with both the Mexica and Pedro de Alvarado's previous attempt at conquest.

TRADING AHEAD

In this section, I argue that Quauhquechollan wished to gain influence over trade in Guatemala as a key futurity underlying their participation in the campaign. This aim becomes apparent in the various depictions of representatives of their altepetl trading in tianguis (marketplaces). The Quauhquecholteca had traded for generations. Some of the earliest Nahuatl-speaking arrivals to the Quauhquechollan area were traders of Toltec origin (Dyckeroff 2003, 190).[47] As waves of conquest at the end of the Postclassic Period took Quauhquechollan—first Huexotcinco and then the Mexica—the Quauhquecholteca directed their attention to trade opportunities in the south, likely as a way to meet tribute obligations. By the time the Quauhquecholteca settled in Almolonga in 1527, they had already engaged in trade between Guatemala and Central Mexico. In fact, a 1543 petitionary letter on behalf of Quauhquecholteca traders to Viceroy Antonio de Mendoza explains that since merchants from Quauhquechollan had already been trading in "las provinçias de guatimala e chiapa e xicalango y piastal tabasco soconusco chilatengo como a otros pueblos y tiangues desta nueva españa" (the provinces of Guatemala and Chiapas, Xicalango and Piastal, Tabasco, Soconusco, Chilatengo, as well as in other towns and markets [tianguis] of this New Spain, they should have official license to continue to do so) (AGN Mercedes, vol. 2, exp. 532, f. 215v–216r). Thus, on the lienzo, the tlacuiloque drew four tianguis glyphs to register their presence as merchants at Chimaltenango, San Miguel Tzacualpan, near

FIGURE 9 Standard glyph of a *tianguis* (marketplace) near Chimaltenango, *Lienzo de Quauhquechollan*. Digital restoration courtesy of Universidad Francisco Marroquín / Banco G&T Continental. © 2007 Universidad Francisco Marroquín, Guatemala.

Lake Quilizinapan, and in Almolonga.[48] Given their experience in trade and their efforts to expand their commerce, I note that the standardized depictions of tianguis in the lienzo represent assertions of their legal authorization to conduct trade (see figure 9).

In addition to depictions of tianguis glyphs, the work of porters (*tlamemehque*; sing. *tlameme*) in the lienzo sheds light on the project of expanding Quauhquechollan's commercial influence. The lienzo's twenty-two depictions of tlamemehque demonstrate the goal of controlling trade routes between Central Mexico and Guatemala (see figure 10). They carried food supplies and weapons and were present at the alliance's visit to tianguis markets, bringing goods and trading them. Military reconnaissance gave one motivation to visit the tianguis: by trading they learned about K'iché and Kaqchiquel maneuvers (Asselbergs 2008, 98). The value of that reconnaissance, I suggest, would endure for the length of the military engagement itself, which the tlacuiloque continued to record in the land surrounding Almolonga even after the founding of the capital. I submit that after helping found Santiago de Almolonga, they anticipated using the trade infrastructure they documented with their images

FIGURE 10 *Tlamemehque*, male and female, between Ollintepeque and Los Encuentros, *Lienzo de Quauhquechollan*. Digital restoration courtesy of Universidad Francisco Marroquín / Banco G&T Continental. © 2007 Universidad Francisco Marroquín, Guatemala.

to increase the income of their altepetl. By depicting the infrastructure of transport and trade, the tlacuiloque show that the unwrapping of the alliance teixiptla meant increasing Quauhquecholteca economic influence.

ALMOLONGA AND AFTERMATH

For thirteen years, 1528–41, the lienzo's representations corresponded to Quauhquechollan's increasing possibilities in Almolonga. They constructed a building that doubled as cabildo and church, and Quauhquecholteca leaders kept minutes of the cabildo meetings there (Lovell 2019, 423). The fighters from Central Mexico received encomiendas and towns in the Valley of Almolonga.[49] Nonetheless, outcomes fell woefully short of expectations. After the dust settled, the Spanish reneged on many of their promises to give lands, titles, and tribute exemptions (Asselbergs 2008, 256; AGCA A1, leg. 73, exp. 1720, f. 8r, f. 19r). Doubtless with bitter disappointment, Quauhquechollan's leaders turned to writing and legal action. They petitioned authorities and the king for better conditions and a coat of arms in recognition of their military service (Castañeda de la Paz 2009, 151). Suddenly, an unexpected event changed the course of Quauhquechollan in Almolonga: on September 10, 1541, a landslide from the Volcán de Agua wiped out the settlement (Otzoy, Otzoy, and Luján Muñoz 1999, no. 174). To my mind, this disastrous turn catalyzed internal Quauhquecholteca deliberations regarding their future.

The landslide shifted the emphasis of the custodians of the lienzo from a means to gain political and economic influence to a mode of historical narrative. The cloth would have enduring importance, particularly for "the children and grandchildren of the former conquistadors" from Quauhquechollan (Asselbergs 2008, 227). Despite frustrated expectations, the Quauhquecholteca and their descendants continued to live in Guatemala. Antonio de Remesal ([1619] 1964, 9) told of "indios mexicanos" honored in a procession in 1557 for helping conquer Guatemala. Even into the eighteenth century, some communities in the Almolonga area remained exempt from tribute (Asselbergs 2008, 118). Caught in the midst of Spanish interests and those of their altepetl, as Nahuas elsewhere, Quauhquecholtecas in Guatemala searched for ways forward "taking sometimes one side, sometimes the other, depending on how they might be better served" (Wood 2003, 9). Despite Almolonga's destruction, the lienzo became a memorial to Quauhquechollan's intense efforts to expand their influence. I also note that the landslide did not destroy the by-definition movable tianguis marketplaces. Even the mass erosion event of 1541 did not entirely erase their economic projects in the region.

Over the remainder of the sixteenth century, colonial administrators moved incrementally from granting privileges to Indigenous warriors to taking them. With the surrender of the Kaqchiquel forces to Pedro de Alvarado in May 1530, he no longer saw the need to compensate the Nahua fighters. Little prevented him from exploiting Nahuas and Mayans.[50] While most Native combatants and porters did not have to pay tribute into the 1540s (AGCA A1.23, leg. 4575, f. 64v, f. 84v), their living conditions did not improve above that of "brute animals."[51] Eventually, the Spanish use of Native labor exceeded what the Alvarado brothers themselves had anticipated at the onset of the campaign. On December 24, 1574, as the final removal of laws protecting Quauhquecholteca fighters and others from Central Mexico, a royal edict (*cédula real*) nullified legislation from 1532 and allowed the Spanish to press the Indigenous conquistadors into draft labor.[52] As with other Nahua communities, the Spanish tended to gain influence over Native affairs through laws and an ever-tightening grip on resources. The alliance with the Spanish did not achieve the expectations of the community. However, as I have shown, through ritual preparations and prowess in battle they showed the kind of strength they could still summon for unknown days ahead as many stayed to forge a life in Guatemala. I now turn to Tepechpan, where tlacuiloque labored over generations to preserve a record of events, which included future aims and expectations.

TIME IN TEPECHPAN

Multiple painters and annotators have contributed to the strips of amatl paper that form the *Tira de Tepechpan*, which measures 625 × 21 cm (246 × 8.26 in.). Two layers of gesso preserve their contributions, which account for more than 288 years of Tepechpan's history (ca. 1302–1596).[53] The tira defies easy categorization as a text for either an Indigenous or Spanish audience, reflecting various contributors' diverse aims during its time in Tepechpan. The document remained with the community until 1743 when the town's leaders sold it to the Italian antiquarian Lorenzo Boturini Benaduci (Diel 2008, 20).[54] The tira represents 117 humans and animals, with ninety-five of them facing right, aligned with ascending year counts. This orientation suggests a long-standing conceptualization of an inherent directionality in time, in which they assumed movement toward the future. The tira combines their traditional year count with Gregorian years added later, demonstrating overlaps of cyclical and linear times significant to the Tepechpaneca and indicating futurities benefiting their ruling houses.

Four painters contributed, whom Diel (2008, 19) calls painters A, B, C, and D. Painter A painted the majority of the images, using an ancestral glyphic style and depicting events from the community's initial migration to the Acolhuacan region north of Lake Texcoco, the time under the Tepanec and later Mexica rule, and the Spanish period up to 1553. Similarly, five different annotators added written glosses in Nahuatl to interpret the tira. The first annotator, likely a Tepechpaneca nobleman, wrote the bulk of this material, sometime between 1590 and 1650 (Diel 2008, 19).

The phases of pictorial representations with alphabetic glosses turned the tira into a palimpsest. I note that additions reveal reinterpretations of their experiences, which helped the town maintain compelling futurities despite rapidly changing circumstances. As time progressed, existing information in the tira became insufficient to explain collective experience. From the beginning, the tira compiled evidence in order to motivate the community toward action. As Diel (2008, 7) has observed, it became "a tool of persuasion commissioned by Tepechpan's elites to support their ambitions. By presenting Tepechpan as a politically and religiously powerful city-state with allegiances to the dominant powers, the tira's patrons and contributors intended to preserve Tepechpan's corporate integrity and community identity." Showing a united front toward the future, they would assure themselves of their noble origins and communicate to potential Spanish readers that their altepetl should hold a place of regional importance. Firm in their resolve, even as times changed, the makers of the multilayered pictorial held that Tepechpan knew how to manage its own resources, rather than relinquishing that responsibility to Texcoco or Tenochtitlan. Not all of the tira has annotations, which suggests that each annotator made deliberate decisions regarding content worth adding (Diel 2008, 113). Thus, I note that the intentionality of the painters and annotators carried complex acts of interpretation and projections of Tepechpaneca futurities. The events the tlacuiloque chose to depict reveal their concerns regarding times ahead. The Nahua futurities of the tira I will examine are the founding of the temple and center of Tepechpan, genealogical dimensions of the text, and ecclesiastical construction projects in the 1530s that the altepetl leaders used to enhance their ability to negotiate with Spanish power.

FOUNDING A LINE

Painter A of the *Tira de Tepechpan* made acts of self-comparison to the Mexica to assert Tepechpaneca nobility, merit, and political autonomy. I am inclined to think that these acts of self-comparison regarding their ritual center served as a starting point for asserting their futurities as preferable over those of Tenochtitlan and other altepeme. Painter A organized parallel histories between the Mexica migration and that of Tepechpan, as both had originally come from the distant northwest. Just as the Mexica overcame hardships and a migration, so had Tepechpan. Through a careful selection of visual cues, the tlacuilo presents Tepechpaneca culture on par, and in ways optimal to, the Mexica (Diel 2008, 123). Tepechpan became a tributary of Tenochtitlan after the latter conquered Azcapotzalco, whose Tepanec Empire controlled the Valley of Mexico prior to 1428 (Hicks 1982, 236). Tepechpan chose to emphasize its alliance with Tenochtitlan during the Tepanec war, ignoring their ethnic ties to nearby Texcoco (Diel 2008, 55). They preferred the horizon of alliance with the more powerful Tenochtitlan, who could lower the risk of falling under Texcoco's control (Lee and Brokaw 2014, 9). Under these political circumstances of the Postclassic Period, the leaders of Tepechpan allied with the Mexica and yet set a ritual horizon distinct from them.

Having previously discussed the importance of animal sacrifice in Tepechpan, I draw attention here to how the tira features additional rituals, in particular, strategic marriages nobles used to build the influence of their royal lineages. In the year 11 Tochtli (1334), the foundation of Tepechpan included noble marriage and animal sacrifice. The tlatoani

FIGURE 11 Founding Tepechpan, *Tira de Tepechpan*. Biblioteque National de France, Fonds Mexicain 13–14.

Icxicuauhtli (His Eagle Claw) and his Toltec wife, Toquentzin (Yellow Feather Garment), founded Tepechpan (see figure 11).[55] Five noble couples attending also witnessed the customary snake, eagle, and butterfly sacrifice (Diel 2008, 40). Long-standing controversy regarding what and how one should sacrifice informed Tepechpan's future-oriented rituals. During the decline of Tollan, a split emerged between Quetzalcoatl, who advocated for animal sacrifice, and Tezcatlipoca, who supported human sacrifice (*Anales de Cuauhtitlan* 1885, 17). Whether these accounts have a historical basis, they introduced a trope that would continue after the Spanish invasion—that of gaining cultural capital by defaming ritual practices of other altepeme. In fact, Guilhelm Olivier (2003, 161) has suggested that Native groups during the sixteenth century attributed "to enemies the invention of practices judged horrifying by the Spaniards." If Olivier is correct, I suspect that attribution explains why respondents from Tepechpan in the *Relaciones geográficas* commented that their only sacrifice was a daily offering of a snake, bird, and butterfly to the sun (Paso y Troncoso 1905–6, 6, 54, 83, 206; Nuttall 1926, 64). Bird sacrifice also appears in the *Codex Borgia* from south of Tlaxcala in the Postclassic Period. Marcy Norton (2024, 8) has pointed out that the *Codex Borgia* emphasizes feeding the energy of a quail's blood to the sun. Their claim parallels the scene, covered in the introduction, when in the year 4 Tecpan (1353) Tepechpaneca leaders and the Mexica migrant couples followed the precedent in Tepechpan of animal rather than human sacrifice.

I observe two futurities that follow from the comparisons the tlacuiloque draw between Tepechpan and nearby groups. The first of these futurities takes place during the Postclassic Period. At that time, the Tepechpaneca were concerned with representing themselves as more attuned to proper sacrifice than the Texcoca. That the bottom register, dedicated to the history of Tenochtitlan and other foreign powers, remained blank in the year of Tepechpan's founding prioritizes the altepetl's vision for rituals. The fact that they show no other event in the founding year reiterates their altepetl-centric perspective: Tepechpan founded their specific ritual time and started their distinctive march toward the future.

The second futurity I see in Tepechpan's self-comparisons with neighbors is the imperative for the leaders to protect their reputation in the altepetl by carefully interpreting their past political and ritual affiliations. As Diel (2008, 40) has observed, when the Spanish took over, it was not advantageous for Tepechpan to emphasize links with Tenochtitlan. While joining forces with the Mexica served their ends during the Tepanec war, now any associations with human sacrifice became counterproductive in the eyes of the Spanish. However, the strength of the early scenes of the tira consists in their polyvalence, allowing for favorable interpretations despite changes in circumstances. I extend Diel's observations, noting that former affiliations with Tenochtitlan must have also presented obstacles to leaders who wanted to convince the altepetl to follow them in the newly imposed colonial order. In other words, leaders knew that giving quarter to Mexica culture in their textual production would damage their tools of persuasion in their community, harming their ability to convince their own town to act. Instead, they chose the flexibility to reinterpret the past to form advantageous relationships, even with Spanish colonizers. Facing the years to come, Tepechpaneca leaders bid on a public, symbolic association with Spain.

EMBLEMATIC CHANGE

As with Quauhquechollan, images accompanying the arrival of the Spanish suggest optimism in Tepechpan regarding times ahead. Most of the tira's alphabetic annotations address events in the colonial period, which demonstrates that "the Spanish colonial present had taken precedent over the Aztec past" (Diel 2008, 123). From the twenty-first century, the retrospective knowledge that the Spanish would not reciprocate the support they had given obscures reasons Nahuas had for their affiliation with Spanish rulers. The tira sheds light on the strength of Tepechpan and how they planned ahead in spite of obstacles colonizers placed before them. In fact, since they had already lived under the rule of outside powers—Tenochtitlan and Texcoco—they had experience with imperialism before the arrival of Spanish hidalgos. Fatigue from years of tribute payments to Tenochtitlan and Texcoco led Tepechpaneca nobles to make strategic appropriations of Spanish culture to maintain their royal identity and gain benefits from signs of Spanish authority, such as the curule chair and European dress that the tlatoani Cristóbal Maldonado used at his accession ceremony in 1540 (Diel 2008, 77) (see figure 12). From this point forward, the Spanish viceroys appear on the upper register along with the rulers of Tepechpan. The local leaders now linked their authority to the Spanish empire rather than the Mexica (Diel 2008, 85–86). In the upper register, the makers of the tira also incorporated events in the Spanish Empire, including the death of Charles V.[56] The passing of the emperor would have caused uncertainty regarding the continuation of legal protections for Natives in tribute and labor requirements that had existed under his reign.[57] As earlier with the use of the Habsburg crest in the *Lienzo de Quauhquechollan*, here the bi-cephalic eagle on the tira's timeline encompasses Tepechpan in its imperial gaze.

FIGURE 12 Tlatoani Cristóbal Maldonado depicted in European clothes and with wooden chair, 1540, *Tira de Tepechpan*. Biblioteque National de France, Fonds Mexicain 13-14.

Tepechpan used a standardized presentation of the imperial blazon, the Habsburg crest, on the upper register in 1541. As in Quauhquechollan, the crest implied the voluntary association of the leaders of Tepechpan with the Spanish, showing their active participation in the reconfiguration of regional authority (Castañeda de la Paz 2009, 128).

Although the crest is an imperial symbol, its use here is the means to the ends Tepechpan has chosen. The crest accompanied a shift in Tepechpan and other altepeme toward the dual use of pictorial representation and alphabetic writing to advocate for their communities in colonial tribunals.[58] Tepechpan thus appropriated Spanish heraldry and alphabetic writing to their advantage to strengthen their altepetl as they entered unknown times. The Tepechpaneca also turned their attention to ecclesiastic construction projects to build their economic stability and political standing.

In the modern town of Tepexpan stands the church of Santa María Magdalena. Its walls of volcanic rock bespeak the labors of thousands of Tepechpaneca who, in the face of demographic loss, epidemic disease, and increasing tribute payments, laid stones and mortar one on top of the other (see figure 13). Finished in 1549, the church and convent became a local instance of the self-motivated mobilization of Indigenous labor, in collaboration with Franciscan friars (Crewe 2018, 489).[59] Tepechpan and dozens of other communities had reasons to build. Since a church

FIGURE 13 Santa María Magdalena, church-and-convent complex in Tepechpan. Manuel Rodríguez Villegas, Wikisource.

would provide "tangible proof that Christianity had indeed laid roots" there, ironically, ecclesiastic building projects became "the most effective resistance" to Spanish colonial control (Crewe 2018, 522). Although the Spanish began to exercise more influence on their daily lives, church building meant that Indigenous leaders stepped in as negotiators before the Spanish had the chance to control the project. Moreover, by building the church on top of the same foundation of their previous *teocalli*, this apparent ideological imposition is perhaps "better understood as the appropriation of introduced institutions, material objects or discourses to strategic effect on the part of colonized peoples" (N. Thomas 1994, 15). In Tepechpan a highly visible, vaulted church served as shorthand for "acceptance of Christianity and, accordingly, Spanish authority, just as the earlier temple to Huitzilopochtli showed its recognition of Mexica hegemony" (Diel 2008, 90–91). Taking the initiative to begin construction before the Spanish suggested it, Tepechpan managed to keep colonizer vigilance at arm's length. Nahua leaders thus led negotiations for the future use of their urban space.

Let us take a further look at factors involved with ecclesiastical building projects that gave Nahuas leverage in the face of pressures from Spanish colonial administrators. From the Spanish standpoint, an ostensibly voluntary acceptance of the faith made a military conquest unnecessary, in contrast to Tenochtitlan (Diel 2008, 75–76). Further legal privileges attended the status of *nuevos cristianos*, which the building of a church would announce to surrounding towns and the countryside. As María Elena Martínez (2008, 92) has observed, "the Native people's acceptance of the Catholic faith made them into a spiritually favored and unsullied population while their voluntary subjection to the Castilian monarch earned them rights similar to those enjoyed by natives of Spanish kingdoms." Moreover, statements from Nahua wills imply that building a church would provide local leaders with a way to protect their wealth from the Spanish. I would suggest that by willing statues, images, banners, and other liturgical objects they had purchased in life to the church, they perhaps protected them from Spanish appropriation.[60] In sum, building a church as a ritual and economic center reveals an astute understanding of the Spanish system. Tepechpan and other altepeme found a way to accrue privilege and distinction safeguarding against the meddling of colonial administrators.

(RE)COLLECTING

Tepechpan faced the seventeenth century with economic and even subsistence concerns they recorded for the first time. Based on its church, its operating cabildo, and its history of a continuous succession of tlatoque, Tepechpan applied for cabecera status. This highest local designation within Spanish law came with the responsibility for collecting tribute payments and sending them to the capital (Diel 2008, 92).[61] Inside their territory, cabeceras also managed draft labor projects and had influence over the use of land and water (Crewe 2018, 508). While a sitting tlatoani alone did not elevate an altepetl's status before the Spanish came, the colonial administration's ignorance of tradition allowed for social mobility.

In the case of Tepechpan, cabecera status offered the chance to raise their economic importance as a tribute collection center, a position that carried with it increased political autonomy (Lee 2014, 84).[62] However, the new status came with mixed results: each cabecera was also responsible for paying its internal administrative costs. This new system additionally ended a tlatoani's ability to use a network of *calpixque* (tribute collectors) to gather resources from beyond the altepetl (Hicks 1992, 1, 5).[63] This restriction led to several petitions to increase the availability of land to Tepechpan for growing crops and raising livestock, all to cover internal costs and pay tribute.[64] Evidently cabecera status did not always increase wealth. However, conferral of cabecera status did depend on the continuous presence of a local ruler (tlatoani) (Diel 2008, 98, 156). Thus, I note that cabecera status did have a perhaps unintended consequence of reinforcing the cohesion of local Native nobles. For Tepechpan, coming together in new adverse circumstances meant astute maneuvering and savvy collection of information regarding the workings of a foreign system. With time, they would need to summon every resource available.

During the second half of the sixteenth century, the *Tira de Tepechpan* gradually shifted to using poverty as an appeal for tribute reduction. The Spanish denied their petitions for cabecera status even with the church and convent they labored to build. Disillusion with the failure of their church, cabildo, and royal lineage to secure their desired future as a cabecera likely led Tepechpan's leaders to advocate for reductions of the ongoing tribute burden. Tepechpaneca leaders had learned that their representations of an illustrious history did not give them status under the Spanish colonial government (Gibson 1964, 188; Diel 2018, 157). Petitions and legal proceedings during the same period reflected this shift in tactics, through efforts to gain land or to prevent its loss to outsiders. In 1578, Tepechpan used the courts to stop a Spaniard from taking two *caballerías* of land from the town, which threatened to reduce their income. Yet the corregidor Francisco de Castañeda, after visiting Tepechpan, sided with the unnamed Spaniard, claiming that the land was uncultivated. Tepechpan's governor explained that because of deaths from a recent epidemic (*cocoliztli*) there were not enough workers to farm the parcels (AGN Tierras 1871, exp. 17, cuaderno 1). Eventually the courts favored Tepechpan when, in 1583, the community petitioned a land grant and this time received it (AGN Tierras 1871, exp. 17, f. 382r, f. 383r).[65] These stark depictions of what life under the Spanish had become contrast with Tepechpan's earlier optimism from the period after the end of Mexica imperial power. As their poverty continued, Nahua futurities moved away from the desire to improve relations with the Crown to finding ways to gain assistance from the viceregal government for their survival.

While depicting misery and illness, Tepechpan nonetheless preserved a horizon of hope that did not relinquish ties to ancestors. Hardships continued in the form of epidemics. In the years 1562, 1564, 1566, 1576, and 1577, Painter C signaled mass death with depictions of skulls (see figure 14). These crania situated in the middle of buildings recall a collective experience that does not separate the deceased from their living community. I recall Bassett's (2015, 24) observation that "animacy functions along a spectrum, and the spectrum encompasses everything in the world—even those entities outsiders might assume dwell beyond the limits of this world." The dead appear here as an enduring future-oriented display of the aftermath of invasion and disease. Thus, while archives tell of land disputes and tenure, the tira discloses a crucial concern of the town's leaders: the realization that demographic crisis had hindered Tepechpan's ability to meet its needs and to pay tribute. With increased tribute and draft labor obligations of the Spanish, securing future income became a primary concern for those who survived the epidemics. Before the eventual sale of the tira to Lorenzo Boturini Benaduci, the community's leaders held a document of hundreds of years of transition and adaptation. Despite their many hardships, Tepechpan had been preparing for

FIGURE 14 Skulls register deaths due to epidemics in the 1560s and 1570s, *Tira de Tepechpan*. Biblioteque National de France, Fonds Mexicain 13–14.

the future for years and had always represented intergenerational efforts toward way-finding, even before colonial challenges.

* * * *

In this chapter, I have examined Nahua futurities in the *Lienzo de Quauhquechollan* and the *Tira de Tepechpan*, focusing on rituals, economics, and political autonomy. Geography, time, and tools of persuasion combine in the *Lienzo de Quauhquechollan*. I have shown how Quauhquechollan strengthened itself by depicting their alliance with the Spanish as the construction of a teixiptla—a collection of calpolli deities and the war banner of the foreigners—in order to expand their territory and trade beyond their previous possibilities. They constructed this deity mosaic on their lienzo in the period before the landslide of 1541 destroyed the capital of Almolonga they built as a new regional center. I have shown how metonymic relationships between community members and between the community and their deities formed a mosaic of powerful beings for conquering Guatemala. In their forays, the Nahuas' collective deity and reciprocal patterns of work earned them success.

Tepechpan also drew on the power of ritual centers to chart a path forward. For Tepechpan, their ritual center anchored their descriptions of the past, including the construction of their temple of the sun, which attracted migrants from Tenochtitlan. After the Spanish, both communities used church and convent construction projects to concentrate their physical strength in architectural emblems of regional influence. By building before the Spanish had requested it, they took control of the project and the conversations surrounding it, making sure that the colonizers did not have the last word about Nahuas' interactions with Catholicism. In each case of ritual life centered on the altepetl, community expectations for how to prepare followed ancestral wisdom.

Amid the restructuring of local life under the Spanish colonial administration, both communities leveraged their ecclesiastical construction projects as evidence that they deserved doctrina status. This strategy provided local prestige as a center of proselytization in the eyes of Spain, which gave a measure of protection from invasive encomenderos. Often, doctrina status as a religious center paved the way for designation as a cabecera, a center of civic and commercial activity (Crewe 2018, 508). While by 1550, Quauhquechollan held cabecera and doctrina status (Crewe 2018, 510), Tepechpan obtained only doctrina status (Paso y Troncoso 1939–42, 16, 90–91). In Quauhquechollan, construction began in the 1530s, and by 1539, the church and convent of San Martín del Caballero became a visible sign of the town's influence in the region south of Popocatepetl (Asselbergs 2012, 225) (see figure 15). Local nobles could gain much from their town's dual designation. The building projects show local nobles still had the loyalty of the macehualli residents, who would

FIGURE 15 San Martín del Caballero, church and convent, Huaquechula, Puebla. Author's photo, 2021.

build a church now as when they built teocalli temples in previous generations (Crewe 2018, 513).[66] The chicahua complex of Nahuatl meant that those who built them would have spoken about the strength they exerted. Thus, the churches as ceremonial structures served as repositories of the energy Nahuas expended to build them.

Both communities placed emphasis on their efforts expended to build their churches. Tepechpan depicted their church in the tira during its construction, highlighting the labor required to build it (Diel 2008, 105). Through an alliance with Franciscans, the nobles of Quauhquechollan preserved regional influence in another vital sense: part of the project was to build subterranean canals from springs on the slopes of Popocatepetl to supply the town with water. By linking their altepetl to the water supply, Quauhquecholteca nobles and the Franciscans consolidated their economic influence (Asselbergs 2012, 227–28).[67] By relying on the traditional association of flowing water with an altepetl, this engineering project used an aspect of ancient knowledge to forge a way ahead.

The Spanish did not keep their promises to Quauhquechollan, and Tepechpan clearly experienced dissatisfaction with their initial optimism. However, both communities used similar economic strategies to gain strength and find balanced ways ahead. They worked to empower themselves as regional economic centers. Demographic decline due to epidemics and Spanish policies of resettlement (*congregación*) led to increased nucleation around the plazas and churches of Spanish-designed pueblos.[68] As discussed, Tepechpan used the tira to document epidemics. While the *Lienzo de Quauhquechollan* does not depict effects of epidemic disease, a colonial administrator in Guatemala reported four severe pestilences from Mexico (Lovell 2019, 418).[69] In Quauhquechollan and Tepechpan, the colonial church, cabildo, and plaza replaced the corresponding functions of the traditional teocalli, tecpan, and tianguis.[70]

Populations in Central Mexico began to descend from the hills to farm in valleys. There, altepeme with cabecera status gained numbers as individuals and families relocated for mutual support (Crewe 2018, 497–98). Perhaps whole calpolli separated and reintegrated in new locations at this time. Today, Tepexpan is a thriving town near Texcoco on the highway to the highly visited Teotihuacan. Huaquechula, although an isolated town near Atlixco in the state of Puebla, has remained there since ancestral times. The fact that both towns have nearly identical names to their ancestral pronunciation and the same urban space shows that their responses to the Spanish—their futurities—supported enduring population centers: not just survival, but life, to a degree, on Native terms.

I have also shown that in the face of population loss and restricted access to natural resources, tribute arose as another concern of Quauhquechollan and Tepechpan. With cabecera status came increased scrutiny from Spanish colonial administrators, who used the cabecera-sujeto system to collect informal information on economic assets in a community. In 1566, the *Tira de Tepechpan* recalls, an official (a *visitador*) came from Mexico-Tenochtitlan to conduct a census (Diel 2008, 105). This visit shows an instance of the administrative shift in the mid-sixteenth century away from tribute in materials and labor to a head tax, in theory an equal amount per tributary (Gibson 1964, 199; Hassig 1993, 226).[71] Annotator 1 of the tira reported another visit in 1578: "otechcalpouh filiphe de valdes" (Felipe de Valdés counted us by house) (Diel 2008, 136, her translation). In both visits, the ravages of epidemics led the Spanish to reassess tribute amounts and Tepechpan to re-evaluate its ability to pay.

By documenting their tax burdens, Quauhquechollan and Tepechpan showed the ability to use writing and images to project a viable course ahead. As the court case from Tepechpan shows, they were successful in gaining access to land that helped them cultivate crops and made tribute payments, thus choosing a path that would help them remain a vibrant Nahuatl-speaking community. Spanish interventions around tribute payment also occurred in Quauhquechollan.[72] State and Church were both interested in assessing the wealth in Quauhquechollan: in 1663, the Franciscan order conducted an inventory (*censo*) of the liturgical objects and books of the Convent of San Martín del Caballero (BNAH Casa 66, Título 6, f. 337r–341v).[73] As before the Spanish, the economic push-and-pull from the imperial capital continued.

Despite increasing reliance on Spanish infrastructure, I have shown that both communities sought to increase their political autonomy. Tepechpan and Quauhquechollan used the double-headed Habsburg eagle as evidence of collaboration with the Spanish and as a sign of political autonomy vis-à-vis surrounding communities. Both towns knew their urban planning mattered. As Castañeda de la Paz and Miguel Luque-Talaván (2010b, 299) have observed, during the sixteenth century, "Indigenous society understood perfectly well the distinction Spanish society made between a city and a town." This early understanding of the law led Nahua communities to use juridical instruments—heraldic devices, probanzas de mérito, and genealogies—to gain the designation of civitas under Spanish law and the rights to manage natural resources and labor drafts that this designation gave. Displays of Nahua lineages also shed light on their futurities. Tepechpan's leaders emphasized their unbroken ruling line along with their experience of generations of self-governance and participation in a tribute system. To announce their autonomy, both communities also appropriated European dress and technologies: the Quauhquecholteca used European weapons and Jorge de Alvarado's crimson banner to aid their attacks in Guatemala, while rulers in Tepechpan gradually appropriated the dress and accouterments of European rulers (Diel 2008, 82–84). Quauhquechollan and Tepechpan both reasoned that association with the Spanish would help free them from the former imperial power, Tenochtitlan, and allow them to make more decisions for themselves moving forward.

By 1560, in Quauhquechollan it was possible to face northward and see the road the Spanish had taken when they first arrived in the 1520s. Now the Franciscan convent and church of San Martín del Caballero broke the skyline, bells pealed out the hours, and three languages—Nahuatl, Latin, and Spanish—were spoken in the town. This transformation occurred within a generation. Yet many changes came through the initiative of Native leaders and residents of the town rather than a unilateral imposition by outsiders. In fact, that the town chose these changes and new sounds adds nuance to Luis Cárcamo-Huechante's (Mapuche) (2013, 51) concept of "acoustic colonialism" as a means the Spanish used to impose their power.[74] In the case of Quauhquechollan, I observe the deft maneuver of Indigenous leaders, who formed another alliance, this time with Franciscan clergy, as a counterbalance to interference from colonial administrators. Quauhquechollan opted to modify its own center to face the challenges ahead. That the town and these buildings stand today shows the vitality of those futurities.

Likewise, in Tepechpan, nobles employed strategic images on their timeline that reveal futurities of political autonomy and economic preparedness. The tira shows that in 1585 a new Tepechpaneca tlatoani used a curule European-style chair. He wore the traditional white tilma of his predecessors and, facing toward the ascending years, his image sits resolute toward forces arrayed against the community. The new tlatoani of Tepechpan was installed in the same year that viceroy Álvaro Manrique de Zúñiga began his tenure in Mexico-Tenochtitlan on the lower register of the tira. Both rulers look pensively forward, suggesting a shared horizon between Tepechpan and the viceregal government. Cynically dismissing the image as oppressive would miss the point: the leaders of Tepechpan worked closely with the makers of the tira to articulate what they perceived as a message of strength. Through legal battles, they advocated for reciprocity between their town and the viceregal government. Even with the viceroy's image, the tlatoani of Tepechpan stays on the upper register, a format that continues to prioritize Tepechpan. After the nearly three centuries of attainments and setbacks, residents of the altepetl represent themselves as the protagonists of their story.

In this chapter, we have seen how Quauhquechollan and Tepechpan confronted problems of perpetuity and expected time to ultimately favor persistent work, careful management of resources, and group cohesion. By keeping their narratives, they kept their futurities. I now turn to the island of Tlatelolco: there we will see an educational institution where in-depth research into Nahua healing practices during the sixteenth century offered ways forward that lived in tension with the desire of Spanish clergy and administrators to domesticate and erase those practices.

CHAPTER 2

• • • •

Futurities of Well-Being in Books 10 and 11 of the *Florentine Codex*

> El médico no puede acatadamente aplicar las medicinas al enfermo sin que primero conozca de qué humor, o de qué causa procede la enfermedad. De manera que el buen médico conviene sea docto en el conocimiento de las medicinas y en el de las enfermedades, para aplicar convenibemente a cada enfermedad la medicina contraria. Los predicadores, y confesores, médicos son de las ánimas, para curar las enfermedades espirituales. (*FC*, Bk. 1, f. 1r)

> [The physician cannot correctly administer medicines to the sick person without first knowing from which humor or from which cause the ailment arises. Thus, the good physician should be expert in the knowledge of medicines and ailments in order to effectively apply to each illness the opposing medicine. Preachers and confessors are physicians of souls for the curing of spiritual diseases.]

The Franciscan friar Bernardino de Sahagún's metaphor of the priest-as-spiritual-physician forms an intersection of medicine and epistemology in the prologue to the compendium on Nahua history and culture, which he called *Historia universal de las cosas de la Nueva España* and is known today as the *Florentine Codex* (1578). Full of meanings not immediately evident to Sahagún, "medicine and ailments" in Book 11 of the codex, which records Indigenous healing and plant cures, implied more than the means of conversion.[1] The many futurities in Book 11 and how they differed from Sahagún's diagnosis of Nahua well-being form the focus of this chapter.

Realities of postinvasion Mexico held disease at the forefront of the friar's mind and those of the many Nahuas who contributed to the project. When Sahagún wrote these opening lines of the twelve-volume codex, a recent epidemic had ravaged Mexico-Tenochtitlan and Central Mexico (Terraciano 2019, 9). The plague of 1576, during the final compilation of the *Florentine Codex*, recalled the 1545 cocoliztli (typhus or smallpox), which had claimed thousands of Indigenous lives and nearly taken his (Terraciano 2019, 1; McDonough 2024, 34; *FC*, Bk. 10, f. 83r). During the final months of writing the monumental linguistic and cultural compendium, even painters and scribes perished in the epidemic (*FC*, Bk. 11, f. 390r; Magaloni Kerpel 2011, 49–51). Perhaps due to these experiences, healing practices had long interested Sahagún, who had worked with the help of Nahua scholars to gather information on Indigenous plant treatments, beginning in the 1540s in Tlatelolco and Texcoco and in the 1550s in Tepepulco.[2] Four Nahua scholars conducted much of this research by consulting healing practitioners called *titicih* (sing. *ticitl*). The scholars Antonio Valeriano, Alonso Vegerano, Pedro de San Buenaventura, and Martín Jacobita conducted a third series of interviews between 1561 and 1565 again in Tlatelolco. The compiled results of interviews of the three rounds during three decades became Books 10 and 11 of the *Florentine Codex* (*FC*, Bk. 2, f. 2r). In 1575, the president of the Council of the Indies in Seville, Juan de Ovando, requested a complete copy of the compendium. Ovando had heard of the collaborative investigation in Tlatelolco into Nahua culture and wished to use the project's findings to help colonial administrators learn more about New Spain and its inhabitants.

Preparing this resource for colonial administrators was already a change of plans: Sahagún had intended to entitle the compendium *Historia universal de las cosas de la Nueva España*, as a manual for clergy in New Spain to help them identify and discourage continuing ancestral beliefs and practices among Nahua converts (Browne 2000, 111–12).[3] The format he envisioned would serve the linguistic needs of priests with "three columns per page, comprising the Nahuatl text, the Spanish translation, and explanatory notes of Nahuatl terms" (Ríos Castaño 2014,

216). In 1558, Francisco de Toral, the prelate of the Franciscan Order, had commissioned Sahagún to write a twelve-volume version of the *Historia universal* "para la doctrina, cultura y manutencia, de la cristiandad, destos naturales" (for the catechesis, teaching of culture, and maintaining Christian customs among these Natives) (*FC*, Bk. 2, f. 1v).[4] With that purpose, the friar asked the four selected Nahua scholars to conduct interviews of elders living near the Franciscan convent in Tepepulco (Terraciano 2019, 6). The materials they wrote there became the drafts of the *Historia universal* and survive as the *Primeros memoriales* in the collection of manuscripts designated as the *Códices matritenses*.[5] The *Florentine Codex* gives a bilingual account in parallel columns of Nahuatl and Spanish, which preserved the left-hand and center columns of the *Primeros memoriales*.

In what sense did Sahagún use the *Historia universal* project to control the future of Nahua culture? By following Francisco Toral's commission to the letter, Sahagún showed a primary concern with indoctrination, and by explaining Nahua culture to an audience of European clergy, he hoped to help them eradicate what he deemed idolatrous. To the extent that the Toral commission aimed to convert, it encouraged cultural erasure (Vásquez 2011, 30). Similarly, Juan de Ovando's commission of the final iteration of the text for administrative purposes aimed at moving the region toward Hispanization. In both cases, translation made culture legible to outsiders, which served the Spanish aim of control (Mignolo 2005, 144). Ovando's desire to translate reveals a desire to possess. As Rolando Vázquez (2011, 33) observes, colonial translation "brings into legibility a double movement: on the one hand, an economy of appropriation and expansion of modernity's epistemic territory, and on the other, the active rejection, the making invisible of modernity's elsewhere, of modernity's others." The *Florentine Codex* thus represents an effort to expand imperial reach.

Even so, in their compiling and editing of Books 10 and 11 of the *Florentine Codex*, Sahagún and the Nahua scholars did inconsistent work when it came to erasing or silencing Native knowledge(s). The ironic turn that motives this chapter is that untranslated lists of parts of the human body in Book 10 and untranslated healing plants in Book 11 of the *Florentine Codex* present fissures in Sahagún's design of persuading Nahuas to abandon their traditional beliefs. Among the plants the Nahua scholars had recorded for the *Primeros memoriales* were *centli* (*cintli*) (dried maize cob) and the hallucinogens *peiotl* (peyote) and *taloa* (datura), all of which treat head fevers within a particular vision of an interconnected body and cosmos, and all of which reappeared in the *Florentine Codex* (López Austin 1971, 63–74).

What the Spanish columns do not contain interests me merely as a point of departure for entering into the Nahuatl text in Books 10 and 11.[6] In Book 10, instead of translating the list of parts of the body Nahua healers had provided, Sahagún included a section titled "Confutación," which focuses on his life's work in Central Mexico. The Confutación does not fill the entire section dedicated to parts of the body, and he left the remaining columns blank (see figure 16). In Book 11, chapter 7, the Spanish column again falls silent regarding plant-based treatments for illnesses, including entries on uses of hallucinogenics.[7] In 150 entries in Book 11, descriptions appear of illnesses and herbal treatments with instructions on how to prepare the plants as drinks or poultices.[8] The first thirty-one of these entries reflect the Nahua conceptualization of the body as a pathway and include the use of psychotropic plants as a diagnostic method.

In light of the foregoing, in this chapter I argue that the Nahuatl descriptions of the human body and healing plants in Books 10 and 11 communicate futurities of healing within a traditional Nahua view of the human body. I observe a precarious balance at work. On the one hand, the formatting of the *Florentine Codex* has fragmented Nahua knowledge(s) on the body and healing, obfuscating them. Kelly McDonough (2020, 396) has explained that "interference" from colonial agents becomes "'colonial static' whose noise renders a message indiscernible or invisible." However, as I show in this chapter, the continuity of material regarding healing plants between the *Primeros memoriales* and the *Florentine Codex* and between the books of the *Florentine Codex* itself indicates a dynamic network of lived practices among the Nahua healers who contributed. In fact, parallels and cross-references join in a network that refers uniformly to future concerns. Understanding the importance of Indigenous authorship as crucial to these sections of the *Florentine Codex*, I also argue that the Nahua healers' contributions, despite the use of preset questionnaires and the subsequent editing of their responses, communicate their collective assumption of the existence of future readers and the future usefulness of the content they contributed. Doing embodied

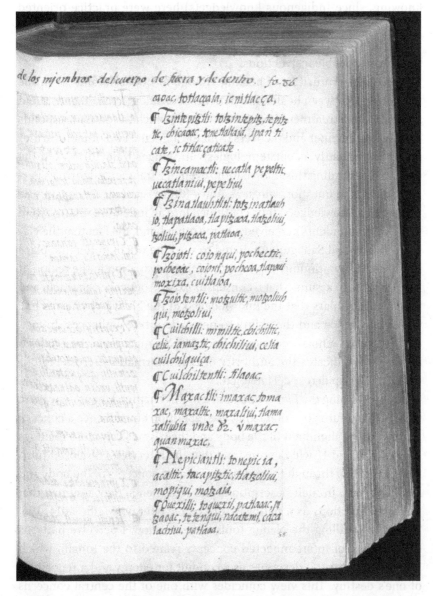

FIGURE 16 Book 10, chapter 27, f. 55v–56r, *Florentine Codex*. This sample text typifies left-hand columns where Sahagún left no Spanish glosses. Folio 56r references functions of the *ihiyotl* (liver). Library of Congress, World Digital Library, accessed April 15, 2024.

knowing, since Indigenous knowledge(s) here were practice-oriented (Maffie 2009, 57). Thus, Nahua healing and bodily well-being form an active, future-oriented path, apt for its format of descriptive writing of specific, actionable instructions.

Three main futurities of healing emerge in Books 10 and 11. In the relationship between healer and patient, I consider that a diagnosis and recommended treatment imagine a future in which the patient responds in a positive manner and recovers from the ailment. Two other futurities figure prominently as epistemologies with longer trajectories. On the one hand, recording this information, even in a fragmented form as part of responses to questionnaires, assumes future readers will consult the text. Nahua knowledge(s) thus continued into an indefinite time, beyond what the respondents perceived. On the other hand, the fact that the Nahua scholars and Sahagún gravitated toward the titicih in the first place illustrates the continuing importance of that occupation in the region. It is reasonable to assume that a consensus existed between the titicih and the Nahua scholars that the knowledge(s) of the Native physicians had utility in practice and the ability to persuade future audiences. In fact, that the Nahua scholars developed Book 11 from material in the *Primeros memoriales* indicates the authority of that information across regions (between Tepepulco and Tlatelolco).

In approaching the *Florentine Codex* in this chapter, I focus on ways in which Nahua futurities of healing use repetition and advance a concern for the proper alignment of the body and the cosmos. My close readings of Books 10 and 11 will demonstrate that the interviews disclosed futurities of healing through the physicians' shared concepts of the body and healing plants. In their descriptions and treatments, they assumed that the body functions as a pathway for cosmic energy (Maffie 2014, 195, 271–72). Recalling the Nahua tools of persuasion, I perceive patterns of repetition of interconnected concepts related to the tonalli, which Book 10, chapter 27, describes as a conduit for energy and a repository of one's destiny. This view coincides with one of the central concerns underlying the plant cures in Book 11, chapter 7, that of alleviating head fevers, which ultimately derive from imbalances of tonalli (solar energy). Descriptions of the body in Book 10 thus provide a framework for the healing instructions of Book 11. My approach agrees with Laura Harjo's (2019, 202) emphasis on healing plants among the Mvskoke; she explains that "teaching another person about medicinal plants and their uses" constitutes an action of "futurity praxis." Harjo has further noted that "futurity is active and constantly being negotiated" (38). The entries of the *Florentine Codex* I examine show titicih communicating instructions on how to heal at a time when they could not take for granted the future of their practices. In this chapter, I consider in detail healing information in the manuscript regarding centli (maize), peyote, and the mushroom teonanacatl. This development of material reveals that the contributing physicians and the scholars had an active role in recording information with future implications for healing.

What is at stake in the examination of these futurities are Indigenous knowledge(s) and their abiding value. Taking for granted that the processes of compilation and editorial filters in the *Florentine Codex* silenced the Nahua physicians in an absolute way risks perpetuating the idea of "the dying, disappearing Indian—a trope that has been necessary for the settler to take Indigenous lands and lives" (Harjo 2019, 201). Instead, here I propose to recenter the Native voices that made the healing content possible in the first place. As McDonough (2020, 402) has observed, "recognizing those whose knowledges and voices are embedded in a text can potentially disrupt centuries of mistranslating academic authority as unequivocal and sole authorship." As a corollary to recognizing Indigenous voices in the text, to not acknowledge the sizable Nahua contributions on healing perpetuates the "appropriation of Indigenous cultural material by non-Indigenous authors" (J. Anderson and Christen 2019, 230). In this case, ignoring Nahua futurities in Books 10 and 11 reifies the conventional notion of Bernardino de Sahagún as the main author. How fitting, then, is it to question the trope of the "dying Indian" with Indigenous knowledge(s) that encourage and sustain life through detailed descriptions of healing?

Before proceeding, I acknowledge that my argument in this chapter touches on colonial entanglements. Primarily, I would like to distance my analysis from any comparisons between Nahua healing practices and Galenic medicine.[9] The Nahuas used a system of dynamic equilibrium based on gradations of heat and cold to diagnose and treat illnesses, and not four humors.[10] For Nahuas, just as there are sicknesses, so are there different states of health, each appropriate for a person at a particular point of life (Chevalier and Sánchez Bain 2003, 24–25). Rather than humors, Nahuas organized states of illness and wellness around foods, conditions, and activities that produce heat or cooling in the body (López Austin 1986, 77, 79). The ever-elusive balance between heat and cold "was the ultimate goal. An individual's activities, environment, emotions, and anything ingested could affect this equilibrium either positively or negatively, as could the emotions of others" (McDonough 2024, 63).[11] These considerations guide my approach to how solar movement affects the tonalli, the center of energy in the head that influences one's destiny, a long-standing concept associated with the tonalpohualli day signs and calendar. It comes as no surprise that the Nahuas have valued knowledge of plants that keep the tonalli attached to the body. Since one's well-being depends on a strong connection between the tonalli and the sun, this traditional knowledge lies at the heart of ancient Nahua views of the future and human action. Within each person's path-seeking in life, the art of the ticitl helped maintain the balance of energy in the body. Recalling Sahagún's quote at the opening of the chapter in which he compared Catholic priests to physicians, it becomes clear that the future Nahua healers anticipated differed profoundly from both the expectations of Sahagún and those of Western medical doctors.

As a parallel to the misaligned tonalli as an infirmity, I also oppose the notion that Nahua healing involves arbitrary conclusions based on private experiences of ritual experts. The contributing titicih (and presumably those who had taught them) formed an intersubjective approach to diagnosis, and their healing knowledge(s) stemmed from common experiences of treatments that produced desired outcomes. Simply put, Nahua healers use cures that work.[12] Nahua scholar Eduardo de la Cruz Cruz shared with McDonough (2024, 16–17) that healers draw on their experience to cure and make predictions and on "ancestral knowledge, which is usually conveyed through modeling and storytelling." These figures practice "a culturally-situated empiricism," within which "personal and collective experience collates with data from dreams, visions, and messages/signs from other-than-humans. In other words, rather than a Western empirical practice, Nahuas learned about and understood the world according to their own frames of reality" (McDonough 2024, 46). Individual healers thus constantly recalibrate their observations of what works and what does not with collective experiences of those who came before, and with the desired end of restoring balance to a patient.

PRECEDENTS FOR THIS STUDY

Existing approaches to Books 10 and 11 of the *Florentine Codex* emphasize how these sections open a window onto future-oriented descriptions of practice that the Nahua healers contributed. Alfredo López Austin's two-volume study (1988) recognizes strong connections between body and cosmos in Book 10 of the *Florentine Codex*. While it is impossible to know why the body parts remained untranslated in Book 10, future ritual implications would have made that information a potential target for clergy such as Sahagún, who was interested in suppressing traditional beliefs. Millie Gimmel (2008a, 171) has elaborated on this tension: "[on] one level there are significant lapses in the translation but on a deeper level the work tries to save and destroy [N]ative culture at the same time; it attempts to serve as a linguistic guide and yet deliberately suppresses certain linguistic information." Gimmel's analysis of Book 11 sheds light on its descriptive approach to cultural phenomena in the Nahuatl text, compared to Sahagún's prescriptive approach.

Beyond the interests of the clergy, studies have also revealed how Spanish functionaries have gained insight from Nahua scholars, healers, and painters regarding the natural world. Marcy Norton (2024, 302–27) explains how Phillip II's promédico Francisco Hernández worked with Nahua scholars in Tlatelolco who generated illustrations and descriptions of flora and fauna that appear both in his "Historiae animalium" and in Book 11 of the *Florentine Codex*. These Nahua scholars drew information for Hernández and for the *Historia universal* from locals with specialized knowledge on plants and animals. For instance, the "atlaca," the "water people," a local, collective source, provided information to Nahua scholars about water animals in Lake Texcoco. The material resulting from these consultations appears in Book 11 of the *Florentine Codex* and in Hernández's *Cuatro libros de la naturaleza y virtudes de las plantas y animales de uso medicinal en la Nueva España* ([1615] 1888) (Norton 2024, 309). Norton's study also shows that, via the publications of Hernández, those Indigenous contributions became precedents for the eighteenth- and nineteenth-century rise of empiricism in Europe.

Other lines of cultural study emphasize Nahua knowledge(s) on their terms. McDonough (2024, 33) applies Susan Star and James Griesemer's (1989) term "boundary object" to the codex, since it is "plastic enough to adapt to local needs and the constraints of the several parties employing them, yet robust enough to maintain a common identity across sites." McDonough's 2024 book delves into Nahua science, their knowledge production, with insightful examinations of the role of sensory input—sight, sound, color, flavor, smell, and tactile elements—in Book 11. The study demonstrates that through a "blend of empirical and inherited knowledges . . . Nahua science was concerned with predicting and influencing future outcomes" as part of their ethical approach to balanced living (McDonough 2024, 22). Complementary to these studies, my examination of futurities in the *Florentine Codex* reveals the contributors' aim to inform Nahua posterity of the materiality and procedures associated with successful plant-based cures. I show how the healers and the Nahua scholars communicated a future vision in which titicih continue to practice their profession. In the cases here, as in the other chapters of this book, Nahuas interpreted their existing knowledge base to chart a future into unknown times. First I give an overview of how the composition of the *Florentine Codex* as a whole sheds light on the content and expectations that informed the context of Books 10 and 11. I then explain findings on the roles of the Nahua healers and scholars vis-à-vis the Colegio de la Santa Cruz de Tlatelolco before I examine Books 10 and 11 of the codex.

FROM *HISTORIA UNIVERSAL* TO *FLORENTINE CODEX*

The investigation of the 1570s into healing plants fell at the end of processes of research and writing that spanned three decades. Using Kevin Terraciano's (2019, 3) timeline, I divide the composition of the *Florentine Codex* into four phases. Circa 1547, in Tlatelolco, Sahagún initiated research into Nahua culture by collecting wisdom sayings of elders (*huehuetlatolli*), which would become Book 6 of the codex. In 1555, he also recorded a Nahua version of the conquest, which later became Book 12. The next stage began with Francisco Toral's commission for Nahuatl-language materials to support evangelization; this portion of research with the Nahua scholars produced the *Códices matritenses*. During the third phase, 1565–70, Sahagún worked independently, organizing the vast quantity of notes that he and the Nahua scholars had accumulated to that point. By 1569, Sahagún had completed a copy of the *Historia universal* in Nahuatl, now lost. In 1570, after a meeting of the regional Franciscan chapter, the provincial Alonso de Escalona confiscated all of Sahagún's materials, suspecting them of containing heresies, and for incurring costs inconsistent with the order's vow of poverty (Terraciano 2019, 7). Escalona scattered Sahagún's manuscripts among the Franciscan clergy of New Spain for their inspection. The final phase opened a brief window that allowed for the production of the *Florentine Codex*. On August 4, 1575, Juan de Ovando's order from the Council of the Indies in Seville to produce a bilingual version of the *Historia universal* reached Mexico City. This order retrieved Sahagún's scattered manuscripts (McDonough 2024, 32) and set in motion the final compilation, editing, and composition of what would become the twelve volumes of the codex.

In the midst of his own aging and the demographic collapse around him, news of Sahagún's project reached Phillip II, who looked askance on Sahagún's cultural research. The codex caused the monarch uneasiness as counterproductive to his promotion of the edicts of the Council of Trent (Browne 2000, 26; Hsia 2005, 48–49). The window closed on the project when on April 22, 1577, the viceroy Martín Enríquez received a *real cédula* from Phillip II to confiscate all of Sahagún's materials and send them to Spain.[13] In the end, Sahagún's vision of the *Historia universal* never materialized as he had imagined. As Terraciano (2019, 14) has observed, "Spanish intentions were seldom fully achieved and were always tempered and compromised by local actors and negotiations. This was true of Sahagún's *Historia general*," whose "final manuscript reflects the profound input and subjectivity of the Nahua artists and writers on whom he depended to complete the project." The many contributors to the codex evince their various perspectives as well as prolonged, iterative processes of drafting and revision.

Regarding the authorship of the codex, the polyphony of voices in the *Florentine Codex* makes Sahagún's ultimately one among many, despite his role of "coordinator, compiler, editor, and translator" (Terraciano 2019, 13). To my mind, a confluence of material by four contributing parties forms the twelve volumes of the codex. Interviewees, usually elders who recalled life before the Spanish, gave answers to questionnaires by Sahagún and the Nahua scholars. In the case of Books 10 and

11, the text lists the names of the titicih intertwined. It is possible that the Nahua scholars also influenced the formation and the articulation of the questions, thus guiding the interviewees within parameters of knowledge(s) acceptable within the project.[14] Victoria Ríos Castaño (2014, 224) has observed that the *Primeros memoriales*, parts of which would appear in plant cures of Book 11 of the *Florentine Codex*, "are undeniably the outcome of a process of linguistic documentation and consultation of Sahagún's assistants, and for this reason they should be credited with a certain degree of co-authorship of this section." By implication, it is reasonable to attribute the role of co-authorship to both the contributing Nahua healers in Books 10 and 11 (Terraciano 2019, 13) and to the Nahua scholars at Tlatelolco for the entire *Historia universal* (Garibay [1954] 1971, 64; León-Portilla 1999; McDonough 2019, 398).[15] The third contribution came from the illustrators, whose some 2,500 images comprise a text in their own right (Gimmel 2008a, 172).[16] Finally, Sahagún contributed prologues to the multiple books and the majority of the Spanish translation in the left-hand columns. His influence over the translation may not be consistent, since the Nahua scholars may have also translated material (Ríos Castaño 2014, 214–28).[17] In the end, the Spanish translation accounts for less than one-third of the finished text (Gimmel 2008a, 176). Adding to these considerations, I recall Michel Foucault's (1969) observation that prior to the eighteenth century, books were almost always considered collective endeavors: the individual author as a legal entity did not exist.[18] Sahagún placed his officiating voice at points of textual inflexion such as the prologues; however, the multiplicity of perspectives and content exceeds the ability of a single author in any era.

As far as textual models, while the *Florentine Codex* bears the marks of European influence, as a point of confluence of Nahua knowledge(s), the compendium also reflects Indigenous organizational elements. The *Codex Mendoza*, a pictorial from the 1530s on Mexica rulers and conquests, tribute that subject altepeme sent to Tenochtitlan, and the daily life of Mexica nobles prior to the Spanish, has parallels with the *Florentine Codex*. In particular, scribes added glosses in Spanish to the painted figures of the text to aid colonial administrators in Spain. (Terraciano 2019, 4–6). In terms of the contents of the twelve volumes, the codex follows the scheme of Isidore of Seville's *Etymologiae* (seventh century), of which the first of its volumes concerned the divine and each book moved downward toward earthly things (Terraciano 2019, 9).[19] Similarly, *De civitate dei* by St. Augustine also orders the cosmos in a vertical manner, as do the books of the *Florentine Codex*.[20] Another Iberian compendium of knowledge, the *General estoria*, which Alfonso X (1930) wrote during his reign of Castailla y León (1252–84), contained a chapter on flora and fauna and compared a Christian present to a polytheistic past: these aspects resonate with the *Florentine Codex* (Terraciano 2019, 11).

Despite the Western organization of the twelve books of the codex, Book 11 at times groups animals by habitat instead of species. For example, the *tzicanantli* serpent appears in an entry next to ants since it usually lives in areas with ant hills (López Austin 2011a, 385). Similarly, the species of otter, the *aitzcuintli* and the *acoyotl*, appear twice—with their species and again among water animals in their natural surroundings. Finally, the *acuitlachtli*, a mammal, appears with waterfowl that live close by (McDonough 2024, 39–40). These arrangements of animals according to where one might find them prioritize sight and sound as organizational criteria, recalling McDonough's observations on Nahua science. As organizational models that built up over the decades of the manuscript's composition, these tendencies allowed the interviewees and the Nahua scholars to organize information in ways specific to their collaborative processes.

THE SCHOLARS, THE HEALERS, AND THE COLEGIO OF TLATELOLCO

The healing knowledge(s) in Books 10 and 11 that I examine recall the role of the Colegio de la Santa Cruz de Tlatelolco. The center of advanced study began in 1536 as a Franciscan project to educate and catechize the sons of Nahua nobles.[21] While the early intent was to train Native clergy, the emphasis of the institution soon shifted to training a trilingual bureaucracy (in Nahuatl, Latin, and Spanish) to assist colonial administrators (Browne 2000, 108). During the 1550s and 1560s, the Colegio gave instruction to around one hundred sons of Nahua nobility in the Renaissance *trivium* (grammar, logic, rhetoric) and another four hundred *parvalitos*, younger boys who learned prayers, music, and basic literacy

(Silvermoon 2007, 75–86). Tlatelolco recalls Homi K. Bhabha's (2012, 31–39) concept of a "third space" within a colonial institution wherein discourses colonizers did not plan could obtain. Students there learned alphabetic writing, which allowed them to preserve information not directly related to religious conversion (Klor de Alva 1992, 26). What began as a project of instruction of the children of leading nobles soon led to ramifications the Spanish did not anticipate.

The final compilation of the *Florentine Codex*, 1575–77, was not the first collaboration between Nahua healers and scholars at Tlatelolco. In 1552, the Nahua healer Martín de la Cruz produced *Libellus de Medicinalibus Indorum Herbis*, an illustrated compendium of plant remedies, in collaboration with Juan Badiano, a Nahua scholar at Tlatelolco who wrote Cruz's work in Latin (Cruz and Badiano [1552] 1991; Zetina et al. 2008).[22] Providing intricate illustrations and binding the volume with red velvet and gold thread, Cruz and Badiano gave it to Phillip II as part of the request for funding for the Colegio. Phillip II and the viceroy Enrique Mendoza both gave financial backing to the college in 1553 (Ríos Castaño 2018, 484–85). Martín de la Cruz had been a ticitl in Tenochtitlan before the conquest (Viesca Treviño 2007, 274). Cruz continued working under the Spanish as an expert in traditional healing: records show he examined Indigenous physicians and conferred licenses for them to practice healing arts in Native communities (Viesca Treviño 2006, 4). In the 1540s, the friars even introduced the healing arts into the curriculum of the Colegio: Martín de la Cruz and Juan Badiano likely taught courses (Ríos Castaño 2018, 486). Adapting their approach, "the friars relied on a regular cohort of Native healers to cater to the ill, whether pupils or themselves" (Ríos Castaño 2018, 483). Thus, by the 1570s, the Colegio de la Santa Cruz had already cemented its association with plant remedies and healing practitioners. When the Nahua scholars interviewed the titicih in the 1570s, a memory existed of Cruz and Badiano's collaboration some twenty years earlier.

The monumental task of compiling data on the human body and plant cures bespeaks the deep involvement of the Nahua scholars in the production of the final manuscript. Although Sahagún's evangelical purposes are clear, why these scholars invested years and their effort in the project remains a matter of speculation. As McDonough (2024, 34) comments, we lack evidence of what prompted the Indigenous elders, authorities, and other Native experts to participate. We know for certain that many of the Nahua scholars and scribes had been Sahagún's students at the Colegio de Santa Cruz de Tlatelolco. They would have been handpicked by the friar for their skill, whether as linguists, historians, or scribes. It is not inconceivable that some of these young men were fervent believers, as they had been educated in this private Catholic boarding school since they were very young. It is not inconceivable that some shared Sahagún's desire to facilitate evangelization of their brethren. Perhaps others simply relished the opportunity to immerse themselves in research and writing. After all, this was a once-in-a-lifetime opportunity to record their history and language in alphabetic writing, to learn about their past from elders, and to create a meaningful resource for future generations of Nahuas.

Despite the lack of an explicit statement of why they wrote, it is clear that the Nahua scholars were enmeshed in a network of Nahua Christians and Spanish clergy who supported their research. From my point of view in this study, the future implications of healing knowledge(s) come to the fore. As epidemics took an increasing toll, the final version of the *Historia universal*, the *Florentine Codex*, provided a pivotal moment for preserving information for coming generations, despite possible tensions with Sahagún over the content. They translated what knowledge they found useful regarding a culture that the clergy simultaneously wished to erase.

At the same time, it is worth considering what we know regarding the Nahua physicians who resided near Tlatelolco. Book 10, chapter 28, of the codex lists the eight titicih who verified the content regarding the parts of the body listed, and Book 11, chapter 7, lists further contributing Native physicians (see table 1). Listing the healers by name, the text shows that the Nahua scholars and the friar had met them. Naming them also signals that residents of Tlatelolco and surroundings would recognize them as professional healers who practiced publicly (Ríos Castaño 2018, 482). In Book 11, the text preceding the list of healers avers that one of them was a scribe, who wrote their names on their behalf. Alfredo López Austin (1972, 131), based on evidence in a personal communication from Howard F. Cline (now lost), claims Pedro Raquena was the scribe, which reduces their numbers by one. I note that the scribe's taking of their names carries with it a further verification that the meetings took place.

TABLE 1 Nahua healers (*titicih*) who contributed to research on healing plants, Books 10 and 11 of the *Florentine Codex*

HEALER (*TICITL*)	COMMUNITY OF ORIGIN
BOOK 10, FOLIO 113 VERSO	
Juan Pérez	San Pablo
Pedro Pérez	San Juan
Pedro Hernández	San Juan
Joseph Hernández	San Juan
Miguel García	San Sebastián
Francisco de la Cruz	Xiuitonco
Baltasar Juárez	San Sebastián
Antonio Martínez	San Juan
BOOK 11, FOLIO 180 VERSO–181 RECTO	
Gaspar Matías	La Concepción
Pedro de Santiago	Santa Inés
Francisco Simón	Santo Toribio
Miguel Damián	Santo Toribio
Felipe Hernández	Santa Ana
Pedro de Raquena	La Concepción
Miguel García	Santo Toribio
Miguel Motolinía	Santa Inés

Thus, a total of fifteen healers brought their accumulated knowledge and practice as well as anticipations of how the information they shared had the potential to impact readers and hearers of the text over time.

Ancestral Nahua healers took an approach to healing and well-being distinct from Western physicians. Alonso de Molina defines a *ticitl* as a "médico o agorero y echador de suertes" (a medical doctor or diviner and caster of lots) ([1571] 2008, 2:113r). Molina pairs the ticitl with *ticiotl*, the "arte de medicina, o cosa de médicos, o adivinación por agueros, agorería, de echar suertes" (the art of medicine, the field of medical doctors, or divination through the reading of signs, augury by casting lots) ([1571] 2008, 2:113r). The enduring practice of casting maize kernels as a central part of diagnosis identifies the Nahua healer.[23] Frances Karttunen (1992, 240) defines the *ticitl* as "physician, prognosticator, healer."[24] Both of these preliminary definitions refer to these specialists' knowledge(s) and their interest in helping others prepare for the future. The *Florentine Codex* also describes this specialist's activities:

> In ticit tepatiani, tlapatiani tlapeleuiani. In qualli ticit tlanemiliani, tlaiximatini, xiuhiximatqui, teiximatqui, quauhiximatqui, tlaneloaioiximatqui, tlaiciecole, tlaztlacole, iztlacole, tlaixieiecoani, tlapaleuia, tepatia, tepapachoa, teçaloa, tetlanoquilia, tlaço tlaltia, tetlalitia, tlaitzmina, texotla, tehitzoma, tecoatiquetza, nextli teololoa. (*FC*, Bk. 10, f. 20r)
>
> The physician [is] a curer of people, a restorer, a provider of health. The good physician [is] a diagnostician, experienced—a knower of herbs, of stones, of trees, of roots. He has [results of] examinations, experience, prudence. [He is] moderate in his acts. He provides health, restores people, provides them splints, sets bones for them, purges them, gives emetics, gives them potions; he lances, he makes incisions in them, stiches them, revives them, envelops them in ashes. (11:30)

As a kind of tlamatini, a ticitl received training in the calmecac, the traditional school for Nahua nobles (Ocaranza 1934, 25; López Austin and Viesca Treviño 1984, 218). He or she diagnosed illness through divination, reading the body and the cosmos to identify the sickness and its remedy (Soustelle [1970] 2002, 194–95).[25] Given the research by Cruz and Badiano, during the work to complete the *Florentine Codex*, the Colegio in Tlatelolco had already gained a reputation for cataloging regional herbs as treatments.

Considering the motives the healers had for participating, although it is impossible to know exactly why they chose to share information with the Nahua scholars who interviewed them, they may have had similar motivations as the respondents to the surveys of the *Relaciones geográficas*, by which the viceregal government registered the geographical features and natural resources of Nahua communities during the sixteenth century. Duccio Sacchi (2000, 304) has suggested that Natives responded to the *Relaciones* questionnaires to speak on behalf of their communities and to officially register the limits of their territories. McDonough (2019, 468) has suggested other possible reasons Nahuas shared information for the *Relaciones*: to establish relationships with "Spanish authorities who would influence future outcomes"; the documents produced would show Spanish recognition of "their authority, thus solidifying or elevating their status"; negative sanctions such as fines may have applied if they did not participate; participation served as an opportunity for reconnaissance, "which would aid in calculating how to best manage their relationships with" the Spanish. Similarly, considering the participation of the titicih in the questionnaires at Tlatelolco, I would add that they may have wished to raise the visibility of their own professional practice by participating in a research project associated with the Colegio de la Santa Cruz; and they may have wished to ensure that their healing practices would survive beyond their lifetimes. While suggesting possibilities does not prove any of them or a combination of them motivated the participation of the titicih, they do show that plausible reasons existed for contributing to efforts to record Nahua healing practices. I now turn to Nahua futurities of well-being in Books 10 and 11 of the *Florentine Codex*.

BODY AND COSMOS

In this section, I show how, beginning with the names of body parts the titicih provided, they represent the human being as a pathway for cosmic energy. According to Nahua pantheism, the energy of the cosmos animates the body and binds each person to the universe (Ortiz de Montellano 1989, 191; McKeever Furst [1995] 1997, 122).[26] The self, according to this conceptualization, is not a permanent entity whose existence continues in an afterlife. This monistic view has implications for individual futures different from the Western or Christian view of the body as joined with a permanent soul or psyche. In the Nahua universe, the human body serves as a site of dynamic confluence of cosmic energies. For the Nahuas, bodily conduits of energy constitute a locus of individuality, which, in the end, is not separate from its surroundings but directs the flow of cosmic energy for a time. As James Maffie (2010, 18) explains,

> At the earth's surface is the only time-place where the three vital forces comprising human beings—tonalli ("inner heat," "vitality," "potency," and "innate personality") concentrated in the head, teyolia ("that which gives life to someone," "that which moves someone") concentrated in the heart,

and ihiyotl ("breath," "wind," "respiration") concentrated in the liver—are fully integrated, and hence the only time-place where humans enjoy the potential for well-being.

Consequently, with the individual and cosmos as aspects of the same continuum, the body becomes humans' principal means for seeking balance and the goals of well-being integrated with cosmic processes. The Nahuas held that three forces animated the human body: the *tonalli* (head), the *yollotli* (heart), and the *ihiyotl* (liver). The list of body parts in Book 10 includes these three entities, which I refer to as animic conduits between body and cosmos.[27] Likewise, Book 11 carries an implicit understanding of the body as a conduit of energy, for the future effectiveness of the remedies that it offers.

In Book 10 of the *Florentine Codex*, the terms that Nahua healers provided relate to the tonalli, the yollotli, and the ihiyotl and reveal their preoccupation with so-called soul loss. Since the body's animic conduits do not firmly attach, interactions with others and with the environment can affect these three entities (McKeever Furst [1995] 1997, 109). A lost soul does not indicate a separation of spirit from matter, since Nahua monism assumes the unity of all reality (Hunt 1977, 55–56). What is at stake is the harmonization of an individual's energies with the cosmos: through training, healers are able to see misalignments that cause illness (C. Pratt 2007, 1:159). In the Postclassic Period, various specialists treated soul loss, especially in children (López Austin 1975, 37). Additionally, Nahuatl-speaking groups have associated strong winds with the condition since the colonial period (Sandstrom 1991, 269–74; McKeever Furst [1995] 1997, 145).

Examining the lists from the Nahuatl columns of the codex in Book 10, chapter 27, reveals allusions to the ancestral views on how the body channels energy from the sun in ways consequential to a person's origins and future. The list begins with the top of the body, which the text describes in metaphysical terms: "Tzontecomatl / totzonteco; / quitoznequi, ilhuicatl" (head / our head / that is to say, the celestial part [*FC*, Bk. 10, f. 72v; 11:99]). The qualifier "quitoznequi" (literally, "it wanted to mean") discloses an interpretive act that links the head to a cosmic reality not immediately apparent. Anderson and Dibble's rendering of "ilhuicatl" as "the celestial part" I take to refer to the link between the body's tonalli and solar heat (*tona*). A flow of energy from the sun into the body occurs at one's birth. The curvature of the head parallels the sun's arc in the sky, linking individuals with the cosmos via the body (Kruell 2016, 9). Below the opening entries, the list further describes the head's qualities.

> Ilhuicatl [the celestial part]
> quitoznequi, totzontecon [that is to say, our head],
> tlalnamiquini [the rememberer],
> tlamatini [the knower],
> tlancaiutl [achievement, destiny],
> tzonquizcaiutl [conclusion, fate],
> mauiziotl [honor],
> mauiztioani [venerable] (*FC*, Bk. 10, f. 73r)

Since the tonalli establishes its connection through the head, the description of the head as a celestial part alludes to the cosmic origins of the life force that illuminates the body and brings with it a specific destiny (Peña 1999, 151; Bassett 2015, 118). The contributors have used a syntactic parallel to explain the interconnectedness of the body and cosmos: "totzonteco / quitoznequi ilhuicatl / ilhuicatl / quitoznequi totzotecon" (the head / that is to say, the celestial part / the celestial part / that is to say, the head [*FC*, Bk. 10, f. 73r; 11:99]). I submit that this construction intends to close any possible conclusion that the head does not relate to the cosmos or that the cosmos does not relate to the head. In this sense, the entry describes a metonymic relationship between the head and the universe. Referring to the head, then, necessarily carries a reference to the cosmic forces that dispose one toward personality traits and a range of possible activities during one's life—one's path.

These descriptions of the head carry with them culturally specific comparisons. By describing the tonalli as an entity connected to solar movement, the titicih refer to the world as they understood it. This mode of writing, working primarily from Nahua referents, "had the potential to create a kind of closed circuit" (McDonough 2024, 44). While McDonough applies the idea of a closed circuit to the plant cures of Book 11, I see the same dynamic at work in descriptions of parts of the human body in Book 10. In fact, Nahua healers' explanations of the head's functions here suggest that they "were not always concerned first and foremost with making their culture legible to outsiders. For them, creating a record of their world, perhaps for future generations of Nahuas, may have been a far more interesting, if not pressing concern" (McDonough 2024, 45). Mindful about representing the body accurately to future audiences of Nahuas, the tonalli wrote descriptions that fell within long-standing views on time and human action from the Postclassic Period or earlier, with the objective of pointing those views forward.

The tonalli maintains a flow of energy characteristic of a person's first day of sunlight, out of the womb. Recalling the importance of the tlamatini as the traditional sage and teacher in the calmecac, the entry explains how the same term applies to the location of the tonalli as the sage of the body. Facing the sun, the head guides the rest of the body, when the body is well. However, it is possible for an animating conduit to become "lost or stuck" outside its proper flows of energy (C. Pratt 2007, 2:458). For the titicih, treating a person suffering from an illness entailed the opening and amplification of their senses to discern to what extent the body's conduits were out of line with the cosmos. In the same passage, the term *tlancaiutl*, which Anderson and Dibble translate as "achievement" and Bernard and Thelma Ortiz de Montellano as "end," recalls how the sum of one's actions occur within the limits set by the proportion of energy received at birth (Maffie n.d., sec. 3b). I note that the position of the head as the "celestial part" implies the preeminence of the tonalli as part of a lifelong bodily economy of cosmic energy. An animic conduit, the tonalli holds future possibilities: the proper functioning of the head allows a person to be in tune with teotl. "It is like your work in life," as one elder described the tonalli to Alan Sandstrom (1991, 258).[28] This work is wrapped up in reciprocity: one expends force in the present for future good. The description continues with *tzonquizcaiutl*, which Anderson and Dibble render as "conclusion," again signaling that one's life represents through actions the tonalli store of energy.[29] One could address the tonalli with "honor" (mauiziotl) and as "venerable" (mauiztioani), implying reverence and caution since certain days of birth stored forces capable of inflicting trouble or sickness on others. Further, both "mauiziotl" and "mauiztioani" recall that teotl is "marvelous" (mahuitzic) (Bassett 2015, 92). While no evidence here suggests the head is itself a deity (teotl), it receives respect associated with a high concentration of energy. By placing it at the start of the list and ascribing to it the function of guiding the body, the titicih and Nahua scholars oriented the head as a locus of movement in space and sensitive to the passage of time.

The description of the body also highlights the importance of the yollotli (heart) as a channel of cosmic energy. If we recall the earlier discussion on the relationship of the heart to the ollin motion of teotl in the sun's path through the sky, deeper meanings of the yollotli in Book 10 become apparent. Several lexical items show the importance of the yollotli: "toiollo / ololtic / totonquj / nemoanj" (our heart / round / hot / that by which there is existence [*FC*, Bk. 10, f. 91v; 11:130]). The roundness, heat, and vital nature of the heart recall the energy released from sacrificial victims, which helped regulate the flow of energy from the earth to the sun (McKeever Furst [1995] 1997, 179; Aguilar-Moreno 2007, 173). That consciousness itself derives from the yollotli shows its indispensability for embodied perception and movement. By synecdoche, the heart stands for the whole body: it allows one to see and orient oneself with a direction in which to proceed. Thus, the heart has the role of a "moral compass" (Dufendach 2019, 630). The list continues and confirms links between the yollotli and life itself: "ioliliztli / teioltia / tenemjtia" (life / it makes one live / it sustains one [*FC*, Bk. 10, f. 91v; 11:131]). Within Nahua pantheism, the body and vital forces are bound together. As the body ages, its animic energy declines until a point when a dim postmortem ember reintegrates into the cosmos.[30] The scribes recapitulate the yollotli portion of the list with the affirmation that "qujcemjtquj yn iollotli" (the heart rules all [*FC*, Bk. 10, f. 91v; 11:131]). Life itself and the ability to perceive surroundings carries with it the awareness of a coming future, the ability to prepare for it, and even to imagine and prepare for times beyond one's life. Keeping the heart in proper working order by reducing emotional and physical stress makes future actions possible.

In addition to the tonalli and the yollotli, the ihiyotl (liver) plays a key role as an animic conduit that eliminates waste (*FC*, Bk. 10, f. 79v). The ihiyotl is a conduit associated with the decaying of a dead body and the dissipation of its energy into the cosmos (McKeever Furst [1995] 1997, 180). By listing and describing these parts of the body, the Nahua physicians established a scheme of the proper functioning of the body in harmony with the cosmos and its local surroundings. These functions of the body go hand in hand with information on healing plants.

HEALING PLANTS

At least two core Nahua futurities of healing undergird Book 11, chapter 7: the aim of healing a patient in the near future and the horizon of the continuation of the role of the ticitl as a specialist. To my mind, the fifteen healers, by providing information to the Nahua scholars and Sahagún, disclosed their aim to continue diagnosis and treatment of infirmities during their lifetimes and to make information on healing procedures available to future readers. Fifteen of the plant remedies in Book 11, chapter 7, treat fevers in the head (tonalli) and show traditional conceptualizations of the body. Together these tonalli treatments comprise 10 percent of the cures in Book 11. Excessive heat in the head indicates a dislodged tonalli, that is, "soul-loss" (McKeever Furst [1995] 1997, 109–10). In the column set aside for the Spanish translation, the scribes have included paintings of the plants they recommended as fever remedies. The fifteen herbs cataloged are 4. centli ina; 6. tlanoquiloni; 7. eloxochineloatl; 9. tlalcacauatl; 10. eloquiltic; 11. chichipiltic; 14. coatli; 15. tzipipatli; 19. coayielli, tememetla, and tesuchitl; 22. xoxouhcapatli; 29. teonanacatl; 30. peiotl; and 31. toloa (*FC*, Bk. 11, f. 139v–142v). This attention to detail in my view suggests the fifteen healers' preparation to continue their occupation. By extension, this impetus to continue suggests consensus within the wider Nahuatl-speaking community regarding the value of the ticitl as a specialist. If there was not a future for the ticitl as a specialist, then the *Historia universal* has fallen into the same predicament identified by Néstor García Canclini (2005, 119) in the display of artifacts in museums—the entries in the codex, torn from the social context that produced them, abstracted from reciprocal relations that integrated rituals, politics, and the economy, would force them into appearing as on the "outside of history." As we shall see, the connections among the plant cures the titicih offered and a future-leaning aspect of their information show that it was not the case that the titicih were frozen in time, nor that they were fading into obscurity.

The first fever-reducing plant in Book 11 has two names that identify it, *centli* or *cintli* (see figure 17). This apparently simple reference to the cob of the corn plant with dried maize kernels belies a range of healing and ritual applications, which form layers of forward-looking meaning. Although three illustrations of bushy plants accompany the description,

FIGURE 17 Three plants representing *centli / cintli*, *Florentine Codex*, Bk. 11, f. 40r. Their roots treated head (*tonalli*) fevers. Library of Congress, World Digital Library, accessed April 15, 2024.

the entry refers to the dried maize cob, when its seeds are ready for storing or planting (Molina [1571] 2008, 2:22v). The text reads: "Centli ina: anoço cintli ina: Tlanelhoatl, iztac, mjmjltic: in jxiuhio cujtlanextic, iuhqujn xivitl ic mochioa quauhtla in muchioa. Ic pati in aqujn motlevia: in cequjn çan mjxcavia in conj, in jquac omotez: cequjn qujneloa in iztac patli tepitoton, yoa iztac patli pitzoac: moteci, conj, in cocoxquj, amo tzoionj" ('The root is white, cylindrical; its foliage is a faded ashen color. It grows like an herb; it grows in the forest. He who has a fever is cured with it. Some drink it just alone, after it has been ground. Some mix it with the small and slender *iztac patli* herb. It is ground. He who becomes sick drinks it. It is not cooked [*FC*, Bk. 11, f. 140r; 12:142]). Corn's ability to correctly orient the tonalli confers sustaining and healing powers beyond its role as a staple food. This reference to corn comes at the culmination of its life cycle when it has accumulated all its energy. Its root is the largest it will be at this point; its dried leaves have spread to their maximum extension, gathering all possible solar energy to store it inside the cintli, the dried kernels suitable for grinding as food.

I note here that the illustrations accompanying centli / cintli only vaguely resemble the description. I propose that the images emphasize the location of the plant (cujtanextic [growing in the forest]) and have a particular role in this case. The plant's cylindrical root resembles that of mature corn; however, its round, clustered leaves do not. Rather than give instructions on how to gather mature corn, the text directs readers to look in the forest. If we recall McDonough's concept of a "closed circuit," the reasons for a differing depiction of a common plant and its placement in the forest may provide clues particularly meaningful to a Nahua audience. The explicit directions for preparing centli clearly indicate future readers. At the same time, the entry's directions include adding iztac patli to make an atole (corn drink) to reduce a fever. The *Codex Badianus* depicts iztac patli with slender leaves and seedpods. Knowing what do to with the plants goes hand in hand with knowing where to find them. Thus, to my mind, the presentation of centli here points to the fifteen healers' shared knowledge with intended readers regarding their surroundings and the healing plants available.

Harjo (2019, 216) refers to this forward-looking effect, which connects the knowledge(s) of the people with the land, as "emergence geographies," which imply recognizing the "community's ability to assert self-determination and to conceive of, act upon, and appropriate the space necessary to realize community aspirations." The text directs information to Nahua audiences, emphasizing a futurity of healing in spaces they knew well. Taking for granted that the Nahua readers and hearers of the text would understand "centli ina açoco cintli ina" as mature, dried corn, in one sense there was no need to provide a direct depiction.[31] Therefore, in my view, the Nahua arrangement of this material avoids Western tampering with a resource by placing corn on the edge of colonial space and the settler epistemological regime. That which is not entirely knowable to Westerners inhabits a liminal space that provides protection moving ahead. By describing centli/cintli as a forest plant, the healers sought to protect maize fields from inspection or harvesting by the Spanish or other outsiders.

Did the Nahua physicians in this manner share with future Nahua readers, while hiding some of their knowledge in a fragmentary presentation? It is impossible to tell for certain. However, what does remain clear are the sacred qualities Nahuas have attributed to mature corn from ancestral times. Nahuatl speakers in the Postclassic Period deified maize and sought its powerful assistance to shape the future. A complex of festivals honored the stages of its life cycle. In the *Florentine Codex*, contributors described how during the month of Huei Tozoztli virgins offered ears of green corn, which they called collectively *Cinteotl* (*FC*, Bk. 2, f. 4v). Inga Clendinnen (1991, 251) has identified these ears of green corn as deities in themselves, gathered in the temple of Chicomecoatl (Seven Snake) in Cinteopan as part of a ritual to bring a plentiful harvest. Molly Bassett (2015, 71) maintains that the green corn in Chicomecoatl's temple were teixiptlahuan that embodied the divine presence of maize. In both cases, the importance of the temple required a group of celibate priests to maintain it. With an eye ever to the future, these priests made requests to Cinteotl for desired outcomes and used oratory to admonish and advise communities (Torquemada 1969, 2:181; Offner 2014, 44–45). Victoriano de la Cruz Cruz (Nahua) (2015, 130) has traced links between Postclassic devotions to Cinteotl and Chicomecoatl and contemporary rituals for Chicomexochitl

(Seven Corn Flower), the main deity of Chicontepec.[32] Today, in the Huasteca region of Veracruz, the festival of Chicomexochitl, the deity of corn, includes offerings of dry maize cobs (Chevalier and Sánchez Bain 2003, 173–78; Cruz Cruz 2015, 134). The observance of an offering of mature corn occurs as well in the Oapan Nahua community of Guerrero (Good Eshelman 2001, 257–60). Consequently, as communities once gathered corn to concentrate its benefits, a complex meaning emerges of this entry in Book 11 regarding centli in support of future healing applications. The root evokes the whole plant, carrying recognition of its sustenance of communities. The titicih articulate the future value of the maize cob's sustaining and healing properties.

The grain that once embodied deities also sustains humans by helping them find the path through life by maintaining reciprocity with their ancestors and the earth. As a viaduct for solar energy, corn energizes the tonalli. The Nahuas of the Postclassic Period referred to corn as *tonacayo*, "our flesh," establishing a link between body and diet. At that time, Nahuas derived an estimated 80 percent of their daily calories from maize (Ortiz de Montellano 1993, 61, 101). Corn tied them to the earth. Alan Sandstrom (1991, 241) explains that for Nahuas individuals "sprout from the earth like the corn plant, and they are placed back in the earth when they die. The earth is womb and tomb, the provider of nourishment and all wealth, home to the ancestors, and the daily sustainer of human life." The sun imparts energy to each person through corn. As maize plants and humans grow, their life cycles intertwine in a series of processes of the gathering and exertion of strength. Chevalier and Sánchez Bain (2003, 23) have commented that humans "must grow up and gather the strength and heat needed to reproduce the seed (corn, food, children) that will sustain them throughout their lives and in their old age. In doing so they gradually wear themselves out, drying up, and dying for the sake of future generations of corn plants and human beings alike. The heat of aging and death is food to the cycle of life." These processes show that a proper path through life requires corn's sustaining energy. The work and strength of one's forebearers provide strength now, and those who live now return that force to the ancestors by giving their bodies back to the ground. The information the codex provides assumes that the body will continue to function as a path for solar energy, within a Nahua futurity of well-being. I turn now to Book 11's description of a plant whose roots help balance the heart.

While a head fever indicates a poorly attached tonalli, temperature changes in the chest can mean a troubled yollotli heart conduit. *Tlacoxivitl* (see figure 18), an herb for treating excessive heat in the body, appears three times in Book 11, chapter 7, in entries 55, 104, and 120:

FIGURE 18 *Tlacoxivitl*, *Florentine Codex*, Bk. 11, f. 148v. Library of Congress, World Digital Library, accessed April 15, 2024.

55. ic cevi in jnacaio. In jaaio ixamopaltic xiuhhiia. [Some drink it, thereby cooling the body. The water of the plant is purple, strong smelling.] (*FC*, Bk. 11, f. 148r; 12:154–55)

104. Auh in jnelhoaio, achi ixtliltic im panj: eoaiotilaoac, in jiollo iztac, nenecutic. [Its root is somewhat black on the surface, thick-skinned; it is white in its interior. It is sweet.] (*FC*, Bk. 11, f. 159v; 12:168)

120: In aqujn in cenca mococoa inacaio, in totonja, in icica, in ic cenca patzmjqui in toiollo: qujcevia in totonquj. [One who is very sick of body, feverish, panting, hence faint of heart, [with this] lessens the fever.] (*FC*, Bk. 11, f. 167r; 12:176)

Despite the disjointed presentation of the herb's properties and effects in three noncontiguous entries, a picture emerges through the repeated entries on how the plant promoted life. Sufferers of heat in the chest could drink the strong-smelling, sweet, purple-colored juice of the tlacoxihuitl roots to cool the yollotli and re-establish the body's animic balance. The collaborating Nahua scholars, who recorded these entries from the titicih, conveyed this knowledge to future readers. In the same untranslated section of Book 11, a group of plants enhance the ability of a ticitl to diagnose illnesses and prescribe remedies.

PERCEPTION AND DIAGNOSIS

If we recall the purpose of the *Florentine Codex* as a reference for colonial administrators who would read the Spanish column, another set of intriguing translation omissions come in the same chapter: those prescribing psychotropic plants. A triad of hallucinogens appears in Book 11, chapter 7, listed as remedies for head fevers. Teonanacatl, peiotl (peyote), and taloa, along with their illustrations, rely on the expertise of the titicih. Hallucinogens formed a routine part of healing practices. Paleopathologists have shown that Indigenous Mexico has used the greatest number of natural hallucinogens to diagnose and treat ailments (Sotomayor Tribín and Cuéllar-Montoya 2007, 52).[33] The role of the ticitl in diagnosing a poorly connected tonalli calls for an amplification of the senses to communicate with the unseen world (C. Pratt 2007, 2:346; see also Olivier 2003, 121; Hoopes and Mora-Marín 2009, 299). Yet the late sixteenth century was a time when it was uncertain whether those practices would continue. Given their established use for diagnosis, it comes as no surprise that psychotropic plants appear as their own group in Book 11. Each Nahuatl entry in this section explains the preparation of a psychotropic plant. These directions in tandem with illustrations represent futurities of alleviated suffering via hallucinogenic diagnosis and treatment.

The section reinforces the ongoing, future-oriented expertise of the ticitl as the practitioner qualified to diagnose illness via ritually enhanced, psychotropic perception (see figure 19). The titicih provided information on how to find and prepare the cactus: "inin peiotl iztac: auh çan yio vmpa in mochioa in tlacochcalcopa, in teutlalpā in mjtoa mjctlanpa" (This peyote is white and grows only there in the northern region called Mictlan [FC, Bk. 11, f. 142v; 12:129]). Peyote today grows in Mexico's northern deserts, but the text here also alludes to the north as the entrance of Mictlan, the place of the dead (León-Portilla 1956, 98–99; Tavárez 2011, 91). In Book 10, chapter 29, of the *Florentine Codex*, communal peyote use appears in Chichimeca rituals, also from northern regions, of dance and singing (FC, Bk. 10, f. 122v). As with the previous fever remedies, the intervention of a ticitl orients readers on where to find the cactus and how to administer its dosage. Titicih used psychotropic plants including picietl, *ololiuhqui*, and peyote (peiotl) in combination with ritual language to diagnose and cure patients (Fellowes 1977, 315–16). In 1620, the Inquisi-

FIGURE 19 Peyote and its ingestion, *Florentine Codex*, Book 11, chapter 7, f. 142v. Library of Congress, World Digital Library, accessed April 15, 2024.

tion would prohibit curanderos from using peyote in diagnostic rituals (AGN Inquisición, vol. 333, f. 35r). However, these attestations of its use in the *Florentine Codex* come from more than forty years prior to that edict.[34] Thus, although peyote was subject to clerical disapproval during the 1570s, formal sanctions had not disrupted its use by a ticitl or its administration to patients. In the seventeenth century, idolatry extirpators worked to eliminate the practice. Hernando Ruiz de Alarcón, while gathering information for his *Tratado de las supersticiones y costumbres gentílicas que hoy viven entre los naturales de esta Nueva España* (1629), found that Nahua physicians continued to use peyote and other hallucinogens.[35] The information the titicih submitted allows for imagining the future use of peyote. These representations also locate the ticitl as the specialist qualified to access unseen realms and redirect misaligned tonalli energy. Further psychotropic substances remain in Book 11.

From peiotl, the titicih documented the fever-reducing effects of the mushroom teonanacatl, found in forest clearings in the mountainous areas of central and southern Mexico (Rai et al. 2012, 476). This time, by recommending a limited dose, the healers provided a cure in a manner that would aid the way-finding efforts of patients who ingest it. The entry also warns to avoid problematic side effects by not exceeding the recommended dosage. The accompanying image (see figure 20) shows a bipedal hummingbird-like figure hovering above a cluster of mushroom tops.

This image forms part of a larger network of references to Huitzilopochtli in the *Florentine Codex*. This anthropomorphic representation may recall the transfer of yollotli energy to the sun, a process associated with Huitzilopochtli (Gimmel 2008a, 174–75). Or it may be that the description of the mushrooms below the standing eagle figure with the prefix "teo-" refers simply to their beauty.[36] While "teotl" as a marvelous visual phenomenon forms part of the hummingbird-man comparisons in Book 11, I cannot ignore other ritual meanings.[37] The same descriptor also recalls the marvelous, sacred characteristics of mushroom that would allow one, through a trance state, to see the workings of cosmic energy (Stone 2011,

FIGURE 20 The mushroom *teonanacatl* with avian conveyor of cosmic energy, *Florentine Codex*, Book 11, chapter 7, f. 142v. Library of Congress, World Digital Library, accessed April 15, 2024.

47–48). The image evokes rituals at variance with Spanish aims of religious conversion (Gimmel 2008a, 175). These considerations lead me to believe that within an adaptable frame the titicih assumed at the time, the bird-man with teonanacatl indicates the potential of the plant to enhance one's vision. Huichol *peyoteros* today continue to call peyote "the flesh of the gods," referring to the cactus peiotl described earlier (Clendinnen 1991, 341; D. Carrasco and Sessions 1998, 139–40). This contemporary connection to the Huichol recalls the etymology of teonanacatl as "sacred flesh." Earlier in Book 11, chapter 7, a description of "nanacatl" appears without the teo- prefix:

> ixtlaoacan, çacatzonititlan in mochioa, quamalacachton, xopiazton, chichicacococ, tozcacacoc: teivintli teiollomalacacho, tetlapololti: atonaviztli, coaciviztli ipaio, çan ontetl, etetl in qualonj, tiolpatzmjcti, tetequijpacho, teamã, techololti: temamauhti, tetlatiti. In aqujn mjec qujqua mjec tlamãtli qujtta temamauhti, anoço tevetzqujti: choloa, momecanja motepexivia, tzatzi, momauhtia. (*FC*, Bk. 11, f. 130v–131r)

> [It grows on the plains, in the grass. The head is small and round, the stem is long and slender. It is bitter and burns; it burns the throat. It makes one besotted; it deranges one, troubles one. It is a remedy for fever, for gout. Only two [or] three can be eaten. It saddens, depresses, troubles one; it makes one flee, frightens one, makes one hide. He who eats many of them sees many things which make him afraid or make him laugh. He flees, hangs himself, hurls himself from a cliff, cries out, takes fright.] (12:130)

These descriptions serve as cautions against undesirable behaviors as a consequence of ingesting the mushroom, including "haughtiness, vanity, and presumptuousness": reasonably, Catholic clergy may have used nanacatl as a metaphor to warn against the dangers of pride and vanity (McDonough 2024, 73).

In light of the forgoing observations on teonanacatl and nanacatl mushrooms in Book 11, to my mind, the titicih sought to provide responsible use of psychotropic mushrooms moving forward. The Nahuatl description, its prescription, and the illustration disclose an imaginary of future healing using the psychotropic mushroom. At the same time, the warnings to avoid too much of this remedy do not portray an overly optimistic view. Would future readers be able to use teonanacatl properly? The titicih and the Nahua scholars did not take for granted that all Nahuas knew how to use the mushroom. Here contributors recount in vivid detail the perceptual effects of the right dosage and the excessive dosage. In any case, come what may, the healing practitioners have considered the risk of side effects worth the plant's fever-reducing and gout-relieving qualities.

Toloa, the remaining hallucinogen from the plant cures with no Spanish translation in Book 11, is a species of datura, a vision quest plant used throughout Mesoamerica and Uto-Aztecan North America (Keoke and Porterfield 2001, 21–22; Brock and Diggs 2013, 112). Attention to the passage and illustration on toloa reveals a futurity of cooperation between titicih and their patients. Entry 31 reads: "Toloa: çan no atonavizpatli cencan auhtic in mj: auh in canjn onoc coaciviztli, oncan ommoteca, oncan ommaloa; qujcevia qujtopeoa, qujquanja: amo mjnecujz: amo no mjhio anaz" (Toloa: It is also a fever medicine; it is drunk in a weak infusion. And where there is gout, there it is spread on, there one is anointed. It relieves, drives away, banishes [the pain]. It is not inhaled, neither is it breathed in [FC, Bk. 11, f. 142v; 12:147]). Like centli/cintli and teonanacatl, toloa is a plant with multiple meanings. Karttunen (1992, 244) explains that the intransitive verb *tōloā* means "to lower, bend down one's head," in distinction to the transitive *toloā*, meaning "to swallow something." Justyna Olko (2014, 164–66) has reviewed a number of ancestral ritual meanings of bowing: those associated with the performance of Christian ritual, and those due to pain or suffering. Recalling expressions deriving from *tōloā* (to bow down), that is, "*-tolol, -malcoch quichihua*," "being sad, afflicted, preoccupied," from Book 4 of the *Florentine Codex*, Olko relates these meanings to physical suffering or strong emotion as a cause to bow or prostrate oneself. From the accompanying illustration, it is clear that the text emphasizes bowing down and not swallowing (see figure 21). A patient crouches and inclines toward a ticitl, who applies a poultice as the passage describes.

FIGURE 21 A *ticitl* gives a topical application of *toloa*, *Florentine Codex*, Book 11, chapter 7, f. 142v. Library of Congress, World Digital Library, accessed April 15, 2024.

Additional commentary supports a reading of the verb *tōloā* as intransitive in this case. Ortiz de Montellano (1990, 156–57) has proposed that toloa is a warm remedy meant to counter the cold effects of gout. "Gout" (*coaciviztli*), in the writings related to Sahagún's research, refers to "joint disorders" in general (Miranda Limón 2021, 476). Earlier, in Book 10, chapter 20, a surgical operation to relieve arthritic pain in the knees recommends lancing and draining the fluid, after which the ticitl applies a poultice of toloa (*FC*, Bk. 10, f. 110v). Thus, the entry describes both the effects of the plant and the knowledge of the Nahua physicians. Considering these factors, I propose that the bowed figure before the ticitl also implies a futurity of these particular practices of the healing specialist. This demonstration via an image and written word reinforces the previously described use of toloa as an anti-inflammatory agent in Book 10. These recurrences together support the expertise of the ticitl as qualified to care for sufferers of arthritic joint pain. That the healers know whether a drinkable infusion or a topical application is necessary means their role in diagnosis forms part of a futurity of healing. Taken together, the hallucinogens in Book 11, chapter 7, form a network of anticipatory knowledge(s): taking for granted the reality of physical pain in the future, the text provides approaches to alleviating suffering and restoring the body's balance.

* * * *

In this chapter, I have demonstrated how representations of traditional Nahua beliefs on the cosmos, ritual practices, and healing plants disclose futurities of bodily balance and well-being in Books 10 and 11 of the *Florentine Codex*. I have argued that omissions in the Spanish column of the Ovando commission of the codex reveal inconsistent editorial attention to cultural practices that supported Nahua beliefs about the cosmos and healing. Consequently, the addition of the information the titicih provided in Nahuatl during the interviews at Tlatelolco in the early 1570s made these sections of the *Florentine Codex* a significantly different intellectual project. An Enlightenment-era articulation of individual authorship is indiscernible in the *Florentine Codex*, and, even by the standards of its time, Sahagún was not its sole author. The untranslated sections of Books 10 and 11 are thus collective texts that draw on Nahua voices from inside and outside its place of composition, the Colegio de la Santa Cruz in Tlatelolco. The content the titicih contributed differed from the future of evangelical work that Sahagún imagined. In light of the evangelical purposes of the earlier Toral commission, Terraciano (2019, 9) signals that the collaboration between Nahua writers, artists, and Sahagún "went far beyond this objective, creating a massive compilation of language and culture that resembles a humanist encyclopedia more than a handbook for extirpation." The confluence of contributions allowed Nahuas to write and paint knowledge(s) for readers in times ahead. The *Primeros memoriales* had already featured plant cures I have examined in this chapter—centli/cintli, peyote, and teonanacatl. However, the instructions and commentary on those healing plants amount to little in comparison to the expanded herbal of the *Florentine Codex*. This difference in the attention devoted to the power of healing plants thus indicates the contribution of material in Nahuatl by the fifteen healers whom Sahagún and the Nahua scholars asked to participate in their information-gathering project but that did not appear in the *Códices matritenses*. Consequently, and even in a fragmented form, the *Florentine Codex* communicates forward-looking perspectives on healing—Nahua futurities of well-being—at the time of its making in the 1570s.

The Nahuatl descriptions of the body and healing plants in Books 10 and 11 draw attention to the ancestral view of the body as a path for the flow of cosmic energy through the animating conduits of the tonalli, the yollotli, and the ihiyotl. To summarize, interlocking evidence in Books 10 and 11 converges in Nahua futurities of well-being:

a. the absence of Spanish translations in Book 10, chapter 27, on the parts of the body, and in Book 11, chapter 7, regarding plant-based treatments for illness;
b. the interconnected knowledge(s) of the titicih regarding the use of toloa in Book 11, chapter 7, as a general topical treatment for gout, and in Book 10, chapter 20, as a postsurgery pain reliever for the knees;
c. the triple entries on tlacoxihuitl as a medication to reduce a chest fever in Book 11, chapter 7, entries 55, 104, and 120;
d. the extended development of the material on healing plants in Nahuatl as compared to the *Primeros memoriales*.

The compilation and editorial processes at work during the final editing of the text led to the preservation of ticitl practices in the form of the diagnosis of sicknesses and their treatments. Parallels between text and image as well as repetition between sections of the *Florentine Codex* strengthen my approach to the entries as fragmented Nahua futurities of well-being. Partial communication of Nahua futurities signals fissures in the colonial project of epistemological erasure Rolando Vázquez (2011) has described. Indigenous healers' knowledges assumed a system of hot/cold disease causation, based on solar energy, and that healing plants properly applied would produce desired animic alignments. My analysis thus reveals that the fifteen titicih who contributed to the list of body parts and the compendium of plant cures used iterative descriptions to weave living links to their predecessors and make information available to future readers.

I have also shown how specific Nahua tools of persuasion advance futurities of well-being in Books 10 and 11. Taken together, these tools of persuasion support futurities of healing despite the fragmenting effects of the compilation and editorial procedures that abstracted them from concrete practices. Syntactic parallels describing the entry on the head (totzonteco) as the body's solar-oriented conduit give that part precedence in relation to a person's activities in life. Since the tonalli in the head aligns with cosmic movement, it faces the celestial rhythms of each day and of each coming day. Thus, within the Nahua view, the head anticipates events that have not yet happened.

The persuasive tool of gathering strength figures prominently in Book 11's entry on centli/cintli. By sustaining the body, dried and ground corn maintains proper alignment of the tonalli with the sun and can even provide a remedy for times when the tonalli is stuck or misaligned. We have also seen references to centli in Book 11 that recall connections to rituals in honor of Centeotl in Book 4 of the *Florentine Codex* and with rituals throughout the Nahua and the wider Uto-Aztecan regions celebrating mature maize. These rituals honor corn and seek future strength for the community from the plant. Repetition also plays a key role in Book 11, chapter 7, paragraph 5, where 15 of the 150 plant cures provided concern anchoring misaligned tonalli conduits to the head. This level of concern reveals that the titicih considered these kinds of head fevers a pressing problem. Even more so, this grouping of entries indicates intentional preparation to address tonalli-based fevers in the future. Repetition also marks representations of psychotropic plants. Toloa as a treatment for joint afflictions appears both in Book 11 and earlier in Book 10, chapter 20. The specificity of instructions discloses an imperative to make that knowledge available to future sufferers of gout and other arthritic aliments.

The opening reference to Sahagún's understanding of proselytization as spiritual medicine ignores the way-keeping emphasis of Nahua futurities among the sixteen healers the Nahua scholars interviewed at Tlatelolco. For these contributors, in a practical sense, paths toward the future would pass through illness. The titicih interwove futurities into the complex exchanges of cosmic energy between the human body, the sun, and the landscape. These imaginaries supported neither Phillip II's vision of orthodoxy nor a triumphalist view of uniform Spanish rule over the territories they claimed to control.

By the time the scriptorium at Tlatelolco finished the lists of body parts and plant remedies, the titicih drew on decades of postinvasion healing practices. Phillip II's confiscation of the *Florentine Codex* limited the diffusion of the Nahua futurities of healing it contains. Nevertheless, as resilient Native concepts of bodily strength, these knowledge(s) on the body and plants have survived centuries of colonialism and the ideological onslaughts of Western religion and biomedical science (Chevalier and Sánchez Bain 2003, xiv). The polyphony of Nahua voices in the *Florentine Codex* has prompted Kelly McDonough (2024, 35) to observe "ironically, the project provided the very means by which Nahuas might always recover or remember who they were." Beyond what the titicih perhaps even imagined, "voices and knowledges that made it to the pages of the *Florentine Codex* became an enduring lifeline for future generations, connecting them—as they do today—to their ancestors, language, histories, and way of life" (2024, 35). Nahua views on health have gained far-reaching influence. The knowledge(s) in the text over time resonate with traditional healing arts in Mexico, the U.S. Southwest, the Iberian world, and beyond. To this day, Nahua futurities of healing in the *Florentine Codex* provide alternative approaches from Western medicine, drawing on Native tradition and experience. The next chapter considers another colonial disruption that catalyzed Nahua futurities. As Mexica nobles in Tenochtitlan confronted vast cultural changes in their city, they resisted tribute, struggled with a leadership crisis, and carefully weighed strategies for negotiating with the Spanish in the years ahead.

CHAPTER 3

• • • •

Warning, Reconnaissance, and Return in the *Anales de Juan Bautista*

On Sunday, December 8, 1566, a Nahua visionary, Juan Teton, forecasted impending doom if his people did not change their future course. His message sparked a riot in Cohuatepec, a village north of Mexico-Tenochtitlan (Reyes García 2001, 157). Teton, a commoner (macehual), warned his listeners to change their diet or face dire consequences:

> Achtopa ye quimilhuiya y ye quimiztlacahuia in cohuatepeca tla xiccaquican yn amehuatin quen anquitohua ca ye anquimati yn quitotihui in tocolhuan yn iquac toxiuhmolpiliz ca centlayohuaz hualtemozque yn tzitzimime in techquazque yhuan yn iquac necuepaloz. Yn omoquatequique yn oquineltocaque yn dios mocuepazque. Yn huacaxnacatl quiqua çan no yehuatl mocuepaz. Yn pitzonacatl quiqua çan no yehuatl mocuepaz. Yn ychcanacatl quiqua çan no yehuatl mocuepaz yhuan yn ichcaayatl quiquemi. Yn quanaca q'[ui]qua ça[n] no yehuatl mocuepaz. (*Anales de Juan Bautista* [*ADJB*], f. 8r–8v)

> [At first, he was lying about it to the people of Cohuatepec [saying], "Hear this: you all know what our grandparents said, that when the end of the year count was tied, that all would become dark and the tzitzimime would come down to eat us. Then many people would be transformed. Those who washed their heads and believed in God will be transformed. Those

who eat the meat of cows will become cows. Those who eat the meat of pigs will become pigs. Those who eat lamb shall turn into lambs, and likewise those who wear woolen cloaks. Those who eat chicken will become that."][1]

This passage from the *Anales de Juan Bautista* (1582) conveys Juan Teton's future expectations. Teton's discourse centers on ritual and a preoccupation with mitigating suffering he had witnessed at the coming of the Spanish and their domesticated animals. Given the profound changes that had transpired during the forty-five years since the surrender of Tenochtitlan in 1521, Teton communicated his concern with securing a harmonious future for his listeners (García Garagarza 2013, 53). This passage illustrates the sweeping economic changes in Mexico-Tenochtitlan and surrounding areas between 1531 and 1582, years on which the Native writing subjects of the text have focused (Reyes García 2001, 23). Imported cattle overwhelmed the people and threatened agriculture in the countryside. The threat could not have come at a worse time. The same annals recount the economic crisis in Mexico-Tenochtitlan in the form of monetized tribute, which the Crown began to charge. In the face of these challenges, the scribes who recorded these events used their writing to lead their community into uncertain times. They also recorded how residents of the region—commoners, nobles, and even crowds interacting with one another—used tools of persuasion to articulate multiple futurities.

This chapter examines the teleological content of the discourse of Juan Teton and others in the *Anales de Juan Bautista*. The title of the text recalls the viceroy Martín Enrique Almanza's 1560 appointment of Juan Bautista, a constable (alguacil), as a collector of Native tribute (Reyes García 2001, 19).[2] Tribute collection motivated its composition, and economic changes the Spanish brought concerned nearly every entity in these annals. However, Juan Bautista the tax collector did not write alone: the text's perspectives reveal that a group of scribes residing in San Juan Moyotlan, the southwest quarter of Mexico-Tenochtitlan, produced the text (Reyes García 2001, 28; C. Townsend 2009, 639).[3] Their collective examination of the effects of monetized tribute and changes in the Indigenous leadership in the city shows that the Native writers used alphabetic script in a strategic manner. As Kelly McDonough (2016, 12–

13) has observed, "writing provided the tactical means by which they could manipulate, contest, or even subvert the hegemonic order. We can assume that young Indigenous men from noble families were trained to read and write by the friars for purposes other than contesting the colonial order, but this was one of the unintended outcomes." Within their official purpose as a tribute register, these annals also grapple with the question of how future readers could maintain balance under the colonial administration's suppression of Nahua economic patterns and their rituals. The scribes drew on the perspectives of Native nobles and commoners, as the Mexica noble houses evaluated the actions of Spanish colonial administrators. This confluence of viewpoints turns the text into a forum for collectively constructing views regarding the future in an increasingly vulnerable Nahua community. They grappled with the encroachment of cattle, the failings of Native leaders, and, above all, with the new cash tax, a sea change from the traditional tribute of labor and goods.[4]

An entry in the annals explains that in January 1564, the viceroy Luis Velasco announced that every adult in the city would be responsible for eight *reales* (one peso) and a half measure of corn per year (*ADJB*, f. 16v). This tribute pressure becomes the central feature in the text's four coinciding accounts of the unrest in the city during September and October 1564 (C. Townsend 2009, 642). Altogether, Natives living in Mexico-Tenochtitlan were required to pay 14,000 pesos annually.[5] The tax the Spanish authorities demanded of every adult meant a loss of influence for Mexica nobles and a hardship for commoners (Reyes García 2001, 58).[6] The Mexica governor, Luis Santa María Cipac, great-grandson of the tlatoani Ahuitzotl, sued to reverse the new tax, but without success. One month after the decree in February 1564, Cipac provided his signature, ratifying the law (Reyes García 2001, 210–13). The tax eroded the Nahua nobles' economic base. Until then, the Spanish exempted them from tribute for their cooperation during the city's surrender (Lockhart 1992, 382; C. Townsend 2019, 159–60). By keeping the Mexica nobles short on cash, the new tax undermined the Native governance of the city.

In this chapter, I analyze three pivotal sections of these annals concerned with communicating Nahua knowledge(s) about the future. I argue that multiple visions of times to come fill the annals' folios. Juan Teton's critique of Spanish diet and religion reorients listeners away from their recent religious conversion and toward preparations needed to survive in times of ritual crisis. Similarly, in the center of Mexico-Tenochtitlan, by recording how the Mexica noble Miguel Tecniuh sparked an anti-tribute riot, the scribes of Moyotlan signaled the futility of direct confrontation with the Spanish. In the wake of the riot, Tecniuh and other nobles resigned themselves to a new regime, one that required approaches of tact and negotiation. Later in the annals, given the failure of the Mexica governor Luis Santa María Cipac, to reduce tribute, the scribes used their writing to fill a leadership role. Moreover, in the absence of stable Indigenous leadership, the same scribes used narrative to build a mosaic of teixiptlahuan, combining the returning Moteuczoma Ilhuicamina, the deity pair of Ehecatl-Quetzalcoatl, and even Christian iconography in expectations of better days ahead. The scribes of Moyotlan preserved in writing critical stances toward colonial policies and reconnaissance for posterity of the actions they took during a crisis.[7] Subsequent readers of the *Anales de Juan Bautista* would know about critical responses to Christianity in the region, the massive manifestations against cash tribute, and the scribe's vision of the restoration of Native governance. Despite Spanish tax policy and failures of Mexica leadership, the annals show how persuasion empowered Moyotlan's community during an economic crisis that permanently altered their lives. My close readings make visible ways in which these Nahua writers interpreted events around them to plan as the future unfolded.

I consider several caveats affecting my approach before proceeding. First and foremost, my intent is to avoid anachronistic, proto-nationalist interpretations of the text. The economic concerns of the Mexica in the mid-sixteenth century have little to do with the notion of mestizaje, an ideology intended to smooth over colonial violence with representations of harmony.[8] Likewise, I do not attempt to discover here—as in María Ángel Garibay's (1945, 155–69) reading—an early Mexican national identity under the influence of Spanish colonialism. I also do not suppose—as did Lorenzo Boturini Benaducci—that the text is guadalupano, although it does record a Marian festival at Tepeyac (Reyes García 2001, 53–55, 160).[9] Instead, I propose that the scribes of Moyotlan used writing to record persuasive speech and actions of other Nahuas who built knowledge about the future.

There is also the question of potential interference from colonial agents. As we have seen, other collective manuscripts, such as the *Florentine Codex*, show clerical interventions, for example. To what extent did Westerners interfere with the writing of the Juan Bautista annals? Compared to the level of Bernardino de Sahagún's involvement in the compilation and editing of the *Florentine Codex*, the *Anales de Juan Bautista* were produced with relative autonomy, making possible the Native writers' repurposing of the tribute register. While supportive of the clergy, the scribes lived and worked in a separate setting, with distance that allowed them to record discourses representative of the goals and concerns of the altepetl of Mexico-Tenochtitlan. The fact that Viceroy Enrique Almanza requested the annals as a tribute register indicates that they produced the text with minimal interventions from Spanish clergy.[10] At the same time, the threat of inquisitorial censure was a reality (García Garagarza 2013, 36). The attention the scribes give to priests, notably Pedro de Gante, and their interactions with them shows that their view of the clergy was largely favorable (C. Townsend 2009, 626).[11] Ecclesiastical agents, while in the background, did not directly control or edit the content.

In my approach to these annals, I recall that Indigenous futurities here as elsewhere focus on what their communities regard as positive outcomes rather than simply the avoidance of pain. Laura Harjo (2019, 107) summarizes this consideration as an intergenerational project of flourishing, explaining that "the project of the people is not solely to work not to get killed and to keep our spirits from being squashed; it is to remember, embark upon, and sustain what should be an even larger project—the original instructions that guide us in achieving a full and rich life. This rich, full life is what our ancestors wanted for us; they asked for it before we were born, and we too should be asking for it for those not yet born." In the Nahua worldview, sometimes the path to the rich life requires pain: one must sacrifice for the community, for future generations, and make sacrifices to deities. This axiological orientation means that being good "has to hurt" now for a desired outcome later (Maffie 2019).[12] That said, the multiple futurities I present here by no means exhaust Nahua futurities present in these annals, and, in my view, all of them tend toward culturally specific positive outcomes.

METHODOLOGY

As in previous chapters, the Nahua tools of persuasion guide my close readings of the *Anales de Juan Bautista*. Gathering strength, reciprocity, repetition, questioning-as-persuasion, and specific features of Nahuatl appear throughout the narrative and dialogues the scribes of Moyotlan wrote down. The scribes elaborated narrative cycles that present their perspectives on turbulent events in Mexico-Tenochtitlan while incorporating a variety of voices around them. Nahua futurities in the *Anales de Juan Bautista*, then, emerge as culturally specific constructs. Harjo (2019, 30) has described this process among the Mvskoke:

> Futurity is space, place, and temporality produced socially by people, including relatives located in the past, present, and future. It invokes many other temporalities, other spaces, and yet-to-be-imagined possibilities: it is a practice of conceiving imaginaries. Indigenous futurity places us in conversation or in a dialectic with the unactivated [*sic*] possibilities of our past, present, and future relatives; these conversations include spaces and places that are rich with meaning and experience.

Concepts from narratology also inform my approaches in this chapter. I draw on work by Mieke Bal (2021) regarding narrative focalization to help me understand effects that come from the tendency in the annals of the narration and speakers to shift from one person to another. A closely related concept of Mikhail Bakhtin (1981), *heteroglossia*, refers to multiple, non-coterminous perspectives that a complex narrative text, like a novel, communicates. Scenes in the Juan Bautista annals are replete with multiple, even contradictory, heteroglot voices. As a last methodological consideration, I take orality and writing as complementary processes in these annals, agreeing with Paul Worley (2013, 6) that Indigenous "literacy should be thought of as both oral and written." After reviewing the annals' origin and analytical precedents for the study of Nahua futurities in this text, I examine the Juan Teton uprising and the tribute riot of Miguel Tecniuh. Next, I examine representations in the annals of omens predicting the return of Moteuczoma Ilhuicamina. I conclude the chapter with remarks on the flexibility of the Mexicas' future-focused discourses and how they used tools of persuasion to forge ahead through demanding times in their capital.

The *Anales de Juan Bautista* take their place among other Nahuatl annals from the sixteenth century, such as the *Annals of Tlatelolco* (1528), the *Historia Tolteca-Chichimeca* (ca. 1550), the *Annals of Cuauhtitlan / La leyenda de los cinco soles* (ca. 1590), and the *Annals of Tecamachalco* (ca. 1590). As I explained in the book's introduction, the colonial annals genre shows parallels from the earlier xiuhpohualli yearly account and thus played an important role in Nahua interactions with Western presentations of linear time.[13] The group of scribes who penned the annals lived in the southwest quarter of the city, San Juan Moyotlan, and had ties with Mexica nobles (C. Townsend 2019, 166). These Native writers in Moyotlan wrote most of their entries in the annals between 1519 and 1586 (Reyes García 2001, 58). Within those sixty-seven years, the concerns of 1564–69 predominate and demonstrate vivid, local effects of Phillip II's empire-wide changes in tribute polices (Reyes García 2001, 29–40). Reminiscent of the tlacuilo codex painter, they recorded events pertaining to their altepetl and lent gravitas to a text meant for use inside their community, similar to the role of codices and murals for previous time untold.

ANALYTICAL PRECEDENTS

Until now, no analysis has centered on Nahua futurities in the three episodes from the annals I examine here. However, existing studies by historians and literary scholars do make visible ways in which the scribes worked to shape their futures. Camilla Townsend's (2019) examination of the reactions of Mexica nobles to Spanish tribute policy in the text highlights the responsibility nobles held to care for commoners. Townsend recalls that Governor Cipac sent emissaries to the scribes of Moyotlan to remind them that they and the other Mexica nobles "in yohualli hitic amo yhuiyan quiqua yn achitzin tlamatzohualli in que[n] quihuicazqu'[ue] yn icuitlapil y iatlapal" (*ADJB*, f. 20v) (suffer anxiety in the night. They don't eat with tranquility, worrying about how they will care for the wings, the tail) (trans. C. Townsend 2019, 167–68). The difrasismo "in cuitlapilli in altapalli" (the wings, the tail) refers to the macehualli, whose future formed a vital concern for the nobles (Molina [1571] 2008, 2:27r; Reyes García 2001, 199n89). William Connell's archival study *After Moctezuma* (2011) includes the administration of Governor Luis Santa María Cipac and dynamics within the Indigenous government of Mexico-Tenochtitlan in the sixteenth century. Although Connell does not analyze the *Anales de Juan Bautista,* his comments on Cipac's tenure inform my reading. Literary analysis of the uprising of Juan Teton also hints at horizons of concern for Teton and for the scribes. Santa Arias (2006, 43) has pointed out that the scribes do not completely censure the message of Juan Teton. By preserving his speech, they showed a degree of ambivalence. They considered elements of Teton's speech worth disseminating, which they show via their use of "free indirect discourse," a technique that narrators can use to place or remove distance between their voices and others they quote. Similarly, León García Garagarza (2013, 52–53) notes the ambiguity of these scribes regarding Teton and argues that his quasi-apocalyptic message belies a palpable fear that European livestock would eradicate Nahua agriculture and with it the age of the Fifth Sun. I now return to Juan Teton and his denunciation of the Spanish-imposed diet.

WARNING: LIFE BEYOND THE FIFTH SUN

The uprising of Juan Teton above all emphasized future actions. His tools of persuasion argue for a future of balance dependent on proper ritual activity. Ever conscious of how the passage of time has weakened the people by turning them into animals, Teton provides a vivid explanation of the dramatic demographic losses and practical solutions for correcting and restoring the people's relationship to the land and the altepetl. First, I consider how Teton warns his listeners of the dangers of uniting oneself with cattle by eating them. I then move to the advice he gives to stave off this and other disasters. I also argue that Teton positions himself at the juncture between a recent past of displacement by Spanish-introduced cattle and a future of group cohesion and strength. As a sufferer himself of this colonial trauma, in my view, he gave voice to widespread and shared consequences of the Spanish invasion.

The scenes with Juan Teton open as denunciations of the ritual washings he conducted of neophyte Christians in Cohuatepec and Atlapolco:

Ce tlacatl mecehualtzintli catca ytoca Juan Teton chane Michmaloyan q'[ui]ntlapololti q'[ui]miztlacahui in cohuatepeca yhua[n] atlapolca q'[ui] npaquilli yn innequatequiliz auh ynic otetlapollolti ynic oteiztlacahui in Juan ynic otequapac oquimilhui yn cohuatepeca atlapolca yn cohuatepeca achto moquapacque auh yn yq[ua]c omoquapacque çatepa[n] quihuallihuaque ymamauh yn Atlapolco ye q'[ui]monometlalli yn altepetl y ye q'[ui] miztlacahuia. (*ADJB*, f. 8r–8v)

[There was a man, a commoner from Michmaloyan named Juan Teton. He deceived, took advantage of the people of Cohuatepec and Atlapolco, making them happy so that he would wash their heads. To cause confusion and fool them, Juan washed their heads. He said this to the Cohuatepeca and Atlapolca. First it was the Cohuatepeca who washed their heads. After they washed their heads, they came bringing this to Atlapolco. Thus, they have cultivated a lie in this altepetl and thus they have fooled you.]

This preface to the words of Juan Teton establishes the attitude of the scribes toward him as one of basic distrust.[14] Since the scribes associated with the Franciscans in Mexico-Tenochtitlan, their description doubly accuses the local leader: they blame him for attempting to dissuade Nahuas from following Christianity and express suspicion toward him for being a resident of the hinterlands who contradicted the sensibilities of the capital.

While at first the text appears to refer to a washing ritual resembling baptism, it is important to recall that Mesoamerican ritual systems contain no such rite. Luis Reyes García (2001, 157), in his translation of the *Anales de Juan Bautista*, has rendered the verbs for washing one's head in the cited passages as denoting baptism. However, Alonso de Molina ([1571] 2008, 2:85v), a Franciscan grammarian working in the sixteenth century, translated *cuatequia* with three meanings: "lavarse la cabeza, o bautizarse, lavar a otro la cabeza" (to wash one's own head, to be baptized, or to wash someone's head). Thus, *cuatequia* can be reflexive or transitive, depending on the context; and context means everything when it comes to baptism. Alternately, Molina ([1571] 2008, 2:85r) translates the verb *quapaca* as simply "lavarse la cabeza" (to wash one's own head). In the quoted passage, the first verb, *cautequia*, forms the preponderance of attestations. Yet these uses of the verb denote a washing that reverses baptism rather than a rite resembling the Catholic sacrament. Indeed, Teton mentions no trinitarian formula but does mention Nahua deities. As we shall see, he aims to prepare his listeners to face malevolent cosmic beings by strengthening themselves through the proper performance of the instructions he will give them. Within these instructions, he counsels his listeners to sever ties with all things foreign as a necessary first step toward a viable future life. That future, within the frame Teton provides, does not occur after death but in the material world of his immediate audience.[15]

By the same token, the return Teton proposes to a Nahua diet and to traditional cultivation of the land does not involve the absolution of wrongdoing according to a Christian paradigm of repentance or penance. According to Julia Madajczak (2017), Sahagún's Christian interpretation of the ritual of *yolmelahua* (heart straightening) in Books 1 and 6 of the *Florentine Codex* has influenced subsequent readings.[16] Similarly, Ulrich Köhler (2001, 126–28) has observed that a mistranslation of the term *ixtlahua* has led to the association of sacrifice with expiation of sin, according to a Western model, a notion that Dibble and Anderson's translation of the *Florentine Codex* has reified. Therefore, the return to ancestral ways Teton promotes here does not reflect a deontological view of morality. Rather, within a consequentialist frame, he warns listeners of what will happen if they do not act as their ancestors did. Concomitantly, I do not argue that Juan Teton aimed to establish a religion or to borrow religious practices from the Spanish. In fact, he positioned himself against the imported rituals he observed. He counseled ritual responses to his people's suffering from threats to their agriculture by colonizers. Teton saw the issue as people suffering due to a lack of ritual preparation rather than as the result of moral transgression. With these considerations in mind, I proceed with the scribes' account of Teton.

Teton begins his speech with a series of repeated warnings, which I quoted at the start of the chapter. It is in the opening of his speech that Teton recalls the coming of the tzitzimime at the end of the Age of the Fifth Sun. He takes for granted his audience's familiarity:

> Ye anquimati yn quitotihui in tocolhuan yn iquac toxiuhmolpiliz ca centlayohuaz hualtemozque yn tzitzimime in techquazque yhuan yn iquac necuepaloz. (*ADJB*, f. 8r–8v)

[You all know what our grandparents said, that when the end of the year count was tied, that all would become dark and the tzitzimime would come down to eat us. Then many people would be transformed.]

The relationship between the extinguishing of the Fifth Sun and the coming of the tzitzimime appears documented elsewhere in the sixteenth century. The *Florentine Codex* contains an often-cited passage: "mitoaia, in tlatlamiz, in qualo tonatiuh: centlaiooaz: oaltemozque, in tzitzimime, tequaquiui" (It was said that if there is a total eclipse, all will end. Together, the tzitzimime will descend in darkness and eat everyone [*FC*, Bk. 7, f. 1v]).[17] By extension, not correctly lighting the New Fire at the end of a fifty-two-year cycle could carry the same consequences (L. Burkhart 1989, 55, 83; Sigal 2011, 123–26; García Garagarza 2013, 38–39). Since the Spanish had toppled the twin temples of Huitzilopochtli and Tezcatlipoca in Tenochtitlan, and the year of his speech coincided with that of the pending New Fire ceremony, Juan Teton had cause for concern (Reyes García 2001, 45; Olivier 2005, 248n4). Seeing this obstacle to ritual timekeeping, Teton advises concerted, collective acts to protect remaining Nahuas.

Teton now turns to diet. I note that by repeating the link between consumed meat and animal alterations, he stresses the cattle's dehumanizing effects. Teton declares,

Yn huacaxnacatl quiqua çan no yehuatl mocuepaz. Yn pitzonacatl quiqua çan no yehuatl mocuepaz. Yn ychcanacatl quiqua çan no yehuatl mocuepaz yhuan yn ichcaayatl quiquemi. Yn quanaca qu'[ui]qua ça[n] no yehuatl mocuepaz. (*ADJB*, f. 8v)

[Those who ate the meat of cows will become cows. Those who ate the meat of pigs will become pigs. Those who ate lamb shall turn into lambs, and likewise those who wear woolen cloaks. Those who ate chicken will become that.]

Repetition of these phrases served to maintain listeners' attention (Ong [1982] 2002, 33–34, 40; Asselbergs 2008, 225). Besides these warnings' immediate effect of drawing his audience to listen, repetition amplifies meaning in Nahuatl. Miguel León-Portilla (2000, 53) observed that syntactic parallels in Nahuatl serve to "strengthen a statement, to amplify an image, or to make an anecdote explicit." Similarly, Ben Leeming (2015, 176) has noted that slight variations in parallelisms agglomerate meaning "by gradually building up a vivid picture layer by layer. Each successive term slightly modifies the previous one as the imagery builds in a linguistic crescendo." Only after Teton repeats the formula four times and varies the farm animals—cows, pigs, sheep, and chickens—does the picture become clear: these meats, these foreign fleshes, have replaced their own bodies, making a metonymical relationship: you become what you eat. Teton further amplifies the idea of substitution, averring, "those who wear woolen cloaks": that is, those who have covered their skins with the skins of the invaders' animals will themselves become sheep. If we recall Molly Bassett's (2015) definition of a teixiptla as "a surface flayed thing," his alarm becomes understandable. On a deep ontological level, the people and the land are becoming unrecognizable threats. Wrapping oneself in a sheepskin meant embodying the ritual energy of that animal. Some teixiptlahuan, according to Teton, pose an existential threat. Teton describes an undesirable but avoidable future of assimilation with otherworldly beasts from across the ocean.

It is easy for me to imagine passersby stopping to listen to Teton's lament at the disappearance of so many people. This explanation of causality likely added an element of persuasion to Teton's message, which accounted for what happened to those who had died. As time wore on, Nahuas disappeared while the population of European cattle exploded.[18] The absences of family, friends, and acquaintances no doubt left the lingering question of what had become of them. Teton offered a compelling explanation of population loss in the altepetl of Xallatlauhco as resulting from the transformation of people into livestock:

Tla xiquimittaca[n] yn xallatauhca yn achto otlaneltocaque yn do[n] Alonso yeh icapa ye ysonbrero mochiuhque yn ipilhua[n] yhuan in teyacanque omochmocuapque[ue] ye moch quaquaque aocmo altepeneçi yn o[n]can onoque ça ixtlahuaca[n] quauhtla y[n] ce[n]mantinemi vacastin. (*ADJB*, f. 8v)

[Just look at the people of Xallatlauhco who were the first to convert. The children of Don Alonso turned into his cape and sombrero, and all the leaders there were transformed and turned into grazing cattle. No longer is the altepetl recognizable, and those who are there now live only in empty land, in forests, where cows have taken over.]

Feeding on foreign food caused metaphysical disorder, and improper nourishment meant the loss of one's humanity. Teton proposed rejecting European ranching and Christianity as threats to traditional life, from his understanding that the animal invasion was killing his people.

Teton has identified the problem at hand. I note here an inflection in his discourse: from this point on he gives instructions for survival in a gloomy, conflictive world. He continues,

In axcan amohuicpa ninoquixtia aocmo huecauh ye mochiuaz yn tlamahuiçolli yn tlaca[m]o anquineltocazque y[n] namechilhuia ca y[n]hua[n] anmocuepazque ynic anpitzque ca namechpaquilliz ynic oanmoquatequique ca namechpopolhuiz ynic amo a[n]miq'[ui]zque ye huel polihuiz. (*ADJB*, f. 8v)

[So today I will fulfill my duty with all of you since there is not much time left before this phenomenal event. Otherwise, if you don't believe what I'm telling you, it is because you also will be transformed. Here there is a remedy. I will satisfy you who washed your heads by destroying it so that you won't die in the utter destruction that is coming.]

As Luis Reyes García (2001, 158) opted for a sacramental translation of the verbs for head washing, here he has also chosen to translate the verb *popolhuia* as "perdonar" (to forgive). Again, this meaning appears as one possibility in Molina's ([1571] 2008, 2:83r) dictionary: the complete definition reads "perdonar a otro la ofensa o destruirle alguna cosa" (to forgive another an offense, or destroy something for someone). Given the orientation of Teton's message toward a future of restored agriculture, I am inclined toward the second meaning in this case.[19] Suffice it to point out that the spaces and places Teton references in this description of the future do not convey a Catholic conceptualization of confession. Teton purports to dissolve and eliminate his listeners' ties to the invaders and their religion. Teton continues his description of coming catastrophes:

Yhua[n] mayanaloz xicpiacan in pipillo in tlalamatl yn xaltomatl y[n] quauhnanacatl yn xillomotzontli y[n] xilloyzhuatl y[n] miyahuatl ceceyacah xiq'[ui]nnahuatican yn macehualtin yhuan y ce[n]ca moneq'[ui] xichautzacan inteçiuhoctli yc a[n]maquiçazque yn iquac antzatzililozque yn Chapoltepec salotica amoxillan ycatiaz yn iquac amechittaz yn Tlantepozyllama yc amechimacaiz yc amo achquaz çan ic amechcahuaz oyuhquihi yn anquicaqui. (*ADJB*, f. 8v–9r)

And there will be a famine. Each one of you, gather food, the leaves that grow on the slopes of volcanoes, wild tomatoes, mushrooms, corn silk, green corn husks, corn tassel flowers. Listen all of you, the people [macehualtin]: it's very necessary that you dry out pulque for when you are called out to Chapultepec. You will carry it in a standing vessel on your stomachs. And when the Tlantepoxyllama sees you, she will be afraid of you and not eat you. This you hear is how it will all happen.

The urgency of the situation required listeners to act for survival by rejecting the foreign diet, gathering regional foods, and preparing for the famine that will come with the extinguishing of the sun. While the foods Teton advises his listeners to gather may appear arbitrary, I observe that once dried, all of them would provide nourishment while traveling. Teton's advice contains instructions about confronting a specific deity among the tzitzimime at Chapultepec. Teton asks listeners to carry jars of dried pulque (xichautzacan inteçiuhoctli) on their stomachs to face Tlantepexillama, a female deity with metal teeth who eats humans. When there is no more sun, it follows that all plants die and death looms over all other living things. In this sense, both the tzitzimime and Tlantepexillama are earth deities who will ultimately devour humans, and Teton's warning is one of common human destiny. This reciprocal relationship appears in succinct affirmations from contemporary Nahua communities: "Nosotros comemos la tierra y la tierra nos come a nosotros" (We eat the earth, and the earth eats us) (Good Eshelman 2001, 273).[20] Nonetheless, how dried pulque will stave off death is not as apparent. Guilhem Olivier (2005, 263–64) sheds light on why Nahuas may have attributed powers of renewal to dried pulque, recalling Diego Muñoz de Camargo's narrative of Camaxtli, a Tlaxcallan who refused to ally with the Spanish. Camaxtli prepared reeds, feathers, and deer nerves to make arrows and set them next to a stone vessel with a single drop of dried breast milk at the bottom. After Camaxtli made offerings, the stone vessel filled with saliva-like foam; the arrows made themselves and began flying under their own power at the Spanish. Olivier (2005, 264–65) further explains that the tzitzimime deities derive their name from "çiçimitl," which the *Codex Magliabechiano* defines as an arrow or dart (*Codex Magliabechiano* 1970, f. 75v).[21] To his observation I add that a contemporary more-than-human Tenantzitzimitl also has connotations of offensive violence: this aggressive grandmother spends her time trying to kill her grandson, Chicomexochitl, the Huastecan maize deity.[22] I also recall the observation of Chevalier and Sánchez Bain (2005, 165–66) that Nahuas may counter the effects of dryness of one kind with dryness of another. Those who would listen to Juan Teton thus endeavor to revive their own flesh and those of future generations by holding the life-giving dried pulque over the womb-midsection of the body. Returning to my main argument, I also observe that Teton's directions articulate a futurity via negotiation with deities, appeasing them to avoid calamity.

Teton envisions further disasters beyond the coming of the tzitzimime and the confrontation with Tlantepexyllama:

> Yhuan in mochiuaz ca ça yyo oncan in y[n] quimochiuilliz in tlalticpaque yn tonacayotl yn nohuiya[n] c[e]m[anaua]c moch huaq'[ui]z yn ixquich qualloni aoctle mochihuaz yxquich nica[n] monamacaquiuh in tenitl yn cuextecatl yc pehuaz in yaoyotl onca[n] momanaz y[n] Matlalxochipa[n] cuitlaxcol atlauhtli yez etc. (*ADJB*, f. 8v–9r)

> [And all of this will happen; the owner of the land [Tlalticaque] will cause all corn, our flesh [tonacayotl] to dry up with all other food. Nothing will grow. Everyone will come here to sell. The foreigner [tenitl], those from the Huaxteca will set out to make war, making their basecamp in Matlalxochipan. There they will fill a canyon with human innards.]

The destruction of which Teton warns is the utter breakdown of the world as he and his contemporaries knew it. A flow of calamities emerges. When the New Fire ceremony fails, the sun does not shine, which causes all plants to die and the people to starve. Any residents who remain, Teton claims, will use trade and, failing that recourse, violence to obtain food. Curiously, Teton turns to an older referent than the Spanish military invasion to articulate to his listeners what is at stake. During the regime of the Mexica, the Huasteca gained a reputation as hard to conquer and hard to rule (Ramírez Sánchez 2018, 36–37). For this reason, Teton refers to Huastecans as foreigners (tenitl), recalling stereotyped images of their nomadic living, drunkenness, and promiscuity (Johansson 2012; Olko 2012). By predicting the ravine they will fill with human innards (cuitlaxcol atlauhtili yez), Teton again evokes the midsection of the body (*ADJB*, f. 9r). Total war of this kind would kill his listeners and devastate their reproductive capacity, foreclosing all possibility of future generations. If we recall the agglomeration of meaning in Nahuatl that Leeming (2015) has described, according to Teton, conversion to Christianity and eating foreign foods had unexpected, disastrous consequences for the listeners present and any of their potential offspring. Baptism, roasted meats, and sheepskin attire disrupted the social and metaphysical order.

How the Spanish handled Juan Teton's uprising shows that in the sense of hegemony and control the age of the Fifth Sun was over. After Teton's speech, the scribes record that the Spanish arrested him, along with five leaders from Cohuatepec and Atlapolco who had joined him: "Cohuatepec gou[ernad]or Don Pedro de Luna, Fran[cis]co Çacayaotl alcalde, Nicolas fiscal, Atlapolco tlatohuani Don P[edro] Xico, fiscal Juan Tecol" (*ADJB*, f. 9r) (The governor of Cohuatepec, Don Pedro de Luna; the mayor Francisco Çacayaotl; the fiscal Nicolas; the ruler of Atlapolco, Don Pedro Xico; the fiscal Juan Tecol). The affiliation of these local leaders with the objectives of Teton posed a threat to the Spanish, particularly since governors and *fiscales* (caretakers of churches) played a key role in tribute collection (Haskett 1987, 212). Thus, the scribes show a level of ambivalence toward Teton by preserving his speech's content and at once repudiating it. As Teton comes into the narrative and disappears into Spanish custody, the scribes' presentation of this figure registers lingering uncertainty regarding diet, the land, rituals, and future survival.

Teton had spoken his truth to power, a trope Foucault ([1982] 2019) has called *parrēsia*. This sort of transgressive truth-telling recalls Santa Arias's (2006) observation that through the use of free, indirect discourse, the scribes of Moyotlan may have distanced themselves from some of Teton's discourse—his rejection of baptizing—while allowing for the expression of frustrations regarding demographic downturn and the people's displacement from their fields by introduced livestock. Perhaps so. While it is not possible to adduce why they considered the speech worth writing down, in my view the pressure of registering tribute may have motivated the scribes to make a record of the ideas of Teton. After all, those ideas led to the arrest of the governors and fiscales of Cohuatepc and Atlapolco, which no doubt made the scribes' collection of tribute more difficult.

In terms of my main argument, the Juan Teton event shows an array of Nahua tools of persuasion. His advice—from breaking away from baptism, to eating proper foods, to preparing to encounter earth deities—supports gathering strength to approach the future. Teton does not counsel return to any static, inert tradition. Instead, he draws on a reserve of ritual acts and adapts them to face coming calamities. By stating that he is doing his duty to help them, Teton evokes reciprocity to convince. Repetition in his warnings regarding each imported farm animal shows the persuasive effect that has identified each troublesome animal separately and brought them together as a single disturbing unit. In the face of an implied question of what had become of absent relatives, Teton provides a response testable against shared experience. Not even the scribes of Moyotlan could escape the question of what was happening to those they once knew. Finally, specific features of Nahuatl worked to persuade. Teton used a cascade of disastrous scenarios to spur his listeners to action, agglomerating details of future scenrios to avoid and providing advice on how to regain ritual balance. The fact that five leaders from the towns he visited followed him shows the partial success of his persuasion. In the next section, I return to the city center, where tension over tribute collection was growing.

RECONNAISSANCE: THE RIOT OF MIGUEL TECNIUH

More than two years prior to Juan Teton's uprising on the evening of February 18, 1564, an angry Miguel Tecniuh entered a meeting with other Mexicas of his noble rank. The purpose of this group's gathering was to deliver the tribute of Mexico-Tenochtitlan to Luis Santa María Cipac, the city's Mexica governor, who would turn it over to Spanish administrators. Viceroy Antonio de Mendoza had appointed Cipac two years earlier, in 1562, meshing his interest in a compliant Native politician with the Mexica interest in self-governance (Lockhart 1992, 28–44). Cipac was a great-grandson of the preconquest tlatoani Ahuitzotl, famed as conqueror of the Mexica's vast territory. Mexica nobles had high expectations that Cipac would help retain their wealth, which had dwindled after the disruption of their tribute networks since the Spanish invasion. Cipac used petitions and litigation to maintain his family's economy and that of the nobles in Moyotlan (Mundy 2015, 156–60).[23] Cipac, for many reasons, had not lived up to his predecessor's reputation. He was ready to help the Spanish goal of tribute collection, provoking tensions with the city's Indigenous nobles and commoners that would prove fatal.[24] Tecniuh's visit quickly turned into a frank conversation with ranking noble authorities about the recently imposed tax. Governor Cipac received the tribute and explained that he and his aides had done their utmost to convince the Spanish to repeal it but without success. Miguel Tecniuh responded bluntly:

> Ca otoconcac in timexicatl in titenochcatl ynic tonmotequitiliz yn iuh oq'uimotlalli yn totlatocatzin in Magestad cuix çan nican omoyocox cuix no ceceme tlatoque nican oquitlalique ca ye ixquich cahuitl yn ticnemitia ye axcan chiquacentetl metztli yn oc nen titlacuepa aoc hueliti aocmo titlahuelcaquililo auh onehuatica yn amotlatocauh cuix aoctle amopan quichihua cuix oamexiccauh cuix oquixicauh yn icuitlapil yn iatlapal auh ye cuel iquac on ye axcan chiquacentetl meztli yn nican anquimocaquiltico auh yn axcan maximoteilhuilli yn timerimo maxiccaquilti yn motlahuilanal maximotecalpanhuilli yn nican ticmocahuilia yn meliotzin. (*ADJB*, f. 35v)

> [You, people from Mexico-Tenochtitlan, have heard that you will pay tribute as our Lord and Majesty has decreed. Was this conceived here? Did each one of the [Indigenous] nobles here decree it? For a while now we have negotiated, for six months now. In vain we contradicted them. It's impossible; our petition is rejected. Now your governor is present here. Does he no longer do anything for all of you? Has he neglected you Mexica? Has he abandoned his subjects? You have come here to listen to what has happened for the last six months. Now you, the *merino*, tell the people; inform those who depend on you; go from house to house, you who turn in the money.]

Miguel Tecniuh's exasperated display to the highest Mexica noble underscores the Native crisis of authority. He employed Nahua tools of persuasion, which the scribes organized and recorded around the narrative focalization of his voice. He draws attention to Cipac's responsibilities, which a ruler has for his people's welfare. While nobles and commoners had respected him and followed his lead, Cipac did not reciprocate by maintaining the earlier tribute exemptions the Spanish had extended to them at the surrender of Tenochtitlan.[25] Tecniuh, whose perspective the scribes privileged, hurled questions that emphasize his superior's lack of competence as a negotiator. Using repetition as a persuasive tool, Tecniuh's series of questions emphasizes answers his listeners already knew. To my mind, here repetition also conveys an implicit yet detailed retelling: assuming at least one of the scribes of Moyotlan was present at the meeting, Tecniuh's speech shows a level of organization that reveals retellings had already occurred prior to its recording in the annals (Lord 1974, 98; Worley 2013, 18–19). As another tool of persuasion, Tecniuh's voice in this retelling identifies the people not as macehualli (commoners) but with the difrasismo "yn icuitlapil yn iatlapal" (the wings, the tail), stressing that the body of nobles depended on broader Mexica cooperation and were responsible for the good of all. The Mexica nobles collectively deferred to Cipac; however, the governor had not fulfilled his duty. In reply, Tecniuh now gave the governor a command: *maximotecalpanhuilli* (you go from house to house).

My observation here regarding Nahua futurity is that Tecniuh's speech signals the construction of noble identity and authority as concerns. His disrespect for Cipac draws a line between those whom he considered trustworthy nobles, who have maintained solidarity and their anti-tribute sentiment, and Cipac, who has ceded unacceptable ground to the Spanish. Luis Santa María Cipac was the last postconquest tlatoani elected and from candidates with a lineage in Mexica houses (Gibson 1964, 605; Lockhart 1992, 610). Tecniuh calls Cipac a merino, the Spanish loan term for a bureaucrat who collected taxes in a calpolli (subdivision of an altepetl), and does not address him as the Native-elected tlatoani (Gibson 1964, 206–7; Lockhart 1992, 43–44).[26] In fact, throughout the city, the Native residents had stopped calling him "Cipactzin" with the traditional honorific suffix, *-tzin* (Chimalpahin 1997, 175).[27] Drawing on features in his language, Tecniuh places another division between

Cipac and the rest of the nobles. He addresses the group of assembled nobles in second-person plural as "aomexiccauh" (you Mexica), separating them from Cipac, whom he refers to in the third-person singular. He speaks to the group of nobles directly, calling them by name and recalling the strength of the city's former rulers. Inevitably, he alludes to the reign of Ahuitzotl, the warrior tlatoani and Cipac's great-grandfather (C. Townsend 2019, 165). This implicit comparison questions Cipac's worthiness compared to Ahuitzotl, who conquered Chiapas and Soconusco. For Miguel Tecniuh and the Moyotlan scribes, the answer is clear: Cipac failed to secure lower tribute, abandoned his people, and exposed them to economic loss.

Wrapping up my thoughts on Miguel Tecniuh's highly organized speech and the futurities it conveys, I note dual forward-looking themes: to denounce what nobles saw as Cipac's ineptitude and to help future leaders avoid his pitfalls. Tecniuh functioned as a figurehead for widely shared concerns regarding economic conditions moving forward. In this manner, by synthesizing several entities' concerns about the future of authority in Mexico-Tenochtitlan, the scribes provided what organization they could in chaotic times through writing. They accomplished a critique of authority through the figure of Miguel Tecniuh, his persuasive questioning, and his derision of Governor Cipac's leadership.

Miguel Tecniuh's confrontation with Governor Cipac set a larger disturbance in motion. The resulting unrest highlights shifts underway in the city's Indigenous hierarchies and provides information on viable courses of action for Nahua leaders. After six months of lobbying in vain against the tribute, the riot becomes a crescendo of meaning, attached to Miguel Tecniuh's invective. A crowd of commoners joined in the manifestation in the governor's patio. One of the most vivid spectacles in the annals, the commotion spans three folios (f. 25v–27r). Through multiple narrative focalizations, this riot further shows the importance the scribes gave Tecniuh's speech and the words of bystanders:

> Auh yn iquac otzonquiz ytlatol niman ye ic neacomanallo auh in goernador oc nen quihualito matlapitzallo niman ye ic netenhuiteco tlacahuaco niman ye hualtemohuac tlatzintla netenhuiteco yhuan mochi tlacatl quito can ticuizque auh ixquich çihuatl yllamatzin in chocaque yhuan cenca quallanque auh ce tlacatl quito ytoca Huixtopolcatl Amanalco chane quito aquinon

tlatohua cuix tlillancalqui cuix quauhnochtli cuix hezhuahuacatl tle mochihua tlapaltontli achac momati ylhuiz tlacauaco conitohua cuix itla quitlanitotihui yn tetecuhtin yn tlatoque yn oquipiaco altepetl. (*ADJB*, f. 25v)

[And when he had finished talking, the people began to riot and the governor cried in vain, "Play music with flutes and wind instruments." Then the people came out from the meeting yelling and beating their mouths. They ran down to the foot of the palace yelling. And everyone said, "How will we handle this problem?" And the elderly women were crying and getting very angry. A man from Amanalco called Huixtopolcatl cried, "Who [in authority] is speaking? Perhaps it is Tlilancalqui. Perhaps it is Quauhnochtli. Perhaps it is Ezhuahuacatl. What has happened to the people here, and what are we to think?" The people were dispersing wildly: he said, "Are the lords and rulers who support the altepetl going to profit from this?"]

The text provides Nahua tools of persuasion during a heteroglossic scene, as the scribes have remembered it. The theme of broken reciprocity continues. Since Cipac did not resolve the tribute issue, the people now look collectively for a solution: "mochi tlacatl quito can ticuizque" (*ADJB*, f. 25v) (everyone said, "How will we handle this problem?"). Commoners now openly criticized the Mexica government for a lack of foresight. The narrative vocalization then passes not to another noble but to Huixtopolcatl, a commoner from Amanalco. I find it telling that singular voices ask questions in these annals: as with Juan Teton, a commoner again signals collective inquietude. Each question Huixtopocatl poses casts doubt on Cipac's ability to govern. Normally, the chief speaker (tlatoani) has the authority to represent the welfare of the people. The silence that meets his questions signals the neglect of duty on Cipac's part. In fact, that something "has happed to the people here" (mochihua tlapaltontli) appears to be a critique of Cipac's lack of care for those around him. What is more, by asking whether the leaders plan to get anything for the altepetl (yn oquipiacoaltepetl), Huixtopocatl signals not only their self-interest but also the poor negotiating abilities even with one another.

Repetitions and parallelisms abound in this brief section. When Miguel Tecniuh finished speaking, the governor "cried in vain" (oc nen quihaulito) for them to play music. This expression mirrors his own words to the Mexica nobles only minutes earlier that "in vain we contradicted them" (yn oc nen titlacuepa). The verb *cuepa* means first "to turn; to return; to bring back" (Karttunen 1992, 70). Cipac recalled the unwillingness of the Spanish to restore the Mexica tribute exemption. However, I note that both Tecniuh and Huixtopolcatl, in the recounting of the scribes, turn Cipac's words back on him. Responding to the governor's desire for music, the group of nobles yell and beat their mouths. Their indignation spreads to women elders next to the palace whose tears morph into anger. Huixtopolcatl asks who is speaking and responds to his own question with syntactic parallels: "cuix tlillancalqui cuix quauhnochtli cuix hezhuahuacatl" (*ADJB*, f. 25v) (Perhaps it is Tlilancalqui. Perhaps it is Quauhnochtli. Perhaps it is Ezhuahuacatl). A *tlilancalqui* was a lower-level judge who began a trial, while a *quauhnochtli* and an *ezhuahuacatl* were executioners (Reyes García 2001, 215n105). As many voices spoke, the scribes positioned perspectives of critique and evaluation of future possibilities. The failure to reduce tribute was a tragic turning point for Cipac and for the Mexica.

In addition to serving as a petition for justice, Huixtopolcatl's cry foreshadowed the eclipse of local leadership. The Spanish restored order, but only by threatening the crowd with bloodshed and by arresting ten Mexica nobles. The annals list the nobles arrested by name. On Monday, July 17, 1564, the Spanish placed wooden stocks in the tianguis and tied the prisoners to them to deter others from speaking poorly of the governor (*ADJB*, f. 26v). After all, "the Audiencia valued above all else the preservation of order" (Connell 2011, 54). Although they voiced their grievances, the tribute riot did not strengthen the shaky Mexica leadership. However, beyond the lives of Tecniuh and the protesters, the account would provide evidence that Mexica leadership did not accept Spanish policies uncritically.

Despite Tecniuh's instigation of the riot in February 1564, by October of the same year he had returned to work as a tribute collector (*ADJB*, f. 36r). Without Indigenous leaders, the Spanish were severely limited in their ability to negotiate with, much less collect taxes from, the city's Nahua residents. Connell (2011, 21) has argued that the viceregal government from the sixteenth to the eighteenth centuries tended to support the Indigenous cabildo in Mexico-Tenochtitlan as pragmatic for maintaining order and tribute collection. He notes that Nahuas in the city worked "to preserve Indigenous control over their own governance within a viceregal system that actively supported them in their efforts." The financial viability of the viceroy ironically depended on the strength of the Indigenous government. Thus, that Tecniuh faced no significant penalty shows that the colonial administration was hard-pressed to find anyone else able to collect tribute in the quarter of Moyotlan besides the Mexica nobles. While I hesitate to affirm Spanish support as sincere, their distance from the Iberian Peninsula forced them to make pragmatic concessions and acknowledge that an uncooperative Native nobility reduced the tribute they could gather.

I further note that Tecniuh's tribute opposition serves as synecdoche for his noble class. He presented the dissent of his cohort yet also participated in a complex and contradictory system that supported his survival. The nobles were now carrying out "negotiation from *within* domination" (Owensby 2010, xii, my emphasis). Cooperation between the Spanish and the Mexica nobles in the capital preserved a fragile civic order—a shifting yet shared goal of the Nahuas and Spanish in the war-torn, disease-ravaged city.[28] The casualties in this arrangement between Nahua nobles and the viceregal government were the macehualli, who "served two masters" by paying tribute to "both the Spanish Crown and Indigenous nobles" (McDonough 2016, 12). The addition of the monetary tribute in Mexico-Tenochtitlan thus took commoners to the edge of what they could pay, provoking open protest in the Juan Bautista annals.

I observe that these scenes of unrest affirm Indigenous scribal agency in recording futurities amid uncertainty. They took it upon themselves to announce the passing of the authority of the Native governor Luis Santa María Cipac. By signaling the decline of Cipac's influence, the scribes also represent narrative focal points involving multiple speakers. In addition to Tecniuh and Huixtopolcatl, Don Martín Ezmallin, another great-grandson of Ahuitzotl, spoke that day. The scribes recall his words, directed at Cipac, after the riot died down: "tihuehue in tixtlamati cenca oticahuilquixti yn altepetl ynic otiquixnamic yx yxco ypac otehuac auh cuix çan aca nican oquitlalli ca ohualla Castillan" (*ADJB*, f. 35v–36r) (You, elder, you who understand things, you have harmed the altepetl by confronting it and rising up. Did anyone here order this? It came from Castile). Ezmallin respected the experience of the Mexica leader above that of the Spanish, since the tlatoani should know better than to place onerous tribute requirements on an altepetl accustomed to receiving and managing tribute. At the same time, Ezmallin recognized the new reality. Counseling expedience, he recommended that the Mexica direct their strength to collecting the 14,000 pesos the Spanish required, for the sake of survival (C. Townsend 2019, 175). The scribes used writing to support the aim of reestablishing Mexica authority in their capital. Documenting the words of Tecniuh, Huixtopolcatl, and Ezmallin, the scribes summarized the anti-tribute actions the Mexica nobility had taken up to that point. They decried the governor's ineffective leadership, while also showing they possessed the words to bring order through the voices they recalled from their altepetl.

I note as well that by recording the tribute riot, the scribes also performed reconnaissance. They learned that the Spanish authorities increasingly did not recognize categories and procedures from the Mexica legal system. Huixtopolcatl's shouting acknowledges that those who had previously administered justice—tlilancalqui, quauhnochtli, ezhuahuacatl—would no longer do so. The scribes and the Mexica nobles now faced the reality that they had reached a point of no return in their diminishing influence. However, I submit that this information would make possible more effective future approaches to negotiating with the Spanish. By including the protest of Tecniuh and the arrests of ten other Nahua nobles in this account, they simultaneously documented their leaders' opposition to tribute and their disapproval of Cipac. They modeled a futurity of group cohesion in the face of uncertainty. Taking for granted their right to speak against tribute, Mexica nobles and commoners found their home city increasingly hostile. Tenochca laws lost their force as the Hispanicized Cuidad de México overshadowed the altepetl of Mexico-Tenochtitlan in a specter of impending cultural erasure (Mundy 2015, 2). Nonetheless, over time, that erasure would prove superficial and incomplete. Mexico City would not displace the altepetl without a struggle.

Amid the Mexica leadership crisis, the scribes of the *Anales de Juan Bautista* recognized there was no going back. Answers to the people's questions and theirs would have to come from days ahead. Cipac's decline in health started when he fell from his roof, an incident that references accounts of the death of Moteuczoma Xocoyotl.[29] Political life had degenerated to an intolerable point, and there was no clear successor to the tlatoani Cipac.[30] The annals record Cipac's last months. In April

1565, under prolonged duress, Cipac hallucinated and climbed on the roof of his palace one night. There he had a sword fight with an invisible enemy, which concluded with his fall from that height, which caused serious injuries (*ADJB*, f. 57v). Next, according to the pictorial *Codex Osuna*, the Spanish official Ceynos put Cipac in prison until he paid a debt of 170 pesos (Chávez Orozco 1947, 77–78). Although he paid, the imprisonment and his compounded trauma depleted him, and he died at the end of December that year (C. Townsend 2019, 178). Even in the face of the demise of Governor Cipac, the scribes of Moyotlan expected the cosmos to find its equilibrium. In the following section, I consider how the scribes engaged Mexica anxieties, offering optimism regarding future governance.[31]

RETURN: PORTENTS OF MOTEUCZOMA

Earlier in 1565, while the government slipped through Cipac's fingers, a series of extraordinary events and appearances of deities pointed to the return of Moteuczoma Ilhuicamina. Here I examine the confluence of cosmic energy the scribes of Moyotlan represent, which recalls the alliance of Quauhquechollan with the Spanish, discussed in chapter 1. As explained there, a wrapped image of deities, warriors, and animated zoomorphic beings functioned as a teixiptla that later unfurled to release its intense energy during the Guatemala campaign. Here, I explain how the scribes of Moyotlan built a similar teixiptla with the written word. In the remaining analysis section in this chapter, I explain how the scribes interpreted extraordinary cosmic events as foreshadowing the return of emperor Moteuczoma Ilhuicamina.

What can a scribal record of omens accomplish? It gives future Mexica and future Nahuas more broadly a precedent for interpreting Spanish rule and other colonial regimes as temporary. Whereas elsewhere in the annals, discourses of futurity come from the mouths of humans, these omens took cosmic dimensions in their strength. The sun, wind, colors, deities, and dynamic sounds came together in an indication of forces stronger than the colonizers. Harjo (2019, 194) includes in her articulation of Indigenous futurity *speculation* and *imagined possibilities*. She explains that by building a "spiral of futurity," that is, an intergenerational account, "these elements operate in the present moment in ways that enact our relatives' unactivated [sic] possibilities, allow us to speculate on future temporalities, and place in motion actions that will bring these imagined possibilities to fruition." Interactions between the ancestors and the living inform the Moteuczoma omens, which together form a similar intergenerational link between the living and previous Indigenous rulers. By imagining a different future, the Mexica could find ways to live with objectives that engaged the potential they already saw in the cosmos around them.

The scribes' narrations of the reemergence of the deceased ruler constitute their response to the problem of Luis Santa María Cipac's death. Bearing in mind the intertwining of politics with their interpretation of extraordinary events, it is worth noting that local cosmologies could become malleable to reflect social realities. Ana Díaz (2020b) has described how the sky served as a medium of representation, changeable based on the social relationships within an altepetl or its relationships with other-than-human beings. Instead of an established, universal, and unalterable cosmography, Nahuas have often constructed representations of interconnected realms using their own communities as models for the sky, the underworld, and the earth, as Timothy Knab (1991) has demonstrated regarding the town San Miguel Tzinacapan. Díaz (2020b) has also explained that regional discourses could project different times into the firmament as well, including important bygone epochs or different moments of their history. The demise of Cipac for the Mexica ruling houses represented an unexpected political shift, which traditionally implied a cosmic shift of destiny. The micropatriotism of the scribes of Moyotlan thus could extend even to the sky over their city.

Loyal to the calpolli (sub-altepetl) of San Juan Moyotlan, the scribes gave an account of the coming return of Moteuczoma Ilhuicamina to restore balance. As Susan Gillespie has shown in *The Aztec Kings* (1989), according to Mexica genealogical documents, times of crisis in their history called forth the return of a Moteuczoma ruler.[32] In the chaotic milieu the *Anales de Juan Bautista* describes, Motuezcoma's return would supersede the authority of Cipac and provide a basis for restoring the disenfranchised Mexica nobility (Ruiz Medrano 2010, 45, 71). The scribes drew on the presence of the ancestors to bring "power, economic clout, dignity, and social identity to descendants" (McAnany [1995] 2014, 168).

Since at the time of the initial invasion Moteuczoma II (Xocoyotl) had failed to stave off the Spanish, as had the late Governor Cipac, the return to order would have to come from a deeper past—that of the prior Moteuczoma, who ruled during times of the Mexicas' ascent and expansion. The scribes recount that on Monday, May 14, 1565,

> yquac ylhuicatitech hualmonexti yuauhcoçamalotl quiyahuallotimoma in tonatiuh yhua ce quixnamic auh in tonatiuh ça tlacaltechpan yetiuh onpa yquiçayanpa yetihuitz auh yn tiquittaqueue aço ye chiuhcnahui hora auh mochitlacatl quittac yn titehuan yhuan españolesme auh yn mocahuato ye nepantla tonatiuh valmocruztecac yn tlanepantla. . . . Auh no yquac hecamalacotl moquetz ynicpac tlaltepehualli yn iglesia mayor caltitlan yuhqui xixitomoni yhuan yuhqui matlequiquiztli ye huehuetzi ynic conittaqueue tlaca yuhqui cacamachallohua tlalli auh yn iquac ye hualtemo hecamalacotl niman quitoque in castilteca ca ye quiça yn Motecuhçoma. (*ADJB*, f. 56v)

> [in the sky there appeared a misty rainbow, which surrounded the sun as it rose; and another rose opposite the sun during the morning. We saw this after nine o'clock. Everyone saw it: we and the Spanish. By midday they came together in the middle [of the sky], the sun, in the shape of a cross in the middle. . . . A whirlwind rose from the mound of dirt next to the main church. There was a flash of lightning and a sound like great gunfire. The people saw the jaws of the earth opening. As the wind died down, the Castilians were saying that Moteuczoma was emerging.]

Nahua tools of persuasion appear as repetition, reciprocity, and the gathering of strength. A double rainbow forms above the city, its two parts rising from the east and the west.[33] As Diana Magaloni Kerpel (2011, 75–76) has observed, rainbows often denote pivotal moments in cosmological time. She has argued that paintings of rainbows in Books 7 and 12 of the *Florentine Codex* link the passing of one age to the beginning of another, a temporal scheme that Nahuas retroactively applied to interpret the Spanish invasion (see figure 22). At first glance, the images evoke a resurrection narrative, perhaps drawing on Franciscan influences (Arias 2006, 45). However, that interpretation of the crossed rainbows does not exhaust the meaning of the scene. The text reads "ye nepantla tonatiuh

FIGURE 22 Rainbows depicted in the *Florentine Codex*, Bk. 7, f. 238v and 404r. Library of Congress, World Digital Library, accessed April 14, 2024.

valmocruztecac yn tlaltepantla" (*ADJB*, f. 56v) (they came together in [the sky], the sun, in the shape of a cross in the middle). Among the many meanings of nepantla, I call to mind the adverb form *nepanotl*, which denotes reciprocity (Maffie 2014, 362). Molina's ([1571] 2008, 2:69r) definition indicates mutual, reciprocal action, "unos a otros, o unos con otros, o los unos a los otros", which Karttunen (1992, 169) has synthesized as "mutuality, reciprocity."[34] Maffie (2014, 362–63) compares the Nahua view of nepantla processes with Victor Turner's well-known concept of liminality. Turner (1979, 237) writes that "this coincidence of opposite processes in a single representation characterizes the peculiar unity of the liminal: that which is neither this nor that, and yet is both." The intersecting rainbows thus also draw on Nahua concepts of symmetry and present the regions of sunrise and sunset in a middling phenomenon, just when the sun is at its highest.

I also note a narrative turning point that occurs at the apex of this middling manifestation of cosmic power, making visible spatial and temporal transitions. The wind whirls on a mound of earth, lightning flashes, accompanied by a loud explosion. For many Nahuas, in addition to sunlight, lightning is often associated with new beginnings. According to one Nahua elder in Veracruz, when lightning strikes Mount Popocatepetl, new deities are born (Sandstrom 1991, 368).[35] I note that these elements lie beyond the control of the Spanish. The earth opens, which recalls how it devours the dead (Brady and Prufer [2005] 2013). At the same time, the opening earth recalls the importance of caves in Mesoamerican origin stories: people often emerge from the ground at the beginning of their histories (Brady and Prufer [2005] 2013).[36] When the elements of the double rainbow scene reach a crescendo of intense light, sound, and symmetry, the text introduces the idea of Moteuczoma's return. News of this event comes not through a third-person narrative focalization but from the Spanish. After all, it was the Castilians who suggested that the emperor was returning: "quitoque in castilteca ca ya quiça y Motecuhçcoma" (*ADJB*, f. 56v) (the Castilians were saying that Moteuczoma was emerging). I submit that the scribes strategically intertwined cosmological elements—sun, rainbows, wind, earth, lightning—along with intensity of light and the sudden explosion, combining them with the more obvious resurrection trope. These depictions show Moteuczoma's reemergence as a cosmic event beyond the grasp of Spanish colonial administrators. Nahua tools of persuasion make the scene into ritual space, which enabled the scribes to narrate a futurity of political autonomy despite the harm the Spanish had inflicted.

This passage, as part of envisioning future political strength, employs cyclical motions to recapitulate Mexica history. Gabriel Kenrick Kruell (2016, 15–16) has noted the connection between solar movement and the Moteuczoma dynasty in the *Crónica mexicayotl* and Diego Durán's accounts:

> El periodo de los reinados de los *tlatoque de Tenochtitlan*, desde el principio con *Itzcoatl* hasta el final con *Moteuczoma Xocoyotl*, se puede asimilar a la curva del sol en el cielo, cuya culminación sería el reinado de *Huehue Moteuczoma*. Los reinos de los gobernantes que siguieron al primer *Moteuczoma*, es decir *Axayacatl, Tizoc, Ahuitzotl* y *Moteuczoma Xocoyotl*, representarían el momento de la decadencia del imperio Mexica, correspondiendo al declive del sol hasta su puesta en el occidente, constituida por la conquista hispana.
>
> [The period of the reigns of the *tlatoque* of Tenochtitlan, from the beginning with *Itzcoatl* until the end with *Moteuczoma Xocoyotl*, can be traced as the arc the sun makes in the sky, the highest point of which would be

the rule of *Huehue Moteuczoma*. The reigns of the kings that followed the first *Moteuczoma*, that is *Axayacatl, Tizoc, Ahuitzotl*, and *Moteuczoma Xocoyotl*, would represent a time of decline of the Mexica empire, as Spain's conquest constituted [as it were] a sinking sun in the west.]

The association of Huehue Moteuczoma Ilhuicamina with midday synchronizes with the solar movement just when the Spanish said that the tlatoani was emerging. The first Moteuczoma embodied the full strength of the dynasty before its descent toward the Spanish invasion. The return of the strongest tlatoani also links with the Mexica's tutelary deity, Huitzilopochtli. According to Guilhem Olivier and Roberto Martínez (2015, 364), "the huey tlatoani (emperor) personified Huitzilopochtli—a deity quite close to Tezcatlipoca—when he assumed royal office. As the patron of the nation, the ruler served as Huitzilopochtli's representative before the people; therefore, the king or tlatoani became the 'likeness of our god Huitzilopochtli.'" It is difficult for me to ignore the scribes' placement of the sun: its midday discharge of energy occurred over the location where Huitzilopochtli's temple stood (Matos Moctezuma 1986, 365–70). The site stands for the entire city as well, since the intersecting rainbows directly above reflect Tenochtitlan's four-calpolli division into Teopan, Cueopan, Moyotlan, and Atzacalco. The combination of the rainbows and the noonday sun thus mark the shift of power away from Luis Santa María Cipac and toward an eventual return to Mexica autonomy. Consequently, the annals suggest that Spanish rule would not be permanent.

After describing the apex of the Mexica tlatoque in the sky, the scribes continued by incorporating Ehecatl, an avatar of Quetzalcoatl (Aguilar-Moreno 2007, 148; Witschey and Brown 2012, 260). The whirlwind recalls spiraling malinalli motions associated with sweeping away tlazolli (ritual impurity) to make way for order and harmony (L. Burkhart 1989, 118). The whirlwind spun "ynicpac tlaltepehualli yn iglesia mayor caltitlan" (*ADJB*, f. 56v) (on top of the mound of earth at the foot of the main church), and the deity Ehecatl appeared:

> Auh ynic mocuep onpa ytztia tlatatacco yhuan çan no onpa polihuito yn icpac tlaltepehualli yn ehecatl yhua ynic quittaque yuhqui yn itlahitic ycatia hehecatl. Auh yn iquac yauhcoçamalotl monexti ylhuicatitech quitoque

yn espanolesme aço ye tlamiz in cemanauac auh cequintin quitoque aço timayanzque anoço yaoyotl topan mochivaz anoço cana ye neci yancuic tlalli, etc. (*ADJB*, f. 56v–57r)

[Coming back, [the whirlwind] came to the place where the hole was made in the ground, and there the wind dissipated over the mound of dirt. They saw that inside of the hole, there stood Ehecatl. When the misty rainbow appeared in the sky, the Spanish said that perhaps the world was coming to an end. Others said that perhaps a famine was coming, or war was upon us, or that somewhere new earth was appearing, etc.]

The strength of the wind materializes as the wind deity. Ehecatl plays a transformative role, clearing away chaos and moving the city toward order. Ehecatl is associated with the movement of air and the generation of life (López Austin 1993, 126). Book 4 of the *Florentine Codex* identifies his ritual pair Quetzalcoatl with the wind itself and the day sign *ce ehecatl* (1 Wind) (*FC*, Bk. 4, f. 260v; Bassett 2015, 121). But what is the function of the church? Primarily, the text refers to it as a landmark, yet in so doing, it also evokes previous times. Twenty-first-century excavations have found the Ehecatl temple next to the Metropolitan Cathedral, confirming the site the passage describes (Matos Moctezuma and Barrera Rodríguez 2011). To my mind, the appearance of Ehecatl as part of the scribes' recollection and interpretation of events proposes that the wind had swept the city clean for a future of renewed order.

Parallelisms also function as persuasive tools in this section. The scribes continue to place predictions regarding times to come in Spanish voices. However, the possible scenario these voices give here parallels one of Juan Teton's warnings from earlier in the manuscript, which I find particularly striking: "quitoque yn espanolesme aço ye tlamiz in cemanahuac" (*ADJB*, f. 57r) (the Spanish said that perhaps the world was coming to an end). The text, however, leaves the question of the end of time open, as it enumerates further scenarios. I also find it striking that the scribes turn now to "others" (cequintin), who anticipate famine or war: "cequintin quitoque aço timayazque anoço yaoyotl topan mochivaz" (*ADJB*, f. 57r) (others said that perhaps a famine was coming, or war was upon us). These warnings repeat those of Teton in the same order in which he presented them earlier (*ADJB*, f. 8r–8v). Are these repetitions of discourses from the Teton uprising part of a persuasive discourse of the scribes? While correlation alone does not show causation, the reality remains that between both scenarios the "others" offer, the altepetl has a longer horizon of action in the advice of Teton. It was possible to confront famine and war. On the other hand, only the Spanish and not the Nahuas imagined an impending end of the world. These implicit comparisons present the scribes and the Mexica as strong, resilient, and in search of an inhabitable future despite setbacks.

• • • •

In this chapter, I have shown that Nahua futurities recorded in the *Anales de Juan Bautista* responded to the economic, political, and ritual crises the Mexica faced in mid-sixteenth-century Mexico-Tenochtitlan. It is crucial to bear in mind that Nahuas did not divide their experience into the categories just mentioned. They considered all living experience as part of their participation in the unfolding of reality. When Native leadership and clerical alliances failed to improve conditions and the disarrayed Nahua leaders did not articulate viable paths forward, the scribes of Moyotlan used writing to process the chaos, record the events of their moment, and describe various future paths before them. They determined to represent habitable futures for their readers and listeners. Similarly to what I have shown in chapter 1, those who produced the text built teixiptlahuan with their writing to marshal strength for the events and challenges they anticipated. The scribes of Moyotlan constructed the presence of deities, ancestors, and omens through their writing.

Juan Teton explained how to avoid the disasters that embracing a foreign diet and religion had brought. With the persuasive tools available, Teton encouraged his audience to gather strength by avoiding foreign meats and collecting regional plants. He used repetition to stress the danger of zoomorphic transformation. By linking the people's transformation into animals and earlier discourses regarding the tzitzimime, Teton explained the demographic decline and the growing presence of European cattle among the Nahuas. He also repeated warnings of famine and gave lists of foods to gather. He recommended appeasing the earth deity Tlantepoxillama in order to build a community ready to survive in the impending darkness ahead. Gaining time meant helping the present generation survive as long as possible in order to keep the possibility of future generations open. Juan Teton's description of the imminent arrival of the tzitzimime recalls that not all deities were benevolent. The scribes thus gave Teton an ambivalent voice. He forecasted a grim future but provided pragmatic advice on survival.

The tribute protest of Miguel Tecniuh confronted corruption in the Spanish authorities' rescinding of earlier tribute exemptions in the capital and denounced Cipac's complicity with the Spanish administrators' plans. Although the scribes placed the speech that sparked the riot in the mouth of Tecniuh, the generalizability of its content makes me suspect a consensus among the scribes and Mexica nobles on the points he outlined. While there are no attestations of the verb *chicahua* in the passage examined, those who confronted Cipac clearly valued strength and integrity in their leaders. The comparisons Tecniuh makes between a governor with integrity and the instability of Cipac, along with the resulting actions of the nobles and commoners who gather to protest, effectively turn the tables, showing their strength vis-à-vis Governor Cipac. A lack of reciprocity between the nobles and between the nobles and the macehualli commoners' cries for redress from Tecniuh's central concerns. The scribes, by representing multiple speakers—Tecniuh, Huixtopolcatl, and Ezmallin—provide a heteroglossic description of the event. Questions-as-persuasion become vitriol and the resulting unrest led the Mexica to the limits of what they were able to accomplish as government functionaries and residents of Mexico-Tenochtitlan under the Spanish.

Nonetheless, the failed tribute negotiations and unsuccessful riot do not preclude their usefulness as reconnaissance. By recording a vivid, detailed version of the tribute riot with dialogues that disclosed interlocutors' attitudes toward the future, the annals provided an example of an ineffective, direct confrontation as a scenario to avoid. The scribes recorded the nobles' disapproval of Luis Santa María Cipac's tribute negotiations with the Spanish. As the riot in Cipac's patio demonstrated, dissatisfied nobles and commoners could not expect justice through open protest of tribute policy.

In the face of failed tribute-reduction efforts and the death of Governor Cipac, the scribes coordinated their efforts to read the movements of cosmic energy (teotl) manifested in solar and meteorological events that heralded a change in authority. That which is marvelous takes over the city in the scribes' recounting of events to remind audiences that the

Spanish as mortals also experience awe at these intense displays of energy in motion. The portents do not bring about the desired future of political autonomy, but they do instantiate the imagination, planning, and speculation necessary for working toward those ends. The representation of the return of Moteuczoma shows that the Native writing subjects interpreted the cosmos in ways counter to Spanish designs, forecasting the ultimate demise of colonial rule. By describing extraordinary events over the city, the scribes evoked the presence of Huitzilopochtli, Quetzalcoatl, and Ehecatl and the reemergence of Moteuczoma Ilhuicamina, in addition to images of resurrection. If we recall Katarzyna Mikulska's (2022) concept of the deity mosaic, the *Anales de Juan Bautista* combine the cross with depictions of ancestral deities to build a collective presence powerful enough to thwart Spanish intentions. Reciprocity spans generations and time. Imagining Indigenous autonomy, even if the observers did not witness it, made its possibility real.

The scribes of Moyotlan wrote futurities that maintained group solidarity. They warned of scenarios to avoid, provided intelligence and strategy based on collective experience, and envisioned a future of growing possibility. Through these futurities, they increasingly gave voice to the concerns of common people as crucial to viable paths ahead for the Mexica leadership. As I will show in chapter 4, similar strategies helped Nahua intellectuals of Tenochtitlan and Amecameca articulate a possible future for education in the aftermath of the Spanish destruction of traditional houses of learning. Despite institutional changes, Nahua voices continued to tell of the ancestors and build spaces of gathering and self-governance. The future, as a discursive field, would allow Nahua nobles and scholars to build reciprocity with each other and with coming generations.

CHAPTER 4

Didactic Horizons in the *Crónica mexicayotl*

Ayc polihuiz ayc ylcahuiz. yn oquichihuaco yn oquitlallico yn intlillo yn intlapallo yn intenyo yn imitolloca yn imilnamicoca. (*Codex Chimalpahin* [*CC*], f. 18v)

[And what they came to do, what they came to establish, their writings, their renown, their history, their memory will never perish, will never be forgotten in times to come.] (Chimalpahin 1997, 1:61)

At the turn of the sixteenth century, the last Mexica elders in the city of Mexico-Tenochtitlan whose parents had told them about life before the Spanish were passing on. These voices became precious for Nahua writers in the capital who continued to generate futurities within their spaces of concern. As those spaces changed, so did their way-finding approaches. In this chapter, I focus on a Nahua educational project that gathered path-seeking efforts of multiple communities, who all faced the threat of the loss of their knowledge by cultural erasure, marginalization from politics and economics, and the ravages of old age. The text I examine, the *Crónica mexicayotl* (1609), represents a collaboration between two Nahuas: Domingo Chimalpahin and Fernando Alvarado Tezozomoc. Chimalpahin and Tezozomoc came from different altepeme. Chimalpahin, the son of a respected, albeit lower-level noble in Amecameca, went to the capital at age fourteen and began working in the church of San Antonio de Abad, where he likely became the fiscal, the property's caretaker (Schroeder 2017, 235). Tezozomoc, a Mexica noble descended from Moteuczoma Ilhuicamina, lived in an enclave of Mexica leaders whose wealth and privilege were declining under the Spanish (Romero Galván 2003, 89).

Both men were interested in preserving the knowledge(s) they inherited from their predecessors. In Chimalpahin's case, that concern motivated him to write a series of annals on Nahua history in the Valley of Mexico.[1] The passage quoted at the beginning of this chapter contains words attributable to Fernando Alvarado Tezozomoc within Chimalpahin's historiographic writing, as I detail later in this chapter. Elsewhere in the vast 1,500 folios of Chimalpahin's lifelong production, he expresses a similar concern that future generations should know of the deeds of his ancestors: "It will never be forgotten. It will always be preserved. We will preserve it, we who are the younger brothers, the children, grandchildren, great-grandchildren, and great-great-grandchildren, we who are the [family extensions]—the hair, eyebrows, nails—the color and the blood, we who are the descendants . . . we who have been born and lived where lived and governed all the precious ancient Chichimeca kings" (Chimalpahin 1998, 2:273). Thus, Chimalpahin, Tezozomoc, and other identified and anonymous contributors brought together information both to enhance their understanding of the past and to keep that knowledge alive for posterity.[2]

Susan Schroeder has examined the oldest copy of the document, which forms part of a larger body of work of Chimalpahin's (*CC*, vols. 1 and 2), and historical writings by Fernando Alva Ixtlilxochitl of Texcoco (see figure 23).[3] Wayne Ruwet discovered these three volumes at Cambridge University in 1983 (*CC*, 1:17–24). Prior to Schroeder's (2011) work, due to earlier misattributions, many scholars held the view that Tezozomoc authored the *Crónica mexicayotl* and expected to eventually find a lost original copy written in his hand.[4] Based on Chimalpahin's distinctive handwriting and characteristic spellings, Schroeder (2007, 2, 7–8; 2011) concluded that he wrote the manuscript, although he did consult Tezozomoc. Chimalpahin compiled data from Chalcan and Mexica sources, including Tezozomoc's introductory material (Schroeder, 2011, 237). At most, Tezozomoc is responsible for the first nineteen folios, seventeen in

Didactic Horizons • 151

FIGURE 23 Opening section known as the *Crónica mexicayotl* in the *Codex Chimalpahin*. INAH, Códices de México.

Spanish and two in Nahuatl: the two folios reiterate in Nahuatl a "Spanish description of the majesty of Mexico-Tenochtitlan that begins the account" and tell "Tezozomoc's purpose, methodology, and attestation as to the authenticity of his information" (Schroeder 2011, 235).[5]

Camilla Townsend describes a highly plausible scenario in which, with his project underway, Chimalpahin paid a visit to Tezozomoc, who was at least seventy at the time in 1609.[6] Since Tezozomoc's voice refers to "vouching for the authenticity of statements," she proposes that "it is very possible that he was reading pictographic statements or reciting aloud to Chimalpahin" (C. Townsend 2019, 197, 283n69). I find Townsend's view compelling of Tezozomoc as a contributor who dictated to Chimalpahin, especially since the content of the first seventeen folios is a genealogy and record of Tenochtitlan's rulers. To realize such a complex project, Tezozomoc and Chimalpahin would have met face-to-face, "especially in an age when *all* important transactions were handled in person" (C. Townsend 2019, 197).[7]

Schroeder (2017) has also described Chimalpahin's historiography as a pan-Nahua project, since he balanced his loyalty to Amecameca with a broader concern for preserving the Nahua history of the Valley of Mexico. Schroeder (2017, 226) observes that Chimalpahin went "beyond his personal patriotism, and undertook an even grander project, a sweeping history of Mexico-Tenochtitlan from its earliest years to the time he was writing, the 1620s." These insights on the text's origins represent advances in the study of the *Crónica mexicayotl*.

Understanding that Chimalpahin deserves credit for the inception and realization of the *Crónica mexicayotl* opens the path to its further analysis as a didactic text. The questions I examine in this chapter concern the shared material of Chimalpahin and Tezozomoc, who begin by informing future generations regarding the Mexica past. In light of the existing texts from which they drew, how did the collaboration between Chimalpahin and Tezozomoc bring to fruition the futurities of ancestors? The *Crónica mexicayotl* outlines the deeds of Mexica rulers and their migration from Aztlan to Tenochtitlan, while also highlighting interventions of Huitzilopochtli, their tutelary deity. How did the text make lessons of the past from Huitzilopochtli relevant to the Nahuas' postinvasion world? On the other hand, can the presentation of these narratives in the form of an alphabetic chronicle in their language offer a stable mode to pass on knowledge as Nahua institutions had formerly done? That is, did the *Crónica* offer a solution to the displacement of houses of learning, chiefly the calmecac, for the education of the tlatoque? While beyond the first nineteen folios, separating the two men's material may prove ultimately impossible, to what extent did micropatriotic viewpoints help or hinder the text's didactic aim?

In this chapter, I argue that the *Crónica mexicayotl* serves as a medium for educating the young, both in ways its makers stated and in ways that expand upon its meaning through a network of ancestors and their connections to coming generations. Since the Mexica inhabited the same space as their ancestors, Tezozomoc's audience formed a "physical network of related individuals" (Cosentino 2002, 120).[8] According to Laura Harjo (2021, 616), communities can enhance their collective outlook by "speculating on a future that their ancestors desired." In this way, Indigenous peoples can participate in dynamic relationships with their forebearers while finding their way forward today. Retelling Mexica history also recentered that narrative on their land as "mexicayotl," the "property of the Mexica," one of the names of the island of Tenochtitlan (Olko 2012, 168). I observe how material Schroeder considers attributable to Tezozomoc in the opening of the *Crónica mexicayotl* addresses future generations directly:

> O ca ye ixquich ynic tamechonpehualtilia yn ticneltilia yn ticchicuaha huehuetlahtolli. huel xiccaquican xicanacan yn antepilhuan yn anteyxhuihuan yn anMexica yn antenochca. yhuan y mochintin yn çaço ac yehuantin yn amotech quiçatihui in yollizque in nemitihui in amotlacamecayohua yezque. (*CC*, f. 19v)

> [Take note of all that we arouse you with as we authenticate and affirm the ancient one's accounts. Listen well; accept them, you children and grandchildren, you Mexica and Tenochca, and all whosoever will issue from you, who will exist, who will be of your lineage.] (Chimalpahin 1997, 65)

Serving as a bridge between ancestors and those who will live after them, the *Crónica mexicayotl* opens with a call for future Mexica readers to keep their ways. This tenacity recalls Michael Chandler's (2013, 86) concept of "persistent indigeneity," which encourages Natives to self-conceptualize as Indigenous so as to pass identity and lifeways to future generations.

The Nahua tools of persuasion guide my analysis. The *Crónica mexicayotl* gathers strength as an example for the young regarding the Mexica's intergenerational migration, culminating with the founding of their capital, Tenochtitlan. For Nahuas, the goal of education is to aid the development of individuals by imparting beneficial knowledge, words, and actions. The expressions *tlacahuapahualiztli*, "the art of strengthening or bringing up men," and *neixtlamachiliztli*, "the act of giving wisdom to the face," demonstrate the Nahua view that human development remains incomplete without study (Maffie 2014).[9] Right knowledge gives strength, while ignorance increases vulnerability. Instilling moral strength through education was also vital for Mexica to fulfill "obligations to family members and creator beings" (Maffie 2019, 12). The text also reinforced preconquest examples of strong rulers (Mexi, Moteuczoma Ilhuicamina, and Axayacatl) and priests (Huitzilopochtli and Tlacaelel) from the historical narrative sections of the *Crónica* and made them relevant to readers in the postconquest world.

Reciprocity as a tool of persuasion occurs on multiple levels. I recall that Chimalpahin and Tezozomoc's shared didactic project draws on their mutual efforts to encourage way-finding through references to and examples from the Mexica past. The text also portrays reciprocity between deities and humans, particularly between Huitzilopochtli and the Mexica. I find it telling that the text relies heavily on ways in which Huitzilopochtli embodies a particular kind of teixiptla, a tlaquimilolli (deity bundle). I speculate for the first time here that the *Crónica mexicayotl* itself mirrors the function of a tlaquimilloli. By wrapping the narrative in an amoxtli historiographic project between altepeme, Tezozomoc protected information from his ancestors for posterity. Repetition of key content underscores its importance, including Tezozomoc's future-tense verbs in the first nineteen folios regarding his plans to teach Mexica history to future generations so that they might pass on that same learning. Material also repeats between the first nineteen folios in Spanish and the Nahuatl of the remaining forty-four folios: the Mexica origins at Chicomoztoc; the pairing of the eagle and cactus with Tenochtitlan; and a genealogy of the Mexica tlatoque, which appears in a concise manner in the Spanish section and with greater detail in the Nahuatl main text. Thus, the *Crónica mexicayotl* brought together techniques of persuasion present in the other texts I have examined in this study for the purpose of encouraging future generations to learn about the Mexica past.

Before I proceed, a number of considerations deserve attention. I do not argue that the chronicle represents a transition to Christianity, based on the convictions of Tezozomoc and Chimalpahin.[10] Elsewhere, I have argued that the text follows a pantheistic view of its deities and the unseen world (Stear 2017). I also eschew the interpretation of the eagle atop the cactus as proto-Mexican patriotism, an anachronistic interpretation with Greco-Roman roots that the Jesuit Francisco Clavijero made iconic, as I discuss later in this chapter. I also clarify that the *Crónica mexicayotl* stood apart from didactic texts Tlatelolco produced with Franciscan supervision and from writings associated with the Real y Pontificia Universidad de México that described the capital of New Spain to readers in the Iberian Peninsula.[11] While scenes in the *Crónica mexicayotl* strike the Western imagination in such familiar ways, I am more interested in the didactic project that Tezozomoc and Chimalpahin have described from their distinct yet interlocking views on the need to instruct the young in Mexica history.

Tezozomoc and Chimalpahin's similar roles in their communities also inform my close readings. Schroeder (2011, 236) explains that Tezozomoc likely inherited the office of tlacuilo from his ancestors:

> Alvarado Tezozomoc tells us as much in his own words: "These accounts of the ancient ones, this book of their accounts in Mexico, we have inherited [... and] are in our keeping." He goes on to describe how he compared and matched the histories and verified them by listening to all that was told him by his father, his uncle, and other elders (CC 1:63, 65). "Such do all the ancient Mexica authors and truthful histories affirm and attest," he added.

The tlacuilo painted pictorials and murals, representing content from the mouth of the tlamatinime for the benefit of rulers and wider society. Ancestral Nahua royal courts further had the position of tlatocapilli dedicated to knowledge transmission via pictorial texts. Tezozomoc possessed multiple pictorials and genealogies at the time of his work with Chimalpahin, and which he references in his preliminary material in the *Crónica*, facts that identify him as a tlatocapilli (Schroeder 2007, 10). In the case of Chimalpahin, many of his ancestors were tlatocapilli, although his father did not inherit the amoxtli of his town of Tzaqualtitlan Tenanco in Amecameca. Eventually gaining access, Chimalpahin used his ancestors' pictorials to write a history of his home altepetl (Schroeder 2007, 9–10). In my view, the eventual acquisition of his altepetl documents represents a key moment in Chimalpahin's study. The impetus to learn the past of his home altepetl parallels his desire to write a history of the Mexica.

ANALYTICAL PRECEDENTS

In addition to Schroeder's 2011 study of the text, José Rubén Romero Galván (2003, 6) has analyzed the *Crónica* as a document of decline, paralleling the gradual rescinding of privileges and status that the Spanish gave the Moteuczoma house after Cuauhtemoc's surrender. Over the course of the sixteenth century, the Spanish gradually took from the Mexica nobles their initial *privilegios de honra*: "the right to carry arms, to wear Spanish clothes, to ride horses, and to use the formal designation of *don*" (Martínez 2008, 107–8). I note the decline likely motivated Tezozomoc to place his message in Chimalpahin's chronicle since he saw firsthand that fall from fortune. In this political environment of erosion of the Mexica hierarchy, it was not the first time Tezozomoc used writing to defend his family.

Tezozomoc was among the second generation of his family adept at the use of the Roman alphabet to write in Spanish and Nahuatl, since his father, Huanitzin, knew Pedro de Gante and had attended the Escuela de San José de los naturales.[12] After his father's death in 1541, Tezozomoc held an important role in the city: he was "Moctezuma's grandson through his mother and his grandnephew through his father" (C. Townsend 2019, 193). The *Crónica mexicayotl* represents the second effort of Fernando Alvarado Tezozomoc to retell his people's history, which he had done previously in Spanish in his *Crónica mexicana* (1598).[13] During his public career, he had also mounted a legal defense for their lands outside Mexico-Tenochtitlan. The *Tlalamatl huauhquilpan* shows how he used his position as a nahuatlato in the Audiencia Real and his skill as a scribe to advocate in favor of land tenure rights for the Moteuczoma family (R. Cortés 2011, 25) (see figure 24).[14] His use of historical documents that he owned to defend the rights of his household show his skill and care in compiling evidence for a legal cause (R. Cortés 2011, 27). As a keeper of documents and as a writer, Tezozomoc fulfilled functions that the tlacuiloque and the calmecac had previously.

I now turn to the *Crónica mexicayotl* and examine its educational content. Tezozomoc emphasized the unity among the ancestors who left them documents: by implication, he called for unity in the face of future uncertainty. Next, the main text of Chimalpahin begins. I focus on the Mexicas' origin at the caves of Chicomoztoc in Aztlan and their journey to Tenochtitlan. Along the way, extraordinary events indicate to me the moments Mexica ancestors designated as pivotal for the realization of their imagined future of finding a permanent location for their altepetl. After examining the foundation of Tenochtitlan, I consider a crucial event from the early years there: the conception of Moteuczoma

FIGURE 24 A Hispanicized portrait of Fernando Alvarado Tezozomoc in the *Tlalamatl Huauhquilpan*. Courtesy of INAH.

Ilhuicamina. In the sections I examine, I will discuss ways that the Mexica have used space and intergenerational ties to kin to build a narrative path from their origins toward a strong and united future within this collaborative historiographical project.

TLATELOLCO: RIVALRY AND REMEMBRANCE

Tezozomoc positions himself as within Mexica nobility and in distinction to Tlatelolco.

> Auh yn tlatilolco ayc ompa ticuililozque ca nel amo ynpiel mochiuhtiuh auh ynin huehuenenonotzaliztlahtolli ynin huehuenenonnotzalizamoxtlacuilolli mexico yn oticahuililotiaque yn huel topial ynin tlahtolli ynic no tehuantin oc ceppa yn topilhuan yn toxhuihuan yn teçohuan yn totlapallohua yn totechcopa quiçazque ynic mochipa no yehuatin quipiezque. Tiquincahuilitiazque yn iquac titomiquilizque. (*CC*, f. 18v)

[And as for Tlatelolco: never will [these accounts] be taken from us, for truly they were not only in the [Tlatelolca's] keeping. But these accounts of the ancient ones, this book of their accounts in Mexico, we have inherited. These accounts are indeed in our keeping. Therefore we too, but especially our sons, our grandsons, our offspring, those who will issue from us, they too will always guard them. We shall leave them for them when we die.] (Chimalpahin 1997, 1:61–63)

The *Crónica mexicayotl*, in part, relates an alternate discourse to Tlatelolcan versions of Mexica history emanating from the Colegio de la Santa Cruz de Tlatelolco.[15] To my mind, Tezozomoc emphasizes here that the recordkeeping activities of the royal court at Tenochtitlan had been at least as dynamic and prolific as those of the Colegio in Tlatelolco. Due to the fact that the Colegio was in decline in the latter decades of the sixteenth century, he perhaps wished to clarify that his family's legacy as keepers of historical accounts would communicate to posterity a set of perspectives as important as those in the texts from Tlatelolco.

Other political and economic conflicts underlie Tezozomoc's declaration. Tenochtitlan and Tlatelolco had a fraught relationship during the Postclassic Period along lines of trade, military expansion, and even a failed royal marriage alliance.[16] As the Mexica expanded their territory with support from Texcoco and Tacuba, they found Tlatelolca resistance a major obstacle to unrivaled control of the region (Bueno Bravo 2005, 144). The Tlatelolca tlatoani Moquixiuh married Chalchiuhnenetzin, the sister of Axayacatl, ruler of Tenochtitlan. Despite best intentions of both rulers, the marriage alliance failed. Moquixiuh mistreated Chalchiuhnenetzin, mocking her in front of his concubines and making her sleep among the metate grinding stones (*CC*, f. 49r.). She complained to her brother Axayacatl, who with his army defeated Moquixiuh, in the end throwing his body down the steps of Tlatelolco's temple (Tezozomoc [1598] 1997, 209–14).[17] I suspect that these rivalries cast a shadow on Tezozomoc's memory and expectations as he dictated to Chimalpahin. The passage thus reinforces Tenochca identity as a basis of stability for their future generations: via kinship links, Tezozomoc's descendants could have a sense of belonging to their island and not to Tlatelolco.

Looking closer at Tezozomoc's declaration on folio 18v, I note a difrasismo with embedded meanings that amplify Nahua futurities of education. Tezozomoc reminded Tenochca nobility of the efforts the ancestors had dedicated to preparing words and passing them on orally and painted in amoxtli folding books. The phrase "ynin huehuenenonotzaliztlahtolli ynin huehuenenonotzalizamoxtlacuilolli," which Anderson and Schroeder translate as "these accounts of the ancient ones, this book of their accounts" (Chimalpahin 1997, 1:63), merits attention, since it refers to educational futurities the ancestors had envisioned. The expanded terms in this diphrastic kenning reflect the tendency in colonial Nahuatl to agglomerate series of parallel phrasings into longer meaning-rich units, what Ben Leeming (2015, 182–83) calls "hyper-trophism." Wrapping units of meaning together in Nahuatl builds complex metaphors (McDonough 2024, 41). In this case, such elaborate bundling sheds light on a sense of urgency that Chimalpahin conveys. This kind of compositional feature can also "create an overwhelming sense of what is being described" (Schwaller 2005, 73). A central morphemic element in this pair is *-nenonotzaliztli-*, which Alonso de Molina ([1571] 2008, 2:68v) translates as "acuerdo, cabildo o enmienda de vida" (agreement, council or correction of one's life). The related term, *nenotzaliztli*, Molina (2:68v) defines as "la reconciliación de los que estauan reñidos" (the reconciliation of those who were at odds). To me these connotations indicate that the ancestors at minimum had deliberated before reaching an agreement regarding their spoken words, *tlatolli*, and regarding what words they would write in their books—their *amoxtlacuilloli*. To my mind, the repetition of tlatolli and amoxtlatolli indicates agreement between the spoken account of the Mexica elders and its pictorial and later alphabetic versions. Perhaps these complex constructions Chimalpahin used reflect conflicts and tensions he had observed among Mexica nobles regarding their history and who had the right to tell it. It is equally possible that the aging Tezozomoc, for his part, saw that any disagreements existing between the remaining Mexica nobles had to cease for the sake of providing information for posterity.[18] In this way, Tezozomoc lived out a futurity that his ancestors had imagined. The work that his ancestors had done to make their records now lay in the hands of Tezozomoc, who acted in a reciprocal manner by passing the accounts on to his children and their future generations.

The second element of the difrasismo, "huehuenenonotzalizamoxtlacuilloli," also emphasizes the material form of knowledge transmission.

After the decline of the Colegio in Tlatelolco and in the absence of traditional educational institutions, save the royal families, custodianship of these accounts in the form of a book offered a solution and a path forward for Tezozomoc and Chimalpahin. By referring to the *Crónica* as an amoxtli—the same word for traditional codices prior to the conquest and applied to Western-style books thereafter—the emphasis is on the text's freestanding, portable nature (Karttunen 1992, 11; Lockhart 2001, 25). The book does not rely on an institution; rather, it rests on Chimalpahin and Tezozomoc's words as representative of Tenochca knowledge. Enclosing the lexical elements just explained, *huehue-* expresses reverence for the elders who have contributed to its content, and *-tlacuilolli* underscores the value of the written word for the compilation and preservation of the text (Karttunen 1992, 84; Molina [1571] 2008, 2:120r). A parallel becomes apparent: as his ancestors had chosen to record their histories on amatl paper, so did Tezozomoc opt to include his genealogy in Spanish and his exhortations, his persuasive speech, in the historiographical project of Chimalpahin. Tezozomoc made an explicit reference to information he gathered from paper texts by his ancestors: "Ayc polihuiz ayc ylcahuiz. yn oquichihuaco yn oquitlallico yn intlillo yn intlapallo yn intenyo yn imitolloca yn imilnamicoca" (And what they came to do, what they came to establish, their writings, their renown, their history, their memory will never perish, will never be forgotten in times to come [*CC*, f. 18v; Chimalpahin 1997, 1:61]). The preservation of the content of his predecessors' paintings was tantamount to preserving their lifeways. As we shall see, the wrapping of words recalls the wrapping of a deity in the form of a tlaquimilolli. From early in the history of the Mexica as the *Crónica mexicayotl* relates it, the nobles wrapped their deity Huitzilopochtli, spoke to it, and heard it speak to them and guide them over vast and varied ground to the permanent location of their altepetl.

BUNDLING THE FUTURE

O ca yehuatl in ynin tlahtolli huehuetque yn nican tictlalllia yn atopilhuan nican anquittazque yhuan yn amixquichtin yn amexica yn antenochca nican anquimatizque yn iuh peuhticatqui yn iuh tzintiticatque yn oticteneuhque in huey altepetl ciudad mexico tenohtitlan yn atlihtic yn tutzallan. yn acatzallan yn oncan otiyolque otitlacatque in titenochca. (*CC*, f. 18v)

[Note well these accounts [of] the ancient ones that we set down here; you who are our children will see them here; and all of your Mexica, you Tenochca here will know that such was the beginning, such was the origin of what we have called the great altepetl, the altepetl of Mexico Tenochtitlan in the midst of the water, among the sedges and the reds, where we Tenochca have lived, [where] we were born.] (Chimalpahin 1997, 1:61–63)

The caves in Aztlan mark the beginning of the Mexica nobles' historical narrative.[19] The single beginning point from the womb of the earth also reminded the Mexica of their shared experience with the Chichimeca groups who emerged from the caves near the same point in their mythic time (Diel 2018, 117).[20] I observe that the seven groups and their settlement throughout Central Mexico complements pan-Nahua themes present in the writings of Chimalpahin. As Schroeder (2017, 230) has observed, "there was hardly a town or people that had not been touched in some manner by Mexica imperialism, whether through trade, tribute exaction, marital alliances, or devastating conquests. The capital, Mexico-Tenochtitlan, was magnificent in its storied appearance and its invincibility. Thus, in many ways, Chimalpahin's history of the great Mexica has come to encompass the story of Nahua life writ large." The groups would eventually settle in Colhuacan, Tenochtitlan, Chalco, and even south of Popocatepetl in Atlixco (Dyckerhoff 2003, 167–68).[21] Membership in these seven groups conferred prestige before and after the arrival of the Spanish. The ability to trace one's origins to Chicomoztoc played a key role in ensuring altepetl autonomy during the colonial era (Schroeder 1991, 123–24; Olko 2012, 183). Each group, once born, embodied their patron deity's character (López Austin 1997, 38). Born together in Chicomoztoc, the Mexicas presented their journey to Tenochtitlan as their wilderness education with Huitzilopochtli. Thus, out of a space of origin, a guiding being began to take shape, a bundle that would shortly speak out the Mexicas' objectives.

Communicating a Nahua futurity of education, the *Crónica mexicayotl* bears the mark of Chimalpahin, the last Nahua to write an extensive historical narrative in his language. Post-Colegio mestizo intellectuals in the Valley of Mexico in the seventeenth century also wrote histories of Indigenous groups.²² However, they tended to write in Spanish and for financial gain (Schroeder 2017, 237).²³ These factors further relegated Native cultures to the past and oriented communities toward a future of Hispanization, an effect Enrique Florescano (1994, 127) has called the "disindigenization" of their history. Contrarily, Chimalpahin wrote to posterity in the hope that they would remember Nahua history in a larger sense.

Huitzilopochtli accompanied the Mexica in the form of a deity bundle, a tlaquimilolli, and in the parallel form of a priest who had his name. The text reads,

> Auh yntlapial catca quitlatlauhtiaya quiteomatia yn aquin quitocayotiaya tetzahuitl huitzilopochtli. ca tlahtohuaya. quinnotzaya. Yhuan oyntlan ne oquinmocniuhtiaya. in yehuatin azteca. (*CC*, f. 20r)

> [And in their keeping was he to whom they supplicated, whom they considered a god, he whom they named the portent Huitzilopochtli. He spoke; he conversed with the Azteca; he lived among them and was their friend.] (Chimalpahin 1997, 1:67)

These dual forms are consistent with his depictions in the *Tira de la peregrinación* (*Codex Boturini*) and the *Codex Azcatitlan*.²⁴ Recalling that Nahuas consciously build their own deities, Bassett (2015, 200) explains that the tlaquimilolli as a living being represented "an ontological transformation [and] an act of exchange." The Mexica ultimately made this bundle and designated the teomameque (deity bearers) who helped the animated object journey with the altepetl (Bassett 2015, 191; Diel 2018, 100).²⁵ In addition, the bundle rewarded their efforts by speaking and providing specific directions to aid their arrival to Tenochtitlan.

The words of Huitzilopochtli serve first to name the leaders of the Mexica, allowing their collective spatio-temporal advance. The text authenticates its claims, referencing individuals to whom readers could trace their ancestry. A central concern is to document the Moteuczoma royal line:

Yn ompa tlahtohuani catca ytoca Moteuhcçoma. Ynin tlahtohuani oncatca omentin ypilhuan. Auh yn iquac ye miquiz niman ye yc quintlahtocatlallitiuh yn omoteneuhque ypilhuan yn tetiachcauh amo huel momati yn itoca yehuatl yntlahtocauh yez yn cuixteca = auh yn teteyccauh yn Mexicatl. çan mitohua Mexi. ytoca chalchiuhtlatonac yehuatl ye quimaca. yn Mexitin. (*CC*, f. 21r)

[He who was ruler there was named Moteucçoma. There were two sons of this ruler. And when he was about to die he then installed these aforesaid sons as his rulers. The elder brother, whose name is not known, was the ruler of the Cuexteca. And to the younger brother, a Mexica, called just Mexi [though] named Chalchiuhtlatonac, he gave the Mexitin.] (Chimalpahin 1997, 1:69)

The narrative thus links the name Mexi with the Mexica and establishes the authority of the Moteuczoma rulers beginning at mythical Aztlan. Those related to the Moteuczoma lineage, such as Tezozomoc and his mother, Francisca, could use this precedent to maintain their leadership roles in the colonial period. In the midst of the Mexica nobles' political uncertainty, the association of the remaining members of the house of Moteuczoma encouraged unity. While at the time of the making of the *Crónica mexicayotl* Chimalpahin had retrospective certainty of the importance of the house of Moteuczoma, he did not know if posterity would. Keeping in mind Chimalpahin's emphasis on Mexica history as Nahua history in a broader sense, I observe the Moteuczoma dynasty as a synecdoche for all that Nahua culture had influenced in Central Mexico, an idea that could strengthen Nahua groups and encourage them to share their lived knowledge(s).

Naming continues as part of this larger pedagogical discourse. From his tlaquimilolli bundle Huitzilopochtli renamed and equipped his people: "ynic axca ye mitohua Mexica. Yhuan oncan no quinmacac yn mitl yhuan tlahhuitolli. Yhuan chitatli yn tleyn aco yauh quimina yn Mexiti" (Hence they are now called Mexica. And he then also gave them the arrow and the bow and the net carrying-bag. Whatever went [flying] above, the Mexiti could shoot easily [*CC*, f. 23v; Chimalpahin 1997, 1:73]). Huitzilopochtli pierced their ears, denoting their noble rank (Olko 2014, 70–73). He painted their faces black, signaling them as warriors, and gave them bows and arrows. These offensive weapons, more suited to ambushes and warfare than to hunting, foreshadowed how the Mexica would gain their status in Mesoamerica (C. Townsend 2019, 24).[26] That Huitzilopochtli gave the Mexica their name recalls how naming ceremonies allowed parents to learn their child's fate (Olivier 2003, 36). Their deity also equipped them as warriors, anticipating their future activities of conquest and expansion.

Huitzilopochtli's speech depicted in the text shows how the deity sustained them on their way to Tenochtitlan. When they arrived at Colhuacan, Huitzilopochtli prevented their death by speaking to them through his tlaquimilolli. He warned them to move away from an ahuehuete tree—a Mesoamerican cypress—where they had encamped. After they relocated to a place still within sight, the tree fell and would have crushed them had they not moved (*CC*, f. 22v). The *Tira de la peregrinación* also records this event, reiterating its importance to the Mexica. From this close call, one could infer that Huitzilopochtli and the cosmos had destined them to survive and flourish. The tlaquimilolli spoke to Mexi, the tlatoani for whom the altepetl and the community were named. Speaking bundles appear elsewhere, contemporary to Chimalpahin and Tezozomoc. The *Florentine Codex* records that the tlatoani consulted the bundle of Tezcatlipoca, asking him to lead "incatlehoatl conchioaz incatlehoatl contocaz" (by the road this one shall take, by the way this one shall follow [*FC*, Bk. 6, f. 13v; Olivier 2003, 25]). These parallel clauses refer to the future and pathways ahead. While the Mexica and, by extension, each Nahua group built their tlaquimilolli, they participated in the construction of their horizons. Each step required reciprocity between the Mexica and their deity.

The voice of Huitzilopochtli also gave oracles, which foretold that the Mexica would gain military strength, become the rulers of an empire, and amass wealth from tribute (*CC*, f. 23v–24r). He also told them the signs that would confirm the site of their capital: an eagle perched on a cactus devouring his food next to a lake. These declarations pointed ultimately to the future construction of Huitzilopochtli's temple in Tenochtitlan. Each time they stopped on their journey, the Mexica built a temporary shrine to their patron: "auh y cana cenca huecahuaya. Moteocaltiaya. oncan quiquetzque yn ical yn inteouh yn huitzilopochtli" (And wherever they tarried long they built a temple; there they constructed the house of their god Huitzilopochtli [*CC*, f. 24v; Chimalpahin 1997, 1:77]). By centering their settlements on the temple to Huitzilopochtli, the Mexica centered themselves as well. Once positioned in space, the group could develop its own sequence of events to enact, its own vision of future actions. Harjo (2019, 46) describes how the positioning of an Indigenous community forms a part of their way-finding:

> Sequencing the concepts of futurity in this way is a pedagogical move for teaching them, with each concept building on the next. First comes understanding one's positionality and the fact that there is richness and value in it. Also important is understanding one's capacities related to autonomy, kinship building, and self-determination. The second step is recognizing that community knowledge and felt knowledge are just as important and valid as positivist models of knowledge production. Third comes in finding that self-determined, felt knowledge can be collectively tapped to generate informal and formal actions that shape community. And finally, the fourth step involves the places in which all of this gets staged and realized—the geographies of emergence.

The sequence of events Harjo describes applies to the Mexica as they oriented themselves toward Tenochtitlan. At the same time, the retelling of this story in the *Crónica mexicayotl* proposes another directionality—the benefit of posterity, or who would be able to access Mexica mythic time and place through the text. Huitzilopochtli and the tlatoani Mexi enacted a map for solidarity among Native elites in the colonial period, by reminding them of the Mexicas' rule from Tenochtitlan. While the rise of the Mexica was clear in hindsight—to Chimalpahin and Tezozomoc—both were unsure whether the young alive at that time or in the future would remember the Mexica sequence of emergence. By recalling that information, the *Crónica mexicayotl* sends a narrative forward to strengthen future generations in return for the ancestors' previous efforts to preserve these accounts.

The arrival of the Mexica to Lake Texcoco and the foundation of Tenochtitlan in 2 Calli (1325) constitute the most important turning points in the migration narrative of the *Crónica mexicayotl*. Here, I emphasize the forward-leaning elements of this well-known passage. Undoubtedly, by the time Chimalpahin recorded these scenes, this moment of recognition of the capital had already gained various layers of embellishment—presumably through countless retellings within Tenochtitlan and the Moteuczoma household. The attention to detail and to keeping a match between what Huitzilopochtli had foretold and what the Mexica elders in the chronicle saw shows the value they attributed to the account. Seeing the eagle and cactus set the Mexica on a path that confirmed their leadership and permanently attached them to the location. While symbolically laden, the eagle does not remain staid or motionless, as the text explains:

> Acatitlan yhacac yn tenochtli. yn oncan oztotenpa yn oquittaque ycpac ca ycpac yhcac. moquetzticac yn quauhtli. in yehauatl yn tenochtli. oncan tlaqua. Oncan quiqua quitzotzopitzticac. yn quiqua. auh in yehuatl yn quauhtli. yn oquimittac. yn Mexica cenca omopechtecac. yn quauhtli. çan huecapa yn conittaque. Auh in itapaçol ynipepech çan moch yehuatl yn ixquichy nepahpan tlaçoyhuitl. yn ixquich yn xiuhtotoyhuitl. yntlauhquecholyhuitl. yn ixquich quetzalli. auh ca no oncan quittaque y noncan tetepeuhtoc. yn intzonteco y nepahpan totome yn tlaçototome. yntzonteco oncan çoçoticate. yhaun cequi totoycxitl. cequi omitl. (*CC*, f. 35r)

> [And when they came upon the rock tuna cactus standing there among the reeds at the cave's mouth, they saw that upon it stood an eagle rising erect on the rock tuna cactus, eating there. There it was eating, picking to pieces what it was eating. And when the eagle saw the Mexica, it humbly bowed low. They saw it only from a distance. And its nest, its bed, was all of varied precious feathers—all cotinga, spoonbill, precious quetzal feathers. And they also saw that the heads of the various birds lay scattered; the heads of the precious birds were strung up there. And there were some birds' feet and some bones.] (Chimalpahin 1997, 1:103)

The oracle's fulfillment forms another iteration of the cave imagery that connects Aztlan to Tenochtitlan and imbues the site of their altepetl with ritual significance (Florescano 1994, 48–49). By revering their presence, the eagle harmonizes with the destiny that Huitzilopochtli revealed. David Carrasco (1984, 163) has observed that by authorizing the foundation of Tenochtitlan, the sky god Huitzilopochtli and the earth god Tlaloc inaugurated the city as the center of the Mexica cosmos. I note that the auspicious bow of the eagle to the elders presages how the group would manipulate life and death from the city center. While Mexica ritual after the Spanish became the target of censure and prohibition, this historical recitation inside a book offered a means to remember the past that evoked ritual spaces, even if they could not use them.

In this sighting, the eagle recognizes the Mexica. It responds to their presence by bowing, a display of respect for the sacrifice, strength, and work they expended in their journey, and hailing the building, ruling, and sacrificing they would conduct there. As previously, I recall that the eagle represents Huitzilopochtli (Mundy 2015, 334). The bird has plenty to eat, which begs a question: what of the snake that the eagle eats in the most iconic representations of this scene? After all, during the composition of the *Crónica mexicayotl* there were contemporary representations of an eagle and snake. In 1576, a drawing of the eagle on a cactus devouring a snake appeared in the *Codex Aubin* (f. 26v).[27] Likewise, a stone has been unearthed from beneath the Palacio Nacional in downtown Mexico City that pictures an eagle standing on a cactus sprouting from a stone that resembles a *chac mool* altar; that eagle is also eating a snake (Montaño 2019). This archaeological find reveals that in the latter part of the Postclassic Period, the Mexica produced examples of the eagle devouring a serpent on top of a cactus. To me it seems that this image would serve at minimum as a place glyph designating Tenochtitlan, among other possible ritual uses.

It would appear that the famous motif sprang from various origins. Perhaps, then, it is better to ask, how did that image proliferate? A partial answer may come from Indigenous appropriations of the literature of Latin antiquity, since the emblem also existed in European memory. Regarding Nahuas who wrote on the Mexica past, Laird (2021, 231) has observed that their "knowledge of Greco-Roman literature may have helped them to mediate and interpret aspects of the pre-Hispanic past." Laird (2021, 233) argues that Cicero's *De divinatio* is a likely source, wherein Marius beholds "an eagle rising from a tree-trunk by the water's edge to tear apart a serpent." Accounts that add the serpent motif thus appear to engage in acts of interpretation similar to those of the Inca Garcilaso, who compared Cusco to Rome and Tawantinsuyu to the Roman Empire (Luque-Talaván 2003, 117).[28] What is certain is that over time the eagle-serpent-cactus grew into the proto-patriotism of Jesuit Francisco Clavijero, who included the icon next to a map of Mexico in his 1804 English translation of *Historia antigua de México*, printed in Philadelphia (Clavijero [1787] 1804; Florescano 2004, 89). Thus, Greco-Roman literature supplemented any existing eagle-serpent-cactus motifs and Clavijero likely helped popularize the iconic scene abroad.

Students at the Colegio in Tlatelolco certainly had exposure to texts in Latin. However, to me both Tezozomoc's repudiation of the Tlatelolca accounts of the Mexica's history and Chimalpahin's autodidacticism explain why they did not introduce a snake into the scene. I speculate that for Chimalpahin and Tezozomoc, the bones of the birds scattered around the eagle sufficed to explain the Mexica destiny of dominance in the Valley of Mexico. The contented, well-fed eagle stands as a herald of things to come for the Mexica elders. The scene also assumes a relationship of reciprocity between Huitzilopochtli and the sun, which would come to form a key aspect of Mexica sacrifice.[29] In turn, the memory of the eagle and cactus could encourage posterity in days becoming increasingly difficult for the Mexica nobles. Perhaps future generations could see the bones as suggestive of the eventual passing of an era of Spanish imperialism as well.

WRAPPING MOTEUCZOMA

As the narrative unfolds, the directions of deities to the Mexica rulers become increasingly complex. Similar to how an oracle established the ritual center of Tenochtitlan, another extraordinary event opened the future of the city to the Mexica noble class. Huitzilopochtli already had brought forth the first Moteuczoma from the cave of Chicomoztoc. Another intervention on the part of Huitzilopochtli would allow the Moteuczoma house to rise. In their early years in Tenochtitlan, the Mexica paid tribute to the Tepanec Empire, whose ruler, Tezozomoctli, governed the valley from Azcapotzalco. They scavenged in the swamps of Texcoco for waterfowl and fish to pay as tribute. A deity again would provide instructions in a dream to a young man who wanted to marry into a royal family of Quauhnahuac (Cuernavaca). After recounting these sequences, my comments focus on connections between the tlaquimilloli of Huitzilopochtli and the written project of the *Crónica mexicayotl* as a tlaquimilloli that safeguarded details on the rise of the Moteuczoma rulers.

Huitzilihuitl, son of Acamapichtli, the ruler who founded Tenochtitlan, desired to marry Miayahuaxihuitl.[30] She was the daughter of Oçomatzin teuhctli, tlatoani of Quauhnahuac, and a sorcerer (nahualli). He forbade Huitzilihuitl from pursuing her and cast spells to cause spiders and fierce animals to guard her palace. Yet in a dream, the spirit Yohualli spoke to Huitzilihuitl:

Yn quinotz yohualli yehuatl yn diablo quilhui ca ompa yn quauhnahuac yn tepan ticallaquizque ompa tiazque yn ichan Oçomatzin teuhctli, ca ticanazque yn ichpoch yn itoca miyahuaxihuitl. (*CC*, f. 42v)

[The devil Yohualli spoke to him. He said to him: We shall penetrate among them in Quauhnahuac; we shall go to Oçomatzin teuhctli's home; we shall take his daughter named Miyahuaxihuitl.] (Chimalpahin 1997, 1:121)[31]

The next day, Huitzilihuitl asked Oçomatzin teuhctli for permission to marry his daughter. The ruler, disdaining the Mexicas' poverty, refused. Yet Yohualli returned and advised Huitzilihuitl to make a spear, to embed a jade stone inside it, and to throw the potent gift into the young woman's palace. Huitzilihuitl pitched the spear and it pierced the roof of Miyahuaxihuitl's chamber. The colorful reed amazed her. She broke it open, swallowed the jade, and became pregnant with none other than Moteuczoma Ilhuicamina (*CC*, f. 43r).[32]

Multiple images of strength accumulate in this passage. I submit that these examples of strength collectively point to the efficacy of the advice of Yohualli. Extraordinary beings counteract the Mexicas' poverty and favor the rise of their future empire, with the Moteuczoma lineage as central to their destiny.[33] The appearance of a spirit, which the passage identifies as a devil, concerns not the imposition of orthodoxy but how they may summon a power greater than that of the sorcerer Oçomatzin teuhctli (Schroeder 1998, 344). That Yohualli appears to Huitzilihuitl in a dream, however, deserves a closer look. As McDonough (2024, 8) observes, Nahuas did not place a dividing line between science and religion. In fact, they tend to evaluate data from all aspects of their experience as relevant to finding a wise manner to proceed in life.[34] The complete name of Yoalli Ehecatl—"Night, Wind"—recalls invocations of the Ometeotl duality, emphasizing ancestral views on the complementarity of aspects of the cosmos (Tena 2009).[35] This account also recalls Huitzilopochtli's birth in Book 3 of the *Florentine Codex* at the dawn of the Fifth Sun when he emerged, fully formed, from the womb of his mother, Coatlicue, to defend her from the attack of Coyolxauhqui and her brothers, the four hundred stars of the south (Centzonuitznahua). Also in the *Florentine Codex*, Book 6, is a prayer to Yohualli-Ehecatl, as an avatar of Tezcatlipoca, asking him to save the supplicant from poverty and to bring abundance (*FC*, Bk. 6, f. 4v–8r). Diel (2018, 123) notes that the *Codex Mexicanus* preserves vital events for the future of the Mexica during the reign of Acamapichtli, including the birth of Ilhuicamina, whose name she translates as "Shooting Arrows Skyward." Thus, the voice of Yohualli, the Ehecatl-Quetzalcoatl complementarity, and evocations of primordial victory of Huitzilopochtli together intensify the meaning of the event. The unfolding of the cosmos favored the rise of the Mexica to power, and multiple deities catalyzed the Moteuczoma dynasty's future potential.

I observe that in this case the wrapping of powerful objects corresponds to the wrapping of Huitzilopochtli at the onset of the Mexica migration sequences. Embedding a precious stone into a reed lance also parallels the embedding of the *Crónica mexicayotl* into the larger amoxtli Chimalpahin wrote. Huitzilihuitl constructed a wrapped projectile, bundling jade inside to affect a marvelous outcome. Princess Miyahauxihuitl's extraordinary conception of Moteuczoma Ilhuicamina thus depended on a tlaquimilolli, a powerfully bundled ritual object that embodied the energy of a deity—in this case reifying the link between Huitzilopochtli's patronage and the Moteuczoma dynasty. The etymology of Ilhuicamina and intertextual references shed light on the key role of Huitzilopochtli. "Ilhuicatl" refers to the sky, and "mina" means to pierce with arrows (Karttunen 1992, 104, 148). These elements combine to recall how the Moteuczoma rulers cooperated with Huitzilopochtli's patronage. I submit that the jade stone inside the arrow functions as a tlaquimilolli to bring about a shared objective between the Mexica and Huitzilopochtli, the continuation of the royal line.[36] Bassett (2005,

190) shares that in their most basic iteration, "tlaquimilolli, like teixiptlahuan and other living creatures, were mere skins and bones. The cloth, clothing, and hides that covered a tlaquimilolli bound together a teotl's corporeal remains and axcaitl (possessions, property) [and] to say that teteo had bodies and property suggests that they were more than metaphors." The extraordinary conception of Moteuczoma Ilhuicamina shows that the property of the reed and then of Miayauhxihuitl was the future of the Moteuczoma house. The precious, gleaming stone had power to overwhelm the magic of Oçomatzin Teuctli.[37] Once ingested, the tlaquimilolli imagery continues: the stone became wrapped in Miayauhxihuitl's body and clothing. As a living tlaquimilloli, she embodied the filiation between the future tlatoani and the deity on whose behalf he spoke.

The arc of the spear traces an optimistic future for the Mexica: overcoming the marriage prohibition, Huitzilihuitl, whose name, "Hummingbird," recalls his patron the "Hummingbird of the South," Huitzilopochtli. The young man achieves the fecund result necessary to raise his people from poverty. As a Nahua tool of persuasion, the repetition of the visits by Yohualli emphasizes the Mexicas' rise as a necessary unfolding of events. Likewise, the repetition of the jade, first inside the spear, inside Miayauxihuitl's mouth, and finally in her womb, shows the ability of the tlaquimilloli to bring about the marvelous effect of continuing the Moteuczoma line. During their imperial years, the Mexica would use tlaquimilolli in rituals, including "the accessions of rulers and New Fire ceremonies" (Bassett 2015, 165). In historical terms, the reign of Itzcoatl marked when the Mexica rose up against Azcapotzalco and stopped paying tribute.[38] From there, they began conquering the region of Lake Texcoco and building their empire.

In narrative terms, I observe that the stone passes from one tlaquimilloli to another, paralleling the passing of information on the Moteuczoma dynasty from Mexica nobles to Chimalpahin. Since the text centers on the importance of telling future generations about what the Mexica accomplished in Tenochtitlan, this account now lies embedded in Chimalpahin's chronicle. It is clear that even with Christianity as the public religion under the Spanish colonial regime, wrapping as a way to signal value continued. Additionally, as with the retelling of the Miguel Tecniuh riot in chapter 3, the accumulation of vivid details and references to further events in the Mexica mythic past leads me to consider this a highly elaborated tale. This foundational episode has passed through many retellings of what the Mexica leaders hold as most valuable: their links to the ruler, to Huitzilopochtli, and to their altepetl of Tenochtitlan. Thus, by wrapping the narrative of the rise of the Moteuczoma dynasty within a larger educational project, the text retains the futurity of education Tezozomoc described, recalling content from the calmecac his ancestors attended.

* * * *

At the opening of the seventeenth century, two Nahua historians from different backgrounds and different altepeme joined their interests in teaching posterity regarding the Mexica past. Tezozomoc, as a representative of the Moteuczoma lineage, desired to make good on his ancestors' aim for him to know of their efforts to find and build Tenochtitlan. Similarly, Chimalpahin desired that future readers in Amecameca and beyond should learn what the ancestors of that region had accomplished. Chimalpahin saw the relevance of looking beyond his altepetl and helping inform coming generations of his fellow Nahuas of the past of the great Chichimeca peoples and in particular the Mexica. Mexico-Tenochtitlan had become a place that Mexica elders did not recognize. They could no longer count on a traditional education for their children. What changed was the postconquest conception of time and place (Florescano 1994, 130–34; Read 1998, 265; Maffie 2014, 419–21). That temporal shift coalesced in the text's presentation of time as spiraling forward, not without precedent, and yet unlived. The *Crónica mexicayotl* envisions coming time as a matter of course and understands that coming generations would not see a return to Tenochtitlan as it was. Yet by retelling these events, they could set an emergent way-finding approach to teaching the young—even those they would never meet.

In this chapter, I have shown that through retelling the stories of the ancestors, Chimalpahin—drawing on contributions from Tezozomoc, Alonso Franco, and possibly other Mexica leaders—engaged in reciprocity with those who lived before and after them. Given the absence of the calmecac, the authors provided a portable, transcribable form of their knowledges with a view to those accounts outlasting their lifetimes. Young Mexicas could learn of the foundations of their altepetl to preserve the integrity of its memory in the face of pressures to convert, assimilate, and suppress expressions of Indigenous identity. The *Crónica mexicayotl* shows that the destruction of ancestral educational centers and the waning of the Colegio de la Santa Cruz de Tlatelolco did not stop Nahuas from using writing to generate their own didactic material. My analysis has additionally made apparent the continuing importance of micropatriotism in articulations of futurities of education. By Tezozomoc's lights, trusting the versions of the past emanating from Tlatelolco would ultimately alienate the Mexica young from their ancestors. What did the ancestors teach Mexica youth? The *Crónica mexicayotl* shows how to live in scarcity and opulence, how to listen to advice, how to engage in reciprocal relationships with humans and deities, and how to bundle and tie together what is precious to their people. Arguably, their words were what they should protect most as basic tools for describing the future.

Nahua tools of persuasion appear in the sections of the *Crónica* I have examined. Features of the vocabulary and syntax in Nahuatl provide understanding of the educational aims of Tezozomoc, who sought to strengthen his fellow nobles and their descendants with their ancestral accounts. Specific features of the Nahuatl language have also shed light on the importance of the tlaquimilolli for safeguarding the Moteuczoma dynasty and its knowledge. In my view, the persuasive approaches of the text culminate with the tlaquimilloli, which serves as an enduring means to express the value of powerful knowledge objects and how to protect those objects moving ahead. Huitzilopochtli gathered strength for the Mexica at their emergence from Chicomoztoc, during their prolonged wilderness journey, at the foundation of Tenochtitlan, and in the conception of Moteuczoma Ilhuicamina. The relationship the Mexica cultivated with the bundle of Huitzilopochtli relied on reciprocity: they built the deity and the deity built them. Repetition comes to bear on multiple occasions: Chimalpahin and Tezozomoc repeat their commitment to communicate information on the past to the young; Huitzilopochtli repeatedly advises the Mexica and allows for their growth as a people. Moreover, the assembly of the deity bundle involved wrapping, iterative turns, which serve to emphasize the importance and potency of Huitzilopochtli's bundle and in the case of the spear, the jade it held. In the end, the *Crónica mexicayotl* enfolds a narrative recalling how Huitzilopochtli spoke to the Mexica through the bundle they made. Tezozomoc wrapped Huitzilopochtli's words in a book with the help of Chimalpahin, understanding that future Mexica generations would read them. Recalling the concept of education as neixtlamachiliztli, "giving wisdom to the face," I ponder that by facing each other and agreeing on what accounts were important to tell, Chimalpahin and Tezozomoc provided the means for future Nahua readers to do the same.

. . . .

Epilogue

How have the Nahua futurities I have examined in these chapters fared over time? What are some approaches Nahuas today have toward the future? Some answers to these questions help close this study and indicate how Nahua futurities continue unfolding. Active Nahua scholars and writers today continue making texts that set forth knowledge(s) regarding days to come.

One of these writers is Sabina Cruz de la Cruz. Her account, "Tepahtihquetl pan ce pilaltepetzin / A Village Healer" (2019), translated by Rebecca Dufendach, represents a collaborative ethnographic project that they undertook to deconstruct the conventional boundary between the Native as the passive possessor of knowledge and the Western ethnographer as the qualified interpreter (Cruz de la Cruz and Dufendach 2019, 647–48).[1] If we consider the work of Clifford Geertz (1973, 452), the intention is not to "read over the shoulders" of Nahuas but to read in a collaborative manner, one that privileges the observations of Natives regarding their own cultures. In Cruz de la Cruz's account, she interweaves her professional accomplishments with daily social life in her hometown of Tecomate, Veracruz. As Cruz de la Cruz explains, she sent money home, which she earned from teaching Nahuatl, and visited her parents on occasion. She became aware that others in the community had started excluding her father from communal work (tequitl), since the men of the village believed that the remittances he received from his daughter gave him an unfair advantage. Cruz de la Cruz fell ill at this news; she sank into depression with heavy fatigue, body aches, and a fever. These symptoms led her to consult healers in her village (Cruz de la Cruz and Dufendach 2019, 653–54).

If we understand that the visible manifestations of an illness represent improper relationships with cosmos and community, a closer look reveals Cruz de la Cruz's condition as similar to animic misalignments underlying illnesses discussed in the *Florentine Codex* (see chapter 2). It soon became clear that hate and envy were to blame for Cruz de la Cruz's symptoms. As she explains, "Axcanah huelih cualli quiittah tlan ichpocatl huan itatahhuan paquih huan axcanah mocualaniah" (They could not stand to see the young woman and her parents happy and that they did not fight amongst themselves) (Cruz de la Cruz and Dufendach 2019, 650, 658).[2] Normally, working together demonstrates unity in Nahua communities (Good Eshelman 2001, 285; 2005, 95).[3] Working communicates enthusiasm, vigor, and personal empowerment (Good Eshelman 2005, 91–92). The disharmony in the village blocked the flow of energy and disrupted her family's patterns of work.

In Sabina Cruz de la Cruz's description of her visit to a healer, I note parallels between her experience and the texts of this study. Like Oxomoco and Cipactonal, the deities who first practiced divination in the *Florentine Codex*, the healer in Tecomate cast maize kernels to see into the future. In this case, the diagnosis of Cruz de la Cruz's depression, body aches, and fever is at stake. As she relates,

> Tepahtihquetl achtohui quichihua ce tlatemoliztli pan ce huapalli zancualli ica cintli ce quezqui itlancoch, ce cantelah huan tomin tlen mahtlactli pezoh, nopayoh pehua motlahtlania ica totiotzitzin nouhquiya, quiihtoama neci tlen quipechia ni inmoconeuh. Nopayoh motiochihua, quimapixtoc cintlancochtli, quitocaxtia macehualli tlen quipahtia, quemman tlamizza huacca quiitzeloa nopa cintli pan huapalli huan nopayoh quiitta tlen quipiya macehualli pan itlacayo huan zampa quimahcahuaz cintli para zampa quiittaz zo motemachiz tlen quiitta pan macehualli itlacayo. (Cruz de la Cruz and Dufendach 2019, 655)

[The healer made a search on a medium board with corn, a few kernels, a candle, and a coin piece of ten pesos. She began to ask the gods to see what worried the woman. She prayed, she had in her hand the kernels of corn, she named the person she was going to cure, when she finished, she dropped the kernels on the board. There she saw what the person had in her body. She threw the kernels once again to confirm what she saw in the body of the person.] (Cruz de la Cruz and Dufendach 2019, 663)

Here multiple potentialities of maize within a ritual context become apparent. Corn, through the eyes of a specialized and trained tepahtihquetl (healer), can show others how to proceed into unknown times. More than mere food for caloric value, the corn seeds will indicate the cause and suggest the remedy for the bodily pain and social disharmony that Cruz de la Cruz suffered. If we recall the descriptions of the root of the dried corn plant (centli/cintli) in Book 11 of the *Florentine Codex* as curative and restorative to sufferers of head fevers, this scene of diagnosis confirms the validity of one Nahua futurity of healing from the sixteenth century. I also note that due to the social aspect of the symptoms Cruz de la Cruz suffered, she sought help from the healer in her community. She has prioritized a Nahua approach to uncertainty over possible solutions from Western medicine. Suzanne Crawford O'Brien (2008, 9) has pointed out that prioritizing Native healing practices over Western medicine entails decolonial thinking: "choosing to be well is to take an active stance against assimilation and colonial control." When Nahuas have control over solutions and paths forward, they generate and follow futurities alternative to Western prescriptions.

After the female tepahtihquetl read the maize kernels, Cruz de la Cruz arranged for her to perform a ritual to remove the objects she had found that hindered the proper flow of energy. The ceremony included Cruz de la Cruz and her family, who, with the guidance of the healer, unblocked what had taken Cruz de la Cruz's strength and disturbed harmony in the village. The ceremony occurred at the house of the healer, who used herbs and a candle to perform a *limpia* (cleaning) on the patient, as Cruz de la Cruz sat in a chair unclothed (Cruz de la Cruz and Dufendach 2019, 655–56). They covered her with a poultice of herbs, recalling cures documented in the *Florentine Codex*, Book 11. The patient bathed and rested. As she slept, the healer identified the objects that blocked energy and removed them. The tepatihquetl instructed Cruz de la Cruz to bathe again, at which point the resolution came:

> Nouhquiya teipan quemman maltiyaya huacca quena quilliah tlen quizqui pan itlacayo:
> > Tomin: Ni tomin eliyaya huehhueyi huan quence huahcapatomin, nouhquiya quipiyaya hueliz miac xihuitl eltoya pan itlacayo, neciyaya yayahuic.
> > Cantelah: Eltoya ome cantelahcotoctli nezqui quence yancuic nocca hueliz yancuic quichihuiltoqueh tequitl tlen axcualli huan yeca queuhquinon nezqui.
> > Omitl: Ome omitl cuecuetzitzin nouhquiya hueliz ayicanah tlahuel huahcahua neciyaya nocca chipahuac.
> > Amatlatehtectli: Ni amatl quizqui hazta yayahuic hueliz huahcauhquiya eltoc pan itlacayo.
> > Tetl: Quizqui ome tetl zan tlen zancualli hueyi, yayahuic huan yehyectzin petlanih huan alaxtique. (Cruz de la Cruz and Dufendach 2019, 657)

> [After bathing then they told her what came out of her body:
> > Pieces of money: the money pieces were large, and they seemed to be from an older time. It also seemed like they had been in her body a long time because they were black.
> > Candle: there were pieces of candle that seemed newer. The pieces must have been from bad works done recently.
> > Bones: two small bones that also appeared newer because they were still white.
> > Paper cuttings: the paper cuttings were black so perhaps they had been in her body a long time.
> > Rocks: two rocks came out that were fairly large. They were black, pretty, shiny, and smooth.] (Cruz de la Cruz and Dufendach 2019, 665)

Three of the five objects removed were dark in color, which Cruz de la Cruz associates with age and duration inside the body. Ancient Nahuas attributed an extraordinary concentration of energy to obsidian and jet stones, fashioning them as ritual objects, including sacrificial knives and mirrors (Bassett 2015, 155, 184, 249n95). The coins and paper cuttings, as fashioned objects used in other ceremonies, here also have a ritual use, albeit malevolent. The rocks also recall the causality of swallowing a stone, as discussed previously in this book. In this case, the stones removed may embody the force of the ehecatl spirits that have blocked the flow of energy in the body.

The tepahtihquetl emerges as a key way-finding figure in the autoethnographic account of Sabina Cruz de la Cruz. The healer provides an inflection point in the narrative as one who expiates negative energy and opens the path ahead. Yet Cruz de la Cruz did not take for granted that one treatment constituted a cure. Cycles of treatment are necessary, since human society ever holds the prospect of malice. As Cruz de la Cruz explains,

> Zan quena tlan quichihua ni tequitl monequi quicencuiliz xihxihuitl, axcanah ma quicahuilli pampa queuhquinon nouhquiya totiotzitzin quipalehuizceh quence axcanah quinilcahuah. Huan nouhquiya pampa tlen tecocoliah axcanah mociauhcahuah, inihhuantin quicencuiliah quichihuah tlen axcualli. (Cruz de la Cruz and Dufendach 2019, 654)

> [But if one does this work, it is necessary to continue it every year. Do not leave it because the gods will help you, they will not forget you. Also, *they who hate do not rest*, they will continue to do bad.] (Cruz de la Cruz and Dufendach 2019, 663, my translation italicized)

Recalling the entry in Book 11 of the *Florentine Codex* on the herb *taloa* (see chapter 2), here a patient also recognizes the present and future need of healers to help maintain balance. She accepts the reality of ill-will but also anticipates treatments to address its effects. The ticitl of the ancestral Nahuas parallels the tepahtihquetl of Chicontepec in this forward-looking manner. Even so, keeping the ways of the healers alive requires sincerity and a high level of engagement on the part of patients and the community, as Cruz de la Cruz advises,

> Zan monequi nelnelliya tictlaliz zo ticchihuaz ica moyollo pampa queuhquinon quena cualli quizaz tlen ta ticnequi ticchihuaz huan cualli tiitztoz,

ticchihuaz tlen quiihtoz tepahtihquetl. (Cruz de la Cruz and Dufendach 2019, 657–58)

[The truth is that one must do it (the ceremonies) with your heart and in this way, things turn out well. If you do what the healer says you will be well and the things you want to do will be good.] (Cruz de la Cruz and Dufendach 2019, 666)

Cruz de la Cruz's estimation of the value of healing specialists shows a degree of success concerning the implicit futurity of their role, evident in the *Florentine Codex*. Nahua healers have been resilient. These specialists in the healing arts have survived the Inquisition, colonial labor drafts and taxation, the Mexican Revolution, waves of catechists in Chicontepec since the 1970s, and continued exclusion from the economy of the modern nation-state. As a bearer and practitioner of intergenerational knowledge(s), the healer performs a vital role for social cohesion and individual well-being in Tecomate, Veracruz, today.

Sabina Cruz de la Cruz depicts sickness and healing as phenomena woven into the social fabric: only the organizing intervention of a tepahtihquetl can set a patient's body right and simultaneously re-establish social relations with the community. Sabina Cruz de la Cruz demonstrates in "Tepahtihquetl pan ce pilaltepetzin" that individual healing includes healing the community. While recognizing the power of the written word as an aid to knowledge transmission, Cruz de la Cruz emphasizes the activities of the healer, of the tepahtihquetl, as the catalyst for restoring balance between body, community, and cosmos. In this account, anger and jealousy disrupted her health; the ill will of some also affected her father and family's ability to participate in tequitl. The diagnosis and extraction of objects blocking chicahualiztli benefited the patient and the altepetl. The stark realism of Cruz de la Cruz's observation that "tecocoliah axcanah mociauhcahuah" (they who hate do not rest) provides an imperative for communities to reconcile differences, drawing on the expertise of the healer to secure a path forward. Cruz de la Cruz's account shows the realization of her ancestors' desire to continue the traditions and lifeways of healing specialists. In addition, she makes clear her desire that future generations should continue to consult these experts. This vivid example shows that preserving balanced living depends not only on studying ancient knowledge(s) but also on planning ongoing acts that will extend the horizon of healing.

NAHUA TOOLS OF PERSUASION

In *Nahua Horizons: Writing, Persuasion, and Futurities in Colonial Mexico*, I have examined Nahua perspectives regarding days to come in various communities: from the southern slopes of Popocatepetl to Guatemala, to the Acolhua region, to Tlatelolco and in Mexico-Tenochtitlan. I have also shown that Nahua futurities follow tendencies of Indigenous futurities as constructs that emerge from practices in everyday spaces (Goodyear-Ka'ōpua 2019, 98; Harjo 2019, 30). These practices strengthen communities' way-finding approaches to the future despite colonial regimes (Harjo 2019, 100). Nahua futurities have also arisen from ritual spaces. Quauhquechollan made an alliance and participated in ecclesiastic building projects to raise its status (see chapter 1). Likewise, the scribes of Moyotlan interpreted portents in the sky and extraordinary events on the street to maintain close links between the Mexica nobles and the city's sacred center (see chapter 3). It has further become apparent that places dedicated to study have generated futurity practices, exemplified in epistemological implications of the *Historia universal* project that reiterated Nahua knowledge(s) regarding the future of their healing practices (see chapter 2). At times, places of study have included one's dwelling, as in the case of Chimalpahin's extensive annals, which included input on the history of the Mexica from Fernando Alvarado Tezozomoc.

It is not enough to envision a futurity. This study has further shown that Nahua writers have used tools of persuasion to convince their communities to act. *Gathering strength* serves as a key persuasive technique as Native writers expressed ways to overcome their groups' vulnerabilities, exacerbated by colonialism. *Reciprocity* between living Nahuas, between ancestors and the living, as well as between living and future generations also characterizes the writings and pictorials I have examined. Invoking deities in displays of reciprocity at times formed part of a mosaic of powerful beings who could come to the aid of Nahua groups. Synecdoche (a deity or ruler stands for the altepetl) or metonymy (elements and agents joined by shared origins or aims) have allowed me to read networks of future-oriented reciprocity. *Repetition* and parallelism in narratives play a vital role in convincing readers, for indicating importance, or to signal the need to address an imbalance. On occasions, *questioning-as-persuasion* also reiterates information listeners/readers already know; for instance, in the heated questions Miguel Tecniuh directed at Luis Santa María Cipac regarding the latter's performance as governor. Additionally, *specific features of Nahuatl* have shed light on future aims and anticipations regarding conditions in times ahead. Even as I enumerate these persuasive techniques, I do not wish to limit the kinds of persuasion in which Nahua writers engage. With time, more can emerge. Rather, in this study, these have served as initial criteria for an approach with great potential for understanding Nahua textual production from the colonial period forward.

A central characteristic of Nahua futurities is their dynamic, changing nature. Since they have arisen as responses to colonial epistemological violence, it comes as no surprise that they have continued to evolve. Alan Sandstrom (1991, 334) has observed that tradition "should not be viewed as the dead hand of the past intruding into the present. Ethnic group members select from traditional cultural elements and recombine them into new patterns that are faithful to ancient Nahua values, but that are also relevant to modern situations." Throughout the years, the strategic appropriation of Western cultural forms was a matter of deliberation and decision. Many choices formed part of views of reality that Spanish colonialism had destabilized. Indigenous scholars have reflected on dynamic futurities. Noelani Goodyear-Kaʻōpua (2019, 87) notes that "praxis is imperative to Indigenous resurgence." The cultural movements in which she participates as a Kānaka Maoli and studies as a scholar emphasize embodied and enacted knowledges as alternatives to "settler or state-directed futurities" (Goodyear-Kaʻōpua 2019, 87). As this study has demonstrated, Nahuas generated futurities in ways that colonial administrators and clergy did not intend. Taking stock of their needs, resources, and history, Nahua groups from the sixteenth century to now have used writing to envision paths ahead.

The pictorials discussed in chapter 1, the *Lienzo de Quauhquechollan* and the *Tira de Tepechpan*, both lay out futurities of economic and political autonomy. Quauhquechollan, a way station for traders, saw the opportunity to gain status as conquerors themselves. The alliance scene their tlacuiloque painted represented their most powerful deities and used gold leaf to communicate the gathering of extraordinary cosmic energy as part of their new possibilities after the previous reign of the Mexica. Likewise, Tepechpan heralded the coming of the Spanish with the Habsburg crest above its timeline and by depicting their rulers seated on European chairs and dressed in Western clothing. While both communities met with bitter disappointment at broken Spanish promises, each one quickly repurposed its document for a new future. Quauhquechollan and Tepechpan rearticulated paths ahead as competent, informed participants, aware of laws that allowed them to accrue status in the Habsburgs' early colonial system. Quauhquechollan finished the narrative map of its conquest as proof of its merit to own land, farm, and trade in Guatemala. Tepechpan documented its successes and challenges and used the painted timeline to supplement evidence in tribunals to defend and advance their causes. Both communities made use of ecclesiastic building projects to reduce scrutiny from Spanish administrators and to gain regional political and economic standing.

In the *Florentine Codex*, Books 10 and 11, a group of Nahua scholars and Native physicians produced guides to the human body and healing practices available for future generations. Given the three animic conduits that give life to the body in the Nahua cosmovision—the tonalli, the yollotli, and the ihiyotl—the information they provided was concerned with helping future Nahuas maintain a balanced flow of cosmic energy. This conceptualization of well-being differed from the humoralism of European medics implicit in Bernardino de Sahagún's understanding of the body. Their vision also stood as distinct to certain Western visions of the body as a vehicle for the soul. I have shown that the detailed information preserved in alphabetic writing with illustrations projected a future different from the orthodoxy and early modern science that the Franciscans wished to inculcate in Nahua students and scholars at Tlatelolco. Processes of the compilation of information from the *Primeros memoriales* in tandem with the deadline of Juan de Ovando's commission of the *Historia universal* resulted in a fragmentary presentation of plant-based treatments. However, repetitions of that healing information, through internal parallels in the *Florentine Codex* and external references, make manifest Nahua futurities of healing of the fifteen Nahua physicians who contributed information.

Fragmentary iterations of Nahua futurities of healing in the *Florentine Codex* recall the confluence of ideas and events in the colonized Native city of Mexico-Tenochtitlan of the mid-sixteenth century, represented vividly in the *Anales de Juan Bautista*. An enclave of scribes from the quarter of Moyotlan who represented interests of the Mexica nobles confronted threats to Nahuas from the Spanish regime. In these annals, they showed a particular regard for rituals, economics, and the law. To transcend the limitations of their contemporary Native leaders, these authors constructed their own scribal authority. Juan Teton's religious rebellion revealed trepidations about Christianity, stemming from the displacement of agriculture by European cattle. Similarly, an anti-tribute riot shows Nahua nobles' frustration with their governor, Luis Santa María Cipac. Furthermore, rumors about Moteuczoma's return confirm that the scribes of Moyotlan developed alternative approaches to leadership, using writing to evoke the presence of a mosaic of powerful beings. The varied content of the *Anales de Juan Bautista* shows how Native Mexico-Tenochtitlan became entangled with the imposed Ciudad de México, a crossroads of the Atlantic and Pacific regions of the Spanish empire, and perhaps the first globalized city. Even in the midst of unprecedented experiences, alphabetic writing allowed the scribes to interpret events around them in ways useful to posterity for strategic interactions with the Spanish. Perhaps coming generations could also draw optimism from knowing the Spanish would not rule in perpetuity. They could also see that those present during the struggles of the mid-sixteenth century took seriously their reciprocal obligations to generations to come.

In chapter 4, the displacement of Native hierarchies and the Hispanization of Mexico-Tenochtitlan also formed the background for my analysis of the *Crónica mexicayotl*. While certainly a concern for Mexica nobles, it was the intervention of a younger outsider that proved decisive for recording the Nahua future of education in the text, Domingo Chimalpahin of Amecameca. I argue that the threat of the disappearance of the knowledge that Mexica nobles had learned in the calmecac and in the telpochcalli school for warriors before the conquest motivated Fernando Alvarado Tezozomoc, a grandson of Moteuczoma Xocoyotl, to collaborate with Chimalpahin.[4] They aimed to preserve Mexica history so that younger generations would not forget. Chimalpahin and Tezozomoc drew from the collective memory of elders and repositioned ancestors' voices. Chimalpahin's project demonstrates that Spanish ideological control of the city would never be total. The Mexica futurity of education provided examples on living in reciprocity with the community and with deities in times of plenty and of scarcity. The volume provided examples of elaborate, courtly speech (tecpilatlatolli), of genealogies, and gave records of Huitzilopochtli's dealings with Mexica nobles—nothing short of a portable calmecac for passing on knowledge(s) as their ancestors desired, yet in circumstances they never imagined. As for Chimalpahin, his overlapping futurity of education involved holding the enclave of Mexica nobles as an example of what Nahuas have accomplished more broadly, adding the *Crónica mexicayotl* to his already prolific writings on the Mexica, on his own altepetl of Tzaqualtitlan Tenanco in Amecameca, and others in the Valley of Mexico.

WRITING AND RESILIENCE

With hindsight, how successful have the Nahua futurities I have examined been over time? As discussed in chapter 1, Quauhquechollan has had greater success than Tepechpan in terms of their futurities coming to fruition. Quauhquechollan's church and monastery complex allowed them to achieve cabecera and doctrina status, which likely encouraged economic activity and offset the loss of income they experienced when the Alvarado brothers broke their promises in Guatemala. Conversely, Tepechpan did not gain cabecera status and experienced greater poverty. Today Quauhquechollan celebrates its lienzo. The seal of the town is the two-headed eagle from the alliance. A community library in the town features information on the locality from the sixteenth century, and the church and convent complex remain open as a museum. Comparatively, the city of Tepexpan today, while sill boasting of the church it built in its bid for cabecera status, during the colonial period was not able to escape the shadow of Texcoco and Mexico-Tenochtitlan. Long ago, the elders of Tepechpan sold their tira to the Italian antiquarian Lorenzo Boturini Benaduci. Today, Avenida Insurgentes going northeast from Mexico City turns into the highway to Teotihuacán. One can easily pass

Tepexpan along the way without realizing their achievements as historians and charters of days ahead.

In both cases, these communities in the sixteenth century were better positioned than they were under the Mexica. However, in the long run, taxation and limited resources would hinder their ability to grow. Despite the narrowing of their horizons, both towns attracted settlement, accrued wealth, and made the most of their placement near main roads leading into and out of the capital. Moreover, in their communities, those who had not lived through the pivotal events their pictorials document would know that their predecessors had them in mind. The recordkeeping of Quauhquechollan and Tepechpan reveals their sense of reciprocity and obligation toward future generations.

Futurities of well-being in the *Florentine Codex*, while fragmented and more subtle to trace, lead to specific practices and a continued valuation of Nahua healing plants (see chapter 2). As we have seen, Sabina Cruz de la Cruz's visit to a female healer who cast maize kernels to diagnose her illness parallels the practices of the titicih in the sixteenth century, as recorded in the *Florentine Codex*. In a broad sense, Nahua healing practices and plant-based knowledge have proven notably resilient. Plant-based treatments of the codex have continued to offer viable paths of healing, particularly in rural areas of Mexico (Aguilar-Moreno 2007, 360). This continuation shows success in the realization of Nahua futurities in the *Historia universal* project. The resulting *Florentine Codex* preserved images and textual directions at a period five decades after the Spanish invasion. That documentation, which countless eyes have seen since Eduard Seler and Francisco Paso y Troncoso revived its study at the end of the nineteenth century, belies the multitudes of anonymous healers (Favrot Peterson 2019, 25). It was through their careful observations and work over five centuries that they have continued to make traditional healing possible.

As for the scribes of Moyotlan, they faced the hard fact that the Mexica nobles would no longer enjoy the legal and fiduciary protections they had at the beginning of Spanish colonialism (see chapter 3). They also had to come to terms with the turmoil resulting from their leadership crisis. They did so with resilience and optimism, by using writing as a means to reconnoiter and document how the Spanish reacted to direct protests and how their options for negotiation with them had narrowed alarmingly and quickly. However, the passing of authority from Cipac to Moteuczoma through the agency of the scribes discloses an intersubjective futurity. Through a balancing effect beyond what the Mexica nobility were able to accomplish, the scribes offered a retelling of events and anticipated a future order in narratives that ran counter to Spanish imperial goals. One could consider this narration merely cathartic, a "teotl ex machina" technique of poetic justice. However, the sequence is more than an a posteriori narrativization. In fact, the standing of key members of the Moteuczoma royal house at the time of the writing of the annals had already proven that the name had a future. As María Elena Martínez (2008, 111) has observed,

> Among the main beneficiaries of the Crown's policies toward Native nobles were the descendants of the Mexica's last supreme ruler (*huey tlatoani*), Motecuhzoma II Xocoyotl ("Moctezuma"), many of whom married Spaniards and moved to the Iberian Peninsula. Throughout the colonial period and as late as the twentieth century, members of this royal lineage in Spain received the titles of count, viscount, duke, and marquis, along with rights to wear royal insignia, bear arms, hold ceremonial acts proper to their rank, collect annual pensions, [and] enjoy tax exemptions.[5]

The last of these privileges provides some vindication of Mexica nobles and the scribes' tribute reduction efforts. Benefits to the house of Moteuczoma continued. Donald Chipman (2005, xiii–xiv) recalls that the Mexican government paid an annual subsidy to the descendants of the Moteuczoma rulers into the 1930s. Other versions of Moteuczoma's return as an immortal, powerful, and sublimated version of his former self have existed since colonial times and across regions of Mexico.[6] Even if Mexicas alive at the time did not live to see Moteuczoma return, they anticipated what eventually did happen: the Spanish regime's departure from Mexico.

The section of the *Codex Chimalpahin* on Mexica history known as the *Crónica mexicayotl* touches an ongoing area of concern, that of Indigenous education in Mexico (see chapter 4). Today, the number of monolingual Nahuas steadily declines. Although interest in the revitalization of language and culture surges, it has not happened at a rate fast enough to offset the overall fading of spoken Nahuatl in Mexico relative to two or three generations ago (Olko and Sullivan 2016, 160). On the other hand, online initiatives, notably the Instituto de Docencia e Investigaciones Etnológicas de Zacatecas (IDIEZ), promote linguistic and cultural growth. In addition to offering language studies, IDIEZ provides on-location cultural immersion and makes the academic publications by its network of Nahua scholars and writers available free of charge. Other online initiatives encourage Nahuatl study, including the partnership between Nahuatl instructors in Río Balsas, Guerrero, and the Anahualcalmecac International College Preparatory Academy in Los Angeles. At that unique school, students learn Nahuatl through online and in-person modalities. Internet-based initiatives allow descendants of the Nahuas and of other Indigenous groups to build identities and consider how language can enliven their futures.

Besides serving as a means to strengthen educational initiatives in the language that are thriving today, the *Crónica mexicayotl* has proven foundational for transnational movements in the Uto-Aztecan language and cultural region. In 1969, the Movimiento Estudiantil Chicano de Aztlán (M.E.Ch.A.), in its well-known "Plan espiritual de Aztlán," took its inspiration in part from the origin account of the emergence of the Mexica from Chicomoztoc in Aztlan in the *Crónica mexicayotl*. The "Plan espiritual" has a noteworthy educational component in its calls for bilingual education and for annual walkouts on September 16, Mexican Independence Day.[7] In the midst of these developments, Chimalpahin's work has received increasing attention due to studies by Susan Schroeder (2007) as well as translations of his histories into English by Susan Schroeder and Arthur J. O. Anderson (*Codex Chimalpahin*, 1997) and into Spanish by Rafael Tena (*Las ocho relaciones*, 1998). These efforts of scholars to make the writings of this Nahua chronicler more accessible still offer a rich, broad, and larely untapped resource for strengthening Indigenous identities.

Even within the context of the *Crónica mexicayotl*, texts were not the only sites of knowledge construction as Nahuas approached the future on the urbanized islands of Lake Texcoco. Despite pressures from taxation and losses from epidemics, Nahuas participated in the colonial economy, acquiring goods and land, and even funding their own building projects. The Nahua community contributed to the reconstruction of the Tecpan of Tlatelolco. The Biblioteca Nacional de Antropología e Historia (BNAH) holds a Spanish translation of the *Códice del Tec-*

pan de Santiago de Tlatelolco (BNAH GO, vol. 12, Annexo "B," FF 1113). According to the document, the residents of the altepetl of Tlatelolco undertook that project in the 1570s with 1,600 silver *reales* they claimed belonged to the emperor Cuauhtemoc himself.[8] The construction of the Tecpan took place from 1576 to 1581 and included nineteen chambers for receiving diplomats and public figures, a tribunal, and two jails: one for men and one for women. The Tecpan stood near the place where Hernán Cortés took Cuauhtemoc prisoner, which was also the ruler's alma mater, the calmecac of Tlatelolco (Baudot 1997, 290; Serna Arnaiz and Castany Prado 2014, 381). The Franciscans would later build a church and the Colegio de la Santa Cruz on that same site. Over the centuries, architectural changes have occurred in Tlatelolco. Today stones from the rebuilt Tecpan remain in the building now belonging to the Secretaría de Relaciones Exteriores, which stands on the same site as the Colegio de la Santa Cruz, the surrender of Cuauhtemoc, and the calmecac of Tlatelolco before (see figure 25). A five-minute walk to the south, the Tecpan is open to visitors as a museum. That such a construction project could begin in the last decades of the sixteenth century illustrates the

FIGURE 25 East side of the Secretaría de Relaciones Exteriores, with a reconstruction of the façade of the Tecpan of Tlatelolco, built with stones from the 1576–1581 project. Author's photo, 2021.

rights of Indigenous nobles under the "*república de indios*" and their skill in making the most of those rights.⁹ I speculate that in this space, Nahuas conversed on political, economic, religious, and cultural topics that mattered to them. By rebuilding the Tecpan, they rebuilt a functional space for discussing their futurities.

The memories Chimalpahin and Tezozomoc preserved also drew on collective reflections over nearly a century of Spanish occupation. My focus on instances in which representations of time and change became problematic for Nahuas captures ways in which they used tools of persuasion to convince readers that the stories of the ancestors deserved retelling and would continue to matter in times to come. What the two produced together, as Camilla Townsend (2019, 204) has noted, "contrary to all expectations, would defiantly remain as part of the world of the Fifth Sun for as long as it might last." Time continued into what Matthew Restall and Kris Lane (2012, 67) have called the "colonial middle" or the "Baroque," explaining that the "Spanish created a string of hierarchical, urban, Catholic societies. Radiating out from colonial cities was a more populous rural, village-oriented world of Indigenous tribute-payers, enslaved African plantation workers, and mine laborers of varying heritage." The overarching economic projects of the Spanish empire turned much of their attention to mining. Silver extracted from mines in Peru and Mexico formed the economic mainstay of Spain's empire (O'Hara 2018, 86–87). Reducing political friction between Indigenous communities was to Spain's advantage. Thus, Native governments in Tlatelolco, Tenochtitlan, and towns throughout the Valley of Mexico were able to continue with a "legal culture, which by the mid-seventeenth century, Native peoples had helped to create" (Connell 2011, 186). Given the silver output of the viceroyalties of Peru and New Spain together with the geographic isolation of many populations, the "colonial middle" provided several generations of legal protections. Under these conditions, Chimalpahin and Tezozomoc articulated their futurity of education.

HORIZONS TO COME

What, then, of things to come for Nahua futurities as an analytical concept? Studying Nahuas' goals and expectations opens paths for further research. Opportunities to apply Nahua futurities and the Nahua tools of persuasion exist with other texts from the colonial period and subsequent years. Texts concerned with preserving the territorial integrity of Nahua communities, notably the *Títulos primordiales* and the responses to questionnaires in the *Relaciones geográficas*, required persuasion and the involvement of multiple communities to write. Both the *Títulos primordiales* and the *Relaciones geográficas* aimed to preserve access to land and resources (Lockhart 1992, 410–17; Mundy 1996). By approaching these texts with Nahua futurities and the Nahua tools of persuasion, we can learn which techniques of communication and organization proved the most effective for promoting community resilience. As related to the area of Nahua critiques of Christianity, Francisco Tenamaztle, a Chichimeca who expressed open disdain toward Spanish invaders and their religion, fought for his own vision of the future (Carrillo Cázares 2000, 163–93). Tenamaztle wrote letters to Phillip II that provide an opportunity for examining his approaches to the days to come. Other Nahuatl alphabetic texts from the sixteenth and seventeenth centuries also invite investigation into their representations of the future, including the *Anales de Tecamachalco* (1398–1590), the *Anales de Tlatelolco* (1540s), and the chronicles of Juan Buenaventura de Zapata y Mendoza in Tlaxcala (1692). Similarly, pictorials including the *Lienzo de Tlaxcala* (1552) and the *Codex Mexicanus* (1580s) provide examples of representations of Nahua futurities, shedding light on the aims and expectations of the communities that generated them.

This study brings to light myriad ways in which Nahua narratives disclose their futurities. If that was true in the sixteenth century, there is no reason to suppose it has not been the case ever since. Futurity is an abiding concern in Indigenous texts from Nahua communities compiled in the nineteenth, twentieth, and twenty-first centuries. Anthropologist Franz Boas collected Nahuatl stories from Milpa Alta (Boas and Arreola 1920; Boas and Haeberlin 1924), south of Mexico City, that open views onto how Nahuas envisioned days to come during the turbulent years of the Porfirio Díaz dictatorship and the revolution. Further stories and biographical narratives come from Milpa Alta through the stories of doña Luz Jiménez in her collection *Life and Death in Milpa Alta* (1972) and *Los cuentos en nahuatl de doña Luz Jiménez* (1979). These examples will reward future research with insight into Nahua futurities informed by doña Luz's perspective as an Indigenous artist, entrepreneur, and collaborator with the muralista movement of the early twentieth century. In addition, contemporary texts by Nahua authors offer a range of opportunities for understanding how writers today envision paths forward. One collection of these authors is the Totlahtol Series, published by IDIEZ and the University of Warsaw. A number of reference tools on Huastecan Nahuatl; stories from communities in Chicontepec, Veracruz; poetry; and children's literature by Nahua writers in the Totlahtol Series work to build a library of meaningful content for linguistic revitalization (Olko and Sullivan 2016, 172). These examples place Native voices at the center of language revitalization efforts. Futurities in these texts also allow me and other non-Indigenous scholars to place ourselves as students who can learn from Nahua scholars and writers today.

Bringing the texts of this study together as I have carries implications, some of which are not as desirable but which I must recognize. Organizing texts around a common thread runs the risk of canon-making, which would do justice neither to the Nahuas who wrote the material nor to their descendants. While I focused on texts with the futurities I have identified, it is my hope that Indigenous scholars will open and critique this approach further and provide interpretations non-Indigenous readers, including me, will miss. Thus, it is not my intention to present a group of writings that would typify or foreclose the expansion of Nahua futurities as an analytical approach. On the other hand, bringing these texts together has brought attention to Indigenous vantage points regarding their textual production in the colonial period. In so doing, I reference James Lockhart's (1992, 7, 375) call to the New Philology, which centers on studying all textual production in Nahuatl, even those modes that do not follow conventional Western ideas of the literary. By bringing together these texts, I have emphasized their persuasive content and the aspirations that those who wrote them communicate.

Just as the tepahtihquetl engages in the healing futurities of making communities and their members whole, Nahua scholars contribute their knowledge(s) and talents to academia. At the time I write, great opportunity exists for Nahua scholars to engage textual futurity on a complex level. Regarding knowledge(s) outside the purview of Western researchers, Laura Harjo (2021, 615) has commented, "while there is research on Indigenous planning and futurity, there is even less written by Indigenous researchers in the planning field; this is imperative, because only an Indigenous researcher can know and feel felt knowledge. [Otherwise, it] remains an outsider-looking-in point of view, narrating Indigenous existence to Indigenous communities." Despite the many obstacles arrayed against them, more Nahuas are accessing higher education and achieving important goals for advancing Indigenous knowledge(s) in academia at the time of this publication. Sabina Cruz de la Cruz holds an MA, teaches Nahuatl at IDIEZ as well as for universities in the United States, and participates in academic conferences on Indigenous healing practices. Victoriano de la Cruz Cruz is the subdirector of research of the Academia Veracruzana de las Lenguas Indígenas, with doctoral work in progress at the University of Warsaw. Abelardo de la Cruz de la Cruz holds his PhD in anthropology from SUNY, Albany, and is currently an assistant professor of religious studies at the University of North Carolina at Chapel Hill. His publications address various aspects of contemporary Nahua rituals, including *el costumbre*, a system of complex, evolving Nahua beliefs and rituals that exists alongside of and in many admixtures with Catholicism in Chicontepec (A. Cruz de la Cruz 2017, 270). Eduardo de la Cruz Cruz also continues his doctoral studies with the University of Warsaw. As director of IDIEZ, Eduardo is an assistant professor of instruction in Nahuatl at the University of Texas at Austin. Their scholarship provides a much-needed and refreshing emic perspective. The opening of their valuable lines of inquiry no doubt will add voluminous insights regarding Nahua views of the future.

During research for this study, I had the honor to visit Eduardo de la Cruz Cruz at IDIEZ in Zacatecas. Our conversation topic was chicahualiztli, a complex term regarding the gathering of strength, and the center of his dissertation research at the University of Warsaw. Eduardo shared with me how maintaining a physical connection between identity and place has helped Nahuas keep their balance. Imbalances in one's life in the present indicate

> un desequilibrio en la vida de la persona en su vida futura, y eso tiene que ver mucho con el cordón umbilical que es el chicahualiztli que se siembra en el suelo. Pero las parteras, sabias, pero que no hacen bien su trabajo la tira, la guarda y se pierde. Entonces hay una creencia local nahua en Chicontepec que dice si tu cordón umbilical se enterró cerca de la casa,

significa—es una creencia de los abuelos—significa que regresarás frecuentemente a casa. O sea, que tú dejastes algo tuyo en el lugar y ese algo tuyo te pide que regreses porque recuerdes. Pero, si esa parte del cordón umbilical no fue enterrado esa persona se pierde. ¿Cómo? Se olvida de dónde es, explora otros horizontes y jamás quiere volver a sus raíces. (Eduardo de la Cruz Cruz, personal communication, May 20, 2021)

[an imbalance in the life of the person in their future life, and that has a lot to do with the umbilical cord, which is the chicahualiztli that is sown in the ground. But midwives, yes *wise*, but who don't do their job well, throw it away; maybe they save it, and then it gets lost. So, there is a local Nahua belief in Chicontepec that says that if your umbilical cord was buried near the house, that means—it's a belief of our elders—that you will come back home often. That is, you left something of yours in that place and that something of yours calls to you and asks you to return, for the sake of its memory. But, if that part of the umbilical cord was not buried, that person is lost. How? By forgetting where he or she is from, exploring other horizons, and never wanting to return to their roots.]

Since one comes from the earth and is going to the earth, there is no need to stray far from one's place of birth. The roots of place and traditional agriculture have marked Eduardo's research on behalf of Chicontepec. The publication of his master's thesis, "Cenyahtoc cintli tonacayo: Huahcapatl huan tlen naman" (2017), with the University of Warsaw amasses knowledge(s) from colonial-era Nahua writings and contemporary practices regarding how his people have grown corn, not with a mentality of scarcity but with one of abundance, supporting a future imaginary of planting and tending the milpas of their communities.

As I close, I reflect that some of the strongest potential I see for Nahua futurities lies in their applications for teaching Nahua texts. The approach makes the Nahuatl word—their tlatolli, which encompasses the language but also all discourses, knowledge(s), advice, and aspirations—central to course content. Consequently, the approach breaks out of the conventional patterns of identifying Nahua elements in song-poems, architecture, narratives, and other objects, consumable within a Eurocentric, cultural studies paradigm. Instead, instructors can give evidence of Native writers' proposals for the best kind of living and with a sense of immediacy that comes with the lived anticipations and expectations of Nahua communities.

    The examples I have studied here are only a start. Students can learn that pictorials like the *Lienzo de Quauhquechollan* and the *Tira de Tepechpan* do not preserve images of a frozen past. They also convey the expectations and plans of their designers. Similarly, the *Florentine Codex* does not simply represent Sahagún's attempts to understand the Nahuas or their incidental expression of their culture. It also represents a compendium of information available to help future generations of Natives maintain their bodily and cosmic well-being. The *Anales de Juan Bautista*, a complex record of tribute collection and contestation, also reveals future plans for Nahua ritual and political engagements that empowers despite pressures from the Spanish, based on the abiding presence of the ancestors and their wisdom. The *Crónica mexicayotl*, although recognizing the impossibility of returning to Mexica hegemony in the city, provides a portable, alphabetic version of traditional knowledge, meant to inform future generations of obstacles their ancestors overcame. Likewise, classes in history, literature, languages, and anthropology can approach the Nahuatl texts I have suggested and others with the same understanding of their forward-looking elements as components of a vision of living well, of *cualli nehnemi*. From Nahua approaches to "extending the path" (Maffie 2011, 75), we can enter more deeply into our analysis of Nahua texts and make our teaching more holistic, accurate, and culturally relevant. As long as Nahuas continue to speak, write, and work their ways forward, fellow Nahuas, members of other Indigenous communities, and non-Indigenous students will learn from one of the hemisphere's most vibrant, resilient intellectual traditions that continues to develop. In his time, Fernando Alvarado Tezozomoc clearly stated his purpose regarding the future of his ancestors' paintings, histories, and memories: "titetlapallohuan yn titechecohan" (we will go on telling of them, we will go on celebrating them [*CC*, 18v]). Given the words of Tezozomoc, Chimalpahin, the Nahua healers, and the hundreds of other voices that inhabit the texts of this study and those yet to be studied, will we listen?

NOTES

INTRODUCTION

1. Traditional Nahua settlements required water and an elevated ritual center. The basic political and territorial unit of the altepetl linked vivifying water (*atl-*) and a local hill (*tepetl*) or high place (García Chávez 2007, par. 6; Lockhart 1992, 14–58). See Marcelo Ramírez Ruiz and Federico Fernández Christlieb's review of the historical development of the altepetl (2006).
2. Xavier Noguez and Fernando Horcasitas (1978, 1:62) suggest that the three animals represent a deity specific to Tepechpan. I would suggest, per findings of Guilhem Olivier (2003, 45–84), that the animals represent three manifestations of Tezcatlipoca: Quetzalcoatl (snake), Itzpapalotl (butterfly/obsidian knife), and Huitzilopochtli ("bird"/eagle).
3. Jerome Offner pointed out to me that the glyphs on the page do not agree with Lori Boornazian Diel's (2008, 36–37) reading. The heart sacrifice on the lower register occurred in Colhuacan rather than Tenochtitlan (Offner, personal communication, October 15, 2022).
4. The *Matrícula de tributos* (1520–30) and the *Codex Mendoza* (ca. 1541) communicate a Mexica perspective of imperial control from Zacatlan in the north to Soconusco in the south.
5. Stephanie Wood (2003) has argued that Nahuas interpreted the invasion as an event manageable within their worldview. My study shows that they did more than interpret the recent past: they used texts to represent the future and propose how to act in it.
6. I draw on Laura Harjo's (2019, 37, 46) concept of the "tools of Mvskoke [Creek] futurity," which she has applied in her community organizing and

cultural reflections. Regarding the period this study covers, Diel (2008, 7) has also used the phrase "tools of persuasion" to describe how the leaders of Tepechpan convinced their town to set economic and political goals.

7. In this study I default to the ACK orthography, named after Richard Andrews, Joe Campbell, and Frances Karttunen. The ACK orthography draws on conventions that sixteenth-century friar-grammarians used and is the basis for the NEH-funded Online Nahuatl Dictionary at the University of Oregon (https://nahuatl.wired-humanities.org/) as well as Karttunen's 1992 *Analytical Dictionary of Nahuatl*. At the same time, I recognize that Nahuatl orthography is a complex topic and that many community-specific variations exist from colonial times to the present. Thus, in this study I also respect and do not alter Nahuatl spellings as they appear in the original sources I quote. It is also important to note that the use of written accent marks (diacritics) continues as a widespread misunderstanding about the Nahuatl language. While diacritics appear in some well-known materials— including Adrián León's 1949 Nahuatl-Spanish bilingual edition of the *Crónica mexicayotl*, discussed in chapter 4—most contemporary scholars do not use them. Using accent marks in such a manner is a direct application of the rules of Spanish orthography. However, Nahuatl's inherent pronunciation naturally places the emphasis on the penultimate syllable with very few exceptions, which makes diacritics unnecessary. For a concise yet thorough introduction to orthographic systems for classical and modern Nahuatl, see Hansen (2016).

8. Michel Launey (2004) has discussed the syntactic flexibility of Nahuatl that allows many parts of speech to function as predicates, depending on the orientation of a phrase. Ben Leeming (2015) has explained hyper-trophism, the tendency of written Nahuatl in the sixteenth century to agglomerate multiple terms and meanings in compound words. Syntactic parallels in Nahuatl appear often with the Spanish names *difrasismos* or *bifrasismos*, and with reference to Mesoamerican languages broadly as *diphrastic kennings*. These parallel structures communicate metaphors, expanded meanings, or complex concepts. On syntactic parallels in Nahuatl and Otomi, see Wright Carr (2011).

9. Joshua Lund (2012, ix–xx) reviews the concept of mestizo in the nineteenth and twentieth centuries. He describes social exclusion resulting from Porfirio Díaz's state-sponsored image of the stoic and loyal mestizo citizen and the transcendentalism associated with the term in Vasconcelos (1925 [2017]).

10. For more on walking as a balancing action with the goal of moving down a path, see Maffie (2012, 10). Among contemporary Nahuas in the Huasteca region, responsibility to maintain reciprocity with the cosmos is collective (Sandstrom 1991, 320–22). *Cualli nehnemi* compares favorably with "not walking well," *ahmo cualli nehnemi* (Knab 2004, 15, 32).

11. Interspersed between the main chapters of McDonough's *The Learned Ones* (2016), contemporary Nahua writers and Native-speaker language instructors provide reflections on the abiding value of their language and culture. Refugio Nava Nava, Victoriano de la Cruz Cruz, and Sabina Cruz de la Cruz each contributed to the volume (McDonough 2016, 30). She continues to highlight continuities and perennial concerns of Nahua scientists past and present in Nahua science, featuring the experiments of Abraham de la Cruz Martínez, *tlayehycolquetl* (scientist, physicist); the painting of Norma Martínez; and the weaving of the Grupo Contraviento Atoltecayotl. In addition, the book features Baruc Martínez Díaz, *ixtlamatiquetl/tlacuilo* (historian/writer) and *chinampanecatl* (chinampa farmer), and Gustavo Zapoteco Sideño, *cuicajpike/tlacuilo* (poet/writer).
12. Yannakakis (2008, 5–11) examines Native intermediaries in colonial Oaxaca: Doña Marina, renowned interpreter who assisted Hernán Cortés and his Tlaxcalteca allies in their invasion of Tenochtitlan (1520–21); and Gaspar Antonio Chi, a Yucatec Maya noble who interpreted for Diego de Landa and later for Landa's rival Francisco de Toral. Chi also mediated between Spanish and Mayan interests while governor of the Mani province.
13. On future making, see O'Hara (2018, 1–17). One of his main points is that constructing the future often meant drawing on older knowledge. See Villella (2016, 1–28) for an overview of that complex identity construction.
14. A word on nomenclature: when possible, I refer to Nahua deities by their proper names (Tezcatlipoca, Huitzilopochtli, Quetzalcoatl, Ehecatl, etc.). In broader references, I primarily use the terms *deity* and *more-than-human* (Harjo's term) to refer to numens specific to an altepetl. *God* in upper case refers to the "Abrahamic God" (Bassett's term) of Western monotheism. Lower-case *god* refers to a numen among a multiplicity of more-than-human beings. In quotations of secondary sources, I leave the original cases for "god" and "God."
15. See the book's final chapter, in which Bassett (2015, 192–201) summarizes how the people build gods and the gods in turn build them up.
16. See also Enrique Florescano's (1994, 100–104) description of the crisis and uncertainties the Spanish destruction of Nahua institutions caused in the early sixteenth century.
17. For another analytical precedent for studying discourses of futurity as key aspects of colonial entanglements, see International Research Training Group, "Temporalities of Future in Latin America: Dynamics of Aspiration and Anticipation," a collaboration that began in 2020 between the Institute for Latin American Studies at Freie Universität Berlin, the Colegio de México, the Universidad Nacional Autónoma de México, the Centro de Investigaciones y Estudios Superiores en Antropología Social, and other German universities (https://www.lai.fu-berlin.de/en/temporalities-of-future/index.html).

18. See Offner's (2014) examination of the Mexica-centric scholarship of the mid-twentieth century as part of the national identity-building efforts of the Partido Revolucionario Institucional (PRI, Institutional Revolutionary Party).
19. All references to pages in the *Florentine Codex* (Sahagún 1578) in this study follow this format: *FC*, Book number, folio number. I have used the digitalized version of the *Florentine Codex*, available through the Library of Congress, https://www.loc.gov/item/2021667837/. Translations by Dibble and Anderson (Sahagún [1578] 1959–82) are given as volume: page.
20. Scholars have observed parallels between the xiuhpohualli and postconquest annals genre (Lockhart 1992, 378–80; Reyes García 2001, 24). See Camilla Townsend's (2009, 638) observations on how the compiler of the *Codex Aubin* (ca. 1578) integrated the Mexica and Western calendars to show the "ancientness and durability" of Tenochtitlan. Anthony Aveni and Gordon Brotherston (1983, 199–203) have commented on how multiple calendars in the *Codex Mexicanus* (ca. 1584) undermine Spanish imperial claims to universal history.
21. Every fifty-two years, the tonalpohualli and the 365-day xiuhpohualli calendars overlapped, which brought about two observances: the xiuhmolpilli tying of the year bundle and the initiation of another fifty-two-year cycle with the New Fire ceremony (Soustelle [1970] 2002, xiii–xv, 108–14; Aguilar-Moreno 2007, 89).
22. While the tonalli is the locus of identity and contains an individual's particular characteristics, it does not survive the death of the body and is not the equivalent of a "soul" (McKeever Furst [1995] 1997, 79; D. Carrasco 2013, 203). Chapter 2 gives an overview of how Nahuas viewed the relationship between the tonalli and the cosmos.
23. As discussed in chapters 3 and 4, the *Anales de Juan Bautista* and the *Crónica mexicayotl* use the Julian and Mexica calendars. See the analysis of Gordon Brotherston (2008, 25–35) as well as Diel's (2018) detailed study of the *Codex Mexicanus*, in which Native writers identified parallels between the Julian calendar, the tonalpohualli, and the European zodiac.
24. Lockhart (1992, 393–94) preferred the term *songs* due to the different conventions they obey as compared to Western poetry. Jongsoo Lee (2008, 153, 164, 167) has translated the genre more literally as "flowers/songs." He followed Ángel María Garibay's ([1940] 2007, 116) rendition of the term as *flor y canto*. I use the terms *songs* and *song-poems* interchangeably.
25. The *Codex Telleriano-Remensis*, for example, shows a female tlacuilo (f. 30r; Quiñones Keber 1995, 63; Rabasa 2011, 3).
26. Colonial Nahua sources recommend steady, dependable behavior for humans on the path above the erratic ways of the deer and the rabbit who leave the path (L. Burkhart 1986, 107–10). In *The Slippery Earth*, Louise

Burkhart (1989, 168) explains the "ethos of moderation," central to Nahua morality (see also McDonough 2024, 68–69).

27. Testimonies Diego Durán (1967, 188–89) collected reflect the link between the sun and ollin motion. Paper banners spattered with rubber tree sap became offerings to Nahua Ollin, "Four Movement" (i.e., the sun). The Mesoamerican ball game had such ritual importance that the ball itself became an avatar of the sun crossing the sky daily and bringing forth maize from the earth (Baudez 1984, 151)

28. The *Annals of Cuauhtitlan* and the *Legend of the Five Suns* foretell the destruction of the Fifth Age as a cataclysmic earthquake, eliminating all solar motion. With hindsight, other approaches have emerged. For example, Nahua scholars Victoriano de la Cruz Cruz and Refugio Nava Nava suggested at the 2012 Meeting of the Northeastern Group of Nahuatl Studies that we may be living under the Sixth Sun (C. Townsend 2019, 208, 285n6).

29. Miguel León-Portilla (1992) first theorized *nepantlismo* as a category for cultural phenomena that emerged in a middle ground between Europe and Amerindian cultures. León-Portilla's term influenced the work of Walter Mignolo (1995) and Gloria Anzaldúa (1999). Mignolo, for a time, enshrined the concept in the cultural studies journal *Nepantla*, which ran from 2000 to 2003. For more on the development of this concept, see L. Burkhart (2017).

30. See Bassett's (2015, 43–60) excellent review of scholarly interpretations of the term *teotl*. She points out that Anderson and Dibble's translation of the *Florentine Codex* calls *teotl* and its various attestations "gods," while León-Portilla (1992, 315) expresses his apprehension with quotation marks ("*dios*") on such an easy equivalence. Bassett points out that one-to-one translations of this kind may also invoke the "Abrahamic God," for which reason various scholars opt for pantheistic interpretations of *teotl*, distanced from Western metaphysical dualism. For more regarding pantheism as the underlying Nahua conceptualization of the sacred, see Hvidtfeldt (1958, 19), Read (1994, 45), López Austin (1997, 7), and Maffie (2007, 16). The recurrence of the term *teotl* as a phoneme in many Nahuatl words likely caught the attention of Catholic priests, who sought to identify and eradicate ancient beliefs (McDonough 2024, 37).

31. Hvidtfeldt's (1958) application of Polynesian mana to Mesoamerica comes from his dissertation.

32. Kalyuta (n.d.) explains that Hvidtfeldt drew from the *Florentine Codex* (Book 2, "The Ceremonies"), the *Primeros memoriales*, the *Anales de Cuauhtitlan*, and Alonso Molina's *Vocabulario en lengua castellana y mexicana*. She notes that these sources form a small foundation for extrapolating cosmological concepts. However, Hvidtfeldt's work has influenced numerous scholars, including Richard Townsend (1979), Jorge Klor de Alva (1979), Elizabeth Boone (1989), and James Maffie (2014), to name a few.

33. See Bassett's (2015, 114–27) explanation of these characteristics, which she synthesizes from the *Florentine Codex*, the writings of Diego Durán, and other colonial ecclesiastical chroniclers, who, logically, focused their attention on Nahua ritual practices.
34. Latour's *On the Modern Cult of the Factish Gods* (2010, 16) examines the ironies of European accusations against religious practices in other continents from the early modern period to the present. He argues that deity representations as well as modern science and innovation do not eliminate earlier beliefs but merely displace them.
35. The eagle and the hummingbird ("bird," per Diel 2008) are common avatars for the Mexica's main deity, Huitzilopochtli (López Hernández 2015).
36. McDonough (2024) draws on explanations by Nahua anthropologist Abelardo de la Cruz (2017, 272): "a Nahua person is just a single piece of the Nahua universe," thus humans and all matter form part of the same monistic conceptualization.
37. Bassett (2015, 132–33) has added the nonspecific personal possessive prefix *te-* (someone), since anything attached to a body is possessed in Nahuatl. On the deity Xipe Totec and the beliefs Mexicas associated with wearing the flayed skin of a sacrificed victim, see Heyden (2001).
38. On the importance of deity embodiment in these bundles, see Bassett's (2015, 162–91) overview of the tlaquimilolli and Guilhem Olivier's (2003, 73–78) overview of the tlaquimilolli of Tezcatlipoca and of Huitzilopochtli.
39. My thanks go to Joe Campbell and James Maffie for providing me access to these findings (Maffie, personal communication, August 31, 2021).
40. See Susan Schroeder's (2016) thorough review on this pivotal figure.
41. Viviana Díaz Balsera (2018) compares the observations of Keith Thomas (1971, 305–22), an English historian, with those of Jacinto de la Serna (1892, 304), an idolatry extirpator in Mexico. For the prevalence of local beliefs and cosmologies in early modern Europe, see Ginzburg (1980).
42. On theological, astrological, and other configurations of time in medieval Europe, see Heiduk, Herbers, and Lehner (2021).
43. Western linear time accompanied Catholic moral doctrine, which emphasized free will, moral obligation, and future judgment (Maher 1909).
44. For an explanation of the central ideological aspects of colonialism and their legacies, see Quijano (2008).
45. *Inter caetera* (1493) designated regions where Spain and Portugal could evangelize and trade. *Regimini Ecclesiae Universale* (1508) allowed the Spanish Crown to appoint clergy. Relevant to Mexico are *Exigit sinceras devotionis affectus* (1478), which gave the Spanish monarchs control of the Inquisition in their territories, and *Eximiae devotionis affectus* (1510), which authorized royal agents to collect tithes to fund evangelization activities, a system later called the Patronato Real. See commentaries by John Schwaller (2011, 46–48) and Enrique Dussel (1981, 38–40).

46. See Florescano's (1992, 309–29) framing of the theological underpinnings of conquest and colonization. On Franciscan polemics surrounding de Fiore's theology, see Phelan (1956, 44–58); see Delno West (1989, 311–13) for an overview of the pamphlet polemics over millenarianism in Franciscan houses in Spain and Italy. Frank Graziano (1999, 16–52) also provides a useful overview of millenarianism in early modern Iberia.
47. Kris Lane (2019, 18, 138–139, 151) discusses the "myth of Potosí's inexhaustibility," which heightened Spain's expectations of future wealth and extraction of the mine's ore.
48. See also chapter 2 of Benedict Anderson's *Imagined Communities* (2016) for the impact of Benjamin's description of time on the development of the secular nation-state. Later Dutch, French, and especially English colonialism gravitated toward linear time and the ethos of linear progress as the very measure of economic, technological, and managerial attainment. This northern European emphasis, which Mignolo (2008, 219) has termed "the second modernity," advances these colonizing nations' self-proclaimed imperatives to put in place around the world European systems for the material and moral improvement of humanity.
49. This spelling of the ruler's name corresponds more closely to its older pronunciation and is the default form I use. Domingo Chimalpahin used the spelling "Moteucçoma" in the *Crónica mexicayotl*, and in the *Florentine Codex* the similar "Motecuhzoma" appears. Lockhart (1993, 70–80, 94–96) also examines orthographic variations of the tlatoani's name. In Hernán Cortés's "Fourth Letter to Carlos V," he at first attempted to reproduce the Nahuatl pronunciation in his spelling but gradually shifted to the Hispanicized "Montezuma" by the letter's close. This process is recognizable in the 1526 copy of the letter held in the Newberry Library in Chicago.

CHAPTER 1

1. Today Hauquechula stands on the same site, southwest of Atlixco in the state of Puebla. In 1520, more than 100,000 people lived in Quauhquechollan, a key trading post en route to the isthmus of Tehuantepec and Guatemala.
2. In Cortés's account of the battle, he helped the Quauhquecholteca oust the Mexica from their town while he gained information on the state of affairs in Tenochtitlan (H. Cortés 1993, 91–92).
3. The Indigenous conqueror, the phenomenon central to new conquest scholarship, receives extensive treatment in Matthew and Oudijk (2007) and Restall and Asselbergs (2007). Matthew Restall (2012) provides an overview of this approach, emphasizing contributions of James Lockhart's (1992) New Philology and perspectives of Natives who participated in Spanish conquests.

4. On benefits Tlaxcala gained via alliance with the Spanish, see Gibson (1952, 158–89).
5. Universidad Francisco Marroquín has made a full-color copy of the lienzo's restoration available. See "Vea el lienzo," Quauhquechollan: El lienzo de la conquista, accessed August 3, 2022, https://lienzo.ufm.edu/vea-lienzo/vea-el-lienzo/.
6. For a full-color copy of the *Tira de Tepechpan*, see the website of the Bibliotheque Nationale de France, Fonds Mexicain 13–14, https://archivesetmanuscrits.bnf.fr/ark:/12148/cc717546.
7. In the *Tira de Tepechpan* each of the four signs—Rabbit (*tochtli*), Reed (*acatl*), Flint (*tecpatl*), and Council House (*tecpan*)—carries a number, 1–13, and every fourth cycle culminates in a fifty-two-year bundle (*tlaquimilpilli*) (Diel 2008, 14).
8. Regarding strategic Nahua interpretations of the past, see also Leibsohn (2009, 21–22) and Boone (2008, 19–27).
9. Whereas early investigators assumed the lienzo focused on Mexico (Paso y Troncoso 1892–93; Noguez 1978), Asselbergs's (2008) study shows that most of its depictions refer to Guatemala (Lovell 2019, 419). Francisco de Paso y Troncoso (1892–93) wrote a description of the lienzo in 1893 assuming the map focuses on areas near Huaquechula, Puebla. Other influential scholars followed his lead (Glass 1964, 90; Glass and Robertson 1975, 116).
10. Nigel Davies (1987, 183) has observed that the primary aim in battle was to destroy the main temple (*teocalli*), "which amounted to final defeat." For this reason, the *Codex Mendoza* dedicates 7.5 of its 72 folios to recounting Mexica conquests through paintings of the destruction of many a teocalli throughout the central highlands. For a study of perspectives from outside Tenochtitlan of the ritual aspects of war, see J. Gillespie (2004, 1–20, 59); see also Lockhart (1992, 203).
11. Optimism gave way to disillusionment. After the landslide destroyed Santiago de Almolonga and a Spanish and Nahua settlement, the latter complained of mistreatment. During archival research, Asselbergs found a letter from Natives to Charles V explaining how the Alvarado brothers forced them to leave their lands, houses, and relatives in Central Mexico. They fought unpaid and then faced enslavement when the Spanish reneged on their earlier pledges of compensation (Asselbergs 2008, 116, citing AGI Guatemala 52, "Indios de Tlaxcala y México a Carlos V," March 15, 1547).
12. I draw on the Kānaka Maoli concept of *Kahiki*, a place of the ancestors, which also represents a future that colonizers do not control (Case 2021, 109).
13. For example, in the early days under the Spanish, local rulers' relative wealth compared to surrounding towns allowed them to commandeer local records for their own aims. On this effect in the altepetl of Texcoco, see Offner (2021, 484).

14. On the advantages of cabecera status, see Gibson (1964, 34) and Menegus (2019). For a case study of the incorporation of Cholula as a cabecera, see Adams (2005).
15. Asselbergs (2008, 21–33) explains her use of narratology in tandem with empirical approaches.
16. Asselbergs draws on Bal (2004) and Prince (2003).
17. Diel (2008) relies on Barthes's (1977, 161) idea of the *intertext*, that each text is embedded in a larger network of discourses and references. Intertexts of the *Tira de Tepechpan* come from other Native texts from the time period, Nahua iconography across regions, archaeological data, and legal documents relating to land tenure and the use of natural resources.
18. Bassett (2015, 78–87) reviews studies of Nahua iconography from the nineteenth century.
19. As Asselbergs (2008, 209) comments on the *Lienzo de Quauhquechollan*, "each person represented in the lienzo must have featured in oral traditions that once accompanied the manuscript, and each must have had his or her own story."
20. Regarding comparisons by historical entities as a humanities research methodology, see Rohland and Kramer (2021).
21. Asselbergs (2008, 218) speculates that up to one-third of the original map is missing, covering modern Antigua, Guatemala City, and perhaps Honduras. As a narrative map the lienzo is comparable to the postinvasion *Codex Xolotl* from the Acolhuacan region (Offner 2014, 52–53).
22. Three other documents come from Quauhquechollan in the sixteenth century: the *Lámina de la genenealogía de Quauhquechollan-Macuilxochitepec*, the *Codex Huaquechula*, and the *Mapa Circular de Quauhquechollan* (kept in the Osterreichische National Bibliotek in Vienna, Austria). In addition, three colonial-era, Native-made maps are in the Archivo General de la Nación (AGN) in Mexico City: the 1571 *Mapa de Tepuxuxumo, Guaquechula, Tezacapan* (AGN Tierras 35, exp. 4, f. 17r), the 1575 *Mapa de Xexotzinco, Guacachula y Yeyetcatepango* (AGN Tierras 2809, exp. 16, f. 22r), and the 1694 *Mapa de San Juan Cuiluco y Guaquachula* (AGN Tierras 158, exp. 1, f. 7r).
23. Other examples of the genre include the *Lienzo de Tlaxcala*, the *Mapa de Cuauhtinchan No. 2*, and the *Lienzo de Analco*. For more on the origins and applications of lienzos, see Boone (2000, 24), Mundy (1996), and Asselbergs (2008, 11–15).
24. For introductions to the Nahua use of heraldic devices of the Habsburg house, see Castañeda de la Paz (2009) and Gutiérrez (2015). By petitioning for the right to use Habsburg heraldry or by informal appropriation, Indigenous communities used the motifs to establish local authority in the colonial legal system. See Florescano (2002) and Castañeda de la Paz and Luque Talaván (2010a).

25. Tlaxcaltecos join Hernán Cortés in the *Lienzo de Tlaxcala* (Glasgow Manuscript, plate 91). Documents from Michoacán show Purépecha alliances with the Spanish—the *Lienzo de Carapan I* (ca. 1690–1710), the *Lienzo de Carapan II* (ca. 1710), and the *Codex Tzintzuntzan* (1595). Alma Rosa Rubí and Sara Altamirano (1989) detail the Purépecha alliances in these lienzos.
26. Asselbergs (2008, 46), during her 1997 fieldwork in Huaquechula, found that oral traditions recalled the walls; she also found their physical remains. During my visit in 2021, I also saw remains of the walls north of town.
27. On the preparation of teixiptla and deity impersonators, see D. Carrasco (2020).
28. The *Matrícula de Huexotzinco* also represents the town of Quauhquechollan with a double-headed bird (f. 716r, f. 868r). See also Marc Thouvenot's (1988, 331–50) study on applications of the eagle as a place glyph in the *Codex Xolotl*.
29. Jane Hill (1992) theorized the Flower World Complex, which manifests itself in blossoms, precious stones, and iridescent natural objects, based on attestations of a flowery world in pottery and songs throughout the Uto-Aztecan region. In the *Florentine Codex*, the hummingbird denotes the reward that a warrior who dies in battle may receive postmortem in Xochitlalpan, an egalitarian garden world (Laack 2019). Local Nahua views of reality varied from altepetl to altepetl in terms of horizontal and vertical elements (Nielsen and Reunart 2020). The idea of Xochitlalpan as a celestial realm may thus be a colonial interpretation by Nahua neophytes who sought to reconcile ancestral and Christian metaphysics. Often, entering Xochitlalpan was a matter of states of consciousness in rituals (Mikulska 2020). On how this complex developed in colonial Mexico, see L. Burkhart (1992).
30. In the Postclassic Period, rulers' gifts to each other could accompany military events. Fernando Alvarado Tezozomoc in the *Crónica mexicana* and Diego Durán record the exchange of gifts between the Mexica tlatoani Itzcoatl and the ruler of Azcapotzalco prior to Mexica occupation of that altepetl (Bassett 2015, 33).
31. Camilla Townsend (2006, 148–71) describes how for Nahuas, Malintzin herself exercised Spanish authority. As a tlatoani (chief speaker) she was the voice of the Spanish. In fact, when addressing Cortés, Nahuas often used the title "Malintzin," fusing the two together (242n3). In the *Lienzo de Tlaxcala*, Malintzin's large relative size shows her importance in the scenes of the alliance between the Spanish and Tlaxcala (E. Aguilera 2014, 13–14).
32. Asselbergs (2008, 141) argues that the figure to the right of Cortés with the banner is Jorge de Alvarado, though she also mentions his possible identification as Cristóbal de Olid.
33. The Mexica carried Huitzilopochtli from Aztlan to Tenochtitlan in the *Mapa de Sigüenza*, the *Tira de la peregrinación*, and the *Codex Aubin*

(1576) as well as the seventeenth-century *Codex Azcatitlan*. An alphabetic narrative of the carrying of Huitzilopochtli appears in the *Codex Chimalpahin* (see chapter 4).

34. Regarding contemporary Nahuas in Oapan, Guerrero, Catharine Good Eshelman (2001, 260) observes, "for the Nahuas, crosses are not religious symbols in themselves, but rather valuable objects charged with a certain kind of power," which she identifies as chicahualiztli (strength).
35. For more on Nahua concepts related to gold, see Klein (1993).
36. In the 1521 precedent to the 1527 campaign, the tlatoque Cuauhtemoc (Mexica) and Ixtlilxochitl (Texcoca) sent ten thousand warriors each with Cortés as fighters and guides to add to the mere three hundred men in the Cortés Company (Brian, Benton, and García Loaeza 2015, 69–70).
37. For this study, I have consulted Berdan and Anawalt (1997).
38. Robert Barlow (1949a, 43) confirmed Ahuitzotl's taking of Chiapan. The tlatoani's conquest of Soconusco appears elsewhere (Jiménez Moreno 1954, 235).
39. According to Daniel Contreras (2004, 70), Kaqchiquel ruler Cahi Yamox became "so disgusted by the new way of life that he was obliged once more to take up arms against the Spaniards." Hence, the Kaqchiquels suffered two conquests—once at Iximché in 1523 and after rebelling against the Spanish in 1524 (Polo Sifontes 2005, 13, 45).
40. Retalhuleu lies between the Sununa and Samalá Rivers (Asselbergs 2008, 151n21), an area abounding with ceiba trees (Gall 1963).
41. While common for scholars of Mesoamerica to view cosmic trees in light of Mircea Eliade's *axis mundi* concept (López Austin 1985, 262; López Luján 2005, 38–39, 178; Granziera 2001, 202), this image derives from Eduard Seler's ([1920] 1961, 9, 15, 17–19) interpretation of the *Codex Vaticanus A* as dividing the universe into thirteen celestial regions, nine underworlds, and the mortal realm in between. Regional variations and Christian influences thus complicate the idea of a generalizable Nahua cosmic model (A. Díaz 2020b). Cosmographies vary, but a broader consensus suggests a preference for order that juxtaposes a "dark and opaque primordial world, nonhuman, full of dangerous and creative divine forces, and another mundane, human world ordered by . . . time and the sun and hence more predictable and secure" (Mikulska 2020, 282).
42. Iximché means "a bunch of trees" (Gall 2000, 343). The Quauhquecholteca gave it the Nahuatl name "Tecpan Cuauhtemallan" (*cuauhtli*, tree, and *lan*, place of an abundance of).
43. When I visited Iximché, its isolation and defensibility struck me. The city is composed of three interconnected plazas with temple complexes that belonged to three royal Kaqchiquel households. The entrance and only access to the city was via a drawbridge, lowered only on market days. Precipices and gorges hundreds of feet deep form the three remaining sides.

44. See Otzoy, Otzoy, and Luján Muñoz (1999, 190, nos. 172–73). Jorge de Alvarado also hanged lords Ch'ikb'al and Nim Ab'aj Kejchún.
45. Archaeological studies describe Tzalcualpa (Fuentes y Guzmán 1932, 39; Lutz 1984, 39, 51).
46. The *Lienzo de Tlaxcala* shows the battle's outcome at Chimaltenango (Acuña 1984, vol. 1, plate 125) and is mentioned in a *Relación geográfica* from Tlaxcala (AGI Justicia 291, f. 97r–97v).
47. Book 9 of the *Florentine Codex* details the gear, actions, ceremonies, and products of *pochteca* (merchants) in Central Mexico. Bassett (2015, 114–15) describes how merchants' products became a part of their property (axcaitl) and carried with them the strength the merchants expended. For more on Nahua trade, see Hassig (1993).
48. Other pictorials from the period that use a standardized glyph for tianguis are the *Matrícula de Huexotcinco* (1560) and the *Codex Mexicanus* (ca. 1578–83).
49. In the archives in Guatemala, Asselbergs (2008, 115) found that "several small towns and parcels of land for cultivation located outside the city of Santiago de Almolonga were granted to the former conquistadores collectively" (AGI Guatemala 168, "Fray Francisco de la Parra a Carlos V"; AGCA A1.23, leg. 4575, f. 48r). Likewise, the Central Mexicans received parcels (*solares*) for farming and exemptions from working on Spanish encomiendas (AGCA A1.23, leg. 4575, f. 48r).
50. When the Kaqchiquel lords Sinacan and Squechul surrendered, Pedro de Alvarado required an immediate gold payment as well as four hundred men and four hundred women to pan for gold and another four hundred men and four hundred women to build up the capital in Almolonga (Otzoy, Otzoy, and Luján Muñoz 1999, 189, no. 165; Lovell 2019, 427).
51. In 1549, Fray Francisco de la Parra described the treatment of the Central Mexican combatants in these terms to Charles V. At the time the clergyman wrote, aging Tlaxcalteca conquistadors lacked even food. William Sherman (1970, 133) and Laura Matthew (2004, 92–93) quote his letter from AGI Guatemala 168, "Fray Francisco de la Parra a Carlos V."
52. Asselbergs (2015, 118) cites the cédula (AGCA A1.23, leg. 1512, f. 457r [Dec. 24, 1574]).
53. The deteriorated ends of the tira suggest that records extended earlier than 1302 and later than 1596. For a detailed explanation of the material and organization of the tira, see Diel (2008, 13–21).
54. After Boturini Benaduci's death in 1753, Fr. José Antonio Pichardo held the tira and made a copy (Noguez 1978, 1:26–28). Jean Waldeck then bought the tira and Pichardo's copy. Waldeck sold the original and Pichardo's copy to Jean Alexis Aubin in 1842. Aubin sold his entire collection to Eugène Goupil. Both Waldeck and Goupil added stamps to indicate their ownership, and Waldeck divided and numbered the tira into twenty plates (Diel

2008, 19). Since 1898, the two documents have resided in the Bibliotheque Nationale de France: *Tira de Tepechpan* (Fonds Mexicain 13–14) and Pichardo's copy (Fonds Mexicain 88–86).

55. The curved hill (Colhuacan) next to Toquentzin shows her noble Toltec origin (Diel 2008, 41).
56. When Charles V died in 1558, the news may have taken time to reach Tepechpan, as the tira shows the funerary bundle a year later, in 1559. The death of Charles V also appears in the *Codex Aubin* (1981, f. 51v), the *Codex Mexicanus* (1952, 83), and the *Codex en Cruz* (1981, 3).
57. On Spanish law under Charles V concerning "los naturales" (natural inhabitants) of the Americas, see Owensby (2011).
58. Xavier Noguez (1978, 1:138) conjectured that the use of the Habsburg crest may refer to the favorable ruling of the Audiencia for Tepechpan in their suit against the nearby Temascalapan. Diel (2008, 88–90) notes the case did not go to the Audiencia until 1552, eleven years after the Habsburg crest appears on the tira. I agree with Diel that the crest instead summarizes Tepechpan's support of the Spanish as a means to gain cabecera status.
59. Crewe (2018) has documented the construction of 251 church-and-monastery complexes from the 1530s to the 1580s. For seventy-two communities that gained doctrina status before 1540, these building projects played a decisive role (Crewe 2018, 508–9).
60. An elder resident describes his work on a church project, as preserved in the *Título primordial* of Sultepeque: "I, don Pedro de Santiago Maxixcatzin, vecino of Quatepec, state that the Franciscan fathers baptized me and my brother don Juan Mecatlal, and they were the ones who founded the church of San Miguel; and we built it, not the Spaniards. And so, my children, I entrust you to care for all of the belongings of the church: the surplice, banner, chalice, [and] bell; all are belongings of Quatepec of San Miguel" (qtd. in López Caballero 2003, 305).
61. Rebecca Horn (1997, 19–110) provides a useful introduction to cabecera status, including its administrative functions and leadership roles it opened to local Indigenous hierarchies.
62. Sixteenth-century Texcocan sources presented their surrounding altepeme as stuck in the past as a means to continue to hold a key economic role under the Spanish (Lee 2014, 77; see also Gibson 1964, 43). Likewise, Juan de Torquemada and Fernando Alva Ixtlilxochitl tended to exaggerate the former holdings of Texcoco (Offner 1979, 238).
63. Frederic Hicks (1992) further explains that prior to the Spanish conquest two systems of tribute existed: one for military service, one for payments of goods and draft labor.
64. For example, petitions came from Tepechpan for "caballerías" of grazing land (AGN Tierras 1871, exp. 17, cuaderno 1) and cultivation (AGN Tribu-

tos 113, vol. 45, exp. 3, f. 14r–17r). Huaquechula used a similar strategy and petitioned for land to increase their crop and livestock production (AGN Tributos, vol. 11, exp. 34, "Carta sobre Huaquechula e Izucar").

65. Tepechpan also used litigation to secure tribute payments from Temascalapan, a small altepetl that traditionally had given them tribute in goods and labor. For an overview of the court battle, which lasted into the eighteenth century, see Gibson (1964, 53–54).

66. Luis Quiab, from Tepechpan, and fifty years old in 1550, testified in court that he participated in a *tequitl* (work) draft for the Mexica tlatoani Ahuitzotl (AGI Justicia, leg. 164, no. 2, f. 261r).

67. The richness of the church's ornaments in Quauhquechollan and the control of water resources helped make the monastery attractive to the Franciscans, who used it until 1642 (Asselbergs 2012, 225). The church continues in use, and the monastery functions as a museum.

68. The tira records a particular epidemic in 1545, which may have been typhus (Gibson 1964, 448–49). Colonial and Indigenous sources mention waves of cocoliztli (illness): in the *Codex en Cruz* and the *Codex Aubin*, victims bled from the nose, a symptom of typhus (Diel 2008, 87). The *Codex Mendoza* and Book 12 of the *Florentine Codex* document skin diseases such as smallpox and chicken pox, which afflicted the Valley of Mexico in waves throughout the sixteenth century. See Charles Gibson's (1964, 448–51) timeline of epidemics compiled from Spanish chronicles and Indigenous sources, 1520–1810.

69. The *Memorial de Solalá* also describes waves of diseases accompanying the Spanish. In an outbreak in 1559, even its scribe reveals the plague struck him while writing (Otzoy, Otzoy, and Luján Muñoz 1999, no. 185).

70. The Spanish either built on top of the previous structures of an altepetl, as in the cases of Tenochtitlan, Tlatelolco, and Cholula, or set up churches in flat areas of valleys in order to bring settlement ("congregación") down from surrounding hills. Cholula made a "pueblo nuevo," as did Puebla, Querétaro, and Valladolid (Morelia). On understanding these distinctions and the juridical processes behind them, see Fernández Christlieb and García Zambrano (2006).

71. The institution of a monetary head tax appears in other pictorials: the *Codex Aubin* (1980, f. 47v), the *Codex en Cruz* (1981, 1:53), and the *Codex Osuna* (Chávez Orozco 1947). An alphabetic text from Mexico-Tenochtitlan in the middle of the sixteenth century, the *Anales de Juan Bautista*, also reports on the unrest the new tax caused among Mexica nobility, as I detail in chapter 3.

72. The *Mapa Circular de Quauhquechollan* (1546) is a pictorial representing the ruling houses of the altepetl. A text accompanies the map and states that in 1546, Don Esteban de Guzmán came to resolve a legal conflict over land boundaries (Asselbergs 2008, 70). Luis Reyes García transcribed Guz-

mán's Nahuatl glosses on the *Mapa Circular* and Asselbergs (2008, 301–3) wrote an English translation.

73. A register of more than one hundred items appears, from priests' liturgical garments to ornaments and even kitchen utensils. In addition, the convent library held more than 160 volumes. This detailed inventory meant a lien or mortgage existed on the convent. These objects could be sold to pay debt (John Schwaller, personal communication, November 11, 2021). To my mind, the presence of these objects also indicates an economy strong enough to allow for their acquisition, despite the many setbacks they had suffered.

74. McDonough (2024, 56) links acoustic colonialism to European interference with Nahua's solar-based-timekeeping, by introducing hours for measuring time.

CHAPTER 2

1. McDonough (2024, 39) points out that as a physician "of souls," the friar used Nahua knowledge in a militant manner "against idolatry and sin." In the prologue of Book 3, Sahagún more explicitly refers to "priests as 'soldiers' whose knowledge of pagan beliefs would be well-guarded weapons."

2. Sahagún subjected the data he and his assistants gathered to a process of three "siftings" (*colaciones*). The research took place in three locations: Tlatelolco and Texcoco (1540s), Tepepulco (1550s), and Mexico-Tenochtitlan (1570s). Only information from elders interviewed that repeated in all three locations made the final copy of the *Historia universal* (Schwaller 2003b). For an overview of Sahagún's editorial processes of data from interviews with elders who lived before the Spanish invasion, see Browne (2000, 120–32).

3. The compendium also provided examples of speech, metaphors, and cultural allusions that would improve their preaching and interactions with the Nahuas (*FC*, Bk. 10, f. vii; Ríos Castaño 2018, 466–67).

4. The funding from Toral allowed Sahagún to write a version of the *Historia universal* with the material the Nahua scholars had collected, which he finished in 1569. The location of the Toral commission of the *Historia universal* remains unknown (Nicholson 1997, 4). Other texts associated with the Toral commission are *Colloquios y doctrina christiana* (ca. 1564); *Adiciones, apéndice a la postilla y exercicio quotidiano* (1579); *Psalmodia christiana* (1569), and *Sermonario de los sanctos del año* (1583); as well as a smaller group of texts on homiletics housed at the Newberry Library in Chicago and the Biblioteca Nacional de México. See Schwaller (1986) for an inventory of texts associated with Sahagún.

5. Two libraries in Madrid hold these materials: the Biblioteca del Real Palacio de Madrid and the Biblioteca de la Real Academia de la Historia. These ma-

terials likely came into the possession of the Crown when Phillip II ordered the confiscation of Sahagún's manuscripts in 1578. Scholarly interest in early manuscript material of the *Historia universal* resurged with the work of Mexican historian Francisco del Paso y Troncoso. As a diplomat and scholar, he resided in Madrid, in 1892–1916, and commissioned a series of glass-plate photocopies of all manuscript materials related to the *Historia universal*. It was Paso y Troncoso who then organized the material into four chapters (Nicholson 1997, 6–7). For this study I have consulted Sullivan et al. (1997).

6. López Austin (1971) and Ríos Castaño (2018) have also noted the silence in the usual Spanish columns in Book 11. Ríos Castaño (2018, 481) has shown that the translated material in Books 10 and 11 formed part of an independent reference work for which Sahagún gathered material in the 1560s. She cites marginalia in the *Códices matritenses* (1907, f. 172r/v) that do not appear in the *Florentine Codex* in which Sahagún refers to the information he was collecting for a "libro de medicina."

7. This was not the only time when the Nahuatl content of the codex remained untranslated into Spanish. He omitted the teocuicatl (songs of deities) that elders provided for Book 1 (*FC*, Bk. 1, f. 137r–144v). Perhaps Sahagún—or the Nahua scholars—saw these chants as too detailed or arcane to translate (León-Portilla 1999, 176).

8. For scientific studies matching the plants in Books 10 and 11 with known species, see Estrada Lugo et al. (1989).

9. The principles of Galenic medicine date from Hippocrates, according to whom good health consisted of balancing four bodily fluids or *humors*: blood, phlegm, yellow bile (choler), and black bile. Vivian Nutton (1997) gives a great introduction to Galenism from antiquity to the eighteenth century.

10. Jacques Chevalier and Andrés Sánchez Bain (2003, xiii, 12, 20–22, 249, 252) have critiqued George Foster's (1953) proposal that a modified Galenism has existed in Latin America since the colonial period. Chevalier and Sánchez Bain point out logical problems in Foster's arguments and ways in which Foster's research differs from their findings among the Nahuas of the Southern Veracruz Huasteca. López Austin (1986, 74–75, 88) also criticizes Foster's likening of Native healing practices to Galenic medicine. The fact that Nahua healers often did not agree with Francisco Hernández's ([1615] 1888, 121, 182, 193–194, 196–197, 253, 256, 363, 371, 488, 550, 664, 708, 713) assessments of hot or cold properties of illnesses nor their treatment gives further evidence against the Galenism hypothesis (McDonough 2024, 63).

11. Chevalier and Sánchez Bain (2003, 22) offer three co-actional principles for understanding Nahua approaches to bodily well-being: (1) equilibrium, not as a fixed point but as a path of moderate action avoiding abrupt mixing

of hot and cold; (2) daily cycles of work and rest; and (3) solar movement, which refers to a lifelong trajectory of age- and movement-appropriate activities, culminating in the twilight of one's life.

12. For scientific analysis of herbal remedies in the *Codex Cruz-Badiano* and the *Florentine Codex*, see Ortiz de Montellano (1975). On prescriptions for herbs in the *Cruz-Badiano* that counteract fright (susto), see Gimmel (2008b, 185) and Dufendach (2019, 631–32).

13. In 1578, the general of the Franciscan order, Rodrigo de Sequera, took the codex to Spain (García Bustamante 1990, 337–39). Philip II held it in the Escorial, eventually giving it to Cardinal Ferdinando di Medici in Florence (Schwaller 2003c, 268–73). This confiscated manuscript is the most-studied version of the *Historia universal* and has remained in Florence ever since, now residing in the Biblioteca Laurenziana. See Eloise Quiñones Keber's ([1988] 1995) annotated bibliography of Sahagún's known writings and their locations.

14. No copy exists of the questionnaires. Yet López Austin, based on patterns of structured responses in the entries of the codex, has proposed questions the Nahua scholars likely employed. Pertinent to this chapter, López Austin (1974, 147) has suggested that the following questions appeared in interviews regarding healing plants: "1. What is it? (In the case of plants: what part of the plant is it?); 2. What does it look like?; 3. What does it cure?; 4. How is the medicine prepared?; 5. How is it administered?; 6. Where is it found?"

15. María Ángel Garibay ([1954] 1971, 64) and Miguel León-Portilla (1999) attributed the authorship of the *Florentine Codex* to the Nahuatl scholars at Tlatelolco, with Sahagún as its editor.

16. See Magaloni Kerpel (2011).

17. As "a secondary consideration," the Spanish "ranges from translating the Nahuatl text verbatim to summarizing or ignoring it" (Terraciano 2019, 12). Elsewhere, Terraciano (2010) describes the Spanish as an independent text within the *Florentine Codex* as it strays in notable ways from the main Nahuatl text.

18. For an introduction to the medieval scriptorium, where books were collective works under the supervision of a head scribe, see Thomson, McKitterick, and Kwakkel (2012).

19. Both the *Florentine Codex* and Francisco Hernández's *Cuatro libros de la naturaleza* ([1615] 1888) show a reliance on the *Naturalis Historia* of Pliny.

20. The organization of the *Florentine Codex* and Sahagún's later writings on the theological virtues suggest he consulted Thomas Aquinas's *Summa Theologiae* (1948; see also Ríos Castaño 2011, 34). Incidentally, the Colegio de la Santa Cruz kept the *Summa* in its library (Mathes 1982, 63). Other classical and medieval models influenced the organization of the *Florentine Codex*, including Aristotle's *History of Animals* (ca. 350 BC). Jacob Mey-

denbach's herbal *Hortus Sanitatis* (1491) also pertains directly to Books 10 and 11 (Bassett 2015, 50).

21. While under the control of Tenochtitlan prior to the Spanish, Tlatelolco by this time had regained some autonomy as an altepetl; the fact that none of the Nahua scholars came from Tenochtitlan reflects their recent political repositioning (Diel 2018, 87).

22. Although conventional scholarship assumes that a lost Nahuatl original existed, based on features of the Latin, Andrew Laird proposes that Badiano interviewed Cruz in Nahuatl and then edited the responses "to fit into the European structure of his text" (personal communication, August 30, 2022). Badiano used Latin since the herbal was a gift to Phillip II; yet the codex retains the Nahuatl names of its plants. See Laird's (2023, 149–55) discussion of the authorship of the *Codex Cruz-Badianus*. For photographic comparisons with the plants the text identifies, see Xavier Noguez's (2013) Spanish translation of the *Cruz-Badiano* in the special issues of *Arqueología mexicana*.

23. The millenarian practice of divining an ailment with corn kernels remains with Nahua healers today and in other Mesoamerican communities. See Rojas (2016a, 2016b).

24. In the Postclassic Period, a ticitl diagnosed a patient by throwing *colorín* seeds and casting spells, or through psychotropic plants and visions (Soustelle [1970] 2002, 192, 194–95). In *Historia de los mexicanos por sus pinturas*, the deities Oxomoco and Cipactonal began this approach to healing at the dawn of the Fifth Sun (Boone 2007, 24). With a diagnosis divined, the treatment often entailed ingesting a liquid the ticitl prepared. In fact, *patli* (medicine) derives from the verb root *pati*, "to dissolve and melt" (Karttunen 1992, 188).

25. Cases of women titicih appear in inquisitorial proceedings. Female titicih were midwives, curers of eye diseases, and had many of the same healing practices as men, a tradition that Hispanization gradually displaced (Polanco 2018). Women titicih appear in the pictorial sources *Codex Magliabechiano* and *Codex Tudela* (Boone 2007, 27).

26. See also López Austin (1988), which is based largely on Book 10 of the *Florentine Codex* and gives detailed linguistic data on the body parts listed in that section. Likewise, Ortiz de Montellano (1990) integrated information from the *Florentine Codex* with colonial and contemporary sources and brought Nahua conceptualizations of health to a wider audience.

27. Ortiz de Montellano (1990, 191, 199–204) calls them "animic forces," which vivify bodies from without. Maffie (2014, 100–113) emphasizes teotl's flowing, dynamic influence on humans. Thus, I conceptualize the tonalli, yollotli, and ihiyotl as conduits between body and cosmos.

28. The elder also explained that such work draws on one's interior strength and vitality (*chicahualiztli*) (Sandstrom 1991, 258).

29. Bernard and Thelma Ortiz de Montellano, in their English translation of Alfredo López Austin's *Tamoanchan, Tlalocan: Places of Mist* (1997, 41–42), also translate tonquizcaiutl as "conclusion."
30. Jill McKeever Furst ([1995] 1997, 175–83) explains the idea of monistic aging among speakers of Uto-Aztecan languages.
31. Nahua scholar Eduardo de la Cruz Cruz's (2017) master's thesis, "Cenyahtoc cintli tonacayo: Huahcapatl huan tlen naman," traces parallels between ancient and current practices and beliefs concerning corn. Cruz Cruz wrote his study in Huastecan Nahuatl. He points out that the *Florentine Codex* and modern Nahua speakers continue to call mature maize by the names "centli" or "cintli" (2017, 9). See also Chevalier and Sánchez Bain's (2003, 191–92) taxonomy of the seventeen stages of the life cycle of corn, according to the Nahuas of the southern Huasteca region.
32. In his *Primeros memoriales*, Sahagún describes rituals for the maize deities Cinteotl, Xochiquetzal, Tocih, Chicomecoatl, Xochipilli, and Xilonen (Sullivan et al. 1997, 58, 66, 83). Durán (1994, 135) also discusses ceremonies for Chicomecoatl, Chalchiuhcihuatl, and Xilonen, which he describes as the principal corn deities. For an overview of maize offerings in colonial-era pictorials, see Mazzetto and Moragas Segura (2015).
33. Francisco Javier Carod-Artal (2015) provides a useful overview of the history of psychotropics in the region.
34. For an overview of Inquisition edicts regarding curanderos' use of psychotropic plants, see Viesca Treviño (2001, 61–62).
35. J. R. Andrews and Ross Hassig published an English translation, *Treatise on the Heathen Superstitions That Live Today Among the Indians of This New Spain, 1629* (Ruiz de Alarcón 1987). See also Díaz Balsera's (2011, 321–49; 2018, 124) examination of healers and hallucinogens in texts by Ruiz de Alarcón. In Ruiz de Alarcón's (1987, 50–51) manual, he explains the use of picietl, ololiuhque, and peiotl as talismans in domestic altars. See also Marin Nesvig's (2022, 160–64) overview on inquisitorial cases from the seventeenth century in Mexico against the use of peyote. Nesvig (2022, 162) argues that among non-Indigenous people in Mexico, peyote use was individualized compared to its communal use among Nahuas and other Indigenous groups.
36. See Montero Sobrevilla (2020) for an analysis of the images of the avatars of this god in Book 11. Montero Sobrevilla details attestations to Huitzilopochtli's visual representations in the codex to signal seasonal changes.
37. Also in Book 11 (f. 48r), an image of a man's body, wearing a loincloth and with a hummingbird head, passes a human heart to a falcon in flight. Norton (2024, 324–26) compares the hummingbird man to a tlamacazqui (sacrificing priest) in the *Codex Borgia*. Norton emphasizes that this avatar of Huitzilopochtli in the *Florentine Codex* and the tlamacazqui in the *Borgia* both feed the energy from human blood to the sun. See Gimmel's

(2008a, 173–75) further treatment of the avatars of Huitzilopochtli in the *Florentine Codex*.

CHAPTER 3

1. For generations, the Mexica had foretold that at the end of age of the Fifth Sun, tzitzimime, zoomorphic beings with fangs and claws, would come to devour humanity (L. Burkhart 1989, 55, 83; Sigal 2011, 123–26; García Garagarza 2013, 38–39). I am grateful to John Sullivan for his translation assistance in this chapter.
2. The annals text makes an early mention of this office, which grew in importance over time. See Connell (2011, 118–149) on the role of the *alguacil amparador* as tribute collector in Mexico City bureaucracy in the seventeenth century.
3. Since the entry identifying the alguacil Juan Bautista is the only one in Spanish, scholars starting with Lorenzo Boturini Benaducci have used his name to identify the manuscript (Townsend 2009, 649n38). Camilla Townsend (2009, 639) proposes an alternative title: *The Annals of the Painters of San Juan Moyotlan*.
4. After the conquest and before the monetization of tribute in 1564, the Mexica had paid through labor and in the form of grains, including corn and wheat (J. Miranda 2005, 197–98).
5. See *Auto proveído por el virrey* (1958).
6. This hardship came in part from "chronic shortages of currency" in New Spain and elsewhere in the silver-rich colonies (O'Hara 2018, 101–2). Spain's appetite for luxuries from India and China and its wars with European powers drove bullion from the Americas to Asia, leaving New Spain and Peru, regions that produced the most sliver, with little hard currency.
7. While it is not central to her analyses of these annals, Camilla Townsend (2009, 639; 2019, 170, 224) references posterity as the intended audience. She observes that the scribes were concerned that future generations should know of their opposition to the new tribute policy.
8. As discussed in the introduction, I am wary of turning "hybrid" alphabetic texts that recall pictorial forms into objects for academic consumption; see Dean and Leibsohn (2003). See Joshua Lund's (2006, xv–xxi) framing of hybridity as a cultural descriptor in Latin America, transferred to racial imaginaries in nineteenth-century discourses on nation building. On this point, see also Cornejo Polar (2011, 89).
9. The manuscript is kept in the library of the Basilica of Guadalupe for its mention of an image of María de Guadalupe shown in Tepeyac in 1555. The entry from that year has no day or month: "Yn ipan xihuitl mill e qui[nient]os 55 a[ñ]os yquac monextitzino in Sancta Maria de Quatalupe yn ompa Tepeyacac" (f. 9r) (In the year 1555, Holy Mary of Guadalupe was reverently

displayed in Tepeyacac). Janette Favrot Peterson (2005, 581) has observed that the verb *monextitzino* refers not to a miraculous apparition but to the display of an object, such as an icon or statue. The verb endings of "-ti" and "-tzino" add meaning: "-ti" indicates an imperfect, long duration (Lockhart 2001, 89), and "-tzino" is a reverential ending in the past (177). The entry does not claim a miracle yet implies that the regular use of Marian icons at Tepeyac dates to at least the mid-sixteenth century.

10. Scholars have proposed classifications of texts based on the presence or absence of clerical intervention. Mark Christensen (2010, 361) proposes three types: texts by "ecclesiastic authors and/or their Indigenous aides" for a large readership of clerics and Natives; texts by "ecclesiastics and/or their Native stewards for more local audiences including religious authorities"; and "unpublished, unofficial texts written by Natives for Natives." Using a similar approach, David Tavárez (2011, 132–39) has termed the *Codex Mexicanus* and other unsupervised texts "clandestine documents."

11. The scribes' location placed them close to the Escuela de San José de los naturales, which Pedro de Gante had established in 1529 (Zepeda Rincón 1972, 51). The scribes show the importance of Gante in their daily lives and mention him several times (Reyes García 2001, 164, 186, 208, 274, 288, 296, 320). Emilio Ros-Fábregas (2012) has commented on Gante's relationship to choral singers, artisans, and the scribes in the *Anales de Juan Bautista*.

12. At the same time, I note that the "reciprocal character of offering or sacrifice" for the Nahuas precludes any notion of "original sin" (Köhler 2001, 126). Rather, the cosmos in its normal functioning instantiates reciprocity, and it is up to humans to decide to what extent they will participate in ongoing universal mutual exchanges.

13. The scribes of Moyotlan used the xiuhpohualli tradition to record their narratives on the effects of monetized tribute (C. Townsend 2019, 179). On how the Juan Bautista annals drew on rotational patterns of Nahua labor, see C. Townsend (2009).

14. The surname Teton that the scribes provide ends with the augmentative -ton, which refers to his low status (García Garagarza 2013, 36; Mendoza 2017, 7–8).

15. Nahua concepts of living well focus on the material present rather than postmortem existence. Their ritual acts aim at attaining the best life they can and not eternal salvation (Klor de Alva 1993; Chevalier and Sánchez Bain 2003, 38).

16. Yolmelahua tended to take place toward the end of one's life. A member of a community told leaders of criminal activities they had committed. However, this ceremony functioned like plea bargaining to lessen the severity of a punishment rather than to expiate malignant effects of wrongdoing (Madajczak 2017, 74–75). Madajczak (2017) examines the dubious pairing of yolmelahua and confession.

17. Translation mine; Dibble and Anderson's reads, "It was thus said: 'If the eclipse of the sun is complete, it will be dark forever! The demons of darkness will come down; they will eat men!'" (Sahagún [1578] 1959–82, 7:2).
18. Elinor Melville (1999) provides an overview of the growth of cattle in Michmaloyan during the Native demographic crisis of the sixteenth century. European cattle caused similar problems by damaging crops during the stint of the second Spanish capital in Guatemala, in Santiago de Almolonga (Matthew and Fowler 2020, 134).
19. That said, on the manuscript's last folio comes an attestation of a woman who addresses a group of men, explaining, "Dios le perdon q[uitoz[n]equi] ma dios q'[ui]motlapopolhuilli" (f. 60v), which Reyes García (2001, 330) translates as "Dios le perdone quiere decir madios quimotlapopolhuilli" (May God forgive him, which means madios quimotlapopolhuilli).
20. This idea recalls Aymara philosopher Fausto Renagas's reflection "El hombre es tierra que piensa" (Man is dirt that thinks) (qtd. in G. R. Cruz 2010, 54).
21. For further attestations of Tlantepuzillama as a tzitzimime from the Postclassic Period to the present, see Olivier (2005).
22. See Eduardo de la Cruz Cruz's "Tlaneltoquilli: Chicomexochitl huan Tenantzitzimitl" (2015), which recounts the origin story and trials of the corn deity at the hands of a merciless antagonist. See also Cecilia Klein's (2000, 16) examination of Citlalincue as the primordial tzitzimime, whose children and grandchildren became stars and other celestial bodies and were also tzitzimime.
23. He also used his influence to defend himself. Not three months earlier, on November 30, 1563, Viceroy Enrique Almanza wrote a *merced* on behalf of Cipac confirming his ownership of a plot in Coatlan, which had belonged to his family since Acamapichtli, since time immemorial (AGN Mercedes, vol. 7, f. 270v). The viceroy's legal intervention shows the Spanish were not eager to lose Cipac as an intermediary between them and the city's Indigenous hierarchy.
24. For more on the political career and demise of Luis Santa María Cipac, see C. Townsend (2019, 155–79).
25. Part of the agreement between Cortés and Company and the house of Moteuczoma was that Mexica nobles and commoners did not have to pay cash tribute in exchange for their cooperation (Ruiz Medrano 2011, 62; C. Townsend 2019, 159–60).
26. The office of merino, interchangeable with the term *tepixque*, carried connotations of corruption as merinos had the reputation of overcharging to top off their salaries and personal living expenses (Connell 2011, 48). The merino held a similar role to the tequitlato (mandón) in charge of draft labor in each calpolli (Molina [1571] 2008, 2:105v; Corominas [1961] 2008,

368; Connell 2011, 269, 62). The Spanish demanded that Mexica nobles collect tribute in the sixteenth century but gradually took that function away. By the eighteenth century all merinos were Spanish (Gibson 1964, 391–97; Connell 2011, 276n25).

27. "Cipac" means "alligator," but many in Tenochtitlan had taken to calling him "Nanacacipac," which means "mushroom alligator": this combination of the psychotropic mushroom and the stately predator led Lockhart (1992, 118) to gloss Nanacacipac as "paper tiger."

28. As Connell (2011, 21) has observed regarding the sixteenth to the eighteenth century, there was "a multigenerational effort by Native peoples in Mexico-Tenochtitlan to preserve Indigenous control over their own governance within a viceregal system that actively supported them in their efforts." See McEnroe (2020), which examines complex relationships between Indigenous and European hierarchies. These tenuous networks upheld the colonial status quo while enabling the survival of Native enclaves across the Americas.

29. Hernán Cortés (1963, 93) purported that when the ruler went out to the edge of his palace rooftop to dissuade his subjects from war with the Spanish, the people gave him mortal wounds by stoning him. For other accounts of the stoning, death, and burial of Moteuczoma Xocoyotl, see Vázquez de Tapia (1953, 42–44), Díaz del Castillo (1968, 390–91), and Aguilar (1980, 88–90). Also useful in this regard is the review and analysis of Matthew Restall (2018, 193–200).

30. At stake was not if Cipac had an heir, since the Mexica nobles elected their ruler from a pool of qualified relations that included brothers or other male relatives of the defunct tlatoani. Thus, they were were not bound to elect the son of a former ruler as the successor (Lockhart 1992, 32; Connell 2011, 19, 34).

31. C. Townsend (2019, 179) notes the scribes' resilience and that they "filled dozens of pages complete with dialogue, detail, anger, and hope."

32. Gillespie (1989, 45–176) explains how the royal line of Moteuczoma I (Ilhuicamina) and II (Xocoyotl) relied on a series of women. At crucial genealogical junctures a "woman of discord" brought harmony by closing cycles of disorder.

33. The proposition that Nahuas uniformly conceived of the cosmos as divided into multiple celestial levels, multiple underworlds with earth in between, began with Seler's ([1920] 1961) interpretation of the *Codex Vaticanus A*. Eric Thompson (1934, 225–26) cemented the view as conventional in Mesoamerican studies (Nielsen and Reunart 2020).

34. See Mikulska's (2020) explanation of the term *chicnauhnepaniuhcan*. The term does contain the number nine (chicnauh-), yet it does not always refer to the vertical arrangement of visual elements or spaces; it may also refer to

a union on a horizontal plane, a "crossing of roads, ways, or whatever other concept, and not precisely the superposition of floors" (Mikulska 2020, 303–4).
35. See V. Cruz Cruz (2016) on lightning as a metaphor for language renewal.
36. In chapter 4, I examine a Mexica origin account from the caves of Chicomoztoc, recounted in a section of the *Codex Chimalpahin* known as the *Crónica mexicayotl* (1609).

CHAPTER 4

1. See Schroeder's (2007) overview of Chimalpahin's annals.
2. Alonso Franco, a mestizo elder the text identified, also informed Chimalpahin (1997) regarding the Mexica origins in Aztlan (*CC*, f. 24r).
3. These manuscripts have since been repatriated. On May 21, 2014, the manuscript of the *Codex Chimalpahin* and Fernando Alva Ixtlilxochitl's *Obras históricas* (1997) were up for auction in London. The Instituto Nacional de Antropología e Historia (INAH) arranged a private purchase and returned the volumes to Mexico (*El Mundo* 2014).
4. Schroeder (2011, 237–39) traces the provenance of the *Crónica mexicayotl*. Chimalphahin's holograph passed through the hands of Carlos Sigüenza y Góngora, then the Jesuit order. In the eighteenth century, the Italian antiquarian Lorenzo Boturini Benaduci made a copy of that manuscript. The original disappeared in the nineteenth century and resurfaced with Ruwet's discovery in 1983. Meanwhile, the astronomer-mathematician Antonio León y Gama acquired Boturini Benaduci's copied manuscript, cited it as part of his study of Mexica calendars, and coined the idea that Tezozomoc had written it. French collectors (Jean Alexis Aubin, then Eugène Goupil) later purchased the Boturini Benaduci copy and took it to Paris. At the end of the nineteenth century, Francisco Paso y Troncoso made glass plate photocopies of this manuscript copy. By now, formatting details (Chimalpahin's typical crosses at the start of a new section) were missing, which allowed authorial misattribution to spread further with Adrián León's ([1949] 1992) Spanish-Nahuatl edition. Ruwet's find in 1983, and Schroeder and Anderson's 1997 English-Nahuatl edition of the *Codex Chimalpahin* (Chimalpahin 1997), of which the *Crónica mexicayotl* is one section, have resolved the problem of misattribution, along with accumulated transcription errors.
5. Schroeder's (2011) work has shifted scholarly focus to the *Crónica mexicayotl* as one of Chimalpahin's manuscripts. Paul Kirchhoff (1951) had argued previously that Tezozomoc was responsible for only the first nineteen folios of the *Crónica mexicayotl* and that Chimalpahin wrote the rest, which corresponded to events in his text *Las ocho relaciones*.
6. The estimate that Tezozomoc was about seventy when he wrote the opening of the *Crónica mexicayotl* is based on his mention of the construction

of the Churubusco-Tenochtitlan aqueduct as taking place in 1470, 128 years before he wrote the introduction to the *Crónica mexicana* in 1598 (Romero Galván 2003, 177); and on the date Chimalpahin gives for the installation of Tezozomoc's father, Huanitzin, as governor of Tenochtitlan in 1538 (Siméon [1889] 1977, 237).

7. The two did know each other. On one occasion, Chimalpahin mentions a theatrical production he saw in which Tezozomoc played the part of Moteuczoma Xocoyotl (Chimalpahin 2006, 67). On the reliability of dictation as a mode for preserving narratives, Albert B. Lord (1974, 149) comments that with "a competent scribe this method produces a longer and technically better text than an actual performance."

8. No genealogical documents from the Postclassic Period survive, though scholars have inferred their existence (Olko 2007; Diel 2008, 75).

9. The *Códices matritenses* explain that a sage (*teixtlamatiani*) imparts wisdom and expands human development (León-Portilla 1956, 65–69). The term *ixtlamatinih* combines the *tlamatini*, a "knower of things," with the notion of *ixila* ("en mi presencia, o en mi tiempo" [Molina (1571) 2008, 2:48r; in my presence, or in my time]) to show how "Nahua intellectuals garner much of their knowledge through lived experience" (McDonough 2016, 8). In Nahua communities in Guerrero today, strengthening children by teaching them, called *huapahua*, emphasizes reciprocity across generations. Adults, by raising children, give them strength that they will in turn receive in their old age (Good Eshelman 2005, 98–99).

10. José Rubén Romero Galván (2003) observes that Chimalpahin subsumes Nahua history within a universalizing, linear, biblical view of time. On the difference between Tezozomoc and Chimalpahin's view of Christianity, Sallie Brennan (1998, 98–99) has noted that "both men claim to be Christian. Tezozomoc, however, brings Christianity into a Mesoamerican idiom, while Chimalpahin sets his Indigenous account into a Christian context."

11. Francisco Cervantes de Salazar's *México en 1554* (1875) served to orient Spaniards who had never seen Mexico-Tenochtitlan on the region's resources and beauty. Ivonne del Valle (2009, 204) has observed that in *México en 1554* Cervantes de Salazar excluded Nahua knowledge "by dividing the space available" and "hierarchically assigning it to different populations."

12. Tezozomoc likely learned alphabetic writing via his household's relationship to Gante. Tezozomoc's father supervised a feather mosaic in 1539 with Gante's support (Estrada de Gerlero 1992, 80; Muñoz 2006, 134–40).

13. At the close of the *Crónica mexicana*, Moteuczoma Xocoyotl spoke with one of his advisors (the tlilancalqui) about the imminent arrival of the Spanish. While the chapter concludes with news that the Spanish had arrived in Tlaxcala, Tezozomoc mentions he would continue his account "en otro cuaderno" (in another chronicle) (Tezozomoc [1598] 2009, 466).

14. The document's title comes from "tlal-" ("tlalli," land) and "amatl" (paper). It is thus a land tenure document, meant to establish the boundaries of the Moteuczoma family's possessions in Huauhquilpan, a municipality in the state of Hidalgo today (R. Cortés 2011, 6).
15. Historical texts written at the Colegio in Tlatelolco highlight the perspective of that altepetl, including Book 12 of the *Florentine Codex* (Lockhart 1993, 27–36) and the *Annals of Tlatelolco* (Berlin and Barlow 1948, 37–42).
16. After both islands overthrew Tepanec control of the valley, Tlatelolco used canoe shipping to become the commercial center of the region with vast tianguis markets, drawing merchandise from as far away as the Mayan zone (Garduño 1997, 86; Bueno Bravo 2005, 136–37).
17. For analysis of this episode within the context of mores and politics between Tenochtitlan and Tlatelolco, see Evans (1998, 174–76).
18. Camilla Townsend (2019, 197) points out that an ancestor of Chimalpahin and an ancestor of Tezozomoc had been enemies: "their great-grandfathers had once been at war with each other. Quecholcohuatl from Amequemecan had knelt in fear before Axayacatl. But those days were gone, and in that fact the two found their common purpose."
19. In the *Codex Mexicanus* the Mexica step out of Aztlan and onto the timeline of their history (Diel 2008, 23). The combination of seven (*chicnahui*) and cave (*moztoc*) may not indicate caves at all (Oudijk 2011, 158, 169n9), although a group's primordial emergence from a cave is a common motif in Mesoamerican creation accounts. Mikulska (2020) has observed that *moztoc*, as a non-pluralizable, inanimate noun, contains a locative that refers to a place with a more profound connotation than a cavern. On problems with numbers in Nahuatl toponyms, see Mikulska (2020).
20. The Mixton War (*la guerra chichimeca*), a series of military campaigns in which the Nahuas helped the Spanish invade the areas northwest of the central plateau, changed the connotation of "Chichimeca" from that of a prestigious past to shorthand for recalcitrant, provincial, and nomadic (Olko 2012, 187). On the origin and extent of the Mixton Wars, see Powell (1996) and Altman (2010).
21. Visual representations of this origin story emphasize the metaphor of birth. An image in the *Historia Tolteca-Chichimeca* of Chicomoztoc depicts the walls of these caves as uterine lining. In the *Códice Vaticano Latino* the Chichimeca emerge from Chicomoztoc and then begin to nurse from breasts that grow on a tree near the mouth of the caves (Báez-Jorge and Martínez 2000, 93). In these sources, nature itself nurtured the future of these seven groups. See Glass and Robertson (1975) for a description of pictorial sources of the migration from Aztlan to Mexico-Tenochtitlan.
22. See Rocío Cortés's (2008, 100–102) excellent overview of texts by post-Colegio Native and mestizo intellectuals.

23. Fernando de Alva Ixtlilxochitl's *Historia de la nación chichimeca* (ca. 1600–1608) inserts the history of Texcoco into a universalizing European vision of history and is concerned with showing merit to the Spanish to enjoy legal privileges as Tlaxcala did (Brading 1991, 274–75). Similarly, Diego Muñoz Camargo, in his *Descripción de la ciudad y provincia de Tlaxcala* ([1585] 1998), sought favor with the Spanish and privileges (Florescano 1994, 126). Amber Brian (2014, 96) observes that Ixtlilxochitl and Muñoz Camargo were part of an intellectual circle that problematizes the distinctions Ángel Rama (1984) made in *La ciudad letrada* between urban spaces of literacy and the oral culture of the countryside.
24. Alphabetic accounts of the Mexica migration by Diego Durán (1994, 31–33) and José Acosta (2006, 391–92) also mention the tlaquimilolli of Huitzilopochtli.
25. The *Codex Boturini* contains multiple depictions of the teomameque, who carried Huitzilopochtli's tlaquimilolli. Their name glyphs in the *Codex Boturini* identify them as Iztac Mixcoatzin, Apanecatl, Tezacoacatl, and Chimalman, a woman (Diel 2018, 100).
26. Archaeological evidence suggests that the Mexica began to use the bow and arrow for war during the reign of Huitzilihuitl, son of Acamapichtli (Hassig 1988, 151; Aguilar-Moreno 2007, 113). On the historical proliferation of these arms in the Uto-Aztecan linguistic region, see Blitz (1988). Georges Baudot (1994, 161–62) observed that war chants (*yaocuicatl*), quoted in the *Crónica mexicayotl*, celebrate Huitzilopochtli as the trainer of a warrior people.
27. Laird (2021, 232) points out that the foundation of Tenochtitlan in the *Codex Mendoza* (1546) shows an eagle perched on the cactus on one foot with another claw extended in the direction of the *tzompantli* (skull rack). Here again, the emphasis is on the coming days in which human sacrifice would play a central religious, economic, and military role in Mexica expansion.
28. On Inca Garcilaso's *Historia de las Indias* and his comparisons between Cusco and Rome, see Asencio (1988). Similarly, Diel (2018, 119) has noted biblical resonances in the Mexica migration in the *Codex Mexicanus*.
29. See Norton's (2024, 323) analysis of the role of the falcon (cuauhtlohtli) in an entry in Book 11 of the *Florentine Codex*. These falcons recall the Mexica migration and their association with Huitzilopochtli, as they brought blood and the sun daily to receive warmth in return. For the origins and development of Mexica ritual sacrifice, see D. Carrasco (1999).
30. The *Codex Mendoza* also depicts Acamapichtli at the foundation of Tenochtitlan.
31. According to Durán (1994, 23), the Mexica asked Huitzilopochtli for permission for a few of their number to stay and live in Pátzcuaro (in modern Michoacán). Huitzilopochtli gave his consent through a dream. In the *Historia de los mexicanos por sus pinturas*, Huitzilopochtli speaks in the dreams

of a number of Mexica who complained about the length of the journey: he encouraged them that they were nearing its end (Icazbalceta 1882).
32. Counting the first Moteuczoma at Chicomoztoc, in the *Crónica mexicayotl* Ilhuicamina is the second Moteuczoma. Hernán Cortés met Moteuczoma Xocoyotl, the third ruler by that name in the text and the maternal grandfather of Fernando Alvarado Tezozomoc.
33. León-Portilla (1985, 38) agreed on the oracular nature of this account in the *Crónica mexicayotl*, as deriving from the *zazanilli* "imaginative prose" genre.
34. McDonough (2024, 7) points to evidence for the importance of dreams as a source of knowledge for Nahuas. McDonough recalls Inga Clendinnen's (1991, 185) summation that "books of dreams were among the Mexica's most valued possessions, and dream-readers among the Mexica's most honoured experts." She also draws on the Standing Rock Lakota scholar Vine Deloria Jr. (1999, 66), who grouped dreams and visions with information worthy of the same analysis and ordering as other observable phenomena in nature. On the epistemological importance of dreams for Nahuas, see also Maffie (2008a, 187).
35. See Graulich (1992, 35), who emphasizes the complementarity of night and wind, and the earlier work of León-Portilla ([1963] 1975, 91, 93), who holds that the movement of *ehecatl* implies transcendence. See also Mikulska (2020), who explains that complementarity between deities parallels complementarity of cosmic regions, including Mictlan and Omeyocan.
36. Fray Andrés de Olmos recorded a Nahua report that in a distant age the sun shot an arrow into the ground: from that hole were born a man and a woman (Thévet 1905, 9; Olivier 2003, 12).
37. Gerónimo de Mendieta ([1595] 1980, 80) observed the manufacture of several tlaquimilolli, each made for a separate deity, each of which included "por corazón unas pedrezuelas verdes" (some small green stones as hearts).
38. On the upset of Tepanec rule in the Valley of Mexico and the beginning of Mexica military expansion, see Schroeder's (2016, 62–75) examination of the military career of Tlacaelel, the Mexica cihuacoatl (royal adviser). Diego Durán, Fernando Alvarado Tezozomoc, and Chimalpahin are the three most extensive sources on Tlacaelel.

EPILOGUE

1. Cruz de la Cruz (2016, 154–59) also published an autobiographical piece in McDonough's *The Learned Ones*. In the same volume, the Nahuatl poet Refugio Nava Nava and the Nahua scholar Victoriano de la Cruz provided autobiographical vignettes in Nahuatl, which are labeled as *Tlen naman* (that which is now), emphasizing the vitality of writing in contemporary Chicontepec. Cruz de la Cruz has also contributed to Stephanie Wood's

NEH-funded project "An Online Nahuatl Lexical Database: Bridging Past, Present, and Future Speakers" as well as to *Tlahtolxitlauhcayotl: Chicontepec, Veracruz* (J. Sullivan et al. 2016), the first monolingual dictionary of Huastecan Nahuatl. As one of the Native-speaker instructors at IDIEZ, Cruz de la Cruz shows how the institute empowers residents of Chicontepec through their language. For information about study opportunities on Huastecan Nahuatl and Classical Nahuatl, see IDIEZ Macehualli, "Instituto de Docencia e Investigación Etnológicas de Zacatecas, IDIEZ A.C.," accessed November 10, 2022, http://www.idiezmacehualli.org.

2. Cruz de la Cruz preferred to narrate her story in the third person (Cruz de la Cruz and Dufendach 2019, 649).
3. When the Nahuas of Río Balsas, Guerrero, say "zan ce imtlayotl" (they have only one maize) and "zan ce imetl" (they have only one metate), they describe how common work and shared domestic space unite groups (Good Eshelman 2005, 92–93).
4. For a survey of the calmecac and the telpochcalli—an academy of the arts of war—see Calnek (1988).
5. Much work exists examining the Moteuczoma lineage. Isabela (Tecuichpotzin) Moteucçoma (daughter of Moteuczoma Xocoyotl) received an encomienda in Tacuba from Hernán Cortés (C. Townsend 2006, 95; Martínez 2008, 111). Other scholars have examined the Moteuczoma family (Cline 1969, 84–88; P. Carrasco 1997, 90–91; Schroeder 2000, 52–53).
6. According to oral accounts in circulation in the twentieth century, Moteuczoma had gone into the earth and was alive still in an abode of tunnels. From there he would re-emerge when his people needed him most and restore order (López Austin 2011b, 47–48). Sandstrom (1991, 240) recorded accounts in the Huasteca describing the earth spirit *montesoma*, who, while unassociated with "the historical person," is a "frightening figure who consumes dead bodies after they have been buried, and who associates with horrifying underworld spirits."
7. For more on the origins and legacy of the M.E.Ch.A. movement, see Hidalgo (2016).
8. See Evans (2005). Juan Miahuatototl donated the amount and claimed the funds belong to Cuauhtemoc (BNAH GO, vol. 12, Annexo "B," FF 1113, f. 2r).
9. The protected category existed during Spain's Habsburg era. In 1697, Charles II emitted a *cédula real* that "upheld the privileged status of the descendants of pre-Hispanic nobles" in Mexico and Peru (Martínez 2008, 118). Richard Konetzke ([1958] 1962) reprinted the *cédula* in *Colección de documents para la historia de la formación social de Hispanoamérica: 1493–1810*, vol. 3, bk. I, 66–69.

REFERENCES

ARCHIVAL SOURCES
Archivo General de la Nación (Mexico City)
AGN Mercedes, vol. 2, exp. 532, f. 215v–216r
AGN Tierras 1871, exp. 17, cuaderno 1
AGN Tierras 1871, exp. 17, f. 382r, f. 383r
AGN Inquisición, vol. 333, f. 35r
AGN Mercedes, vol. 7, f. 270v
AGN Tierras 35, exp. 4, f. 17r
AGN Tierras 2809, exp. 16, f. 22r
AGN Tierras 158, exp. 1, f. 7r
AGN Tributos 113, vol. 45, exp. 3, f. 14r–17r
AGN Tributos, vol. 11, exp. 34, "Carta sobre Huaquechula e Izucar"

Biblioteca Nacional de Antropología e Historia (Mexico City)
BNAH GO, vol. 12, Annexo "B," FF 1113 (*Códice del Tecpan de Santiago de Tlatelolco*)
BNAH Casa 66, Título 6, f. 337r–341v

Archivo General de las Indias (Seville, accessed online)
AGI Justicia 291, f. 97r–97v
AGI Justicia, leg. 164, no. 2, f. 261r

Archivo General de las Indias (Guatemala City, referenced in secondary sources)

AGI Guatemala 52, "Indios de Tlaxcala y México a Carlos V," March 15, 1547
AGI Guatemala 168, "Fray Francisco de la Parra a Carlos V"

Archivo General de Centro América (Guatemala City, referenced in secondary sources)

AGCA A1, leg. 73, exp. 1720, f. 8r, f. 19r
AGCA A1.23, leg. 4575, f. 64v, f. 84v
AGCA A1.23, leg. 4575, f. 48r
AGCA A1.23, leg. 1512, f. 457r [Dec. 24, 1574]

PUBLISHED SOURCES

Acosta, José de. 2006. *Historia natural y moral de las Indias*. Mexico City: Fondo de cultura económico.

Acuña, René, ed. 1984. *Relaciones geográficas del siglo XVI: Tlaxcala, Descripción de la ciudad y provincia de Tlaxcala de la Nueva España y las Indias y del mar océano para el buen gobierno y ennoblecimiento dellas.* 2 vols. Mexico City: Instituto de Investigaciones Antropológicas, UNAM.

Adams, Francisco. 2005. "De tecpan a cabecera: Cholula o la metamorfosis de un reino soberano nahua en ayuntamiento indio del rey de España durante el siglo XVI." *Dimensión antropológica* 12 (33): 7–67.

Aguilar, Francisco de. 1980. *Relación breve de la conquista de la Nueva España*. Mexico City: Instituto de Investigaciones Históricas, UNAM.

Aguilar-Moreno, Manuel. 2007. *Handbook to Life in the Aztec World*. New York: Oxford University Press.

Aguilera, Elizabeth. 2014. "Malintzin as a Visual Metaphor in the *Lienzo de Tlaxcala*." *Hemisphere: Visual Cultures of the Americas* 7 (1): 8–24.

Alfonso X, el Sabio. 1930. *General estoria*. Pt. 1. Edited by Antonio G. Solalinde. Madrid: Centro de Estudios Históricos.

Altman, Ida. 2010. *The War for Mexico's West: Indians and Spaniards in New Galicia, 1524–1550*. Albuquerque: University of New Mexico Press.

Anales de Cuauhtitlan: Noticias históricas de México y sus contornos compiladas por José Fernando Ramírez y traducidas por los señores Faustino Galicia Chimalpopoca, Gumesindo Mendoza y Felipe Sánchez Solís. 1885. Mexico City: Anales del Museo Nacional.

Anales de Tecamachalco. (1398–1590) 1992. Edited by Eustaquio Celestino Solís and Luis Reyes García. Mexico City: FCE.

Anderson, Benedict. 2016. *Imagined Communities: Reflections on the Origin and Spread of Nationalism*. New York: Verso.

Anderson, Jane, and Kimberly Christen. 2019. "Decolonizing Attribution: Traditions of Exclusion." *Journal of Radical Librarianship* 5 (1): 113–52.
Anzaldúa, Gloria. 1999. *Borderlands: [The New Mestiza] = La Frontera*. San Francisco: Aunt Lute Books.
Aquinas, Thomas. *Summa Theologiae*. 1948. Taurini, Italy: Marietti.
Arias, Santa. 2006. "La visión Nahua ante la conquista espiritual: Milenarismo e hibridez en los Anales de Juan Bautista." In *Ensayos de cultura virreinal latinoamericana*, edited by Juan Zevallos Aguilar, Takahiro Kato, Luis Millones, and the Latin American Indian Literatures Association, 33–52. Lima: Fondo Editorial de la Facultad de Ciencias Sociales UNMSM.
Aristotle. *History of Animals in Ten Books*. 1862. Translated by Richard Creswell. London: Henry Bohn.
Asensio, Eugenio. 1988. "El Inca Garcilaso: Dos tipos coetáneos de historia." In *Historia y crítica de la literatura hispanoamericana*, edited by Cedomil Goic, 177–81. Barcelona: Grijalbo.
Asselbergs, Florine. 2008. *Conquered Conquistadors: The Lienzo de Quauhquechollan: A Nahua Vision of the Conquest of Guatemala*. Boulder: University Press of Colorado.
Asselbergs, Florine. 2012. "El Mapa Circular de Quauhquechollan." *Tlalocan* 17 (1): 219–33.
Auto proveído por el virrey. 1958. In *Sobre el modo de tributar los indios de Nueva España a Su Majestad, 1561–1564*, vol. 5, edited by France Vinton Scholes and Eleanor Adams, 116–18. Mexico City: Porrúa.
Aveni, Anthony, and Gordon Brotherston, eds. 1983. *Proceedings of the Forty-Fourth Meeting of the International Congress of Americanists, Manchester, 1982: Calendars in Mesoamerica and Peru: Native American Computations of Time*. Oxford: B.A.R.
Báez-Jorge, Félix, and Arturo Gómez Martínez. 2000. "Los equilibrios del cielo y de la tierra: Cosmovisión de los nahuas de Chicontepec." *Desacatos* 5:79–94.
Bakhtin, Mikhail. 1981. *The Dialogic Imagination*. Translated by Caryl Emerson and Michael Holquist. Austin: University of Texas Press.
Bal, Mieke. 2004. *Narrative Theory: Critical Concepts in Literary and Cultural Studies*. London: Routledge, 2004.
Bal, Mieke. 2021. *Narratology in Practice*. Toronto: University of Toronto Press.
Barlow, Robert. 1949a. *The Extent of the Empire of the Culhua Mexica*. Berkeley: University of California Press.
Barlow, Robert. 1949b. "Relación de Zempoala y su partido, 1580." *Tlalocan* 3:29–41.
Barthes, Roland. 1977. *Image-Music-Text*. Edited and translated by Stephen Heath. New York: Hill and Wang.
Bassett, Molly. 2015. *The Fate of Earthly Things: Aztec Gods and God-Bodies*. Austin: University of Texas Press.

Baudez, Claude. 1984. "Le Roi, La Balle et le Mais, Images due Jeu de Balle Maya." *Journal de Société des Americanistes* 70:139–52.
Baudot, Georges. 1994. "Identité mexicatl, conscience d'altérité cosmogonique et mexicayotl." *Caravelle* 62:155–62.
Baudot, Georges. 1997. "Los franciscanos etnógrafos." *Estudios de Cultura Náhuatl* 27 (1): 275–307.
Benjamin, Walter. 1973. *Illuminations*. Edited and with an introduction by Hannah Arendt. Translated by Harry Zohn. London: Fontana.
Berdan, Frances. 2014. *Aztec Archaeology and Ethnohistory*. Cambridge: Cambridge University Press.
Berdan, Frances, and Patricia Anawalt. 1997. *The Essential Codex Mendoza*. Berkeley: University of California Press.
Berlin, Heinrich, and Robert Hayward Barlow. 1948. *Anales de Tlatelolco: Unos anales históricos de la nación mexicana y Códice de Tlatelolco*. Vol. 2. Mexico City: Porrúa.
Bhabha, Homi K. 2012. *The Location of Culture*. New York: Routledge.
Bierhorst, John. 2010. *Ballads of the Lords of New Spain: The Codex Romances de los Señores de la Nueva España*. Austin: University of Texas Press.
Blitz, John. 1988. "Adoption of the Bow in Prehistoric North America." *North American Archaeologist* 9 (2): 123–45.
Boas, Franz, and José María Arreola. 1920. "Cuentos en mexicano de Milpa Alta, D.F." *Journal of American Folklore* 33 (127): 1–24.
Boas, Franz, and Herman Haeberlin. 1924. "Ten Folktales in Modern Nahuatl." *Journal of American Folklore* 37 (145/146): 345–70.
Boone, Elizabeth. 1989. *Incarnations of the Aztec Supernatural: The Image of Huitzilopochtli in Mexico and Europe*. Transactions of the American Philosophical Society 79. Philadelphia: American Philosophical Society.
Boone, Elizabeth. 1992. "Guías para vivir: Los manuscritos adivinatorios pintados de México." In *Azteca Mexica*, edited by José Alcina Franch, 333–38. Madrid: Centro Cultural de la Villa.
Boone, Elizabeth. 1994. "Introduction: Writing and Recording Knowledge." In *Writing Without Words: Alternative Literacies in Mesoamerica and the Andes*, edited by Elizabeth Boone and Walter Mignolo, 3–26. Durham, N.C.: Duke University Press.
Boone, Elizabeth. 2000. *Stories in Red and Black: Pictorial Histories of the Aztec and Mixtec*. Austin: University of Texas Press.
Boone, Elizabeth. 2005. "In Tlamatinime: The Wise Men and Women of Aztec Mexico." In *Painted Books and Indigenous Knowledge: Manuscript Studies in Honor of Mary Elizabeth Smith*, edited by Elizabeth Boone, 9–25. New Orleans: Tulane University.
Boone, Elizabeth. 2007. *Cycles of Time and Meaning in the Mexican Books of Fate*. Austin: University of Texas Press.

Brading, David. 1991. *The First America: The Spanish Monarchy, Creole Patriots, and the Liberal State 1492–1867*. Cambridge: Cambridge University Press.

Brady, James, and Keith Prufer. (2005) 2013. *In the Maw of the Earth Monster: Mesoamerican Ritual Cave Use*. Austin: University of Texas Press.

Brennan, Sallie Craven. 1988. "Cosmogonic Use of Time and Space in Historical Narrative: The Case of the *Crónica Mexicayotl*." PhD diss., University of Rochester.

Brian, Amber. 2014. "The Original Alva Ixtlilxochitl Manuscripts at Cambridge University." *Colonial Latin American Review* 23 (1): 84–101.

Brian, Amber, Bradley Benton, and Pablo García Loaeza. 2015. *The Native Conquistador: Alva Ixtlilxochitl's Account of the Conquest of New Spain*. University Park, Pa.: Penn State University Press.

Brock, Kerry, and George Diggs. 2013. *The Hunter-Gatherer Within: Health and the Natural Human Diet*. Fort Worth: Botanical Research Institute of Texas Press.

Brotherston, Gordon. 2008. "America and the Colonizer Question: Two Formative Statements from Early Mexico." In Moraña, Dussel, and Jáuregui 2008, 23–42.

Browne, Walden. 2000. *Sahagún and the Transition to Modernity*. Norman: University of Oklahoma Press.

Bueno Bravo, Isabel. 2005. "Tlatelolco: La Gemela en la Sombra." *Revista Española de Antropología Americana* 35:133–48.

Burkhart, Brian Yazzie. 2003. "What Coyote and Thales Can Teach Us: An Outline of American Indian Epistemology." In *American Indian Thought: Philosophical Essays*, edited by Anne Waters, 15–26. Malden, Mass.: Blackwell.

Burkhart, Louise. 1986. "Moral Deviance in Sixteenth-Century Nahua and Christian Thought: The Rabbit and the Deer." *Journal of Latin American Lore* 12 (2): 107–39.

Burkhart, Louise. 1989. *The Slippery Earth: Nahua-Christian Moral Dialogue in Sixteenth-Century Mexico*. Tucson: University of Arizona Press.

Burkhart, Louise. 1992. "Flowery Heaven: The Aesthetic of Paradise in Nahuatl Devotional Literature." *RES: Anthropology and Aesthetics* 21 (1): 88–109.

Burkhart, Louise. 2010. *Holy Wednesday: A Nahua Drama from Early Colonial Mexico*. Philadelphia: University of Pennsylvania Press.

Burkhart, Louise. 2017. "Introduction." In Tavárez 2017, 4–28.

Bustamante García, Jesús. 1990. *Fray Bernardino de Sahagún: Una revisión crítica de los manuscritos y de su proceso de composición*. Mexico City: UNAM.

Busto, Rudy. 1998. "The Predicament of Nepantla: Chicana/o Religions in the Twenty-First Century." *Perspectives* 1:7–21.

Calnek, Edward. 1988. "The Calmecac and Telpochcalli in Pre-Conquest Tenochtitlan." In Klor de Alva, Nicholson, and Quiñones Keber 1988, 169–77.

Camargo, Diego Muñoz. (1585) 1998. *Historia de Tlaxcala: Manuscrito 210 de La Biblioteca Nacional de París*. Vol. 5. Edited by Luis Reyes García. Tlaxcala, Mexico: Gobierno del Estado de Tlaxcala.

Campbell, Joe. 1985. *A Morphological Dictionary of Classical Nahuatl and Morpheme Index to the Vocabulario en Lengua Mexana y Castellana of Fray Alonso de Molina*. Madison, Wis.: Hispanic Seminary of Medieval Studies.

Canclini, Néstor García. 2005. *Hybrid Cultures: Strategies for Entering and Leaving Modernity*. Minneapolis: University of Minnesota Press.

Carballo, David. 2020. *Collision of Worlds: A Deep History of the Fall of Aztec Mexico and the Forging of New Spain*. Oxford: Oxford University Press.

Cárcamo-Huechante, Luis. 2013. "Indigenous Interference: Mapuche Use of Radio in Times of Acoustic Colonialism." *Latin American Research Review* 48 (1): 50–68.

Carod-Artal, Francisco Javier. 2015. "Hallucinogenic Drugs in Pre-Columbian Mesoamerican Cultures." *Neurología* 30 (1): 42–49.

Carrasco, David. 1984. *Quetzalcoatl and the Irony of Empire: Myths and Prophecies in the Aztec Tradition*. Chicago: University of Chicago Press.

Carrasco, David. 1999. *City of Sacrifice: The Aztec Empire and the Role of Violence in Civilization*. Boston: Beacon Press.

Carrasco, David. 2013. *Religions of Mesoamerica*. Long Grove, Ill.: Waveland Press.

Carrasco, David. 2020. "The Imagination of Matter: Mesoamerican Trees, Cities, and Human Sacrifice." In *Wiley Blackwell Companion to Religion and Materiality*, edited by Vasudha Narayanan, 258–73. Malden, Mass.: Wiley-Blackwell.

Carrasco, David, and Scott Sessions. 1998. *Daily Life of the Aztecs: People of the Sun and Earth*. Westport, Conn.: Greenwood Press.

Carrasco, Pedro. 1997. "Indian-Spanish Marriages in the First Century of the Colony." In *Indian Women of Early Mexico*, edited by Susan Schroeder, Stephanie Wood, and Robert Haskett, 87–103. Norman: University of Oklahoma Press.

Carrillo Cázares, Alberto. 2000. *El debate sobre la guerra chichimeca, 1531–1585: Derecho y política en la Nueva España*. 2 vols. Zamora: El Colegio de Michoacán.

Case, Emalani. 2021. *Everything Ancient Was Once New: Indigenous Persistence from Hawai'i to Kahiki*. Honolulu: University of Hawai'i Press.

Castañeda de la Paz, María. 2009. "Central Mexican Indigenous Coats of Arms and the Conquest of Mesoamerica." *Ethnohistory* 56 (1): 125–61.

Castañeda de la Paz, María, and Miguel Luque Talaván. 2010a. "Heráldica Indígena: Iconografía tipo códice en los escudos de armas tepanecas." *Arqueología mexicana* 18 (105): 70–75.

Castañeda de La Paz, María, and Miguel Luque-Talaván. 2010b. "Privileges of the 'Others': The Coats of Arms Granted to Indigenous Conquistadors." In *The International Emblem: From Incunabula to the Internet Selected Proceedings of the Eighth International Conference of the Society for Emblem Studies, 28 July–1 August, 2008, Winchester College,* edited by Simon McKeown. Newcastle, UK: Cambridge Scholars Publishing. 283–316.

Chandler, Michael. 2013. "On Being Indigenous: An Essay on the Hermeneutics of 'Cultural Identity.'" *Human Development* 56 (2): 83–97.

Chávez Orozco, Luis, ed. 1947. *Códice Osuna acompañado de 158 páginas inéditas encontradas en el Archivo General de la Nación.* Mexico City: Instituto Indigenista Interamericano.

Chevalier, Jacques, and Andrés Sánchez Bain. 2003. *The Hot and the Cold: Ills of Humans and Maize in Native Mexico.* Toronto: University of Toronto Press.

Chimalpahin, Domingo. 1997. *Codex Chimalpahin: Society and Politics in Mexico Tenochtitlan, Tlatelolco, Texcoco, Culhuacan, and Other Nahua Altepetl in Central Mexico: The Nahuatl and Spanish Annals and Accounts Collected and Recorded by don Domingo de San Antón Muñón Chimalpahin Quauhtlehuanitzin.* Vol. 1. Edited and translated by Arthur Anderson and Susan Schroeder, with introduction by Wayne Ruwet. Norman: University of Oklahoma Press.

Chimalpahin, Domingo. 1998. *Las ocho relaciones y el Memorial de Cohuacan.* 2 vols. Edited by Rafael Tena. Mexico City: Cien de México.

Chimalpahin Cuauhtlehuanitzin, Domingo Francisco de San Antón Muñón. 2006. *Annals of His Time: Don Domingo de San Antón Muñón Chimalpahin Quauhtlehuanitzin.* Edited and translated by James Lockhart, Susan Schroeder, and Doris Namala. Stanford, Calif.: Stanford University Press.

Chipman, Donald. 2005. *Moctezuma's Children: Aztec Royalty Under Spanish Rule, 1520–1700.* Austin: University of Texas Press.

Christensen, Mark. 2010. "The Tales of Two Cultures: Ecclesiastical Texts and Nahua and Maya Catholicisms." *The Americas* 66 (3): 353–77.

Cicero, Marcus Tullius. 1921. *De divinatio.* Vol. 1. Urbana: University of Illinois Press.

Clavijero, Francisco. (1787) 1804. *The History of Mexico: Collected from Spanish and Mexican Historians, from Manuscripts, and Ancient Paintings of the Indians. Translated from the Original Italian by Charles Cullen.* 2 vols. Philadelphia: Thomas Dobson.

Clendinnen, Inga. 1991. *The Aztecs: An Interpretation.* Cambridge: Cambridge University Press.

Cline, Howard. 1969. "Hernando Cortés and the Aztec Indians in Spain." *Quarterly Journal of the Library of Congress* 26 (2): 70–90.

Codex Aubin. 1980. Edited by Alfredo Chavero. Mexico City: Innovación.

Codex Azcatitlan. 1995. Edited by Michel Graulich and Robert Barlow. Paris: Bibliothèque Nationale de France Société des Américanistes.

Codex en Cruz. 1981. Edited by Charles Dibble. 2 vols. Salt Lake City: University of Utah Press.

Codex Huaquechula. 1945. Mexico City: Fototeca Nacional de México.

Codex Magliabechiano. 1970. Graz: Akademische Druck–u. Verlagsantalt (ADEVA).

Códice matritense de la Real Academia de la Historia: Memoriales en tres columnas con el texto en lengua mexicana de cuatro libros (VIII á XI) de los doce que componen la obra general. 1907. Edited by Francisco del Paso y Troncoso. Madrid: Hauser y Menet.

Codex Mexicanus. 1952. "Commentaire du *Codex Mexicanus,* nos. 23–24 de la Bibliothèque Nationale de Paris." Edited by Ernest Mention. *Journal de la Société des Américanistes* 41:387–498.

Codex Vaticanus 3738 (Codex. Vaticanus. A, Codex. Ríos). 1979. Biblioteca Apostolica Vaticana; Farbreproduktion des Codex in verkleinertem Format. Graz: Akad. Dr.- u. Verl.-Anst.

Códice Vaticano Latino 3738/Códice Vaticanus Ríos. 1964. *Antigüedades de México basadas en la recopilación de Lord Kingsborough* 3:7–313.

Connell, William. 2011. *After Moctezuma: Indigenous Politics and Self-Government in Mexico City, 1524–1730.* Norman: University of Oklahoma Press.

Contreras, Daniel. 2004. "Sobre la Fundación de Santiago de Guatemala y la rebelión de los Kaqchikeles." In *El Memorial de Sololá y los inicios de la colonización en Guatemala,* edited by J. Daniel Contreras R. and Jorge Luján Muñoz, 45–64. Guatemala City: Academia de Geografía e Historia de Guatemala.

Cornejo Polar, Antonio. 2011. *Escribir en el aire: Ensayo sobre la Heterogeneidad Socio-Cultural en las Literaturas Andinas.* Lima: Centro de Estudios Literarios "Antonio Cornejo Polar": Latinoamericana Editores.

Corominas, Joan. (1961) 2008. *Breve diccionario etimológico de la lengua castellana.* Madrid: Gredos.

Cortés, Hernán. 1526. *La quarta relaciõ que Fernãndo cortes gouernador y capitã general por [s]u mage[s]tad en la nueua E[s]paña del mar oceano ẽbio al muy alto y muy potenti[ss]imo inuciti[ss]imo [s]eñor don Carlos emperador [s]emper agu[s]to y rey d'Spaña nro señor. en la qual e[s]tan otras cartas y relaciones quelos capitanes Pedro de aluarado e Diego godoy embiaron al dicho capitan Fernardo cortes.* Valencia: George de Costilla.

Cortés, Hernán. 1963. *Cartas y documentos.* Mexico City: Porrúa.

Cortés, Hernán. 1993. *Cartas de relación.* Edited by Ángel Delgado Gómez. Madrid: Editorial Castalia.

Cortés, Rocío. 2008. "The Colegio Imperial de Santa Cruz de Tlatelolco and Its Aftermath: Nahua Intellectuals and the Spiritual Conquest of Mexico." In *A Companion to Latin American Literature and Culture,* edited by Sara Castro-Klaren, 86–105. Oxford: Blackwell.

Cortés, Rocío. 2011. *El nahuatlato Alvarado y el Tlalamatl huauhquilpan: Mecanismos de la memoria colectiva de una comunidad indígena.* New York: Hispanic Seminary of Medieval Studies.

Cosentino, Delia Annunziata. 2002. "Landscapes of Lineage: Nahua Pictorial Genealogies of Early Colonial Tlaxcala, Mexico." PhD diss., University of California, Los Angeles.

Crawford O'Brien, Suzanne. 2008. "Introduction." In *Religion and Healing in Native America: Pathways for Renewal*, edited by Suzanne Crawford O'Brien, 1–12. Westport, Conn.: Praeger.

Crewe, Ryan. 2018. "Building in the Shadow of Death: Monastery Construction and the Politics of Community Reconstitution in Sixteenth-Century Mexico." *The Americas* 75 (3): 489–523.

Cruz, Gustavo Roberto. 2010. "El soplo vital del indianismo revolucionario: Fausto Reinaga (1906–1994)." In *Perfil de Bolivia (1940–2009)*, edited by Gaya Makaran, 43–70. Mexico City: Centro de Investigaciones sobre América Latina y el Caribe, UNAM.

Cruz, Martín de la, and Juan Badiano. (1552) 1991. *Libellus de Medicinalibus Indorum Herbis: Manuscrito Azteca de 1552*. 2 vols. Mexico City: FCE.

Cruz Cruz, Eduardo de la. 2015. "Tlaneltoquilli: Chicomexochitl huan Tenantzitzimitl." In *Tototatahhuan ininixtlamatiliz*, edited by Eduardo De la Cruz, 41–69. Warsaw: University of Warsaw; Zacatecas: Instituto de Docencia e Investigación Etnológicas de Zacatecas (IDIEZ).

Cruz Cruz, Eduardo de la. 2017. "Cenyahtoc cintli tonacayo: Huahcapatl huan tlen naman." University of Warsaw.

Cruz Cruz, Victoriano de la. 2015. "Chicomexochitl y el Maíz entre los Nahuas de Chicontepec: La Continuidad del Ritual." *Politeja-Pismo Wydziału Studiów Międzynarodowych i Politycznych Uniwersytetu Jagiellońskiego* 12 (38): 129–47.

Cruz Cruz, Victoriano de la. 2016. "Tlen naman 3: Tlapepetlaca (Lightning Strikes Again and Again)." In McDonough 2016, 116–19.

Cruz de la Cruz, Abelardo de la. 2017. "The Value of El Costumbre and Christianity in the Discourse of Nahua Catechists from the Huasteca Region in Veracruz, Mexico, 1970s–2010s." In Tavárez 2017, 267–88.

Cruz de la Cruz, Sabina. 2016. "Cihuatequiuh (Women's Work)." In McDonough 2016, 154–59.

Cruz de la Cruz, Sabina, and Rebecca Dufendach. 2019. "Tepahtihquetl pan ce pilaltepetzin / A Village Healer." *Ethnohistory* 66 (4): 647–66.

Davies, Nigel. 1987. *The Aztec Empire: The Toltec Resurgence*. Norman: University of Oklahoma Press.

Dean, Carolyn, and Dana Leibsohn. 2003. "Hybridity and Its Discontents: Considering Visual Culture in Colonial Spanish America." *Colonial Latin American Review* 12 (1): 5–35.

Deloria, Vine. 1999. *Spirit and Reason: The Vine Deloria, Jr., Reader*. Edited by Barbara Deloria, Kristen Foehner, and Sam Scinta. Golden, Colo.: Fulcrum.

Díaz, Ana. 2020a. "Dissecting the Sky: Discursive Translations in Mexican Colonial Cosmographies." In Díaz Alvarez 2020b, 100–140.

Díaz, Ana, ed. 2020b. *Reshaping the World: Debates on Mesoamerican Cosmologies*. Boulder: University Press of Colorado.
Díaz Balsera, Viviana. 2008. "Celebrating the Rise of a New Sun: The Tlaxcalans Conquer Jerusalem in 1539." *Estudios de Cultura Náhuatl* 39 (1): 311–30.
Díaz Balsera, Viviana. 2011. "Atando dioses y humanos: Cipactonal y la cura por adivinación en el tratado sobre idolatrías de Hernando Ruiz de Alarcón." In *Estudios Coloniales Latinoamericanos en el Siglo XXI: Nuevos Itinerarios*, edited by Stephanie Kirk, 321–49. Pittsburgh, Pa.: Instituto Internacional de Literatura Iberoamericana.
Díaz Balsera, Viviana. 2018. *Guardians of Idolatry: Gods, Demons, and Priests in Hernando Ruiz de Alarcón's Treatise on the Heathen Superstitions*. Norman: University of Oklahoma Press.
Díaz del Castillo, Bernal. 1968. *Historia verdadera de la conquista de la Nueva España*. 2 vols. Mexico City: Porrúa.
Diel, Lori Boornazian. 2008. *The Tira de Tepechpan: Negotiating Place Under Aztec and Spanish Rule*. Austin: University of Texas Press.
Diel, Lori Boornazian. 2018. *The Codex Mexicanus: A Guide to Life in Late Sixteenth-Century New Spain*. Austin: University of Texas Press.
Dillon, Grace. 2012. *Walking the Clouds: An Anthology of Indigenous Science Fiction*. Tucson: University of Arizona Press.
Dufendach, Rebecca. 2019. "'As if His Heart Died': A Reinterpretation of Moteuczoma's Cowardice in the Conquest History of the *Florentine Codex*." *Ethnohistory* 66 (4): 623–45.
Durán, Diego. 1967. *Historia de las Indias de Nueva España e Islas de la Tierra Firme*. 2 vols. Mexico City: Porrúa.
Durán, Diego. 1994. *The History of the Indies of New Spain*. Translated by Doris Heyden. Norman: University of Oklahoma Press.
Dussel, Enrique. 1981. *A History of the Church in Latin America*. Translated by Alan Neely. Grand Rapids, Mich.: Eerdmans.
Duverger, Christian. 2000 *Mesoamérica: Arte y antropología*. Paris: Américo Arte Editores.
Dyckerhoff, Ursula. 2003. "Grupos étnicos y estratificación socio-política: Tentativa de interpretación histórica." *Indiana* (2003): 155–96.
Easthope, Antony. 1991. *Literary into Cultural Studies*. London: Routledge.
Estrada de Gerlero, Elena Isabel. 1992. "Una obra de plumaria de los talleres de San José de los Naturales." In *Arte y coerción: Primer Coloquio del Comité Mexicano de Historia del Arte*, edited by Comité Mexicano de Historia del Arte, 97–107. Mexico City: UNAM.
Estrada Lugo, Erin, Efraín Hernández Xolocotzi, Teresa Rojas Rabiela, and Emil Engleman. 1989. *El Códice Florentino: Su información etnobotánica*. Montecillo, Estado de México: Colegio de Postgraduados, Institución de Enseñanza e Investigación en Ciencias Agrícolas.

Etymologies of Isidore of Seville. 2006. Edited and translated by Stephen Barney, W. J. Lewis, J. A. Beach, and Oliver Berghof. Cambridge: Cambridge University Press.

Evans, Susan Toby. 1998. "Sexual Politics in the Aztec Palace: Public, Private, and Profane." *RES: Anthropology and Aesthetics* 33 (1): 166–83.

Evans, Susan Toby. 2005. "The Aztec Palace Under the Spanish Rule: Disks Motifs in the *Mapa de México de 1550 (Uppsala Mapa* or *Mapa de Santa Cruz*)." In *The Postclassic to Spanish-Era Transition in Mesoamerica: Archaeological Perspectives*, edited by Susan Kepecs and Rani Alexander, 14–33. Albuquerque: University of New Mexico Press.

Exigit sincere devotions affects. 1478. Sixtus IV. Portal de Archivos Españoles. http://pares.mcu.es/ParesBusquedas20/catalogo/autoridad/46283.

Eximiae devotionis affectus. 1510. Adrian VI. Arquivo nacional, Torre do Pombo. Direção-geral do livro, dos arquivos e das bibliotecas. https://www.papalencyclicals.net/alex06/alex06inter.htm.

Farriss, Nancy. 1987. "Remembering the Future, Anticipating the Past: History, Time, and Cosmology Among the Maya of Yucatan." *Comparative Studies in Society and History* 29 (3): 566–93.

Favrot Peterson, Jeanette. 2005. "Creating the Virgin of Guadalupe: The Cloth, the Artist, and Sources in Sixteenth-Century New Spain." *The Americas* 61 (4): 571–610.

Favrot Peterson, Jeanette. 2019. "Images in Translation: A Codex 'Muy Historiado.'" In Favrot Peterson and Terraciano 2019, 21–36.

Favrot Peterson, Jeanette, and Kevin Terraciano, eds. 2019. *The "Florentine Codex": An Encyclopedia of the Nahua World in Sixteenth-Century Mexico*. Austin: University of Texas Press.

Fellowes, William. 1977. "The Treatises of Hernando Ruiz de Alarcón." *Tlalocan* 7:309–55.

Fernández Christlieb, Federico, and Ángel Julián García Zambrano. 2006. "La policía, de los indios y la urbanización del altepetl." In *Territorialidad y paisaje en el altepetl del siglo XVI*, edited by Federico Fernández Christlieb and Ángel Julián García Zambrano, 114–62. Mexico City: FCE.

Florescano, Enrique. 1992. "Concepciones de la historia." In *Filosofía iberoamericana en la época del encuentro*, edited by Laureano Robles, 309–29. Madrid: Trotta.

Florescano, Enrique. 1994. *Memory, Myth, and Time in Mexico: From the Aztecs to Independence*. Translated by Albert Bork. Austin: University of Texas Press.

Florescano, Enrique. 1999. *The Myth of Quetzalcoatl*. Translated by Lysa Hochroth. Baltimore: Johns Hopkins University Press.

Florescano, Enrique. 2002. "El canon memorioso forjado por los *Títulos primordiales*." *Colonial Latin American Review* 11 (2): 183–230.

Florescano, Enrique. 2004. *Quetzalcóatl y los mitos fundadores de Mesoamérica*. Mexico City: Taurus-Santillana Ediciones Generales.
Foster, George. 1953. "Relationships Between Spanish and Spanish-American Folk Medicine." *Journal of American Folklore* 66 (261): 201–17.
Foucault, Michel. 1969. "What Is an Author." Translated by Josue Harari. In *Textual Strategies: Perspectives in Post-Structuralist Criticism*, edited by Josue Harari, 141–60. Ithaca, N.Y.: Cornell University Press.
Foucault, Michel. (1982) 2019. "*Parrēsia*: Lecture at the University of Grenoble, May 18, 1982." Translated by Nancy Luxon. In *Discourse and Truth and Parrēsia*, edited by Henri-Paul Fruchaud and Daniele Lorenzini, 1–38. Chicago: University of Chicago Press.
Fuentes y Guzmán, Francisco Antonio de. 1932. *Recordación Florida: Discurso historial y demostración natural, material, militar y política del Reyno de Guatemala*. Edición conforme al códice del siglo XVII que original se conserva en el archivo de la municipalidad de Guatemala. 3 vols. Guatemala City: Biblioteca Goathemala de la Sociedad de Geografía e Historia de Guatemala.
Gall, Francis, ed. 1963. *Título del Ajpop Huitzilzin Tzunún: Probanza de méritos de los de León y Cardona*. Ministerio de Educación Pública 11. Guatemala City: Centro Editorial José de Pineda Ibarra.
Gall, Francis. 1967. "Los Gonzalo de Alvarado, Conquistadores de Guatemala." *Anales de la Sociedad de Geografía e Historia* 40 (3–4): 38–49.
Gall, Francis, ed. 2000. *Diccionario geográfico de Guatemala*. Guatemala City: Instituto Geográfico Nacional. CD.
García Chávez, Raúl. 2007. "El altepetl como formación sociopolítica de la cuenca de México: Su origen y desarrollo durante el Posclásico Medio." *Arqueoweb: Revista sobre arqueología en internet* 8 (2): n.p.
García Garagarza, León. 2013. "The Year the People Turned into Cattle: The End of the World in New Spain, 1558." In *Centering Animals in Latin American History*, edited by Martha Few and Zeb Tortorici, 31–61. Durham, N.C.: Duke University Press.
Garduño, Ana. 1997. *Conflictos y alianzas entre Tlatelolco y Tenochtitlan, siglos XII a XV*. Mexico City: INAH.
Garibay, Ángel María. (1940) 2007. *La llave del náhuatl*. Mexico City: Porrúa.
Garibay, Ángel María. 1945. "Temas guadalupanos II: El diario de Juan Bautista." *Revista Ábside* 9 (2): 155–69.
Garibay, Ángel María. (1954) 1971. *Historia de la literatura náhuatl*. Vol. 1. Mexico City: Porrúa.
Geertz, Clifford. 1973. *The Interpretation of Cultures*. New York: Basic Books.
Gell, Alfred. 1998. *Art and Agency: An Anthropological Theory*. Oxford: Clarendon Press.
Gibson, Charles. 1952. *Tlaxcala in the Sixteenth Century*. Stanford, Calif.: Stanford University Press.

Gibson, Charles. 1964. *The Aztecs Under Spanish Rule: A History of the Indians of the Valley of Mexico, 1519–1810*. Stanford, Calif.: Stanford University Press.

Gillespie, Jeanne. 2004. *Saints and Warriors: Tlaxcalan Perspectives on the Conquest of Tenochtitlan*. New Orleans: University Press of the South.

Gillespie, Susan. 1989. *The Aztec Kings: Construction of Rulership in Mexican History*. Tucson: University of Arizona Press.

Gimmel, Millie. 2008a. "An Ecocritical Evaluation of Book XI of the *Florentine Codex*." In *Early Modern Ecostudies: From the Florentine Codex to Shakespeare*, edited by Thomas Hallock, Ivo Kamps, and Karen L. Raber, 167–80. New York: Palgrave Macmillan.

Gimmel, Millie. 2008b. "Reading Medicine in the Codex de la Cruz Badiano." *Journal of the History of Ideas* 69 (2): 169–92.

Ginzburg, Carlo. 1980. *The Cheese and the Worms: The Cosmos of a Sixteenth-Century Miller*. Baltimore: Johns Hopkins University Press.

Glass, John. 1964. *Catálogo de la colección de codices del Museo Nacional de Antropología*. Mexico City: INAH.

Glass, John, and Donald Robertson. 1975. *A Census of Native Middle American Pictorial Manuscripts*. In *Handbook of Middle American Indians*, vol. 14, edited by Robert Wauchope, 81–252. Austin: University of Texas Press.

Goldie, Terry. 1995. "The Representation of the Indigene." In *The Postcolonial Studies Reader*, edited by Bill Ashcroft, Gareth Griffiths, and Helen Tiffin, 259–63. New York: Routledge.

Good Eshelman, Catharine. 1994. "Trabajo, intercambio y la construcción de la historia: Una exploración etnográfica de la lógica cultural nahua." *Cuicuilco: Nueva Época* 1 (2): 139–53.

Good Eshelman, Catharine. 2001. "El ritual y la reproducción de la cultura: ceremonias agrícolas, los muertos y la expresión estética entre los nahuas de Guerrero." In *Cosmovisión, ritual e identidad de los pueblos indígenas de México*, edited by Johanna Broda and Félix Báez-Jorge, 239–97. Mexico City: FCE.

Good Eshelman, Catharine. 2005. "Ejes conceptuales entre los nahuas de Guerrero: Expresión de un modelo fenomenológico mesoamericano." *Estudios de Cultura Náhuatl* 36 (1): 87–113.

Goodyear-Kaʻōpua, Noelani. 2019. "Indigenous Oceanic Futures: Challenging Settler Colonialisms and Militarization." In *Indigenous and Decolonizing Studies in Education*, edited by Linda Tuhiwai Smith, Eve Tuck, and K. Wayne Yang, 82–102.

Gossen, Gary, and Miguel León-Portilla, eds. 1993. *South and Mesoamerican Native Spirituality: From the Cult of the Feathered Serpent to the Theology of Liberation*. New York: Crossroads.

Granziera, Patrizia. 2001. "Concept of the Garden in Pre-Hispanic Mexico." *Garden History* 29 (2): 185–213.

Graulich, Michel. 1992. "Quetzalcoatl-Ehecatl: The Bringer of Life." In *Ancient America: Contributions to New World Archaelogy*, edited by Nicholas Saunders, 33–38. Oxbow Monograph 24. Oxford, UK: Oxbow Press.

Graziano, Frank. 1999. *The Millennial New World*. New York: Oxford University Press.

Gruzinski, Serge. 2013. *The Mestizo Mind: Intellectual Dynamics of Colonization and Globalization*. New York: Routledge.

Gutiérrez, Gerardo. 2015. "Indigenous Coats of Arms in títulos primordiales and Techialoyan Códices: Nahua Corporate Heraldry in the Lienzos de Chiepetlan, Guerrero, Mexico." *Ancient Mesoamerica* 26 (1): 51–68.

Hajovsky, Patrick Thomas. 2015. *On the Lips of Others: Moteuhczoma's Fame in Aztec Monuments and Rituals*. Austin: University of Texas Press.

Hansen, Pharo Magnus. 2016. "How to Spell Nahuatl? Nawatl? Nauatl?" Blog, July 26. http://nahuatlstudies.blogspot.com/2016/07/how-to-spell-nahuatl-nawatl-nauatl.html.

Harjo, Laura. 2019. *Spiral to the Stars: Mvskoke Tools of Futurity*. Tucson: University of Arizona Press.

Harjo, Laura. 2021. "Indigenous Planning: Constellating with Kin and Urban Futurity." *Planning Theory and Practice* 22 (4): 615–20.

Haskett, Robert. 1987. "Indian Town Government in Colonial Cuernavaca: Persistence, Adaptation, and Change." *Hispanic American Historical Review* 67 (2): 203–31.

Hassig, Ross. 1988. *Aztec Warfare: Imperial Expansion and Political Control*. Norman: University of Oklahoma Press.

Hassig, Ross. 1993. *Trade, Tribute, and Transportation: The Sixteenth-Century Political Economy of the Valley of Mexico*. Norman: University of Oklahoma Press.

Hassig, Ross. 2001. *Time, History, and Belief in Aztec and Colonial Mexico*. Austin: University of Texas Press.

Heiduk, Matthias, Klaus Herbers, and Hans-Christian Lehner, eds. 2021. *Prognostication in the Medieval World: A Handbook*. Berlin: Walter de Gruyter.

Hernández, Francisco. (1615) 1888. *Cuatro libros de la naturaleza y virtudes de las plantas y animales, de uso medicinal en la Nueva España*. Edited by Francisco Ximénez and Antonio Peñafiel. Mexico City: Oficina tipográfica de la Secretaría de Fomento.

Hester, Thurman Lee. 2012. "American Indians, Transhumanism and Cognitive Enhancement." In *The Routledge Companion to Religion and Science*, edited by James Haag, Gregory Peterson, and Michael Spezio, 602–10. New York: Routledge.

Hester, Thurman Lee, and Jim Cheney. 2001. "Truth and Native American Epistemology." *Social Epistemology* 15 (1): 319–34.

Heyden, Doris. 1991. "Dryness Before the Rains: Toxcatl and Tezcatlipoca." In *To Change Place: Aztec Ceremonial Landscapes*, edited by David Carrasco, 188–202. Ann Arbor: University of Michigan Press.

Heyden, Doris. 2001. "Xipe Totec." In *The Oxford Encyclopedia of Mesoamerican Cultures: The Civilizations of Mexico and Central America*, edited by David Carrasco, 3:353–54. Oxford: Oxford University Press.

Hicks, Frederic. 1982. "Tetzcoco in the Early Sixteenth Century: The State, the City, and the Calpolli." *American Ethnologist* 9 (2): 230–49.

Hicks, Frederic. 1992. "Subject States and Tribute Provinces: The Aztec Empire in the Northern Valley of Mexico." *Ancient Mesoamerica* 3 (1): 1–10.

Hidalgo, Jacqueline. 2016. *Revelation in Aztlán: Scriptures, Utopias, and the Chicano Movement*. New York: Palgrave Macmillan.

Hill, Jane. 1992. "The Flower World of Old Uto-Aztecan." *Journal of Anthropological Research* 48 (2): 117–44.

Historia Tolteca-Chichimeca. 1976. Edited by Paul Kirchhoff, Lina Odena Güemes, and Luis Reyes García. Mexico City: INAH.

Holland, William. 1963. *Medicina maya en los altos de Chiapas: Un estudio del cambio socio-cultural*. Mexico City: CONACULTA.

Hoopes, John, and David Mora-Marín. 2009. "Violent Acts of Curing: Pre-Columbian Metaphors of Birth and Sacrifice in the Diagnosis and Treatment of Illness 'Writ Large.'" In *Blood and Beauty: Organized Violence in the Art and Archaeology of Mesoamerica and Central America*, edited by Heather Orr and Rex Koontz, 291–330. Los Angeles: Cotsen Institute of Archaeology.

Horn, Rebecca. 1997. *Postconquest Coyoacan: Nahua-Spanish Relations in Central Mexico, 1519–1650*. Stanford, Calif.: Stanford University Press.

Hsia, R. Po-Chia. 2005. *The World of Catholic Renewal, 1540–1770*. Cambridge: Cambridge University Press.

Huerta Ríos, César. 1981. *Organización socio-política de una minoría nacional: Los triquis de Oaxaca*. Serie de Antropología Social 62. Mexico City: Instituto Nacional Indigenista.

Hunt, Eva. 1977. *The Transformation of the Hummingbird: Cultural Roots of a Zinacantecan Mythical Poem*. Ithaca, N.Y.: Cornell University Press.

Hvidtfeldt, Arild. 1958. *Teotl and Ixiptlatli: Some Central Conceptions in Ancient Mexican Religion, with a General Introduction on Cult and Myth*. Copenhagen: Munksgaard.

Icazbalceta, Joaquín García. 1882. "Historia de los Mexicanos por sus pinturas." *Anales del INAH* 1882:85–106.

Inter Caetera. 1493. Alexander VI. *Papal Encyclicals Online*. https://www.papalencyclicals.net/alex06/alex06inter.htm.

Ixtlilxochitl, Fernando Alva. 1976. *Codex Ixtlilxochitl, Bibliothèque Nationale, Paris (Ms. Mex. 65–71): Reproduktion des Manuskriptes im Originalformat = Reproduction du Manuscrit en Format Original*. Edited by Jacqueline de Durand-Forest and Jay Kislak. Graz, Austria: Akademische Druck- u. Verlagsanstalt.

Ixtlilxochitl, Fernando de Alva. 1997. *Obras históricas: Incluyen el texto completo de las llamadas Relaciones e Historia de la nación chichimeca en una nueva versión establecida con el cotejo de los manuscritos más antiguos que se conocen*. Edited by Edmundo O'Gorman and Miguel León-Portilla. Toluca, Mexico: Instituto Mexiquense de Cultura, UNAM.

Jiménez, Luz. 1972. *Life and Death in Milpa Alta: A Nahuatl Chronicle of Díaz and Zapata from the Recollections of Luz Jiménez*. Translated and edited by Fernando Horcasitas. Norman: University of Oklahoma Press.

Jiménez, Luz. 1979. *Los cuentos en nahuatl de doña Luz Jiménez*. Edited by Fernando Horcasitas and Sarah Ford. Serie Antropológica. Mexico City: Instituto de Investigaciones Antropológicas, UNAM.

Jiménez Moreno, Wigberto. 1954. "Síntesis de la historia precolonial del Valle de México." *Revista mexicana de estudios antropológicos* 55 (14): 219–36.

Johansson, Patrick. 2012. "Teoxihuitl: Turquoise in Aztec Thought and Poetry." In *Turquoise in Mexico and North America: Science, Conservation, Culture, and Collections*, edited by J. C. H. King, Max Carocci, Caroline Cartwright, Colin McEwan, and Rebecca Stacey, 135–44. London: Archetype Publications in Association with the British Museum.

Kalyuta, Anastasia. n.d. "What Is Teōtl?" Accessed June 2, 2024. https://www.academia.edu/40717355/What_is_te%C5%8Dtl_Some_Observations_the_Meaning_of_One_Word_in_Classical_Nahuatl.

Karttunen, Frances. 1992. *An Analytical Dictionary of Nahuatl*. Norman: University of Oklahoma Press.

Kellogg, Susan. 1995. *Law and the Transformation of Aztec Culture, 1500–1700*. Norman: University of Oklahoma Press.

Keoke, Emory, and Kay Porterfield. 2001. *Encyclopedia of American Indian Contributions to the World*. New York: Facts on File.

Kirchhoff, Paul. 1951. "El autor de la segunda parte de la *Crónica mexicayotl*." In *Homenaje al Doctor Alfonso Caso*, edited by Juan Comas, 225–27. Mexico City: Nuevo Mundo.

Kirchhoff, Paul. 1960. Review: "Teotl and Ixiptlatli: Some Central Conceptions in Ancient Mexican Religion, with a General Introduction on Cult and Myth. Hvidtfeldt Arild. Munksgaard, Copenhagen, 1958. 182 Pp. Danish Kr. 24." *American Antiquity* 25 (3): 438–39.

Klein, Cecelia. 1993. "Teocuitlatl, 'Divine Excrement': The Significance of 'Holy Shit' in Ancient Mexico." *Art Journal* 52 (3): 20–27.

Klein, Cecelia. 2000. "The Devil and the Skirt: An Iconographic Inquiry into the Pre-Hispanic Nature of the Tzitzimime." *Ancient Mesoamerica* 11 (1): 1–26.

Klor de Alva, Jorge. 1979. "Christianity and the Aztecs." *San Jose Studies* 5 (3): 6–22.

Klor de Alva, Jorge. 1992. "Nahua Colonial Discourse and the Appropriation of the (European) Other." *Archives de Sciences Sociales des Religions* 37 (77): 15–35.

Klor de Alva, Jorge. 1993. "Aztec Spirituality and Nahuatized Christianity." In Gossen and León-Portilla 1993, 173–97.

Klor de Alva, Jorge, Henry Nicholson, and Eloise Quiñones Keber. 1988. *The Work of Bernardino de Sahagún: Pioneer Ethnographer of Sixteenth-Century Aztec Mexico*. Albany: Institute for Mesoamerican Studies, University at Albany, State University of New York.

Knab, Timothy. 1991. "Geografía del inframundo." *Estudios de Cultura Náhuatl* 21: 31–57.

Knab, Timothy. 2004. *The Dialogue of Earth and Sky: Dreams, Souls, Curing, and the Modern Aztec Underworld*. Tucson: University of Arizona Press.

Köhler, Ulrich. 2001. "'Debt-Payment' to the Gods Among the Aztec: The Misrendering of a Spanish Expression and Its Effects." *Estudios de Cultura Náhuatl* 32 (1): 125–33.

Konetzke, Richard. (1958) 1962. *Colección de documentos para la historia de la formación social de Hispanoamérica: 1493–1810*. 3 vols. Madrid: Consejo superior de investigaciones científicas.

Kruell, Gabriel Kenrick. 2016. "La concepción del tiempo y la historia entre los mexicas." *Estudios mesoamericanos* 1 (12): 5–24.

Laack, Isabel. 2019. "The (Poetic) Imagery of 'Flower and Song' in Aztec Religious Expression: Correlating the Semiotic Modalities of Language and Pictorial Writing." In *Language and Religion*, edited by Christopher Lehrich, Courtney Handman, and Robert Yelle, 349–81. Berlin: De Gruyter Mouton.

Laird, Andrew. 2021. "Classical Learning and Indigenous Legacies in Sixteenth-Century Mexico." In *Brill's Companion to Classics in the Early Americas*, edited by Maya Feile Tomes, Adam J. Goldwyn, and Matthew Duquès, 209–41. Boston: Brill.

Laird, Andrew. 2023. *Aztec Latin: Renaissance Learning and Nahuatl Traditions in Early Colonial Mexico*. New York: Oxford University Press.

Lámina de la genealogía de Quauhquechollan-Macuilxochitepec. 1940. Fototeca Nacional de México, Mexico City. http://mediateca.inah.gob.mx/repositorio/islandora/object/fotografia:282799.

Lane, Kris. 2019. *Potosí: The Silver City That Changed the World*. Oakland: University of California Press.

Latour, Bruno. 2010. *On the Modern Cult of the Factish Gods*. Durham, N.C.: Duke University Press.

Launey, Michel. 1992. *Introducción a la lengua y a la literatura nahuatl*. Mexico City: Instituto de Investigaciones Antropológicas, UNAM.

Launey, Michel. 2004. "The Features of Omnipredicativity in Classical Nahuatl." *Sprachtypologie und Universalienforschung (STUF)* 57 (1): 1–17.

Lee, Jongsoo. 2008. *The Allure of Nezahualcoyotl: Pre-Hispanic History, Religion, and Nahua Poetics*. Albuquerque: University of New Mexico Press.

Lee, Jongsoo. 2014. "The Aztec Triple Alliance: A Colonial Transformation of the Prehispanic Political and Tributary System." In Lee and Brokaw 2014, 63–91.

Lee, Jongsoo, and Galen Brokaw, eds. 2014. *Texcoco: Prehispanic and Colonial Perspectives*. Boulder: University Press of Colorado.

Leeming, Ben. 2015. "'Micropoetics': The Poetry of Hypertrophic Words in Early Colonial Nahuatl." *Colonial Latin American Review* 24 (2): 168–89.
Leibsohn, Dana. 2009. *Script and Glyph Pre-Hispanic History, Colonial Bookmaking and the Historia Tolteca-Chichimeca*. Washington, D.C.: Dumbarton Oaks.
León, Adrián, trans. (1949) 1992. *Crónica mexicáyotl*. Mexico City: UNAM.
León-Portilla, Miguel. 1956. *La filosofía náhuatl*. Mexico City: Instituto Indigenista Interamericano.
León-Portilla, Miguel. 1962. "Nepantla. La palabra clave de la tragedia de un pueblo." *Periódico Excélsior*, January 23.
León-Portilla, Miguel. (1963) 1975. *Aztec Thought and Culture: A Study of the Ancient Nahuatl Mind*. Translated by Jack Emory Davis. Norman: University of Oklahoma Press.
León-Portilla, Miguel. 1985. "Nahuatl Literature." In *Literatures: Supplement to the Handbook of Middle American Indians*, vol. 3, edited by Robert Wauchope, Munro S. Edmonson, and Patricia A. Andrews, 7–42. Austin: University of Texas Press.
León-Portilla, Miguel. 1992. "Have We Really Translated the Mesoamerican 'Ancient Word'?" In *On the Translation of Native American Literatures*, edited by Brian Swann, 313–38. Washington D.C.: Smithsonian Institution Press, 1992.
León-Portilla, Miguel. 1993. "Those Made Worthy by Divine Sacrifice: The Faith of Ancient Mexico." In Gossen and Léon-Portilla 1993, 41–64. New York: Crossroad.
León-Portilla, Miguel. 1999. *Bernardino de Sahagún: Pionero de la antropología*. Mexico City: UNAM.
León-Portilla, Miguel. 2000. *Fifteen Poets of the Aztec World*. Norman: University of Oklahoma Press.
Lienzo de Analco. 1945. Edited by Franz Ferdinand Blom. Mexico City: Cuadernos Americanos.
Lienzo de Tlaxcala. 1983. Edited by Josefina García Quintana, Carlos Martínez Marín, and Mario de la Torre. Mexico City: Cartón y papel.
Lockhart, James. 1985. "Some Nahua Concepts in Postconquest Guise." *History of European Ideas* 6 (4): 465–82.
Lockhart, James. 1992. *The Nahuas After the Conquest: A Social and Cultural History of the Indians of Central Mexico, Sixteenth Through Eighteenth Centuries*. Stanford, Calif.: Stanford University Press.
Lockhart, James, ed. and trans. 1993. *We People Here: Nahuatl Accounts of the Conquest of Mexico*. Berkeley: University of California Press.
Lockhart, James. 2001. *Nahuatl as Written: Lessons in Older Written Nahuatl, with Copious Examples and Texts*. Cambridge: Cambridge University Press.
López Austin, Alfredo. 1971. *Medicina Náhuatl*. Mexico City: Secretaría de Educación Pública.

López Austin, Alfredo. 1972. "Textos acerca de las partes del cuerpo humano y de las enfermedades y medicinas en los *Primeros Memoriales* de Sahagún." *Estudios De Cultura Náhuatl* 10 (November): 129–53.

López Austin, Alfredo. 1974. "The Research Method of Fray Bernardino de Sahagún: The Questionnaires." In *Sixteenth-Century Mexico: The Work of Sahagún*, edited by Munro S. Edmonson, 111–49. Albuquerque: University of New Mexico Press.

López Austin, Alfredo. 1975. *Textos de medicina nahuatl*. Mexico City: Instituto de Investigaciones Históricas, UNAM.

López Austin, Alfredo. 1985. "El texto sahaguntino sobre los mexicas." *Anales de Antropología* 22 (1): 287–335.

López Austin, Alfredo. 1986. "La polémica sobre la dicotomía frío-calor." In *La medicina invisible: Introducción al studio de la medicina tradicional de México*, edited by Xavier Lozoya and Carlos Zolla, 73–90. Mexico City: Folios Ediciones S.A.

López Austin, Alfredo. 1988. *The Human Body and Ideology: Concepts of the Ancient Nahuas*. 2 vols. Salt Lake City: University of Utah Press.

López Austin, Alfredo. 1993. *The Myths of the Opossum: Pathways of Mesoamerican Mythology*. Translated by Bernard Ortiz de Montellano and Thelma Ortiz de Montellano. Albuquerque: University of New Mexico Press.

López Austin, Alfredo. 1997. *Tamoanchan, Tlalocan: Places of Mist*. Translated by Bernard Ortiz de Montellano and Thelma Ortiz de Montellano. Boulder: University Press of Colorado.

López Austin, Alfredo. 2011a. "Estudio acerca del método de investigación de fray Bernardino de Sahagún." *Estudios de Cultura Náhuatl* 42 (February): 353–400.

López Austin, Alfredo. 2011b. "Los reyes subterráneos." In *La Quête du Serpent à Plumes: Arts et Religions de l'Amérique Précolombienne: Hommage à Michel Graulich*, edited by Nathalie Ragot, Sylvie Peperstraete, and Guilhem Olivier, 39–56. Turnhout, Belgium: Brepols.

Lopez Austin, Alfredo, and Carlos Viesca Treviño. 1984. *La historia general de la medicina en México*. Vol. 1, *México Antiguo*. Mexico City: UNAM.

López Caballero, Paula. 2003. *Los Títulos primordiales del centro de México*. Mexico City: CONACULTA.

López Hernández, Miriam. 2015. "El colibrí como símbolo de la sexualidad masculina entre los mexicas." *Itinerarios: Revista de estudios lingüísticos, literarios, históricos y antropológicos* 21 (1): 79–100.

López Luján, Leonardo. 2005. *The Offerings of the Templo Mayor of Tenochtitlan*. Translated by Bernard Ortiz de Montellano and Thelma Ortiz de Montellano. Albuquerque: University of New Mexico Press.

López Wario, Luis Alberto. 2008. *Lenguaje en piedra: Manifestaciones gráfico rupestres registradas por la Dirección de Salvamento Arqueológico*. Mexico City: INAH.

Lord, Albert. 1974. *The Singer of Tales*. New York: Atheneum.
Lovell, George. 2019. "Presidential Address: A Rainbow of Spanish Illusions: Research Frontiers in Colonial Guatemala." *Ethnohistory* 66 (3): 409–35.
Lund, Joshua. 2006. *The Impure Imagination: Toward a Critical Hybridity in Latin American Writing*. Minneapolis: University of Minnesota Press.
Lund, Joshua. 2012. *The Mestizo State: Reading Race in Modern Mexico*. Minneapolis: University of Minnesota Press.
Luque-Talaván, Miguel. 2003. *Un universo de opiniones: La literatura jurídica indiana*. Mexico City: CIESAS.
Lutz, Christopher. 1984. *Historia sociodemográfica de Santiago de Guatemala, 1541–1773*. Guatemala City: CIRMA.
Madajczak, Julia. 2017. "Towards a Deconstruction of the Notion of Nahua 'Confession.'" In Tavárez 2017, 63–81.
Maffie, James. 2007. "The Centrality of *Nepantla* in Conquest-Era Nahua Philosophy." *Nahua Newsletter* 44 (1): 11–31.
Maffie, James. 2008a. "Thinking with a Good Heart." *Hypatia* 23 (4): 182–91.
Maffie, James. 2008b. "Watching the Heavens with a 'Rooted Heart': The Mystical Basis of Aztec Astronomy." *Journal of the History of Astrology and Cultural Astronomy* 12 (1): 31–64.
Maffie, James. 2009. "'In the End, We Have the Gatling Gun, and They Have Not': Future Prospects of Indigenous Knowledges." *Futures* 41 (1): 53–65.
Maffie, James. 2010. "Pre-Columbian Philosophies." In *A Companion to Latin American Philosophy*, edited by Susana Nuccetelli, Ofelia Schutte, and Octávio Bueno, 9–22. Malden, Mass.: Wiley-Blackwell.
Maffie, James. 2011. "Double Mistaken Philosophical Identity in Sahagún's *Colloquios y Doctrina Cristiana*." *Divinatio* 34 (1): 63–92.
Maffie, James. 2012. "In *Huehue Tlamanitiliztli* and *la Verdad*: Nahua and European Philosophies in Fray Bernardino de Sahagún's *Colloquios y doctrina Cristiana*." *Inter-American Journal of Philosophy* 3 (1): 1–33.
Maffie, James. 2014. *Aztec Philosophy: Understanding a World in Motion*. Boulder: University of Colorado Press.
Maffie, James. 2019. "The Role of Hardship in Mexica Ethics: Or, Why Being Good Has to Hurt." *American Philosophical Newsletter on Native American and Indigenous Philosophy* 18 (2): 8–17.
Maffie, James. n.d. "Aztec Philosophy." *Internet Encyclopedia of Philosophy*. Accessed September 13, 2023. https://iep.utm.edu/aztec-philosophy/.
Magaloni Kerpel, Diana Isabel. 2011. "Painters of the New World: Processes of Making the Florentine Codex." In *Colors Between Two Worlds: The Florentine Codex of Bernardino de Sahagún*, edited by Gerhard Wolf, Joseph Connors, and Louis Alexander Waldman, 47–78. Florence: Kunsthistorisches Institut in Florenz, Max-Planck-Institut.
Maher, Michael. 1909. "Free Will." In *Catholic Encyclopedia*, vol. 6. New York: Robert Appleton Company. http://www.newadvent.org/cathen/06259a.htm.

Mathes, Miguel. 1982. *Santa Cruz de Tlatelolco: La primera biblioteca académica de las Américas*. Mexico Ciy: Archivo histórico mexicano.

Martínez, María Elena. 2008. *Genealogical Fictions: Limpieza de Sangre, Religion, and Gender in Colonial Mexico*. Stanford, Calif.: Stanford University Press.

Matos Moctezuma, Eduardo. 1986. *Muerte a filo de obsidiana*. Lecturas mexicanas 50. Mexico City: SEP.

Matos Moctezuma, Eduardo, and Raúl Barrera Rodríguez. 2011. "El templo de Ehecatl-Quetzalcoatl del recinto sagrado de México-Tenochtitlan." *Arqueología mexicana* 18 (108): 72–77.

Matrícula de tributos. 1980. Edited by Luis Reyes García and Frances Berdan. Graz, Austria: Akademische Druck.

Matthew, Laura. 2004. "Neither and Both: The Mexican Indian Conquistadors of Colonial Guatemala." PhD diss., University of Pennsylvania, Philadelphia.

Matthew, Laura. 2012. *Memories of Conquest: Becoming Mexicano in Colonial Guatemala*. Chapel Hill: University of North Carolina Press.

Matthew, Laura, and William Fowler. 2020. "A Tense Convivencia." In *The Global Spanish Empire: Five Hundred Years of Place Making and Pluralism*, edited by Christine Beaule and John Douglass, 130–49. Tucson: University of Arizona Press.

Matthew, Laura, and Michel Oudijk. 2007. *Indian Conquistadors: Indigenous Allies in the Conquest of Mesoamerica*. Norman: University of Oklahoma Press.

Mazzetto, Elena, and Natalia Moragas Segura. 2015. "Contexts of Offerings and Ritual Maize in the Pictographic Record in Central Mexico." *Scripta Instituti Donneriani Aboensis* 26 (1): 82–100.

McAnany, Patricia. (1995) 2014. *Living with the Ancestors: Kinship and Kingship in Ancient Maya Society*. Cambridge: Cambridge University Press.

McDonough, Kelly. 2014. "Performances of Indigenous Authority in Postconquest Tlaxcalan Annals: Don Juan Buenaventura Zapata y Mendoza's *Historia cronológica de la noble ciudad de Tlaxcala*." In *Coloniality, Religion, and the Law in the Early Iberian World*, edited by Santa Arias and Raúl Marrero-Fente, 71–90. Nashville: Vanderbilt University Press.

McDonough, Kelly. 2016. *The Learned Ones: Nahua Intellectuals in Postconquest Mexico*. Tucson: University of Arizona Press.

McDonough, Kelly. 2019. "Indigenous Technologies in the 1577 *Relaciones geográficas* of New Spain: Collective Land Memory, Natural Resources, and Herbal Medicine." *Ethnohistory* 66 (3): 465–87.

McDonough, Kelly. 2020. "Intercultural (Mis)Translations: Colonial Static and 'Authorship' in the *Florentine Codex* and the *Relaciones Geográficas* of New Spain." In *The Routledge Hispanic Studies Companion to Colonial Latin America and the Caribbean (1492–1898)*, edited by Yolanda Martínez-San Miguel and Santa Arias, 393–405. New York: Routledge.

McDonough, Kelly. 2024. *Indigenous Science and Technology: Nahuas and the World Around Them*. Tucson: University of Arizona Press.

McEnroe, Sean. 2020. *A Troubled Marriage: Indigenous Elites of the Colonial Americas*. Albuquerque: University of New Mexico Press.
McKeever Furst, Jill. (1995) 1997. *The Natural History of the Soul in Ancient Mexico*. New Haven, Conn.: Yale University Press.
Melville, Elinor. 1999. *Plaga de ovejas: Consecuencias ambientales de la conquista de México*. Mexico City: FCE.
Mendieta, Gerónimo de. (1595) 1870. *Historia eclesiástica Indiana*. Edited by Joaquín García Icazbalceta. Mexico City: Porrúa.
Mendoza, Celso Armando. 2017. "Those Who Have Been Baptized, Those Who are Believers in Dios Will Transform [Into Animals]: New Perspectives on Juan Teton, the Would-Be Nahua Messiah of Early Colonial Mexico." Master's thesis, University of California, Los Angeles.
Menegus, Margarita. 2019. *Los indios en la historia de México*. Mexico City: FCE.
Mignolo, Walter. 1995. *The Darker Side of the Renaissance: Literacy, Territoriality, and Colonization*. Ann Arbor: University of Michigan Press.
Mignolo, Walter. 2005. *The Idea of Latin America*. Malden, Mass.: Blackwell.
Mignolo, Walter. 2008. "Geopolitics of Knowledge and the Colonial Difference." In Moraña, Dussel, and Jáuregui 2008, 225–58.
Mikulska, Katarzyna. 2020. "The Sky, the Night, and the Number Nine: Considerations of the Nahua Vision of the Universe." In A. Díaz 2020b, 282–318.
Mikulska, Katarzyna. 2022. "The Deity as a Mosaic: Images of the God Xipe Totec in Divinatory Codices from Central Mesoamerica." *Ancient Mesoamerica* 33 (3): 432–58.
Miranda, José. 2005. *El tributo indígena en la Nueva España durante el siglo XVI*. Mexico City: Colegio de México.
Miranda Limón, Juan Manuel. 2021. "Rheumatological Therapy in Prehispanic Mesoamerica." *Reumatología Clínica* 17 (8): 475–81.
Molina, Alonso de. (1571) 2008. *Vocabulario en lengua castellana y mexicana y mexicana y castellana*. 6th ed. Mexico City: Porrúa.
Montaño, Héctor. 2019. "Águila, nopal y serpiente, antes, durante y después de la Conquista: Lucha de siglos que rescató la iconografía biodiversa y simbólica." Gobierno de México, September 20. https://www.gob.mx/semarnat/articulos/aguila-nopal-y-serpiente-antes-durante-y-despues-de-la-conquista.
Montero Sobrevilla, Iris. 2020. "The Disguise of the Hummingbird: On the Natural History of Huitzilopochtli in the Florentine Codex." *Ethnohistory* 67 (3): 429–53.
Moraña, Mabel, Enrique Dussel, and Carlos Jáuregui, eds. 2008. *Coloniality at Large: Latin America and the Postcolonial Debate*. Durham, N.C.: Duke University Press.
El Mundo. 2014. "México recupera un códice del siglo XVII, origen de su historiografía." September 26. https://www.elmundo.es/la-aventura-de-la-historia/2014/09/26/5425293622601d10248b456c.html.

Mundy, Barbara. 1996. *The Mapping of New Spain: Indigenous Cartography and the Maps of the Relaciones Geográficas*. Chicago: University of Chicago Press.

Mundy, Barbara. 2015. *The Death of Aztec Tenochtitlan, the Life of Mexico City*. Austin: University of Texas Press.

Muñoz, Santiago. 2006. "El 'arte plumario' y sus múltiples dimensiones de significación: La Misa de San Gregorio, Virreinato de la Nueva España, 1539." *Historia crítica* 31 (1): 121–49.

Nesvig, Martin. 2021. "Sandcastles of the Mind: Hallucinogens and Cultural Memory." In *Substance and Seduction*, edited by Stacey Schwartzkopf and Kathryn Sampeck, 27–54. Austin: University of Texas Press.

Nesvig, Martin. 2022. "Forbidden Drugs of the Colonial Americas." In *The Oxford Handbook of Global Drug History*, edited by Paul Gootenberg, 153–75. New York: Oxford University Press.

Nichols, Deborah, and Enrique Rodríguez-Alegría. 2017. *Oxford Handbook of the Aztecs*. Oxford: Oxford University Press.

Nicholson, Henry. 1967. "A 'Royal Headband' of the Tlaxcalteca." *Revista mexicana de estudios antropológicos* 21 (1): 71–106.

Nicholson, Henry. 1997. "Introduction." In Sahagún, 1997, 3–14.

Nielsen, Jesper, and Toke Sellner Reunert. 2020. "Colliding Universes: A Reconsideration of the Structure of the Precolumbian Mesoamerican Cosmos." In A. Díaz 2020b, 31–69.

Noguez, Xavier. 1978. *Tira de Tepechpan: Códice Colonial Procedente del Valle de México*. 2 vols. Mexico City: Biblioteca Enciclopédica del Estado de México.

Noguez, Xavier, ed. 2013. *Códice de la Cruz-Badiano*. Special issues of *Arqueología Mexicana* 50 and 51.

Norton, Marcy. 2024. *The Tame and the Wild: People and Animals After 1492*. Cambridge, Mass.: Harvard University Press.

Nuttall, Zelia. 1926. "Official Reports on the Towns of Tequizistlan, Tepechpan, Acolman, and San Juan Teotihuacan Sent by Francisco de Castaneda to His Majesty, Philip II, and the Council of the Indies, in 1580." *Papers of the Peabody Museum, Harvard University* 11 (2): 45–83.

Nutton, Vivian. 1997. "Humoralism." In *Companion Encyclopedia of the History of Medicine*, vol. 1, edited by W. F. Bynum and Roy Porter, 281–91. London: Routledge.

Ocaranza, Fernando. 1934. *El Imperial Colegio de Indios de la Santa Cruz de Santiago Tlatelolco*. Mexico City: UNAM.

Offner, Jerome. 1979. "A Reassessment of the Extent and Structuring of the Empire of Techotlalatzin, Fourteenth Century Ruler of Texcoco." *Ethnohistory* 26 (3): 231–41.

Offner, Jerome. 2014. "Improving Western Historiography of Texcoco." In Lee and Brokaw 2014, 25–61.

Offner, Jerome. 2021. "Empires of Xolotl: Two Opening Compositions of the *Codex Xolotl.*" *Ethnohistory* 68 (4): 455–91.
O'Hara, Matthew. 2018. *History of the Future in Colonial Mexico*. New Haven, Conn.: Yale University Press.
Olivier, Guilhem. 2003. *Mockeries and Metamorphoses of an Aztec God: Tezcatlipoca, Lord of the Smoking Mirrors*. Boulder: University Press of Colorado.
Olivier, Guilhem. 2005. "Tlantepuzilama: Las peligrosas andanzas de una deidad con dientes de cobre en Mesoamérica." *Estudios de Cultura Náhuatl* 36 (1): 245–72.
Olivier, Guilhem, and Luz María Guerrero Rodríguez. 1998. "Tepeyóllotl, 'corazón de la montaña señor del eco': El dios jaguar de los antiguos mexicanos." *Estudios de Cultura Náhuatl* 28 (1): 99–141.
Olivier, Guilhem, and Roberto Martínez. 2015. "Translating Gods: Tohil and Curicaueri in Mesoamerican Polytheism in the *Popol Vuh* and the Relación de Michoacán." *Ancient Mesoamerica* 26 (2): 347–69.
Olko, Justyna. 2007. "Genealogías indígenas del centro de México: Raíces prehispánicas de su florecimiento colonial." *Itinerarios: Revista de estudios lingüísticos, literarios, históricos y antropológicos* 6:141–62.
Olko, Justyna. 2012. "El 'otro' y los estereotipos étnicos en el mundo nahua." *Estudios de Cultura Náhuatl* 44 (1): 165–98.
Olko, Justyna. 2014. *Insignia of Rank in the Nahua World: From the Fifteenth to the Seventeenth Century*. Boulder: University Press of Colorado.
Olko, Justyna, and John Sullivan. 2016. "Bridging Divides: A Proposal for Integrating the Teaching, Research, and Revitalization of Nahuatl." In *Language Documentation and Conservation in Europe*, edited by Vera Ferreira and Peter Bouda, 159–84. Honolulu: University of Hawai'i Press.
Ong, Walter. (1982) 2002. *Orality and Literacy*. New York: Methuen.
Ortiz de Montellano, Bernard. 1975. "Empirical Aztec Medicine: Aztec Medicinal Plants Seem to be Effective if They Are Judged by Aztec Standards." *Science* 188 (4185): 215–20.
Ortiz de Montellano, Bernard. 1989. "The Body, Ethics and Cosmos: Aztec Physiology." In *The Imagination of Matter: Religion and Ecology in Mesoamerican Traditions*, edited by David Carrasco, 191–209. Oxford: B.A.R.
Ortiz de Montellano, Bernard. 1990. *Aztec Medicine, Health, and Nutrition*. Newark, N.J.: Rutgers University Press.
Ortiz de Montellano, Bernard. 1993. *Medicina, salud y nutrición aztecas*. Mexico City: Siglo Veintiuno.
Otzoy, Calí, Simón Otzoy, and Jorge Luján Muñoz. 1999. *Memorial de Sololá*. Guatemala City: Comisión Interuniversitaria Guatemalteca de Conmemoración del Quinto Centenario del Descubrimiento de América.
Oudijk, Michel. 2011. "Elaboration and Abbreviation in Mexican Pictorial Manuscripts: Their Use in Literary Themes." In *Their Way of Writing: Scripts, Signs,*

and Pictographies in Pre-Columbian America, edited by Elizabeth Boone and Gary Urton, 149–74. Washington, D.C.: Dumbarton Oaks.

Owensby, Brian. 2010. "Foreword." In *Negotiation Within Domination: New Spain's Indian Pueblos Confront the Spanish State*, edited by Ethelia Ruiz Medrano and Susan Kellogg, xi–xvi. Boulder: University Press of Colorado.

Owensby, Brian. 2011. "Pacto entre rey lejano y súbditos indígenas. Justicia, legalidad y política en Nueva España, siglo XVII." *Historia Mexicana* 61 (1): 59–106.

Paso y Troncoso, Francisco de. 1892–93. *Catálogo de los objetos que presenta la República Mexicana en la Exposición Histórico-Americana de Madrid*. 2 vols. Madrid: Rivadeneyra.

Paso y Troncoso, Francisco de. 1905–6. *Papeles de la Nueva España publicados de orden y con fondos del Gobierno Mexicano*. 7 vols. Madrid: Rivadeneyra.

Paso y Troncoso, Francisco de. 1939–42. *Epistolario de Nueva España*. 16 vols. Mexico City: Porrúa.

Peña, José Carlos. 1999. "Pre-Columbian Medicine and the Kidney." *American Journal of Nephrology* 19 (2): 148–54.

Phelan, John. 1956. *The Millennial Kingdom of the Franciscans in the New World: A Study of the Writings of Gerónimo de Mendieta, 1525–1604*. Berkeley: University of California Press.

Polanco, Edward Anthony. 2018. "'I Am Just a Tiçitl': Decolonizing Central Mexican Nahua Female Healers, 1535–1635." *Ethnohistory* 65 (3): 441–63.

Polo Sifontes, Francis. 2005. *Los cakchiqueles en la conquista de Guatemala*. Guatemala City: Editorial Cultura.

Porter, Camarin. 2010. "Time Measurement and Chronology in Medieval Studies." In *Handbook of Medieval Studies*, vol. 2, *Terms-Methods-Trends*, edited by Albrecht Classen, 1350–68. Berlin: Walter de Gruyter.

Powell, Phillip. 1996. *La guerra chichimeca 1550–1600*. Mexico City: FCE.

Pratt, Christina. 2007. *An Encyclopedia of Shamanism*. 2 vols. New York: Rosen.

Pratt, Scott. 2002. *Native Pragmatism: Rethinking the Roots of American Philosophy*. Bloomington: Indiana University Press.

Prince, Gerald. 2003. *A Dictionary of Narratology*. Lincoln: University of Nebraska Press.

Quijano, Aníbal. 2008. "Coloniality of Power, Eurocentrism, and Social Classification." In Moraña, Dussel, and Jáuregui 2008, 181–224.

Quiñones Keber, Eloise. (1988) 1995. "The Sahaguntine Corpus: A Bibliographic Index of Extant Documents." In Klor de Alva, Nicholson, and Quiñones Keber 1988, 341–45.

Quiñones Keber, Eloise. 1995. *Codex Telleriano-Remensis: Ritual, Divination, and History in a Pictorial Aztec Manuscript*. Austin: University of Texas Press.

Rabasa, José. 2011. *Tell Me the Story of How I Conquered You: Elsewheres and Ethnosuicide in the Colonial Mesoamerican World*. Austin: University of Texas Press.

Rai, Mahendra, Geoffrey Cordell, José Martínez, Mariela Marinoff, and Luca Rastrelli. 2012. *Medicinal Plants: Biodiversity and Drugs*. Boca Raton, Fla.: CRC Press.
Rama, Ángel. 1984. *La ciudad letrada*. Hanover, N.H.: Ediciones del Norte.
Ramírez Ruiz, Marcelo, and Federico Fernández Christlieb. 2006. "La policía de los indios y la urbanización del altepetl." In *Territorialidad y paisaje en el altepetl del siglo XVI*, edited by Federico Fernández Christlieb and Ángel Julián García Zambrano, 31–113. Mexico City: FCE.
Ramírez Sánchez, María Guadalupe. 2018. "La conquista de la Huasteca a través de la perspectiva nahua del siglo XVI." *Diacronías* 11 (19): 29–43.
Read, Kay. 1994. "Sacred Commoners: The Motion of Cosmic Powers in Mexica Rulership." *History of Religions* 34 (1): 39–69.
Read, Kay. 1998. *Time and Sacrifice in the Aztec Cosmos*. Bloomington: Indiana University Press.
Read, Kay Almere, and Jason González. 2002. *Mesoamerican Mythology*. New York: Oxford University Press.
Recollet, Karyn. 2016. "Gesturing Indigenous Futurities Through the Remix." *Dance Research Journal* 48 (1): 91–105.
Regimini Ecclesiae Universae. Constitutio Apostolica de Romana Curia. 1968. Paul VI. Vatican Library Online. Accessed November 7, 2014. https://www.vatican.va/content/paul-vi/la/apost_constitutions/documents/hf_p-vi_apc_19670815_regimini-ecclesiae-universae.html.
Remesal, Antonio de. (1619–20) 1964. *Historia general de las Indias occidentales y particular de la gobernación de Chiapa y Guatemala por Fray Antonio de Remesal, O.P.I.* Edited by Carmelo Sáenz de Santamaría. Biblioteca de Autores Españoles 175. Madrid: Atlas.
Restall, Matthew. 2012. "The New Conquest History." *History Compass* 10 (2): 151–60.
Restall, Matthew. 2018. *When Montezuma Met Cortés: The True Story of the Meeting That Changed History*. New York: HarperCollins.
Restall, Matthew, and Florine Asselbergs. 2007. *Invading Guatemala: Spanish, Nahua, and Maya Accounts of the Conquest Wars*. University Park, Pa.: Penn State University Press.
Restall, Matthew, and Kris Lane. 2012. *The Riddle of Latin America*. Farmington Hills, Mich.: Gale Cengage Learning.
Reyes García, Luis. 2001. *¿Cómo te confundes: Acaso no somos conquistados? Anales de Juan Bautista*. Mexico City: CIESAS, Biblioteca Lorenzo Boturini, Insigne y Nacional Basílica de Guadalupe.
Reygadas Robles, Pedro. 2020. "Semiótica de la carnalidad sentipensante en la cultura nahua." *Refracción: Revista sobre lingüística materialista* 2 (1): 177–202.
Ríos Castaño, Victoria. 2011. "Translating the Nahuas: Fray Bernardino de Sahagún's Parallel Texts in the Construction of Universal History of the Things

of New Spain." *Bulletin of Latin American Research: Journal for the Society of Latin American Studies* 30 (1): 28–37.

Ríos Castaño, Victoria. 2014. "From the 'Memoriales con escolios' to the *Florentine Codex*: Sahagún and His Nahua Assistants' Co-Authorship of the Spanish Translation." *Journal of Iberian and Latin American Research* 20 (2): 214–28.

Ríos Castaño, Victoria. 2018. "The Herbal of the *Florentine Codex*: Description and Contextualization of Paragraph V in Book XI." *The Americas* 75 (3): 463–88.

Rohland, Eleonora, and Kirsten Kramer. 2021. "Introduction: On 'Doing Comparison'—Practices of Comparing." In *Contact, Conquest and Colonization: How Practices of Comparing Shaped Empires and Colonialism Around the World*, edited by Eleonora Rohland, Angelika Epple, Antje Flüchter, and Kirsten Kramer, 1–16. New York: Routledge.

Rojas, Araceli. 2016a. "Casting Maize Seeds in an Ayöök Community: An Approach to the Study of Divination in Mesoamerica." *Ancient Mesoamerica* 27 (2): 461–78.

Rojas, Araceli. 2016b. "Reading Maize: A Narrative and Psychological Approach to the Study of Divination in Mesoamerica." *Journal for the Study of Religions and Ideologies* 15 (43): 102–24.

Romero Galván, José Rubén. 2003. *Los privilegios perdidos: Hernando Alvarado Tezozómoc, su tiempo, su nobleza y su Crónica mexicana*. Mexico City: Instituto de Investigaciones Históricas, UNAM.

Ros-Fábregas, Emilio. 2012. "'Imagine All the People . . .': Polyphonic Flowers in the Hands and Voices of Indians in Sixteenth-Century Mexico." *Early Music* 40 (2): 177–89.

Rubí, Alma Rosa, and Sara Altamirano. 1989. *El Lienzo de Carapan: Estudio histórico, iconográfico y de restauración*. Vol. 2. Mexico City: Dirección de Restauración del Patrimonio Cultural, INAH.

Ruiz de Alarcón, Hernando. 1987. *Treatise on the Heathen Superstitions That Today Live Among the Indians Native to This New Spain, 1629*. Translated by James Andrews and Ross Hassig. Norman: University of Oklahoma Press.

Ruiz Medrano, Ethelia. 2010. "Fighting Destiny: Nahua Nobles and Friars in the Sixteenth-Century Revolt of the Encomenderos Against the King." In *Negotiation Within Dominion: New Spain's Indian Pueblos Confront the Spanish State*, edited by Ethelia Ruiz Medrano and Susan Kellogg, 45–77. Boulder: University Press of Colorado.

Ruiz Medrano, Ethelia. 2011. *Mexico's Indigenous Communities: Their Lands and Histories, 1500–2010*. Boulder: University Press of Colorado.

Ruiz Medrano, Ethelia. 2016. "History, Tradition, Myth and Territory in a Nahua Village (Guerrero, Mexico)." In *Places of Power and Memory in Mesoamerica's Past and Present: How Sites, Toponymns, and Landscapes Shape History and Remembrance*, edited by Daniel Graña Behrens, 255–74. Berlin: Gebr. Mann.

Russo, Alessandra. 2002. "Plumes of Sacrifice: Transformations in Sixteenth-Century Mexican Feather Art." *RES: Anthropology and Aesthetics* 42 (1): 226–50.

Sacchi, Duccio. 2000. "Gathering, Organization, and Production of Information in Sixteenth-Century Mesoamerica." *Review (Fernand Braudel Center)* 23 (2): 293–308.

Sáenz de Santa María, Carmelo, ed. 1991. *Libro viejo de la fundación de Guatemala*. Guatemala City: Academia de Geografía e Historia de Guatemala.

Sahagún, Bernardino de. (1569) 1993. *Bernardino de Sahagún's Psalmodia Christiana*. Translated by Arthur Anderson. Salt Lake City: University of Utah Press.

Sahagún, Bernardino de. 1578. *General History of the Things of New Spain by Fray Bernardino de Sahagún: The Florentine Codex*. 3 vols. World Digital Library, Library of Congress. https://www.loc.gov/item/2021667837/.

Sahagún, Bernardino de. (1578) 1959–82. *Florentine Codex: General History of the Things of New Spain*. Translated and edited by Charles Dibble and Arthur Anderson. 13 vols. Santa Fe, N.Mex.: School of American Research; Salt Lake City: University of Utah Press.

Sahagún, Bernardino de. 1997. *Primeros Memoriales: Paleography of Nahuatl Text and English Translation*. Edited by Henry Nicholson, Arthur Anderson, Charles Dibble, Eloise Quiñones Keber, and Wayne Ruwet. Translated by Thelma Sullivan. Norman: University of Oklahoma Press.

Salazar, Francisco Cervantes de. (1554) 1875. *México en 1554: Tres diálogos latinos que Francisco Cervántes Salazar escribió é imprimió en México en dicho año*. Edited by Joaquín García Icazbalceta. Mexico City: Andrade y Morales.

Sandstrom, Alan. 1991. *Corn Is Our Blood: Culture and Ethnic Identity in a Contemporary Aztec Indian Village*. Norman: University of Oklahoma Press.

Schroeder, Susan. 1991. *Chimalpahin and the Kingdoms of Chalco*. Tucson: University of Arizona Press.

Schroeder, Susan. 1998. "The First American Valentine: Nahua Courtship and Other Aspects of Family Structuring in Mesoamerica." *Journal of Family History* 23 (4): 341–54.

Schroeder, Susan. 2000. "Jesuits, Nahuas, and the Good Death Society in Mexico City, 1710–1767." *Hispanic American Historical Review* 80 (1): 43–76.

Schroeder, Susan. 2007. "The Annals of Chimalpahin." In *Sources and Methods for the Study of Postconquest Mesoamerican Ethnohistory, Provisional Version*, edited by James Lockhart, Lisa Sousa, and Stephanie Wood, 1–13. Eugene: University of Oregon.

Schroeder, Susan. 2011. "The Truth About the *Crónica Mexicayotl*." *Colonial Latin American Review* 20 (2): 233–47.

Schroeder, Susan. 2016. *Tlacaelel Remembered: Mastermind of the Aztec Empire*. Norman: University of Oklahoma Press.

Schroeder, Susan. 2017. "Writing the Nahuatl Canon." In *To Be Indio in Colonial Spanish America*, edited by Mónica Díaz, 219–41. Albuquerque: University of New Mexico Press.

Schwaller, John. 1986. "Nahuatl Manuscripts in: The Newberry Library (Chicago), The Latin American Library, Tulane University, The Bancroft Library, University of California, Berkeley." *Estudios de Cultura Náhuatl* 18:315–83.

Schwaller, John Frederick, ed. 2003a. *Sahagún at 500: Essays on the Quincentenary of the Birth of Fr. Bernardino de Sahagún*. Berkeley, Calif.: Academy of American Franciscan History.

Schwaller, John. 2003b. "Introduction." In Schwaller 2003a: ix–xiii.

Schwaller, John. 2003c. "Tracking the Sahagún Legacy: Manuscripts and Their Travels." In Schwaller 2003a, 265–74.

Schwaller, John. 2005. "The Pre-Hispanic Poetics of Sahagun's *Psalmodia Christiana*." *Estudios de Cultura Náhuatl* 36:67–86.

Schwaller, John. 2011. *The History of the Catholic Church in Latin America: From Conquest to Revolution and Beyond*. New York: New York University Press.

Schwaller, John. 2019. *The Fifteenth Month: Aztec History in the Rituals of Panquetzaliztli*. Norman: University of Oklahoma Press.

Seler, Eduard. (1920) 1961. "Mythus und Religion del Alten Mexikaner." In *Gesammelte Abhandlungen*, 4:1–167. Graz, Austria: Akademische Druck- und Verlagsanstalt.

Serna, Jacinto de la. 1892. *Manual de ministros de indios para el conocimiento de sus idolatrías y extirpación de ellas*. Madrid: José Perales y Martínez.

Serna Arnaiz, Mercedes, and Bernat Castany Prado. 2014. *Historia de los indios de la Nueva España por Fray Toribio de Benavente, Motolinía*. Madrid: RAE, Centro para la edición de los clásicos españoles.

Sherman, William. 1970. "Tlaxcalans in Post-Conquest Guatemala." *Tlalocan* 6:124–39.

Sigal, Pete. 2011. *The Flower and the Scorpion: Sexuality and Ritual in Early Nahua Culture*. Durham, N.C.: Duke University Press.

SilverMoon. 2007. "The Imperial College of Tlatelolco and the Emergence of a New Nahua Intellectual Elite in New Spain (1500–1760)." PhD diss., Duke University, Durham, N.C.

Siméon, Rémi. (1889) 1977. *Diccionario de la lengua nahuatl o mexicana*. Translated by Josefina Olivia de Coll. First Spanish edition of *Dictionnaire de la lengue nahuatl ou mexicaine*. Mexico City: Siglo veintiuno.

Sotomayor Tribín, Hugo, and Zoilo Cuéllar-Montoya. 2007. *Aproximaciones a la paleopatología en América Latina*. Bogotá: Convenio Andrés Bello.

Soustelle, Jacques. (1970) 2002. *Daily Life of the Aztecs*. London: Phoenix.

Star, Susan Leigh, and James Griesemer. 1989. "Institutional Ecology, 'Translations,' and Boundary Objects: Amateurs and Professionals in Berkeley's Museum of Vertebrate Zoology, 1907–1939." *Social Studies of Science* 19 (3): 387–420.

Stear, Ezekiel. 2017. "Between the Glosses: Devils and Pantheism in the Crónica Mexicayotl." *Latin Americanist* 61 (2): 247–71.
Stone, Rebecca. 2011. *The Jaguar Within: Shamanic Trance in Ancient Central and South American Art*. Austin: University of Texas Press.
Sullivan, John, Eduardo de la Cruz Cruz, Abelardo De la Cruz De la Cruz, Delfina de la Cruz De la Cruz, Victoriano de la Cruz Cruz, Sabina Cruz de la Cruz, Ofelia Cruz Morales, Catalina De la Cruz, Manuel De la Cruz Cruz. 2016. *Tlahtolxitlauhcayotl: Chicontepec, Veracruz*. Warsaw: IDIEZ.
Sullivan, Thelma, and Timothy Knab. 2003. *A Scattering of Jades: Stories, Poems, and Prayers of the Aztecs*. Tucson: University of Arizona Press.
Tavárez, David. 2011. *The Invisible War: Indigenous Devotions, Discipline, and Dissent in Colonial Mexico*. Stanford, Calif.: Stanford University Press.
Tavárez, David, ed. 2017. *Words and Worlds Turned Around: Indigenous Christianities in Colonial Latin America*. Boulder: University Press of Colorado.
Tedlock, Barbara, and Dennis Tedlock. 1985. "Text and Textile Language and Technology in the Arts of the Quiché Maya." *Journal of Anthropological Research* 41 (1985): 121–46.
Tedlock, Dennis. 1985. *Popol Vuh: The Definitive Edition of the Mayan Book of the Dawn of Life and the Glories of Gods and Kings*. New York: Simon & Schuster.
Tena, Rafael. 2009. "La religión mexica: Catálogo de dioses." *Arqueología mexicana, Edición especial* 30:n.p.
Terraciano, Kevin. 2010. "Three Texts in One: Book XII of the *Florentine Codex*." *Ethnohistory* 57 (1): 51–72.
Terraciano, Kevin. 2019. "Introduction. An Encyclopedia of Nahua Culture: Context and Content." In Favrot Peterson and Terraciano 2019, 1–18.
Tezozomoc, Fernando Alvarado. (1598) 1997. *Crónica mexicana*. Edited by Gonzalo Díaz Migoyo and Germán Vázquez. Madrid: Historia 16–Información e Historia.
Thévet, André. 1905. "Histoyre du Mechique, manuscrit français inédit du XVIe siècle." Edited by Edouard de Jonghe. *Journal de la Société des Américanistes*, nouvelle série 2: 1–41.
Thomas, Keith. 1971. *Religion and the Decline of Magic: Studies in Popular Beliefs in Sixteenth- and Seventeenth-Century England*. London: Folio Society.
Thomas, Nicholas. 1994. *Colonialism's Culture: Anthropology, Travel, and Government*. Melbourne: Melbourne University Press.
Thompson, Eric. 1934. *Sky Bearers, Colors, and Directions in Maya and Mexican Religion*. Contributions to American Archaeology 10. Washington, D.C.: Carnegie Institution of Washington.
Thomson, Rodney, Rosamond McKitterick, and Erik Kwakkel. 2012. *Turning Over a New Leaf*. Leiden: Leiden University Press.
Thouvenot, Marc. 1988. "Codex Xolotl. Étude d'une des composantes de sonécriture: les glyphes. Dicctionnaire des éléments constitutifs des glyphes." PhD diss., Université de Lille III.

Tira de la peregrinación: Códice Boturini. 1990. Tepic, Nayarit: Gobierno del Estado de Nayarit.

Torquemada, Juan de. (1615) 1986. *Monarquia indiana*. 3 vols. Mexico City: Porrúa.

Torquemada, Fray Juan de. 1969. *Monarquía indiana*. 3 vols. Mexico City: Porrúa.

Townsend, Camilla. 2006. *Malintzin's Choices: An Indian Woman in the Conquest of Mexico*. Albuquerque: University of New Mexico Press.

Townsend, Camilla. 2009. "Glimpsing Native American Historiography: The Cellular Principle in Sixteenth-Century Nahuatl Annals." *Ethnohistory* 56 (4): 625–50.

Townsend, Camilla. 2019. *Fifth Sun: A New History of the Aztecs*. New York: Oxford University Press.

Townsend, Richard. 1979. *State and Cosmos in the Art of Tenochtitlan*. Washington, D.C.: Dumbarton Oaks.

Turner, Victor. 1979. "Betwixt and Between: The Liminal Period in Rites of Passage." In *Reader in Comparative Religion: An Anthropological Approach*, 4th ed., edited by William Lessa and Evon Vogt, 234–42. New York: Harper and Row.

Umberger, Emily Good. 1981. "Aztec Sculptures, Hieroglyphs, and History." PhD diss., Columbia University, New York.

Valle, Ivonne del. 2009. "On Shaky Ground: Hydraulics, State Formation, and Colonialism in Sixteenth-Century Mexico." *Hispanic Review* 77 (2): 197–220.

Vasconcelos, José. (1925) 2017. *La raza cósmica*. Mexico City: Porrúa.

Vázquez, Rolando. 2011. "Translation as Erasure: Thoughts on Modernity's Epistemic Violence." *Journal of Historical Sociology* 24 (1): 27–44.

Vázquez de Tapia, Bernardino. 1953. *Relación de méritos y servicios del conquistador Bernardino Vázquez de Tapia, vecino y regidor de esta gran ciudad de Tenustitlán, México*. Vol. 1. Mexico City: Antigua Librería Robredo.

Viesca Treviño, Carlos. 2001. "*Curanderismo* in Mexico and Guatemala: Its Historical Evolution from the Sixteenth to the Nineteenth Century." In *Mesoamerican Healers*, edited by Brad Huber and Alan Sandstrom, 47–65. Austin: University of Texas Press.

Viesca Treviño, Carlos. 2006. "La formación del buen médico: La historia y el porvenir." *Revista de la Facultad de Medicina UNAM* 49 (1): 3–9.

Viesca Treviño, Carlos. 2007. *Historia de la medicina en México*. Mexico City: UNAM.

Villella, Peter. 2016. *Indigenous Elites and Creole Identity in Colonial Mexico, 1500–1800*. Cambridge: Cambridge University Press.

Wallerstein, Immanuel. 1974. *The Modern World-System I: Capitalist Agriculture and the Origins of the European World-Economy in the Sixteenth Century*. New York: Academic Press.

Wallerstein, Immanuel. 1979. *The Capitalist World-Economy*. Cambridge: Cambridge University Press.

West, Delno. 1989. "Medieval Ideas of Apocalyptic Mission and the Early Franciscans in Mexico." *The Americas* 45 (3): 293–313.

White, Hayden. 1987. *The Content of the Form: Narrative Discourse and Historical Representation*. Baltimore: Johns Hopkins University Press.

Witschey, Walter R. T., and Clifford T. Brown. 2012. *Historical Dictionary of Mesoamerica*. Lanham, Md.: Scarecrow.

Wood, Stephanie. 1991. "The Cosmic Conquest: Late-Colonial Views of the Sword and Cross in Central Mexican *Títulos*." *Ethnohistory* 38 (2): 176–95.

Wood, Stephanie. 2003. *Transcending Conquest: Nahua Views of Spanish Colonial Mexico*. Norman: University of Oklahoma Press.

Worley, Paul. 2013. *Telling and Being Told: Storytelling and Cultural Control in Contemporary Yucatec Maya Literatures*. Tucson: University of Arizona Press.

Wright Carr, David Charles. 2011. "La tinta negra, la pintura de colores: Los difrasismos metafóricos translingüísticos y sus implicaciones para la interpreción de los manuscritos centromexicanos de tradición indígena." *Estudios de Cultura Náhuatl* 42:285–98.

Yannakakis, Yanna. 2008. *The Art of Being In-Between: Native Intermediaries, Indian Identity, and Local Rule in Colonial Oaxaca*. Durham, N.C.: Duke University Press.

Zepeda Rincón, Tomás. 1972. *La educación pública en la Nueva España en el siglo XVI*. Mexico City: Progreso.

Zetina, Sandra, José Luis Ruvalcaba, Tatiana Falcón, Eumelia Hernández, Carolusa González, Elsa Arroyo, and Marimin López Cáceres. 2008. "Painting Syncretism: A Non-Destructive Analysis of the *Badiano Codex*." Presentation, Ninth International Conference on Nondestructive Investigation and Analysis of Art, Jerusalem, Israel, May 25–30. https://www.ndt.net/article/art2008/papers/121Ruvalcaba.pdf.

INDEX

ACK orthography, 198n7
Acolhuacan (region), 62, 181, 205n21
acoustic colonialism, 76, 211n74
Ahuitzotl (Mexica tlatoani), 52, 117, 132, 134, 137, 207n38
Almanza, Enrique (viceroy), 116, 118, 218n23
altepetl (altepeme, pl.): main characteristics, 3–5, 197n1; mentions, 15, 22, 24–25, 37, 39, 41–43, 65, 74, 137, 156, 161, 206nn29–30
Alvarado, Jorge de, 33, 43, 50, 54–55; executions of Kaqchiquel rulers, 56, 208n44; as synecdoche for alliance, 57
Alvarado, Pedro de, 33, 47, 52–53; exploitative labor practices of, 61, 208n50; at Iximché 56
Amecameca (region), 149, 155, 172
amoxtli (codex/book): mentions 14, 17, 155, 160, as tool of persuasion, 154, 159–60, 170
Anahualcalmecac International College Preparatory Academy, 188
Anales de Juan Bautista, 31, 115–16, 119, 121; naming of, 216n3; narrative cycles in 120–21; role of clergy in 119, 217n11; as similar to other Nahua annals, 121, 191
animal sacrifice: political role of, 4, 23, 26, 63–65, 197n2; in Tollan, 64
animic conduits, 15, 96–97, 99–100, 111, 214n27. *See also* tonalli; yollotli
animic misalignment, 99, 111–12, 176
Antigua (Guatemala), 205n21
Aragón, Fernando de. *See* reyes católicos
Asselbergs, Florine, 40, 204n9, 208n49
atlaca ("water people"), 87
Atlapolco, 122–23, 130–31
Atlixco, 161, 203n1
Aubin, Jean Alexis, 208n54, 220n4
Audiencia Real, 136, 156, 209n58
Axayacatl (Mexica tlatoani), 26, 143–44, 153–54, 158, 222n18
axis mundi, 207n41
Azcapotzalco (altepetl), 63, 168, 171, 206n30
Aztecs. *See* Mexica
Aztlan, 152, 156, 161, 188, 206–07n33, 222n19. *See also* Chicomoztoc

Badiano, Juan, 92, 95, 214n22
Bal, Mieke, 120

Basílica de Guadalupe, 216–17n9
Bassett, Molly, 24, 71, 162, 170–71; traits of teotl, 20–21
Bautista, Juan (alguacil/constable), 116–17, 216n2
Benjamin, Walter, 29
Bhabha, Homi K., 92
Boas, Franz, 191
body, as cosmic energy pathway, 84, 96–100, 179, 183
Boturini Benaducci, Lorenzo (antiquarian), 62, 118, 208n54, 216n3, 220n4
bow and arrow, 116, 223n26
Brennen, Sallie Craven, 221n10
Buenaventura de Zapata y Mendoza, Juan, 191

cabecera status, 38; in Quauhquechollan, 185; Tepechpan's petitions for, 70, 209n58
Cahi Yamox (Kaqchiquel ruler), 207n39
calmecac (school for nobles), 16–17, 95, 99, 156, 185, 189
calpixque (tribute collectors), 70
calpolli (altepetl division), 46–47, 218n26; in Quauhquechollan 47; Tenochtitlan 144
Camaxtli, 128–29
Campbell, Joe, 25, 198n7, 202n39
Case, Emalani, 10
Castañeda de la Paz, María, 75–76
Castilla, Isabella de. *See* reyes católicos
caves, in Mesoamerican origin accounts, 143, 222n19
Centeotl, 112
centli/cintli, 101–4, 112, 215n31
Cervantes de Salazar, Francisco, 221n11
Chalchiuhnenetzin (sister of Axayacatl), 158
Chalchiuhtlatonac. *See* Mexi
Chalco (region), 161
Chandler, Michael, 153
Charles V, 35, 204n11, 208n51; death of, 66, 209n56

Chi, Gaspar Antonio, 199n12
Chiapas/Chiapan, 33, 52, 134, 207n38
chicahua (to strengthen), 7, 14, 25, 56, 74
chicahualiztli, 14, 180, 193–94, 207n34, 214n28
Chichicastenango, 57
Chichimeca, 222n20
Chicomecoatl, 103–4, 215n32
Chicomexochitl, 103–4, 129
Chicomoztoc (seven caves of), 154, 161, 173, 222n21, 224n32
Chicomoztoc-Colhuacatepetl, 26
Chicontepec, 103–4, 193–94
Chimalpahin, Domingo, 149–52, 220n4; pan-Nahua themes of, 161–62; view of history, 221n10
Chimaltenango, 56–58, 208n46
Cipac, Luis Santa María (Mexica governor), 117, 121–22, 131–39, 147, 218n23, 219n27; death of, 140
Cipactonal, 176, 214n24
civitas (legal status of city), 76
Clavijero, Francisco, 168
Coatlicue, 170
cocoliztli. *See* epidemics
Codex Aubin, 200n20, 209n56, 210n71
Codex Chimalpahin, 187–88, 220n3
Codex Cruz-Badianus, 214n22
Codex Mendoza, 90; foundation of Tenochtitlan in 223n30; Mexica conquests in, 52, 197n4, 204n10
Codex Mexicanus, 170, 191, 200n23; as a "clandestine document," 217n10; death of Charles V in, 209n56; tianguis glyph in, 208n48
Codex Xolotl, 205n21
Códices matritenses, 81, 88–89, 111, 212n6, 221n9
Cohuatepec, 115, 121–23, 130
Colegio de la Santa Cruz de Tlatelolco, Nahua scholars of, 87, 91–93; mentions, 30, 91–93, 110–11, 189, 222n15
Colhuacan, 161, 197n3, 208n55

collective teixiptla. *See* mosaic deities
coloniality of power, 28
colonial middle/Baroque, 190
comparison, as tool of persuasion: in *Crónica mexicayotl*, 158; in *FC*, 98–100; in Quauhquechollan and Tepechpan, 41, 52, 63, 65–66
congregación (resettlement), 74–75, 210n70
Connell, William, 136, 190, 219n28
Cortés, Hernán, 33–35, 49–50, 189, 203n2, 206n25, 207n36, 224n32
costumbre, el, 193
Council of Trent, 89
Coyolxauhqui, 170
Crawford O'Brien, Suzanne, 177
Crewe, Ryan, 35
Crónica mexicayotl: authorship, 150–52, 220n4; mentions, 153–74 passim
cross: as chicahualiztli, 207n34; of Santiago, 50, 55
Cruz, Martín de la. *See* Colegio de la Santa Cruz de Tlatelolco
Cruz, Victoriano de la, 103–4, 193, 201n28, 224–25n1
Cruz Cruz, Eduardo de la, 86, 193–94, 215n31, 218n22
Cruz de la Cruz, Abelardo de la, 193, 202n36
Cruz de la Cruz, Sabina, 175–76, 179–80, 186, 193, 199
cualli nehnemi (walking well), 11, 195, 198n9
Cuauhtemoc (Mexica tlatoani), 156, 189, 207n36, 225n8
Cueopan, 144
curanderos, 106–7, 215n34

Díaz, Porfirio, 191, 198n9
Diel, Lori Boornazian, 35, 62
Difrasismo. *See* diphrastic kenning
Dillon, Grace, 9
diphrastic kenning, 14, 16, 41–42, 121, 133, 159–60, 198n8

disindigenization, 162
divination, 15–16; by casting corn kernels, 94, 176–77, 186, 214n23
doctrina status, 73
domesticated animals. *See* European cattle
double mistaken identity, 9
dreams. *See* Indigenous knowledge(s)
Durán, Diego (fray), 19, 143–44, 201n27

eagle-and-cactus motif, 154, 166–68
education, of Mexica nobles, 161–62, 171–72; pan-Nahua views on, 153–54, 159
ehecatl, 224n35; ehecatl spirits, 179
Ehecatl/Quetzalcoatl, 118, 144–45
emergence geographies, 35, 103, 165
Enríquez Almanza, Martín (viceroy), 89, 116, 119, 218n23
epidemics, 210n68–69; epidemic (1576), 80
Escalona, Alonso de (Franciscan provincial), 89
Escuela de San José de los naturales, 156, 217n11
European cattle, 116, 125–26; damaged caused by, 218n18
Ezhuahuacatl, 135–36, 138
Ezmallin, Martín, 137–38, 147

Fifth Sun, 18, 44, 122–25, 130, 170, 190, 201n28, 214n24, 216n1
Final Judgment, 29
Fiore, Joachim de, 28
Florentine Codex (FC), 14; authorship of, 89–90, 91–96, 213n15; as boundary object, 87–88; composing of, 80–82, 88–91, 211n2; origin of name, 213n13; reconstructed questionnaires of, 213n14; textual models for, 90–91, 213nn19–20; timeline of composition, 88–89
Flower World Complex, 206n29
Franco, Alonso (Mexica elder), 172, 220n2
future: as Franciscan polemic, 203n46; as Nahua polemic, 5, 29

futurities/futurity: in *Anales de Juan Bautista*, 146–48; in *Crónica mexicayotl*, 172–74; Indigenous, 9–11, 40, 119–20, 139–40, 181–82; Nahua, 5–9, 11, 14–18, 21; in Quauhquechollan and Tepechpan, 72–77; of well-being in *FC*, 101–5, 110–11

Galenic medicine, 85, 212n9; debates concerning, 212n10
Gante, Pedro de, 119, 156, 217n11, 221n12. See also *Anales de Juan Bautista*
García Canclini, Néstor, 101
Geertz, Clifford, 175
Gimmel, Millie, 87
Goldie, Terry, 8
Good Eshelman, Catharine, 207n34
Goodyear-Kaʻōpua, Noelani (Kānaka Maoli), 9–10, 182
gout, 108–11, 113
Gruzinski, Serge, 13
Guadalupe, María de, 216n9
Guatemala, 33–34; Antigua and Guatemala City, 205n21

Habsburg crest, Indigenous use of, 44–45, 66–68, 209n58
hallucinogenics: for diagnosis, 105–6, 214n24; in *FC*, 82, 105–10; as talismans, 215n35
Harjo, Laura (Mvskoke), 35, 85, 119–20, 153, 192–93; on futurity praxis, 84–85; on spiral of futurity, 139–40; on tools of Muskoke futurity, 197–98n6
Hassig, Ross, 27
heat, as aging and death, 104
heraldic devices, Indigenous use of, 205n24. See also Habsburg crest
Hernández, Francisco (protomédico), 87, 212n10
Hispanic Christianity, 28
Hispanization, 81, 184
Historia universal. See *Florentine Codex*

Huanitzin (father of Fernando Alvarado Tezozomoc), 156, 206n26, 220–21n6, 221n12
Huaquechula, 74, 203n1, 209–10n64
Huasteca, 198n10, 212n10, 215n31; Mexica view of, 130
Huastecan Nahuatl, 224–25n1
Huauhquilpan (altepetl), 222n14
huehuetlatolli (sayings of elders), 88, 153
Huitzilihuitl (Mexica tlatoani/son of Acamapichtli), 169, 223n26
Huitzilihuitl River, 33
Huitzilopochtli: avatars of, 23, 107, 197n2, 202n35, 206n29, 215–16n37, 223n29, 223n29; birth of in *FC*, 170; mentions, 25, 48, 144, 148, 152, 160–68, 170–74, 185, 199n14, 223n26; as Mexica tutelary deity, 144; temples of, 69, 125; as tlamacazque (sacrificing priest), 154, 215–16n37
Huixtopolcatl, of Amanalco, 134–36, 138
human sacrifice, 22; in Tenochtitlan 24, 223n27; in Tollan, 64–65
Hvidtfeldt, Arild, 20–21, 201n32
hybridity, criticisms of, 8, 216n3
hyper-trophism, 159, 198n8

Iberian Peninsula, 28, 137, 155, 187
Icxicuauhtli. See marriage alliances in Tepechpan
ihiyotl, 83, 97, 100, 183, 214n27
Inca Garcilaso, 167, 223n28
Indigenous knowledge(s) (IK): in academia, 193; dreams as, 10, 22, 86; oracles as 223–24n31, 224n33–34; as practice-oriented, 84–85. See also Nahua knowledge(s)
Indigenous maps, 35, 39; from Quauhquechollan/Huaquechula, 205n22. See also emergence geographies
intertext, 205n17
Itzcoatl (Mexica tlatoani), 26, 143
Itzpapalotl, 197n2

Iximché (Kaqchiquel kingdom), 53, 56–57, 207nn42–43
Ixtlilxochitl, Fernando de Alva, 150, 209n62, 220n3, 223n23

Jiménez, doña Luz, 191–92

Kahiki (Kānaka Maoli concept), 204n11
Kalyuta, Anastasia, 20, 201n32
Karttunen, Frances, 94, 198n7
Kenrick Kruell, Gabriel, 143–44
Kirchhoff, Paul, 20, 220n5

Laird, Andrew, 167, 214n22, 223n27
Lake Texcoco, 3, 34, 87, 165, 171, 188. *See also* atlaca ("water people")
land tenure: Huauhquilpan petitions for, 156, 222n14; Tepechpan petitions for, 71, 205n17
Leeming, Ben, 126. *See also* hyper-trophism
León-Portilla, Miguel, 22, 125–26
León y Gama, Antonio, 220n4
Lienzo de Qauahquechollan, 42–43
Lienzo de Tlaxcala, 191, 205n23
lightning, 141–43, 220n35
limpia (animic cleaning), 177
López Austin, Alfredo, 93; on body and cosmos, 87
Luque-Talaván, Miguel, 75–76

Maffie, James, 96, 202n39; on movements of teotl, 17–20, 100
Magaloni Kerpel, Diana, 141
mahuitzic (marvellous), 21, 46, 99
maize, deification of, 103–4
Maldonado, Cristóbal (tlatoani of Tepechpan), 66
Malintzin (Marina), 50–51, 199n12, 206n31
Manrique de Zúñiga, Álvaro (viceroy), 77
Marina. *See* Malinztin
marriage alliance in Tepechpan, 63–64

Martínez, María Elena, 69, 187
McAnany, Patricia, 140
McDonough, Kelly, 12, 85, 92–93, 95–96; Indigenous epistemologies, 8, 82, 87–88, 98–99, 221n9, 224n34; Indigenous map-making, 40; Indigenous writing in Tlatelolco, 113, 116–17
Medici, Ferdinando di (cardinal), 213n13
Mendieta, Gerónimo de (fray), 24, 224n37
Mendoza, Antonio de (viceroy), 58, 92
merino, 132–33, 218–19n26
mestizaje, as ideology, 118, 198n9
metonymy, as tool of persuasion, 7, 41, 52, 65, 98, 205n19. *See also* synecdoche
Mexi (elder, Mexica namesake), 154, 163
Mexica (Aztecs), 3, 26–27, 33, 46, 90, 161, 171; Huitzilopochtli's naming of, 163–64; noble houses, 117, 152, 219n30. *See also* Moteuczoma house
Mexico, Valley of, 3, 150, 152
Mexico-Tenochtitlan, 35, 165–68, 211n2
Miahuatototl, Juan, 225n8
Miayahuaxihuitl (daughter of Oçomatzin teuhctli), 169
Michmaloyan, 123
Mictlan, 106, 224n35
Mikulska, Katarzyna, 23, 37, 48, 207n41
Milpa Alta, 191
Molina, Alonso de (fray), 55, 94, 123, 159
Moquixiuh (tlatoani of Tlatelolco), 158
mosaic deities (collective teixiptla), 23, 37, 43, 48–49, 118
Moteuczoma house: conception of 168–72; Moteucçoma, Isabela (Tecuichpotzin), 225n5; Moteuczoma I (Ilhuicamina) (Mexica tlatoani), 26, 52, 139, 141; Moteuczoma II (Xocoyotl) (Mexica tlatoani), 138, 219n29; origins of, 162–63; overview of 143–44; re-emergence accounts of, 225n6; spelling of, 203n49
Movimiento Estudiantil Chicano de Aztlán (M.E.Ch.A.), 188

Moytlan, scribes of, 118–19, 133, 135, 139; associations with clergy, 217n10–11; micropatriotism of, 140; use of xiuhpohualli 217n13
Muñoz de Camargo, Diego, 128, 223n23
Mvskoke (Creek), 11, 35, 84–85, 120

Nahua demographic crisis, 71, 126, 218n18
Nahua healers. *See* ticitl
Nahua knowledge(s) 6, 84, 87–88, 90–91, 180, 194. *See also* Indigenous knowledge(s)
Nahua tools of persuasion, 6–8, 21, 135, 181–82; in *Anales de Juan Bautista*, 120–22, 131, 133, 141–43; in *Crónica mexicayotl*, 153–54, 173; in *FC*, 84–85, 112–13; in other Nahua texts, 190–91; in Quauhquechollan, 37–38, 42–43; in Tepechpan, 38–39, 65–66
nanacatl (mushroom), 108, 219n27
narrative focalization, 40, 120, 133–34, 143
nepantla, 19–20, 141–42,
nepantlismo, 19–20, 201n29
new conquest scholarship, 203n3
New Fire ceremony, 18, 125, 129, 200n21
New Philology, 192, 203n3
New Spain, 80–81, 89, 154–55, 190, 216n6
Nim Ab'aj Kejchún, 208n44
Norton, Marcy, 65, 87
nuevos cristianos (legal category), 69

Oaxaca, 12, 33
Oçomatzin teuhctli (tlatoani of Quauhnahuac), 169
Offner, Jerome, 42
ollin, movement, 18, 100, 201n27
Olmos, Andrés de (fray), 24–25, 224n36
Ometeotl, 170
Omeyocan, 224n35
oracles. *See* Indigenous knowledge(s)
Ovando, Juan de (president, Council of the Indies), 80–81, 89, 110, 183
Oxomoco, 214n24

pantheism: in Mesoamerica, 20; Nahua views on, 18, 51, 96, 100
Parra, Francisco de la (fray), 208n49, 208n51
parrēsia (speaking truth to power), 130–31
Paso y Troncoso, Francisco del, 47, 212n5, 220n4
peyote/peiotl, 106–8, 215n35
peyoteros, Huichol, 108
Philip II (king), 213n13
Pichardo, José Antonio, 208n54
Popocatepetl, 33–34, 73, 142, 161
porter. *See* tlameme
Postclassic Period, 13–14, 65; politics of, 26, 63, 206n30, 221n8; rituals of, 103–4, 214n24
Primeros memoriales, 81–84, 90, 111, 215n32. *See also Florentine Codex*
privilegios de honra, 156, 223n23
psychotropic plants. *See* hallucinogenics
Purépecha (ethnic group), 206n25

Quauhnahuac (Cuernavaca), 168–69
Quauhnochtli, 135–36, 138
Quauhquechollan (altepetl), 33–34, 203n1; deity of, 48; economic interests of, 59–61; mentions, 43–51 passim; organization of, 45–46; ritualized alliance in, 42–43
Quetzalcoatl: avatars of, 23, 197n2; Totec lord, 64; tutelary deity of Toltecs, 16. *See also* Ehecatl

rainbow, 141–45 passim
Raquena, Pedro (scribe), 93–94
Real y Pontificia Universidad de México, 154–55
reciprocity, with deities, 19–20, 23, 154, 164; gift-giving, 49, 206n30; Huitzilopochtli and the sun, 168; intergenerational, 181–82; with land 38; between Mexica and Huitzilopochtli, 173; Nahua views on, 7, 99; between nobles and commoners, 147

Relaciones geográficas, 40, 95–96; questionnaires of 191
Remesal, Antonio de (fray), 60
Renaga, Fausto, 218n20
repetition, as tool of persuasion, 7, 41, 125–26; in *Anales de Juan Bautista*, 133; in *Crónica mexicayotl*, 171; in *FC*, 84, 112–13,
Retaluhleu. *See* Soconusco
reyes católicos, 28
Reyes García, Luis, 127
Río Balsas, 188, 225n3
Ruiz de Alarcón, Hernando, 107

Sacchi, Duccio, 95–96
Sahagún, Bernardino de (fray), 30, 186
San Antonio de Abad (church), 149–50
Sandstrom, Alan, 99, 104, 182
San Juan Moyotlan, 31, 119, 121, 140, 216n3
San Martín del Caballero (church and convent), 73, 75–76
San Miguel Tzalcualpan, 58
San Miguel Tzinacapan, 140
Santa María Magdalena (church), 68–69
Santiago de Almolonga: foundation of, 56–58; mentions 34, 37, 56–61 passim
Schroeder, Susan, 150–52
Schwaller, John, 211n73
secularization, 28–29
Sequera, Rodrigo de, 213n13
Sigüenza y Góngora, Carlos de, 220n4
Soconusco (Retaluhleu), 52–54, 58, 207n38
susto, 213n12. *See* tonalli
syncretism, criticisms of, 8
synecdoche, as tool of persuasion, 42, 52, 100
syntactic parallel, as tool of persuasion, 198n8; in *Crónica mexicayotl*, 136; in *FC*, 98. *See also* repetition

Tacuba, 158, 225n5
Tecniuh, Miguel, 118, 131–38

Tecomate, Veracruz (altepetl), 175–76, 180
Tehuantepec, 42, 52, 203n1
teixiptla (embodied deity, teixiptlahuan, pl.): in *Anales de Juan Bautista* 126, 139–46; mentions, 21–22, 24, 206n5; in Quauhquechollan, 46–47
telpochcalli (school of warriors), 25–26, 184
Temascalapan (altepetl), 210n65
Tenantzitzimitl, 129
Tenochca, in *Anales de Juan Bautista*, 132, 138; in *Crónica mexicayotl*, 158–61
Tenochtitlan, foundation of, 164–68, 169, 223n27, 223n30; in Postclassic Period, 22, 26–27, 33–34, 143–44, 152–54, 158, 161–62, 171–72, 214n21; surrender of, 125, 133, 199n12
teocuitlatl (sacred excrement), 51
teomameque (deity bearers, sing. teomama), 162, 223n25
teonanacatl, 107–9. *See also* nanacatl
Teopan, 144
teotl (teteo, pl.), 18; as metaphysics, 17–20, 147, 214n27; as phenomenology, 20–25, 171; scholarly interpretations of, 20–25, 201n30
tepahtihquetl (village healer), 176–77, 179–80; *See also* ticitl
Tepanec Empire, 63, 168, 222n16, 224n38
Tepechpan (altepetl), 185–86; alliance with Tenochtitlan, 63, 65–66; mentions, 3–4, 35, 68–77 passim
Tepepulco, 80–81, 211n2
Tepexpan, 68
Tepeyac, Marian festival, 118, 216–17n9
tequitl (rotational work), 176, 178–80, 210n66
Terraciano, Kevin, 88–89, 213n17
Teton, Juan, 115–18, 122–25, 129–31, 145–47, 217n14
Texcoco (altepetl) 63, 204n13, 209n 62, 211n2, 223n23

Tezcatlipoca, avatars of, 197n2
Tezozomoc, Fernando Alvarado, 149–50, 156–57, 195, 206n30, 224n32; Francisca (mother), 163
Tezozomoctli (tlatoani of Azcapotzalco), 168
tianguis (marketplace), 51–52, 58–59, 61, 74, 136, 222n16; its glyph, 208n48
ticitl (Nahua physician, titicih, pl.), 16, 89–90, 92, 93–96, 179; diagnosis by, 80, 86, 94–95, 101, 105–7, 109–10, 214n24; titicih, female, 214n25
time, in *Crónica mexicayotl*, 172; as cyclical, 15, 27–28, 207n41; as homogeneous and empty, 29; as linear, 27–28, 37, 121, 202n43, 203n48, 211n74, 221n10; mythic, 161; as spiraling, 172; in Tepechpan, 62–63, 204n7
time-place, 14–15, 96–97
Tira de la peregrinación (*Codex Boturini*), 46, 164
Tira de Tepechpan: physical description of, 61–62, 204n6; mentions, 6, 30, 38, 205n17; tlacuiloque and annotators of, 38, 62–63
Tlacaelel, cihuacoatl (royal adviser), 26–27, 154, 224n38
Tlacopan, 45
tlacuilo (painter-scribe, tlacuiloque, pl.): female 200n24; mentions, 17, 30, 34–35, 37–39, 45–46, 48–55 passim, 57–61, 63, 65, 155, 199
Tlalamatl huauhquilpan, 156–57
Tlaloc, 166
tlalticpac, 17
tlamacehua, 22
tlamatini (sage, tlamatinime, pl.), 16–18, 22, 95, 98, 155, 221n9
tlameme (porter, tlamemehque, pl.), 59, 61
Tlantepexillama, 128–29
tlaquimilolli (deity bundle): of Huitzilopochtli, 154, 162, 206–7n33, 223n24;
mentions, 24, 224n37; of Tezcatlipoca, 24–25
Tlatelolco (altepetl), calmecac of, 189; mentions, 93, 96, 189, 211n2, 214n21, 222n16; as rival of Tenochtitlan, 157–60; tecpan of, 188–90
tlatoani (ruler, tlatoque, pl.), 42, 52–53, 70, 204n31
tlatocapilli (royal historian), 155
Tlaxcala/Tlaxcalans, 33–34, 204n4, 206n31, 208n46s
Tlilancalqui, 135–36, 221n13
toloa, 109–10
tona (solar heat), 15, 97–98
tonalamatl (books of divination), 15–16, 29
tonalli, 15, 84, 86, 101, 112; dislodged, 97, 101. *See also* animic misalignment
tonalpohualli (calendar), 13, 15, 27, 86, 200n21, 200n23
tonalpouhque (diviners), 13, 16
tools of Mvskoke (Creek) futurity, 197–98n6
tools of persuasion, 197–98n6
Toquentzin. *See* marriage alliances
Toral, Francisco de (Franciscan provincial), 81, 88, 199n12, 211n4
Totlahtol Series, 192
Townsend, Camilla, 53, 151–52, 190, 200n20, 206n31, 216n3
tribute exemptions, of labor/goods, 117, 209n63; mentions, 60–61, 133, 136, 147; monetized, 116–17, 137, 216n3; of Moteuczoma house 218n25; in Quauhquechollan and Tepechpan, 75
trivium, 91
Turner, Victor, 142
Tzalcualpa, 56
Tzaqualtitlan Tenanco, (altepetl), 155
tzitzimime, 115–16, 124–25, 128–29, 146–47, 216n1, 218n22

Uto-Aztecan, region, 112, 206n29

Valeriano, Antonio. *See* Colegio de la Santa Cruz de Tlatelolco
Valle, Ivonne del. 221n11
Vásquez, Rolando, 81
Vegerano, Alonso. *See* Colegio de la Santa Cruz de Tlatelolco
Velasco, Luis de (viceroy), 117
Volcán de Agua, 57, 60; landslide of 1541, 60–61

Waldek, Jean, 208n54
Wallerstein, Immanuel, 28–29
way-finding, 10–11, 38–39, 40, 107, 165, 179

way-keeping, 113
Worley, Paul, 120

Xipe Totec, 45
xiuhpohualli (yearly account), 15, 27, 29, 121, 200n20, 217n13
Xochitlalpan, 206n29
xochiyaoyotl (flower war), 26

yaocuicatl, (war songs) 223n26
Yazzie Burkhart, Brian, 11
Yohualli, (avatar of Tezcatlipoca), 169–70
yollotli, 26, 97, 100, 105

ABOUT THE AUTHOR

Ezekiel G. Stear's publications examine how the Nahuas of Mexico and other Native writers in colonial Spanish America played an active and decisive role in shaping culture by using writing to persuade their communities. By highlighting the future-oriented writing of Nahuas, he challenges the widespread assumption that Spanish colonialism erased Indigenous culture. Stear teaches Spanish and the literature of colonial Spanish America at Auburn University.